LARRY GARIFO

OS JCL

OS JCL

Wayne Clary

Mike Murach & Associates, Inc.
4222 West Alamos, Suite 101
Fresno, California 93711
(209) 268-8438

Development Team

Editor: Judy Taylor
Book designer: Michael Rogondino
Production coordinator: Debbie Lowe
Artist: Steve Ehlers

Thanks to International Business Machines Corporation for permission to reprint the following materials: figures 1-3, 1-5, 1-10, and 6-1.

© 1980, Mike Murach & Associates, Inc.
All rights reserved.
Printed in the United States of America.

Library of Congress Catalog Card Number: 80-82867

Contents

Preface — vii

PART 1 Required Background — 1

Chapter 1 Introduction to the System/360-370 and Its Operating System — 3
  Topic 1 System/360-370 Hardware — 4
  Topic 2 The Operating System for the System/360-370 — 19
  Topic 3 Data-Management Services — 37

PART 2 The Core Content — 45

Chapter 2 Job-Control Language: A Basic Subset — 47
  Topic 1 Coding Rules and Standards — 47
  Topic 2 The Syntax of the Language — 54
  Topic 3 Examples of Job Streams — 79

Chapter 3 Expanding the Basic Subset: Advanced JCL — 91
  Topic 1 JCL Coding Techniques — 91
  Topic 2 Advanced JCL Parameters — 104

PART 3 OS JCL for Specific Applications — 129

Chapter 4 Advanced File Handling — 131
  Topic 1 Indexed Sequential Files — 132
  Topic 2 Direct Files — 151

Chapter 5	Libraries and Procedures	165
Topic 1	Libraries	165
Topic 2	JCL Procedures	178
Chapter 6	JCL for OS/VS Environment	207
Topic 1	Conceptual Background and Additional JCL for Virtual Storage Systems	207
Topic 2	Virtual Storage Access Method (VSAM) File Handling	216
Chapter 7	OS Utilities and the Sort/Merge	231
Topic 1	OS Utility Programs	231
Topic 2	The OS Sort/Merge Program	254
Chapter 8	Language Translators and the Link-Edit Program	269
Topic 1	Language Translators	269
Topic 2	The Link-Edit Program	287
Chapter 9	Extended File Handling Capabilities of the DD Statement	299
Appendix		321
Index		327

Preface

In the mid-1960s, a new concept developed that would forever change the way we view computers. That concept is the operating system. Briefly, an operating system is a collection of computer programs to control the computer's resources. As application programs are read into the system, they are executed under the direct control of the operating system.

The IBM full Operating System (OS) for the System/360, 370, and 303X computers is one of the most advanced operating systems ever implemented. By using job-control language (JCL), we tell OS what we want it to do with our programs and files. As a result, a knowledge of OS JCL is critical to the effective use of this operating system.

What this book does

In this book, you'll learn how to code JCL for the applications that occur in the real world of data processing. You'll learn to use JCL to execute utility, sort/merge, language translator, and link-edit programs; you'll learn how to code JCL for advanced file handling and for the virtual storage environment; and you'll learn how to use timesaving techniques that can reduce coding errors. In short, you'll learn to code JCL the way the professionals use it. In addition, you'll be introduced to a standard method of "structuring" your JCL code so it will be easier to read and modify.

To fully appreciate the value of this book, you should be aware of some of the alternative training methods and materials used in industry. Typically, a new programmer (or an old one converting to OS for the first time) picks up bits and pieces of JCL in a very inefficient way. As each new JCL application or problem presents itself, the programmer learns what's needed by studying the IBM manuals, by copying the shop standards, or (usually) by asking the resident JCL expert or "guru" for help in a specific area. When a formal training course is available, it is likely to be poorly conceived and poorly presented. As a result, experience becomes the best teacher. (How well I remember my first error-filled attempts at writing JCL!)

The books and courses currently on the market that cover OS JCL are usually more theory than application. They present the parts without ever showing the whole. Sometimes, they present an academic overkill of a subject that is complicated enough on its own. This book, in contrast to other training materials on this subject, presents the basics of JCL, adds to that foundation little by little, and applies each area of JCL to the kind of data processing work that's done in industry.

Who this book is for

Simply stated, this book is for people who need to write OS JCL. This includes beginning programmers who have had a programming course (or are taking a concurrent course in a programming language); the experienced programmer who is new to the OS environment; and the experienced programmer, systems analyst, data control specialist, or computer operator who may be familiar with some parts of OS JCL through experience, but who has never mastered it. So if you have occasion to use a System/360-370 computer system running some version of OS, this book is for you.

Some features of this book

Content selection In deciding what to cover throughout this book, I've kept my sights set on a usable, "professional subset" of the language. Too many times, books will tend to cram everything into the course with a resulting loss in educational effectiveness. In contrast, this book is designed to be meaningful to the working programmer or systems analyst. In chapter 2, a subset of the language is presented. Since this is the foundation upon which the rest of the course is built, only the basics of JCL are covered here. I don't want you to be so overwhelmed by the complexities and intricacies of the language in the first part of the book that you become discouraged. In later chapters, as required, other elements of the language are introduced.

Illustrations We know from experience that a complex subject like OS JCL cannot be learned without extensive illustrative material. In fact, we believe the illustrative material is more important than the descriptive material. So this book contains hundreds of illustrations—illustrations that show you not only how to code certain JCL parameters, but also when they are required because of a particular application. What's more, the illustrations are examples of real systems that I have worked on myself or have some knowledge of. Since the names used for files, programs, and jobs are important in a real data processing environment, I've used real file names, program names, and job names in the examples. In short, I've tried to keep the emphasis on usefulness and practicality in planning and coding the illustrations.

Educational approach In general, there are two basic approaches to teaching any computer language subject—the parts-to-the-whole method and the modular method. The first teaches the separate elements of the language until a great deal of detail has been covered, and only at that time are a few of these elements put together as a complete job. Using this approach, it isn't uncommon for the first complete JCL job that the student actually understands to be found halfway through the book.

As I indicated a minute ago, this book uses the second (modular) approach for teaching OS JCL. After some background material is provided in chapter 1 (some of which may be review), chapter 2 presents a basic subset of OS JCL, including several complete jobs that are indicative of the kind of data processing work done in industry. As soon as you understand this basic subset, you can begin writing significant JCL job streams of your own.

Following the basic subset presented in chapter 2, chapter 3 adds advanced techniques and elements of the language to form an extended subset on which the rest of the book is based. Once a student has completed chapter 3, the most demanding part of the course is over. Then in the next part, chapters 4 through 9, the student (or instructor) can choose the sequence of subjects to be covered.

Learning aids by topic Because learning depends on what you do, more than upon what you see or hear, there are self-checking aids and exercises at the end of each topic in this book. Specifically, each topic is followed by terminology lists, behavioral objectives, and, whenever relevant, problems and their solutions.

The terminology lists are listings of the new words presented in the text of the topic. The intent is for you to scan the list to check your comprehension of the terminology. If you understand the words, you can proceed. If you feel that you don't have a clear understanding of a term, you can reread applicable sections or note the term so you can question its meaning in class or at work with your supervisor. In any case, the intent of the list is for use as a quick review; you're not expected to write definitions of the words.

Following the terminology lists are behavioral objectives that describe the activities a student should be able to do upon completion of the topic. The intent here is to give you a clear picture of what your learning goals should be. Since this book deals with OS JCL, the primary objectives have to do with solving various types of problems involving the writing of job-control language. In addition, there are objectives that deal with related skills such as coding utility control statements.

When the objectives deal with problem solving, they are followed by problems and their solutions. These problems are intended to give practice in the skills described by the objectives. As much as possible, these problems have been designed to show how the elements and techniques described in the text and illustrated by the figures are used in a different context. For the most part, then, the problems presented are the kind of problems you'll be asked to solve on the job as a programmer or systems analyst.

So that there is immediacy to the problem-solving activity, solutions are presented immediately after the problems. This has the advantage of letting you know that you are right when you are right, and, just as important, of letting you know right away when you're wrong. Although testing the JCL streams on a computer system has the same effect as doing the problems and checking the solutions, studying the solutions of a professional can correct many false notions and bad habits before problems are actually tried on a computer system.

How to use this book

As I said earlier, the modular approach to teaching JCL improves learning effectiveness. In addition, it gives the student or teacher some choice as to the sequence in which the subjects will be covered. Here is the general plan of the book:

Part	Chapters	Title	Prerequisite parts	Design
1	1	Required Background	—	Sequential
2	2-3	The Core Content	1	Sequential
3	4-9	OS JCL for Specific Applications	1,2	Random

This means that after you have read chapters 1 through 3, you can read the remaining chapters in any sequence you want. I would suggest, though, that you read over chapter 5 before too long, since libraries and procedures are referred to in several other chapters.

If you are reading this book on your own, this is important to you because you may only be interested in certain applications. For example, you may want to skip over the advanced file handling chapter so you can read about how to compile a program. This way, you can study the parts you want to study.

If you are in charge of training for your company, or if you're an instructor at a college, I think you'll find that the modular approach will allow you to design the course around your own requirements and resources. Because of the modular organization and the thoroughness of the material, the course can be split into two classes or semesters, one for the beginning JCL students and one for the more advanced.

Whether you are studying the book on your own or as part of a class, you will be able to write significant JCL streams that will be structured and easy to read and maintain when you have completed this book. In fact, you have our word on it. If you can't learn how to write OS JCL by using this book alone, you can return any and all books for a full refund, no matter how long you've had them.

Conclusion

I'm excited about this OS JCL book for two reasons. First, it represents the only product on the market that teaches OS JCL the way it's used in the day-to-day operations of an OS shop. Second, because of the structure of the book, it will be a desk reference that will serve you for years after you've mastered the JCL basics.

Although we have tried very hard to make this book as effective as possible, I know that any product can be improved. That's why I welcome your comments, criticisms, suggestions, and questions...about the subject of OS JCL, about the method I used to present the material, or about any other aspect of the book. If you have any, feel free to use the postage-paid comment form near the end of this book. With the help of your feedback, I hope we can improve not only this product, but future products as well.

Wayne Clary
Fresno, California
July, 1980

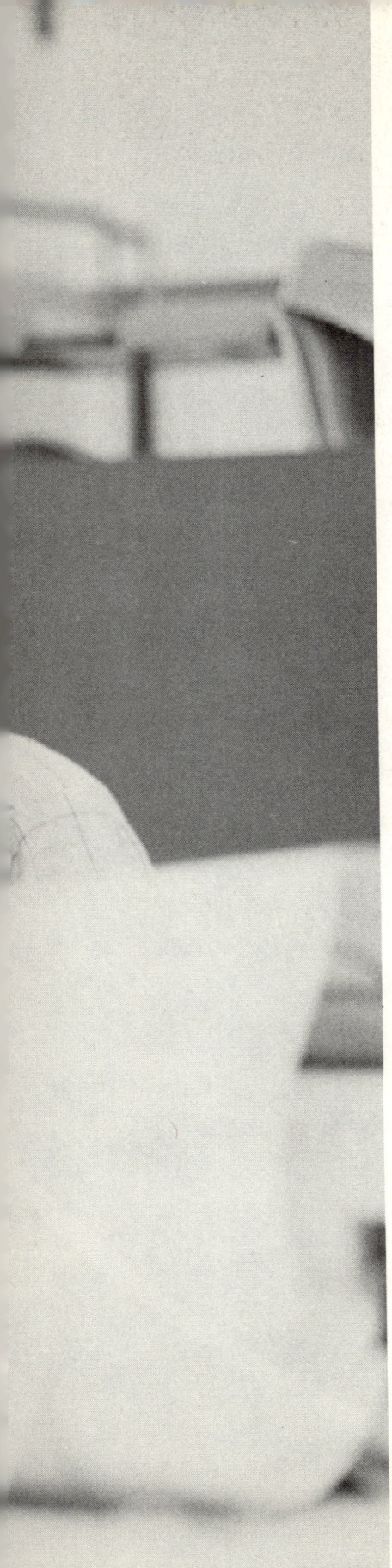

PART 1

Required Background

Before you can understand how to code the OS job-control language to run a program, you need to understand some basic concepts about the System/360-370 and IBM's full Operating System. As a result, this part presents that necessary background. If you've already had experience with a System/360-370 operating under OS, you may be familiar with much of the material in this part. If so, you can use this material as a review.

1

Introduction to the System/360-370 and Its Operating System

Before you can start learning about job-control language (JCL) for IBM's full Operating System (OS), you need to understand some basic concepts. As a result, this chapter provides the required background information. Topic 1 presents a brief description of the equipment used in an IBM System/360-370 computer installation; topic 2 presents an overview of the operating system; and topic 3 introduces the data-management concepts you'll need in order to understand some of the file handling functions performed by OS.

If you are already familiar with these subjects through a previous course or job experience, you probably won't need to study this chapter. To help you decide whether or not to skip a topic, review the terminology lists and behavioral objectives at the end of each topic.

On the other hand, if this material is new to you, you may feel overwhelmed when you have completed this chapter. If so, go on to chapters 2 and 3; then come back and reread the parts you are having trouble with. After you have gained some experience with the features and concepts of the System/360-370, you'll have no difficulty in understanding this elementary description.

Chapter 1

TOPIC 1 System/360-370 Hardware

The IBM System/360 is probably the most widely used computer in history. Because its central processing units (CPUs) are available in many different sizes and can be combined with many different input/output devices, the System/360 can be used in relatively small businesses as well as in the largest businesses in the world.

The System/370 is the successor to the 360. Because it makes use of more recent technological developments, the cost of computer processing can be lower with the 370 than with the 360. Like the 360, the 370 is available in many model sizes and configurations.

Still another series, the IBM System/303X, is the successor to the 370. It allows further savings in terms of CPU cost by doubling the amount of main storage for about half the cost of a System/370. Since the operating system and job-control language are basically the same for any of these systems, the term System/360-370 is used throughout this book to refer to either the System/360, 370, or 303X.

In this topic, I'm going to briefly describe the equipment, or *hardware*, components that make up a typical System/360-370. Then, I'll explain how a piece of equipment called a channel enables the system to make better use of its components in terms of processing time.

A TYPICAL SYSTEM

A typical System/360-370 computer installation has two major types of components: a CPU and input/output devices. The *CPU* is the *central processing unit* in which calculations, data manipulation, and the control of logic are performed. The *input/output devices* (or *I/O devices*) transmit data to and receive data from the CPU. The common types of I/O devices found on a System/360-370 are the operator console, card reader, card punch, printer, magnetic tape drives, and direct-access devices.

The *operator console* is either a television-like screen with a keyboard or a typewriter-like device with a continuous roll of paper. Through it, the system sends messages to the operator, and the operator sends responses and messages to control or monitor the system.

Although many installations are eliminating punched cards as the primary form of input to the computer, *card readers* and *card punches* are still common. They are used to read control decks and small files of data into the computer and to punch program decks and data for external manipulation. The reader and punch may be separate physical units, but they are often combined into one unit called a *reader/punch*.

The *printers* that operate on the System/360-370 can print from several hundred to more than one thousand lines per minute. And they have the capability of skipping to appropriate lines before printing. For example, when printing an invoice, the printer can print detail lines for each item ordered and then skip down to the last line to print the total balance due. This capability is commonly called *forms control*. The printer can also be adjusted to forms of many widths and lengths, so it can be used to print very small forms such as mailing labels as well as 16-inch-wide management reports. In short, it can meet the printing requirements of almost all business forms.

The card reader, card punch, and printer are all known as *unit record devices*. A System/360-370 operating under OS uses them only as input or output media. The other two major types of I/O devices available on the System/360-370—magnetic tape devices and direct-access devices—are used for storing data as well as for transmitting data to the CPU and accepting data from it. As you will see in the chapter that follows, OS requires more information in the job-control language when you're using these devices than it does when you're using unit record devices. So I'm going to cover them here in detail. You should be aware, however, that many of the characteristics of magnetic tape apply to unit record equipment as well.

Magnetic tape devices

The *magnetic tape* used in computer operations is similar to the tape used in home tape recorders. Magnetic tape is a continuous strip of plastic coated on one side with a metal oxide. For the System/360-370, this tape is one-half inch wide and usually comes in 250, 600, 1200, and 2400 foot lengths on plastic reels of varying sizes. Figure 1-1 illustrates a reel of tape.

Data is recorded on the coated surface of the tape as patterns of magnetized spots called *bits*. These bits correspond to the computer's internal storage. Each pattern represents one character, or *byte*, of data. For example, one pattern represents the letter A, while another represents the digit 1.

A number of bytes are strung together to form a *record*—that is, a collection of related data fields. For example, the data from a file of 80-column punched cards can be recorded on tape so that each tape record corresponds to an individual card. In this case, each tape record will be 80 bytes long. If the last 15 columns of the cards aren't used, however, you might want to make the tape records only 65 bytes long. In general, tape records can be as short or as long as needed.

Between individual data records on the tape are spaces where no data is recorded, as shown in figure 1-1. These spaces are called *interrecord gaps*, or *IRGs*. An IRG is only .06 of an inch long on most IBM tapes, and this gap is down to .03 of an inch on tapes for the latest tape equipment.

6 Chapter 1

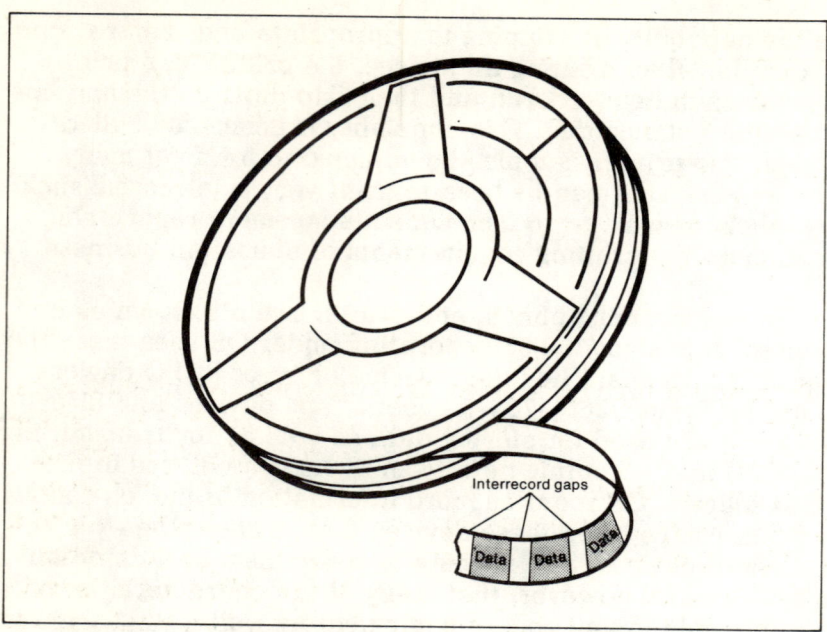

Figure 1-1 A magnetic tape

Tape capacity and speed The capacity of a reel of tape (how much data it can hold) depends on the length of the tape and the *density* of the tape. Density is a measure of the number of bytes of data that can be recorded on one inch of tape. The most common models of tape drives used on the System/360-370 have a density of either 800 or 1600 *bpi* (bytes per inch).

Blocking also affects the capacity of a tape. When records are blocked, more than one record is stored between IRGs. Figure 1-2, for example, shows how a *block* of five records would look on tape. Since blocking reduces the number of IRGs, it reduces the amount of wasted space on the reel of tape, so there's more room to store data.

Blocking also affects the speed with which tape records can be accessed. When the tape device reads a record, it reads the data between two IRGs. So for unblocked records, it must start and stop for each record in the file. When the records are blocked, there are fewer IRGs, so the device doesn't have to start and stop so often. Instead, a whole block of records is read at one time.

The tape drive Figure 1-3 illustrates one of IBM's 2400 series *tape drives*. Tape drives are the hardware units that read and write data

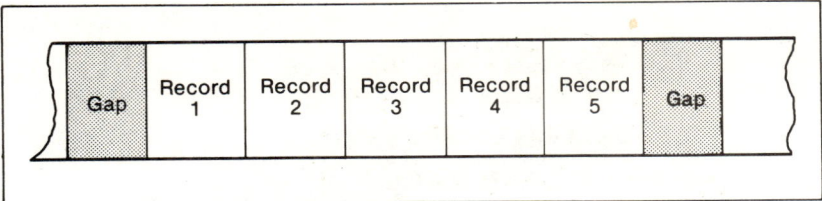

Figure 1-2 Blocked records

on tape. To mount a tape on a drive, the computer operator threads the tape through a read/write mechanism in the center of the unit and then onto an empty takeup reel. The process is similar to mounting tape on a home reel-to-reel tape recorder. Once the tape has been mounted, tape records can be read or written under the control of a program. When data is read from tape, the data that is on the tape remains unaltered, so it can be read many times. When data is written on the tape, it replaces (and thus destroys) any data that was on the tape.

Processing and use Whenever a tape drive operates on a tape, it processes the tape records in sequence, from beginning to end. In other words, before you can access the 50th record in a tape file, you have to process the preceding 49. This is called *sequential processing*.

Although limited to sequential processing and handicapped by slow mounting and data-access rate, magnetic tapes are the least expensive form of external storage and they can be used to pass data from one type of computer system to another. As a result, they are widely used in the computer industry, and most System/360-370 installations have magnetic tape drives.

Direct-access devices

A substantial majority of today's data processing systems have direct-access capabilities. *Direct-access devices* provide large amounts of storage with fast access to any of the records stored. Unlike sequential devices like card readers and tape drives, any record on a direct-access device can be read or written without having to read or write the records that precede it. In other words, to process the 500th record in a direct-access file, only the 500th record has to be read.

Since disk drives are the most common form of direct-access device in use today, this discussion will be directed towards disk

8   Chapter 1

Figure 1-3   The tape drive

storage devices. You should realize, however, that there are many IBM direct-access devices that can be attached to the System/360-370. These include several models of disk drives and drums. Although drums differ significantly from the disks in physical characteristics, many of the same principles apply. For example, in a moment, I'll introduce you to the notion of cylinders and tracks for forming a direct-access address. This same notion applies whether you are using a disk or drum for storing your file. From the programmer's point of view, then, the concepts are much the same, although the hardware may differ.

Disk devices   The *disk pack* is the device upon which the data is recorded; the *disk drive* is the hardware unit that reads and writes the data on a disk pack. A typical disk pack, schematically illustrated in figure 1-4, consists of a central spindle with a number of permanently affixed metal disks that spin at a constant speed in the disk drive. Except for the top surface of the top disk and the bottom surface of the bottom disk, data can be recorded on both sides of the disks that make up the disk pack.

On each of the individual recording surfaces are concentric circles called *tracks*, as illustrated in figure 1-5. The disk in the figure

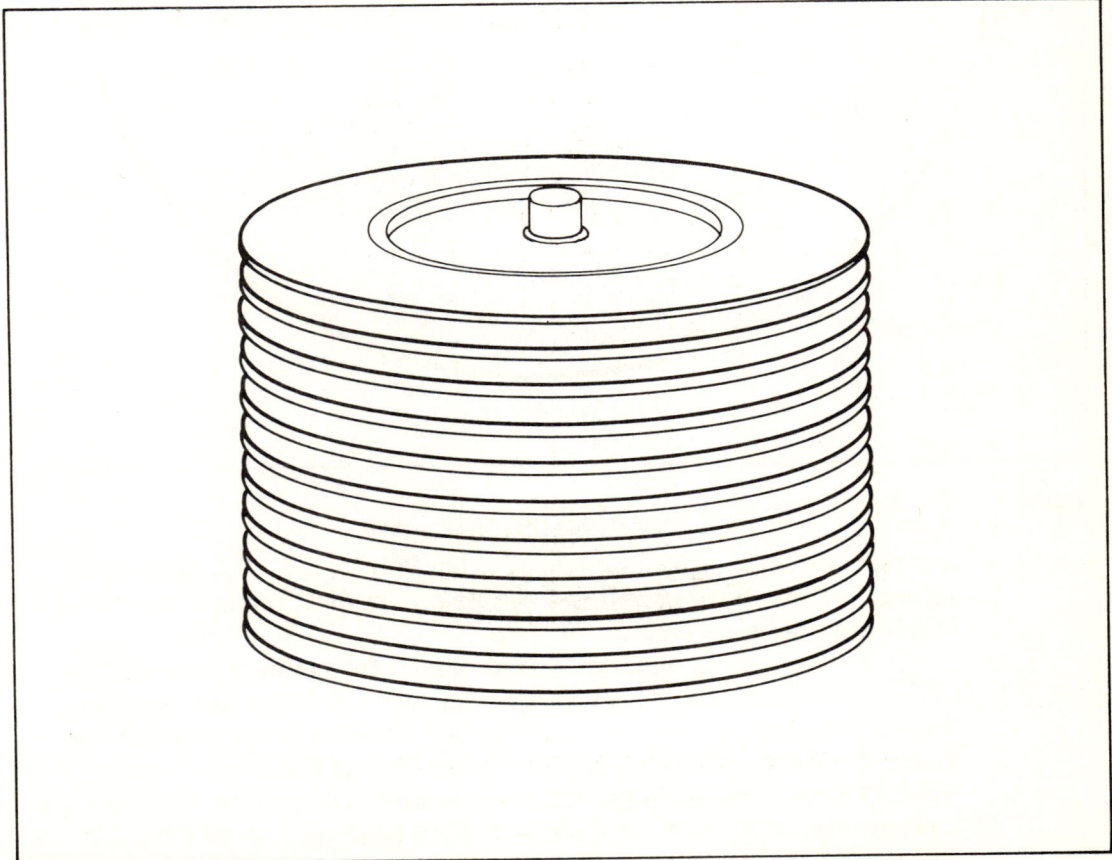

Figure 1-4   The disk pack

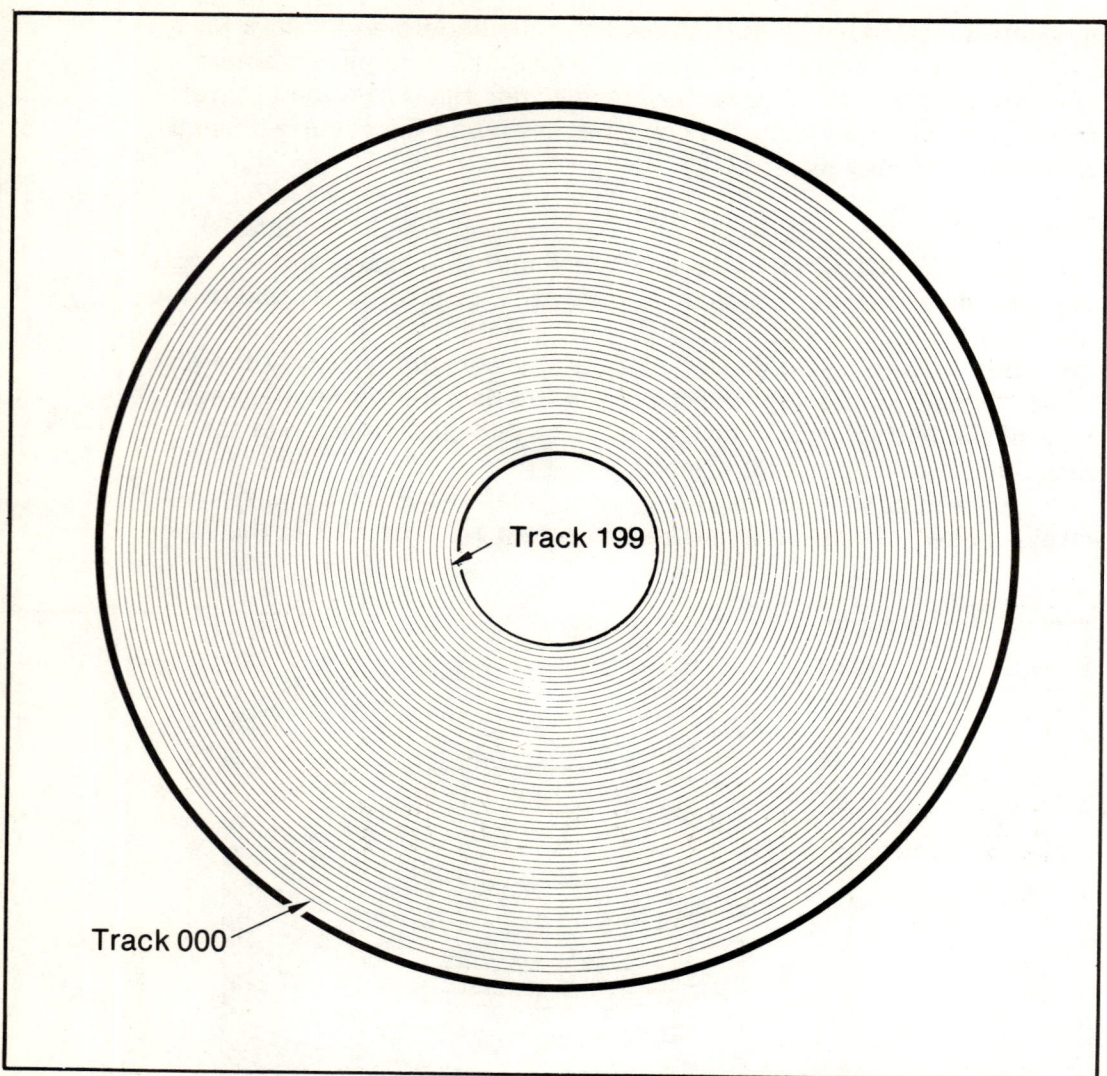

Figure 1-5 Tracks on a disk surface

consists of 200 tracks, numbered from 000 to 199. Although these tracks get smaller toward the center of the disk, each of the tracks can hold the same amount of data.

The recording surfaces are accessed for reading and writing data by an *access mechanism* like the one shown in side view in figure 1-6. As you can see, there is one *read/write mechanism*, or *head*, for each recording surface. Only one of the heads can be turned on at any one time; thus, only one track can be operated upon at one time. Each of the heads can both read and write data but can do only one operation at a time.

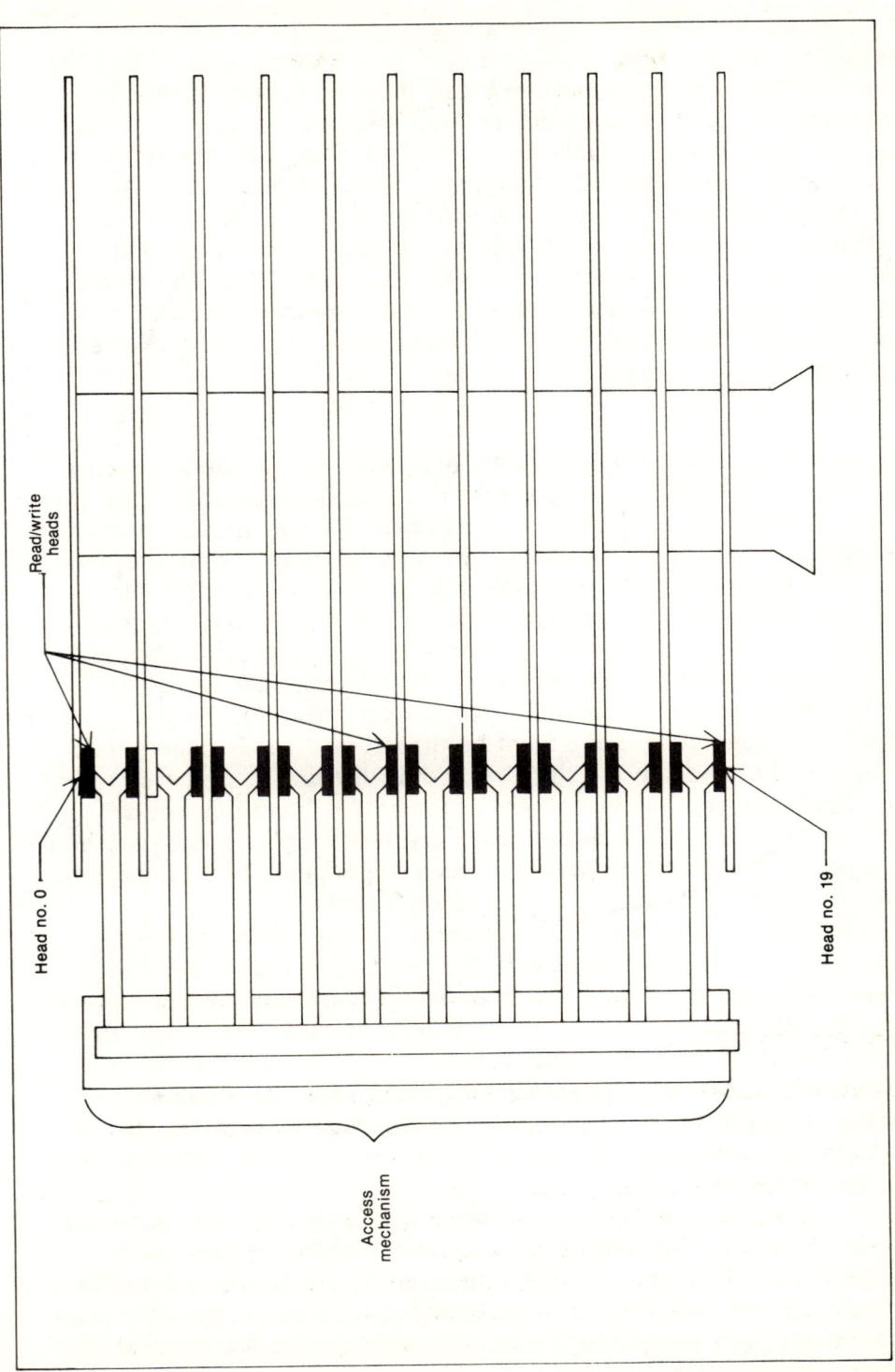

Figure 1-6 Side view of the access mechanism

In order to operate on a recording surface, the access mechanism moves to the track that is to be operated upon. When the access mechanism moves, all the heads move in unison so that they are positioned at the same track on each of the recording surfaces. Then, all these tracks, which are said to make up one *cylinder* of data, can be operated upon, one right after another, without the access mechanism having to move to another setting. In other words, if the access mechanism is positioned at the 75th cylinder, the 75th track on each recording surface can be read or written, one track right after another. Assuming there are 200 cylinders on the disk pack shown in figure 1-6, the access mechanism is positioned at approximately the 65th cylinder.

Accessing a record When directly accessing and reading a record on a disk, there are four phases that the disk drive goes through. During the first phase, called *access-mechanism movement*, the access mechanism moves to the cylinder that is going to be operated upon. The time required for this movement depends on the number of cylinders moved. If it is just one cylinder, the time is much shorter than it would be to move 199 cylinders. In both cases, though, the time is measured in thousandths of a second, or milliseconds.

Once the heads are moved to the correct cylinder, the appropriate read/write head must be turned on. This is called *head switching*. If a track on the third recording surface is supposed to be read, head number 2 is turned on. In figure 1-6, head number 2, which is on, is white while the others are black. Since head switching takes place at electronic speeds, it has a negligible effect on the total amount of time required to read or write a record.

After the head is turned on, there is a delay while the appropriate record rotates around to the head. This phase is called *rotational delay* (or *latency*). If the desired record has just passed under the head, the rotational delay will be equal to the time it takes for one complete rotation of the disk. On the other hand, if the appropriate record is just reaching the head when the head is switched on, rotational delay will be 0 milliseconds. So rotational delay varies between 0 and the number of milliseconds required for a complete rotation.

The last phase in the process of accessing and reading a record is called *data transfer*. Here, data is transferred from the disk to storage in the CPU. The *transfer rate* on System/360-370 disk devices varies by device. For example, the 2314 has a transfer rate of 312,000 bytes per second, or 312KB. In contrast, the 3330 has a transfer rate of 806KB.

An Introduction to the System/360-370 and Its Operating System

When accessing and writing a record, the same four phases are completed. First, the access mechanism is moved; second, the appropriate head is turned on; third, rotational delay takes place; and fourth, the data is transferred from storage to disk. In either a reading or writing operation, access-mechanism movement and rotational delay are by far the most time-consuming phases.

File organization and blocking As I've already pointed out, disk files differ from tape files in that they don't have to be processed sequentially. Instead, they can be given a file organization that will allow them to be accessed directly (in other words, you only have to access the record you want to work on). If you don't know much about the different types of file organization that can be used for disk files, don't worry about it right now. You'll learn about them as you write programs that use different types of files. And you'll learn the JCL considerations in later chapters of this book.

The only reason I bring up file organization at all here is so I can talk about blocking. In some cases, the file organization requires that the file records be unblocked. But if the records can be blocked, they often are, for the sake of processing efficiency. Because more than one record is read or written by a single read or write command when the records are blocked, blocking reduces the time required for these I/O operations. Specifically, only one rotational delay is required for each block of records in contrast to one rotational delay for each record when unblocked records are processed. Thus, by reducing rotational delay, blocking can significantly reduce the time required to read the records in a disk file. In addition, blocking allows you to store more data per track on the disk pack.

OVERLAP AND I/O PROCESSING

Before the System/360, most computer systems could perform only one operation at a time. For instance, a typical small system read a card, processed it, and printed an output line on the printer. It then repeated this sequence for the next card record. Similarly, a typical tape system read input, processed it, and gave output—but only one operation at a time. The trouble with this method of processing was that most of the components of the computer system were idle, even though the system was running.

To overcome the problem of having idle components, systems that could *overlap* I/O operations with CPU processing were developed. The difference between nonoverlapped and overlapped processing is illustrated in figure 1-7. On system A, the nonoverlapped system, nine time intervals are required to read, process, and write three records.

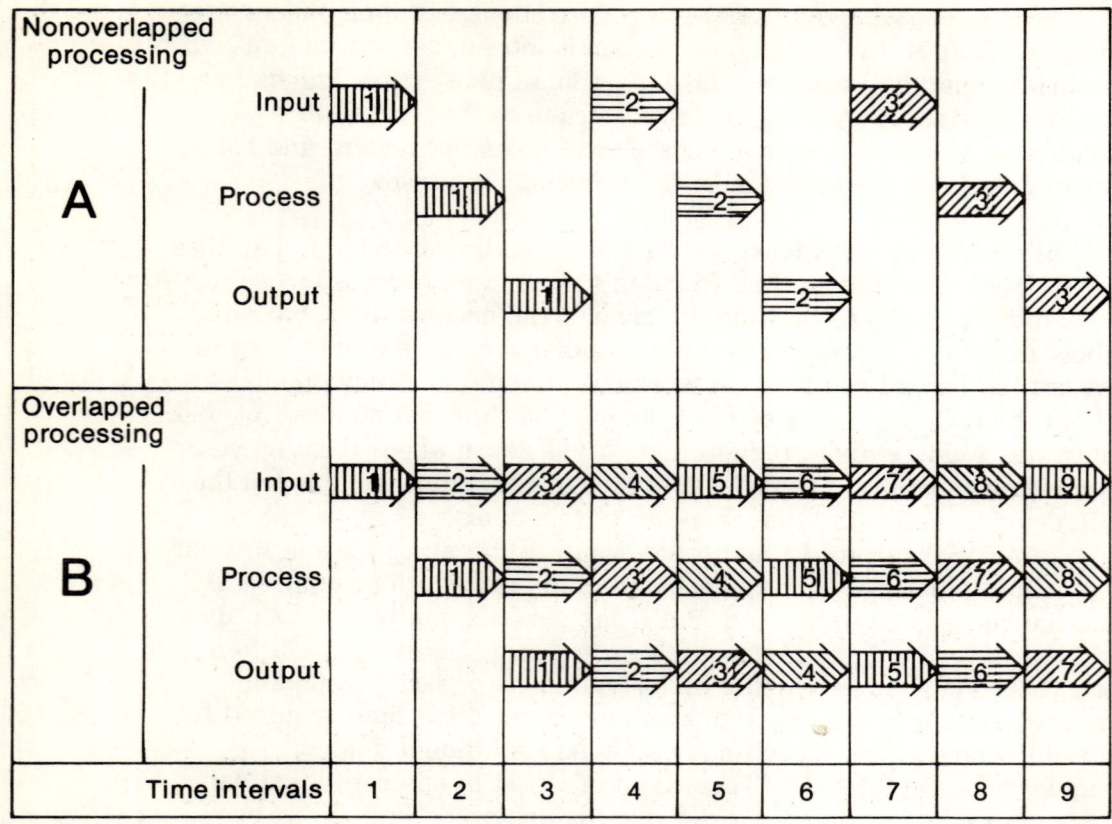

Figure 1-7 Overlapped and nonoverlapped processing

On system B, the overlapped system, nine records have been read, eight have been processed, and seven have been written at the end of nine time intervals. Although this example makes the unlikely assumption that reading, processing, and writing take equal amounts of time, the message is clear: overlap can significantly increase the amount of work that a computer system can do.

Channels One reason earlier computers weren't able to overlap is that the CPU executed all of the instructions of a program, one after the other. In contrast, the CPU of an overlapped system like the System/360-370 doesn't execute I/O instructions. Instead, *channels* are used to execute the I/O instructions, while the CPU executes processing instructions (like performing calculations). The I/O instructions that the channels execute are called *channel commands*. Figure 1-8 illustrates the components of an overlapped system: one channel executes an input command, a second channel executes an output

An Introduction to the System/360-370 and Its Operating System

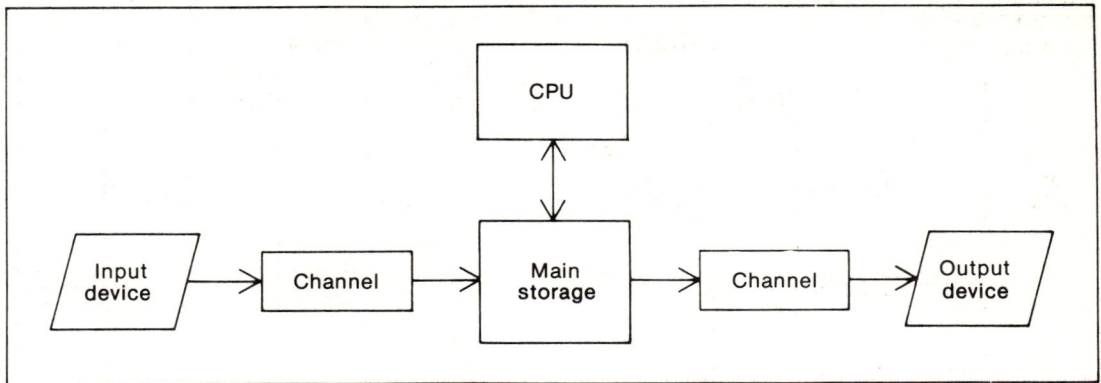

Figure 1-8 Computer system with overlap capability

command, and the CPU executes other instructions of the program—all at the same time. (Although the CPU is generally considered to consist of storage and control circuitry, the CPU and storage are drawn separately in this figure to show that both CPU and channels can access data from storage.)

Whenever data is transferred from a channel to storage or from storage to a channel, CPU processing is interrupted for one *storage access cycle* (or just *access cycle*). Because of the tremendous difference between access-cycle speeds and I/O speeds, however, this is a minor interruption. To illustrate, suppose cards read by a 600-card-per-minute card reader are being processed by a computer that transfers two storage positions (or bytes) of data during each access cycle. If each access cycle takes one microsecond (millionth of a second), CPU processing will be interrupted for a total of 40 microseconds to read all 80 card columns into storage. In contrast, the card reader takes 1/10 of a second, or 100,000 microseconds to read all 80 card columns. This means that while each card is read, the CPU can spend over 99 percent of its time—99,960 seconds out of 100,000 to be exact—executing other instructions of the program.

Although tape and disk devices are many times faster than card readers and printers, this same type of inequality is likely to exist between the speeds of these I/O devices and the access-cycle speeds. For example, a tape drive with a 50,000 byte-per-second transfer rate reads or writes one byte of data every 20 microseconds. If the CPU requires one-half microsecond to transfer the byte to or from storage, 19.5 microseconds per byte are available for other processing. In other words, because of the overlap capability, the CPU can spend 97.6 percent of its time executing other instructions.

Since a channel, like the CPU, can execute only one operation at a time, the number of overlapped operations that a system can have is limited by the number of channels on the system. For instance, a one-channel system can overlap one I/O operation with CPU processing, while a three-channel system can overlap three I/O operations with CPU processing. The one exception to this is the *multiplexor channel*, which can read or write on two or more slow speed I/O devices at one time.

The multiplexor channel has the ability to alternate between several I/O devices. If, for example, a card reader, card punch, and printer are attached to a multiplexor channel, the channel can accept one byte of data from the card reader, send one byte to the card punch, send one byte to the printer, and then return for another byte from the card reader. By switching from one device to another, the single channel makes possible the overlapping of several different devices. Here again, this is possible because of the extreme difference in speeds between I/O devices and access cycles.

Figure 1-9 is a typical OS level System/370 configuration. All of its slow speed devices—the console, card reader, card punch, and printer—are attached to a multiplexor channel while the tape drives and disk drives are attached to the other kind of channel, a *selector channel*. This system, then, can overlap card reading, card punching, printing, console operations, reading or writing on one tape drive, and reading or writing on one disk drive. Because a selector channel can only do one operation at a time, however, operations on two disk drives cannot be overlapped, nor can operations on two tape drives be overlapped. In general, a System/360 or System/370 consists of one multiplexor channel and one or more selector channels.

Dual I/O areas One programming complexity resulting from overlap is that two I/O areas in storage must be used for each I/O operation. If only one input area of storage were used for a card-reading operation, for example, the second card would be read into the input area while the first card was being processed—thus destroying the data from the first card. Instead, the second card must be read into a second input area of storage while the first card is being processd in the first input area. Then, the third card is read into the first input area. This switching from one input area to the other, which is shown schematically in figure 1-10, must be continued throughout the program. Similarly, dual I/O areas (or *buffers*, in OS terminology) must be used for all other I/O operations that are overlapped.

In most cases, OS will automatically provide the number of buffers you need. In some cases, though, you may want to control how the buffers are assigned. So I'll talk again about buffering in later chapters of this book as it applies to specific applications.

An Introduction to the System/360-370 and Its Operating System 17

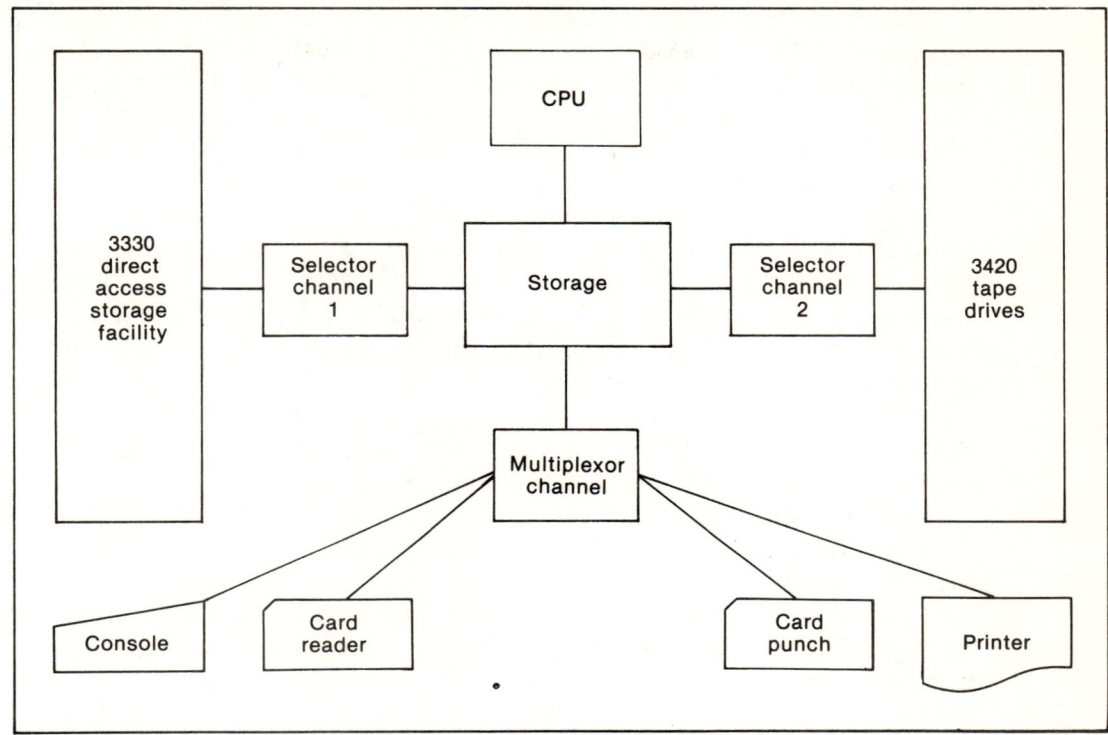

Figure 1-9 A typical System/370 configuration

DISCUSSION

At this point, you may be wondering what all this hardware material has to do with OS job-control language. In fact, you may feel confused as to just what OS and job-control language are. But trust me. You need to be familiar with the information in this topic in order to understand when and how to code the JCL in the chapters that follow. And I'll be using the terms presented here again and again throughout the rest of the book, so you need to understand them. As for OS and job-control language, I'll describe them completely in topic 2.

Terminology

hardware
CPU
central processing unit
input/output device

I/O device
operator console
card reader
card punch

18 Chapter 1

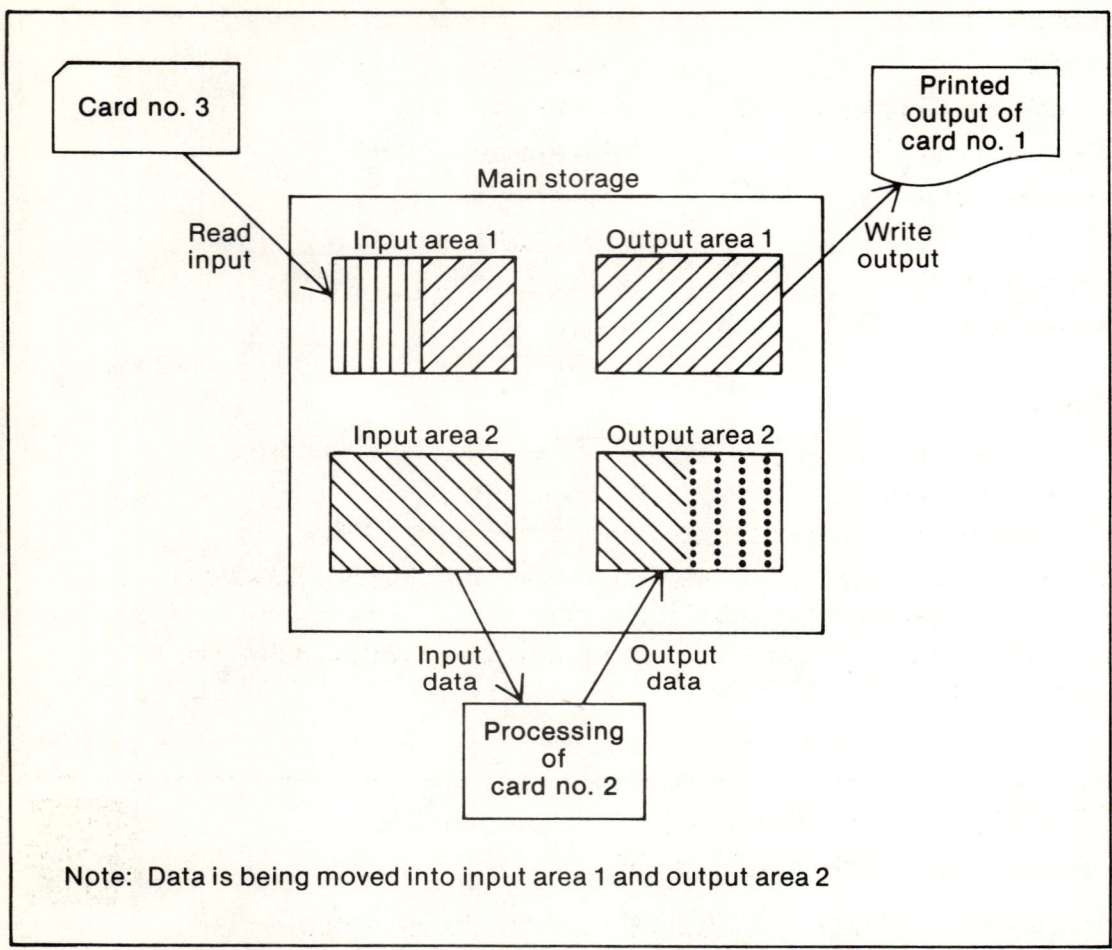

Figure 1-10 Use of dual I/O areas (buffers) for overlapped processing

reader/punch	bpi
printer	blocking
forms control	block
unit record device	tape drive
magnetic tape	sequential processing
bit	direct-access device
byte	disk pack
record	disk drive
interrecord gap	track
IRG	access mechanism
density	read/write mechanism

read/write head
cylinder
access-mechanism movement
head switching
rotational delay
latency
data transfer
transfer rate

overlap
channel
channel command
storage access cycle
access cycle
multiplexor channel
selector channel
buffer

Objectives

1. Describe the differences between a magnetic tape and a direct-access device.
2. Describe the effect of blocking records on tape or disk.
3. List and describe the physical operations required by a disk drive to access and read or write a record in a file.
4. Describe how overlapped I/O operations are accomplished on the System/360-370.

TOPIC 2 The Operating System for the System/360-370

At one time, computer manufacturers first designed a computer and then decided what programming support should be supplied with it. About the mid-1960s, however, the manufacturers realized that the programming support, or *software*, was almost as important as the equipment, or hardware. They then began to design software in conjunction with the hardware. One result was the development of operating systems, which today are supplied along with computer systems.

An *operating system* is a collection of programs designed to improve the efficiency of a computer installation. These programs affect both operating and programming efficiency. For instance, some of the programs of the operating system are designed to reduce operator intervention so the system's idle time is reduced. Other programs are designed to make it easier for a programmer to prepare a tested program.

Although two major operating systems are available on the System/360-370, this book only deals with one of them: IBM's full Operating System (*OS*). It comes in four different versions, as I'll explain later in this topic. First, though, I want to introduce you to some of the common programs that make up OS, regardless of which version you're using, so you'll have a better idea of what an operating system does. Although I've categorized these programs into two basic types—those that improve the computer's operating efficiency and those that improve programming efficiency—you should be aware that the distinctions aren't all that easy to make. The operating system is just too complicated and the programs are too interrelated. But I hope this division will make the discussion a little more manageable.

IMPROVING THE COMPUTER'S OPERATING EFFICIENCY

Stacked-job processing

Before *stacked-job processing* was developed, a computer system stopped when it finished executing a program. The operator removed the program output, such as card decks or magnetic tapes, and made ready the I/O units for the next program. He then loaded the program and placed any cards to be processed in the card reader. The program was then ready to be executed.

The trouble with this intervention by the operator between programs is that it wastes computer time. If a company runs 120 programs a day and the operator takes 30 seconds to set up each program, one hour of computer time is lost. With the current cost of computer time, that lost time can be very expensive.

When stacked-job processing is used, the computer rather than the computer operator loads programs. To make this possible, all of a company's programs can be stored in *libraries* on a *system-residence device*, which is usually a disk device. As a result, programs can be directly accessed from the system-residence device and loaded into storage at a high rate of speed.

At the start of a day's computer operations, then, the computer operator loads a *supervisor program* into storage, and control of the computer is transferred to this program. The supervisor program, which is one of the programs of the operating system, is responsible for (1) loading all of the other programs to be executed from the system-residence device and (2) starting all I/O operations. In short, the supervisor remains in storage throughout the day and controls the overall operation of the computer system.

Job-control language   To tell the supervisor which programs are to be executed, the operator places a stack of *job-control cards* such as the stack in figure 1-11 in the card reader. These cards contain *job-*

An Introduction to the System/360-370 and Its Operating System

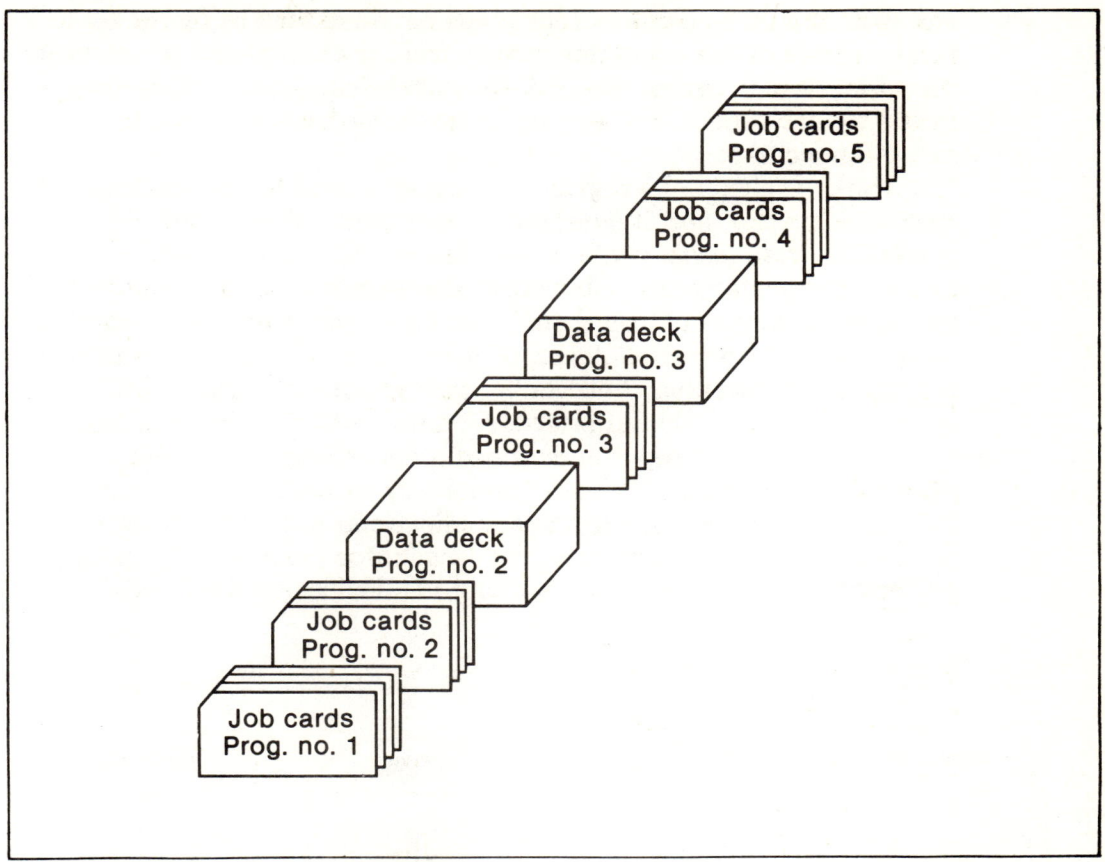

Figure 1-11 A job deck

control statements that give the names of the programs to be executed, along with information such as which tape should be mounted on which tape drive. Because job-control statements require specifications that are in a sense a language of their own, the code used in job-control statements is often referred to as *job-control language*, or *JCL*. The object of this book, of course, is to teach you how to code the JCL you need to run programs on an OS system.

There are several job-control cards for each program to be executed, and, if a program requires card input, the data deck follows the job-control cards. In figure 1-11, programs 2 and 3 require card input, while programs 1, 4, and 5 do not. The stack of job-control cards is commonly referred to as a *job deck*.

Program execution and the job-scheduler program When the computer finishes executing one program, loading and executing the next one typically takes place in four steps as illustrated in figure 1-12. First, control of the computer passes from the completed program to the supervisor program. Second, the supervisor loads a program called the *job-scheduler program* from the system-residence device and passes control to it.

The job-scheduler program is another one of the programs of the operating system, and it consists of three parts: the *reader/interpreter*, the *initiator/terminator*, and the *output writer*. The reader/interpreter reads job-control statements from an input device, analyzes them, and places them in an *input queue* on disk according to job class and priority. (An input queue is a sequence of statements waiting to be executed. And you'll learn about job class and priority later in this topic.) The initiator/terminator selects individual jobs (programs) from the input queue, again according to job class and priority, and performs the tasks necessary to start the job processing. This usually requires storage space allocation and I/O device allocation. When the job is complete, the terminator portion of the program performs de-allocation of storage and I/O devices. If the program

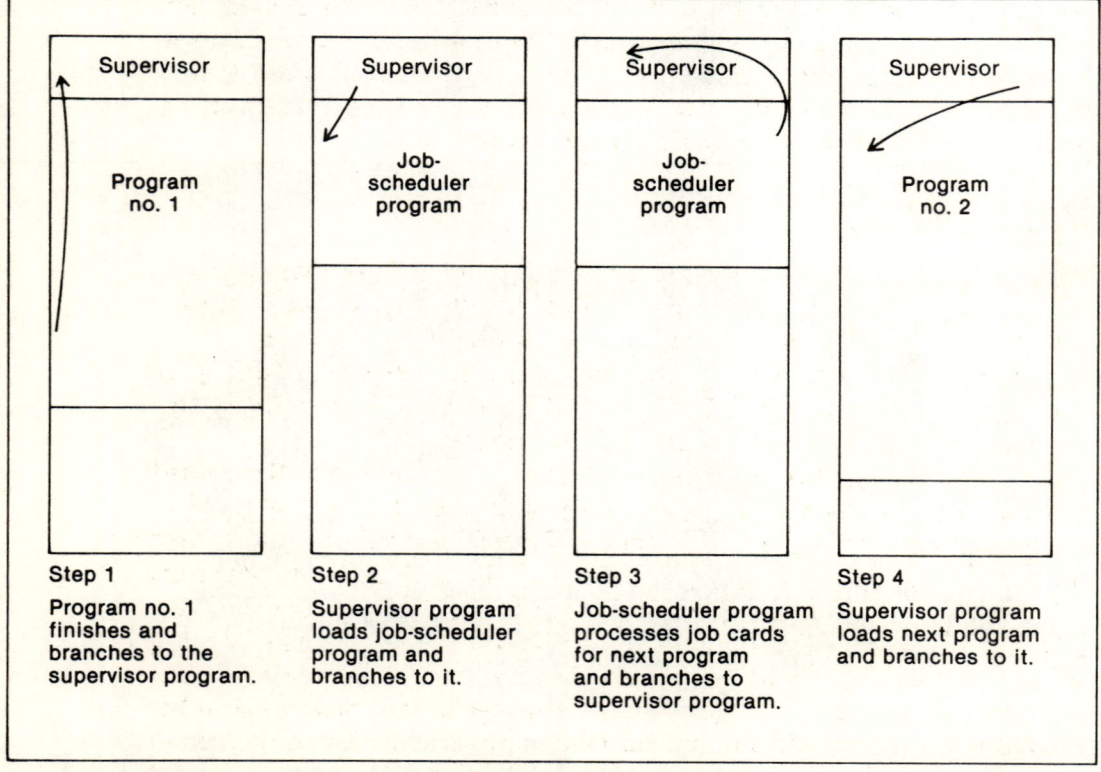

Figure 1-12 Job-to-job transition in stacked-job processing

generated some output in the *output queue*, this data is released to the output writer for printing or punching as required.

In the third step in figure 1-12, then, the job-scheduler program processes all the job-control statements used to request the execution of the next program and checks the availability of the required input and output devices. If a job-control statement is invalid, the job-scheduler program prints an error message so the job deck can be corrected and rerun. When all the job-control statements for the next program have been processed with no errors found, control returns to the supervisor. Then, as shown in the last step in figure 1-12, the supervisor loads the next program from the system-residence device and passes control to its first instruction.

The master-scheduler program Even though stacked-job processing means the system takes care of loading and executing programs, that doesn't mean the computer operator has no control over its operation. The *master-scheduler program* (another program of the operating system) serves as a communication link between the operator and the system through the operator console. The system can send messages to the operator and accept his replies, or the operator can initiate messages to the computer. Thus, through a set of system commands, the operator can monitor and control the operation of the system. He can alter the storage space allocations, the assignment of job classes and priorities, and the availability of I/O devices. He can start and stop some OS functions like reading the input and writing the output. He can even suspend job scheduling altogether.

Multiprogramming

Multiprogramming means the simultaneous execution of more than one program. Actually, this is misleading, because what really happens is that, simultaneously, multiple programs are present in separate parts of storage, but only one program executes at any given time. The others wait for input or output operations to be completed, or simply wait to be given control by the supervisor.

Multiprogramming is valuable because it can increase the overall productivity of a computer system. As you learned earlier, internal processing operations can be executed thousands of times faster than input or output operations. Since it is the nature of business programs to have little internal processing between I/O operations, the CPU is normally idle a great percentage of the time with the program waiting for an I/O operation to be completed. In an effort to make use of this idle time, multiprogramming systems allow additional programs to be in storage so their instructions can be executed while the first program waits for its I/O operations to be completed.

Later in this topic, when I explain the different versions of OS, I'll show you how multiprogramming works. For now, I just want you to see that multiprogramming provides for making better use of CPU storage space, CPU time, and I/O devices.

Managing CPU storage space OS attempts to maximize storage space utilization in two primary ways. First, whenever possible, only the space actually required for a program is allocated to it. If, for example, a program that needs 40K of storage (K refers to approximately 1000 storage positions) is allocated a 50K area and another program that needs 68K is allocated 80K, there is 22K of storage that isn't available to accommodate another program. Through both job-control language and operator commands, OS allows dynamic allocation of storage to permit a higher level of storage utilization. Again, I'll cover this in detail when I talk about the versions of OS.

The second technique used by OS to maximize storage utilization is shared programs. Figure 1-13 illustrates the effect of multiple programs sharing I/O modules. In the first case, the supervisor and two user programs are stored in 65K of storage. The tape-to-printer program requires a total of 10K: 5K for the program code and 5K for the tape and printer I/O modules. The disk update program requires 10K for program code and 10K for disk, tape, and printer I/O modules, a total of 20K. Since the supervisor requires 30K, a total of 60K is occupied when these two programs are in storage. There is still 5K of storage available for use, but none of the programs that can run at this time will fit into this space.

The second case shown in figure 1-13 demonstrates the effect of sharing the tape and printer I/O modules. Since only one copy of each is required, an additional 5K of storage space is available for a third program. If one of the programs that can be run at this time needs 10K or less of storage, it can be loaded and executed with the tape-to-printer and disk update programs. To get this increased storage usage, OS allows you to make the most heavily used program modules permanently resident in storage and causes them to be shared by both system and user programs.

Managing CPU time As I mentioned, multiprogramming was developed to make better use of CPU time, which is measured in access cycles. When one program is waiting for an I/O operation to finish, the supervisor branches to another program in storage to see whether it needs any of the available access cycles. As a result, cycle use improves as the number of programs in storage increases, until all cycles are used. For instance, the first case in figure 1-13 might have a low CPU time utilization. That's because only two programs

An Introduction to the System/360-370 and Its Operating System

```
                                                     Leftover 5K is too
       ┌─────────────────────────────────────┐       small for a program
       │  Unused                        5K   │
       │  Tape & printer I/O modules    5K   │
       │  Disk I/O modules              5K   │
       │                                     │
  65K  │  Disk update program           10K  │
       │                                     │
       │  Tape & printer I/O modules    5K   │
       │  Tape-to-printer program       5K   │
       │                                     │
       │  Supervisor                    30K  │
       │                                     │
       └─────────────────────────────────────┘
                Duplicate I/O modules


                                                     Leftover 10K is
       ┌─────────────────────────────────────┐       large enough for
       │  Third program area            10K  │       a third program
       │                                     │
       │  Disk I/O modules              5K   │
       │                                     │
  65K  │  Disk update program           10K  │
       │  Tape-to-printer program       5K   │
       │  Tape & printer I/O modules    5K   │
       │  (shared)                           │
       │                                     │
       │  Supervisor                    30K  │
       │                                     │
       └─────────────────────────────────────┘
                Shared I/O modules
```

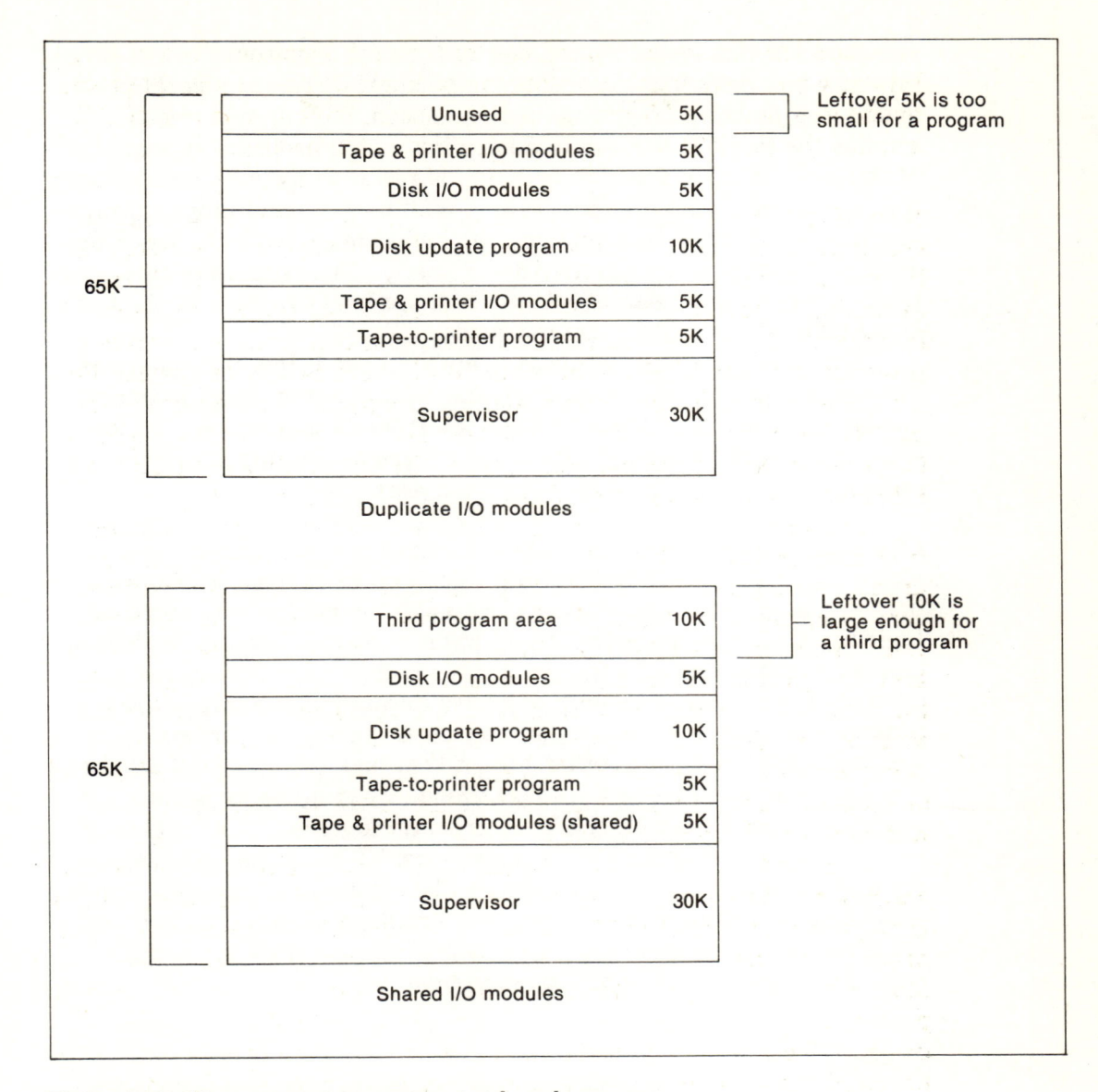

Figure 1-13 Storage space management—shared programs

are in storage. The CPU time utilization will automatically improve when a third program is added. This is illustrated in the second case.

But effective management of CPU time goes beyond just using as many CPU cycles as possible: the cycles must be applied to the most important job first and the least important job last. To do this, OS uses a priority scheme that permits distribution of processing time according to the user's needs. Jobs to be executed under OS are assigned *job classes* and *priorities* by the user according to his definition of what work is most or least important. Then, as several programs are placed into storage for execution, the OS supervisor applies the priority scheme to determine which program gets control of the CPU. If the highest priority job is ready to execute instructions, it is given control. If that program is waiting for something (perhaps for an I/O operation to complete), the supervisor checks to see if the second program in the priority list is ready. This continues until all of the programs have been checked. Then the first program in the list is checked again to see if it is now ready.

This task selection process is repeated each time the supervisor has control of the CPU. If desired, special allocation considerations can be included to prevent any one job from using too many of the CPU cycles and "starving" the other programs waiting for CPU cycles.

Managing I/O device usage The effects of multiprogramming are also evident at the I/O device level. Since more of the devices (tape drives, disk drives, card readers, etc.) will be used at any one time, their utilization is increased. In addition to this, individual devices can serve more than one program. This is true primarily of the disk devices. For instance, instead of a disk drive spinning idly while a program processes a record just retrieved from it, the drive can be reading a record from another file on that disk for a second program.

OS also permits one file to be shared by multiple programs. For example, records can be retrieved from an inventory file by two different programs running at the same time. This is especially useful for maintaining program libraries on disk: more than one user can be executing jobs that require a common program library file. Even so, OS includes safeguards to prevent two programs from updating a record on a common file at the same time.

Spooling

Even with several programs running simultaneously, there is still usually more CPU time available than can be used because of the difference between internal processing speed and the speed of the I/O units. In a further effort to make better use of the available CPU time, *spooling programs* serve as an interface between the very slow I/O devices—the card readers, punches, and printers—and the processing programs. When the processing program attempts to print a line on the printer, for example, the output writer portion of the job-scheduler program acts as a spooling program to cause the line to be written as a record on a disk file instead. Since a disk device is much faster than the printer, it allows the problem program to resume processing much sooner. Later, the output writer prints out the lines that were temporarily stored on disk.

The same spooling procedure is used in reverse for card input files through the reader/interpreter portion of the job-scheduler program. The reader/interpreter first places the data in the cards on disk. Then, when the processing program tries to read a card from the card reader, it is actually read from the disk, and the program thus waits a much shorter time for I/O completion.

Figure 1-14 is a schematic illustration of the concept of *spooling*. Quite simply, the job deck, which consists of job-control statements plus data cards, is read by the reader/interpreter portion of the job-scheduler program and converted to a number of disk files. These disk files can then be processed by the job-scheduler program for the job-control statements and by the processing programs for the data files. When an application program is executed, it processes the appropriate disk file for the original card deck just as though it were the card deck itself. For output, the lines intended for the printer are written in a disk file area reserved for printer output. Later, when the output writer portion of the job-scheduler program processes the output disk file for this application program, the disk file is converted to printed output.

Incidentally, spooling takes place even though the programmer may be completely unaware of it. In fact, the processing programs are written as though they are using card input and printer output, even though they are actually using disk input and output. The operating system itself makes the necessary adjustments so that spooling takes place automatically.

Virtual storage

Virtual storage is another OS facility. It allows simulation of a very large CPU on a much smaller one by using disk storage as an extension of internal storage. In a typical virtual storage system, for example, a computer with 256K bytes of *real storage* might appear to the

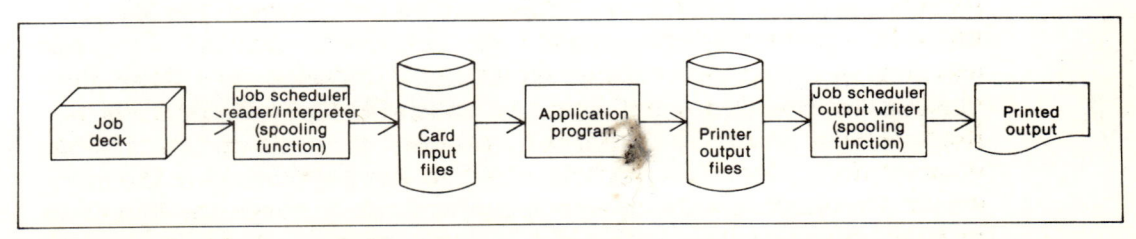

Figure 1-14 Spooling is used to place the job deck on disk and to write output from disk to the printer

user to have 512K bytes; it is thus said to consist of 512K bytes of virtual storage.

During processing, only small portions of the programs being executed are present in real storage. The parts of the progams that aren't currently being used are stored on disk. As additional portions of programs are required, parts that are no longer needed are replaced by the portions now required. In chapter 6, we'll cover virtual storage in more detail, and you'll see how it's accomplished.

The advantage of virtual storage is that more programs can be multiprogrammed, thus increasing the efficiency of the computer system. Although the operating system itself is less efficient because of the additional control routines demanded of it, the overall productivity of the computer system is increased. From the programmer's point of view, the computer functions as though it were a traditional system without virtual storage.

IMPROVING PROGRAMMING EFFICIENCY

Language translators

Language translators are the assemblers and compilers supplied with an operating system. For example, an OS system might include COBOL, FORTRAN, PL/I, and RPG compilers. The translators take the source program written by the programmer and translate it into an *object program*. The object program contains machine-language instructions that can be executed by the computer itself.

The intent of the translators is to reduce the programming time required to prepare a working object program. As a result, all of the translators print diagnostic (error) listings to aid in correcting clerical errors in the source program and often provide debugging statements to aid in testing and correcting the object program. You'll learn how to use the language translators in chapter 8.

The loader program and the linkage editor

When a program is compiled or assembled on a System/360-370, the object program is in relocatable form. This means that the object program must be assigned to storage locations different than those given during the compilation before it can be loaded and executed. For instance, most compilers will create an object program designed to be loaded into storage starting with the first byte of storage in the computer. However, the supervisor occupies these first storage bytes. As a result, the object program must be reassigned to the area of storage in which it will actually be loaded and executed.

Under OS, you can use either the loader program or the linkage-editor program for this purpose. The *loader program* relocates the object program and executes it. If you want to execute the same object program later, you have to run it through the loader program again. The *linkage-editor program* creates a *load module* with the proper storage addresses out of the object program and places it in a library. Then, the load module can be executed again and again from that library.

Besides converting a single object program into a load module, the linkage editor can combine two or more segments of an object program (called *object modules*) into a single load module. For instance, a programmer who is writing an inventory program may want to make use of an available object module that calculates square roots; otherwise, he would have to write this routine himself. In this case, the inventory program is the main program and the square-root module is a *subprogram*. Before testing the inventory program, then, the linkage editor would be used to combine the main program and subprogram into a single load module. In a case like this, the linkage editor not only relocates the object modules, it also resolves all references between the modules; that is, it makes sure that all the fields in one module are addressed properly by instructions in another module. You'll learn how to execute both the loader and the linkage editor in chapter 8.

Sort/merge programs

In any computer installation, much of the processing requires that records be in certain sequences. As a result, two or more tape or direct-access files often have to be merged into one file, or one tape or direct-access file has to be sorted. Although this sorting and merging may take as much as 40 percent of the total running time of a computer system, the programs themselves are very much the same. They differ primarily in the number of files to be merged, the length of the records in the files, the blocking factors used, the length and location of the field on which the file is to be sequenced, and the number of I/O devices to be used.

To take care of these functions, OS provides *sort/merge programs*. These are generalized programs that can be used for many different jobs. The user simply supplies coded specifications and the sort/merge program adjusts accordingly, thus eliminating the need for sort programs to be written by the computer user. You'll learn how to run the sort/merge in chapter 7.

Utility programs

Many of the programs of a typical computer installation are relatively simple ones that convert data from one I/O form to another; for example, printing the contents of a file of tape records or converting a disk file to a tape file. To eliminate the need for a computer user to write such programs, OS provides *utility programs*, in which the user need only specify in coded form the characteristics of the files involved. The utility programs then adjust accordingly and do the desired processing. Thus, routine programs such as card-to-printer, card-to-tape, card-to-disk, tape-to-printer, tape-to-tape, and many others are supplied by OS. You'll learn more about what utilities are available and how to use them in chapter 7.

Library maintenance To reduce duplication of programming effort within a company, an operating system provides for segments of both source and object code to be stored in libraries on the system-residence device. Thus, if a programmer writes a payroll routine for finding a job rate when the job class is known, it can be stored either as source code or as object code in one of the system's libraries. Any other program that involves this routine can then retrieve it from the appropriate library. If the routine is stored as object code, the object code of the main program and the object code of the payroll routine can be combined before execution by the linkage editor. To take care of maintaining the libraries, OS provides special utility programs that can be used to add, modify, delete, and list the segments or members of libraries. You'll learn how to use them in chapter 5.

Data-management services

Another way in which OS saves programmer time and effort is by providing *data-management services*. As the name suggests, these services have to do with handling the data files that pass through the system. They determine such things as how the files are labelled, accessed, and stored, how space is allocated to them, how errors in file handling should be taken care of, and so on. These services are activated either by statements a programmer codes in a source program or by job-control statements. Because the way in which files are handled is critical to OS JCL, the data-management services are covered in detail in topic 3 of this chapter.

VERSIONS OF OS

OS is currently used in five basic versions. Two are designed to control System/360 facilities and the three more recently developed versions are for the System/370. The two System/360 versions are *OS/MFT* (Multiprogramming a Fixed Number of Tasks) and *OS/MVT* (Multiprogramming a Variable Number of Tasks). The three 370 versions, OS/VS1, OS/VS2, and OS/MVS, are very similar to OS/MFT and OS/MVT, except they operate in a virtual storage environment. (Some 370s also operate under OS/MVT or other operating systems that are variations of these basic operating systems.)

OS/MFT

OS/MFT is designed to support System/360 systems ranging from a 128K model 40 up through a 1024K model 75. In practice, however, it is seen on a small range of systems—from a 256K model 40 to a 512K model 50. Similarly, although OS/MFT was designed to multiprogram up to 15 jobs, practical considerations (storage and I/O device limitations) usually limit this to from two to seven programs executing concurrently.

MFT manages the computer's storage space by dividing it into blocks called *partitions* as shown in figure 1-15. The partition with the highest storage address (partition zero or P0) has the highest priority and is the first to be allocated CPU cycles by the supervisor. The next lower partition (P1) has the second priority for CPU cycles, and so on down to the last partition. The number and size of the partitions are set at the time MFT is generated. Although these standard sizes are usually in effect, they can be altered by the operator to meet any special processing needs.

The number and the sizes of the partitions are chosen to best suit the range of jobs to be run by the computer during normal operations. For example, a small partition with a relatively high priority might be specified to allow quick processing of small, short jobs. Usually these jobs are heavily *I/O bound*—that is, the speed of the jobs is determined primarily by the speed of the I/O operations they require. Because these jobs have little processing between I/O operations, they use few CPU cycles. As a result, they can be assigned a high priority because most of the CPU cycles offered by the supervisor will be made available to lower-priority jobs while the high-priority ones wait for I/O completion.

A partition with middle-level priority might be reserved for programs that have a more balanced internal-processing-to-I/O ratio.

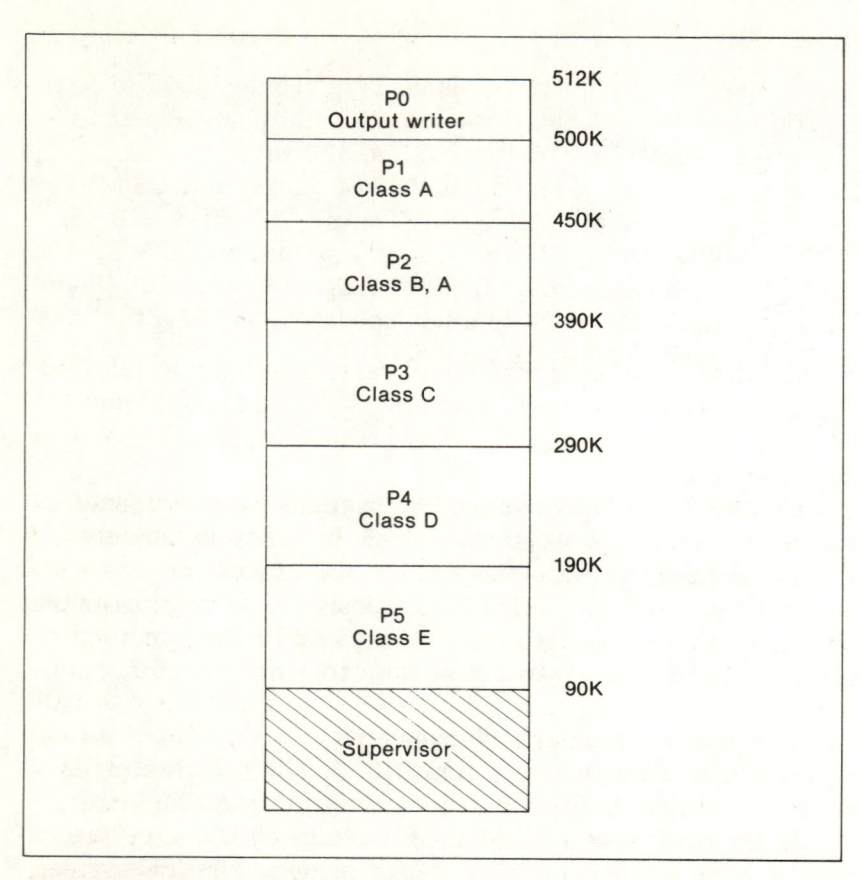

```
                    512K
    ┌─────────────┐
    │     P0      │
    │Output writer│
    └─────────────┘ 500K
    │     P1      │
    │   Class A   │
    └─────────────┘ 450K
    │     P2      │
    │  Class B, A │
    │             │
    └─────────────┘ 390K
    │     P3      │
    │   Class C   │
    │             │
    └─────────────┘ 290K
    │     P4      │
    │   Class D   │
    │             │
    └─────────────┘ 190K
    │     P5      │
    │   Class E   │
    │             │
    └─────────────┘ 90K
    │ Supervisor  │
    └─────────────┘
```

Figure 1-15 Sample OS/MFT storage map

Even then, it is likely that these programs will spend some time waiting for I/O completion, so some of the CPU cycles are available for lower-level partitions. These extra CPU cycles can then be used by a low-priority partition containing a program with a high level of internal processing activity. Many engineering and scientific programs are of this nature.

Figure 1-15 represents the storage map of an MFT system whose partitions are allocated for the type of workload just described. The 90K supervisor resides permanently in the lowest address area of the 512K of storage. The rest of storage is divided into six partitions. Partition zero (P0) is set at a standard size of 12K and normally contains an output writer to print or punch the output generated by the processing program partitions. Even though P0 is the highest priority, it will use only a small percentage of the CPU cycles made available to it since it will be waiting for the printer to complete an I/O operation most of the time.

Partition 1 (P1) is allocated 50K and is set up to run only class A jobs. (Job classes will be defined in chapter 2.) The installation may allow users to assign job class A only to I/O-bound programs that require 50K storage or less and will complete in less than five minutes.

Class A jobs might also be permitted to run in partition 2 (P2) if no class B jobs are in the input queue. Class B jobs would perhaps be less I/O-bound and run longer than class A jobs.

Since P1 and P2 are reserved for small, short jobs, P3 might accommodate the larger or longer jobs that must be run by the installation. I'll call them class C jobs. Large-file loads or updates, lengthy report generations, and large-field sorts are likely to fall into this class. It is the nature of these programs to be highly I/O-bound, thereby allowing a sufficient number of CPU cycles to reach the lower-priority partitions.

Partition 4 (P4) might be reserved for class D jobs: program compilation and testing by the programmers. This partition is likely to get enough CPU cycles so the compilations don't take a very long time to complete. Since the language translater programs do a large amount of input and output, however, CPU cycles will still be available for partition 5.

The lowest partition, P5, would be used to execute the programs with a heavy amount of internal processing, job class E. This insures that a very small precentage of the total CPU cycles will be wasted because all the partitions are waiting for I/O completions. "Number cruncher" jobs, like engineering calculations or scientific analyses, would have the requirement for cycle utilization that's intended here.

Figure 1-16 shows this MFT system in operation. The output writer, residing permanently in P0, prints the output placed in the output queue by the processing programs. At the start of the day's operations, a reader/interpreter job is started in P1 to process the input stream. It would remain there as long as there is more input stream to process. But once the initial input stream has been processed, P1 can also be used for processing programs. At some later time, when more input stream is available, a reader/interpreter task can be started in any available partition to load more jobs in the queue.

Once an initiator task has been started for each of the processing partitions, jobs of the proper class will be selected from the input queue and processed. As each job is completed, the output that it has generated is made available to the output writer for printing, and the initiator is again loaded to select another job from the input queue. This process continues until there are no more jobs in the input queue or until the system is shut down by the operator.

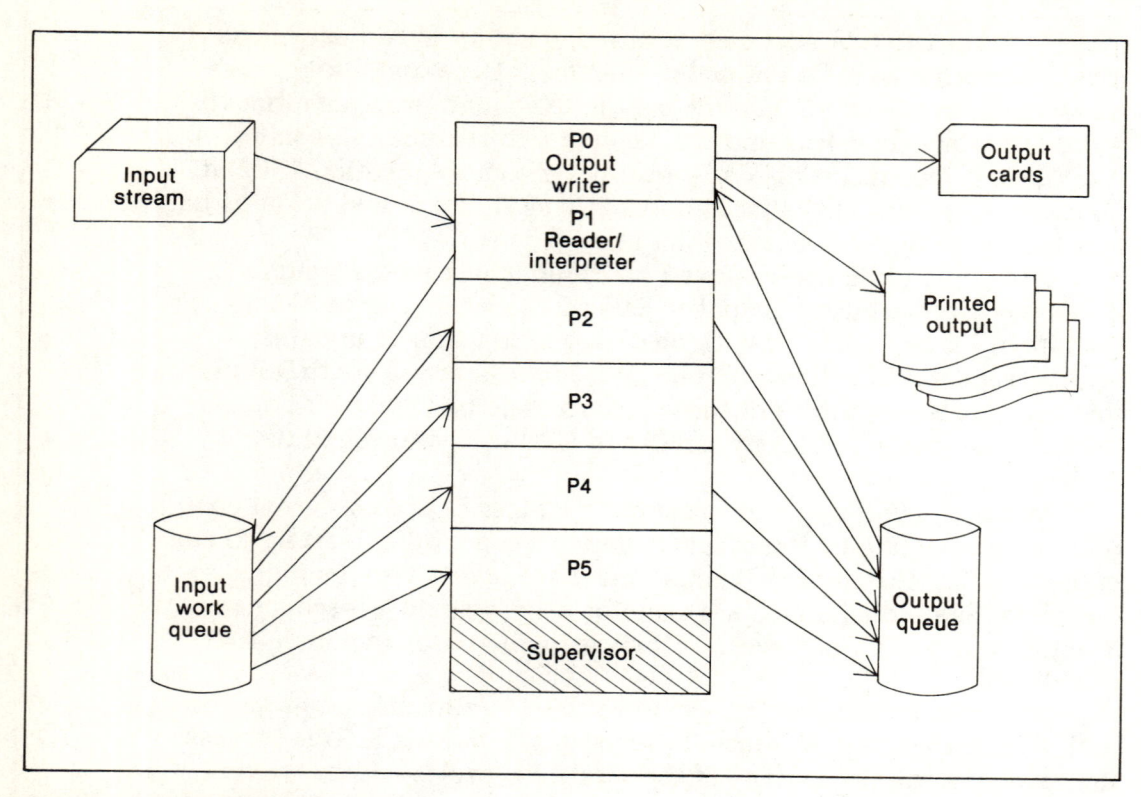

Figure 1-16 OS/MFT in operation

OS/VS1 In chapter 6, you'll be introduced to OS/VS1—a virtual storage version of OS/MFT. Briefly, VS means that the programs currently being executed are divided into segments, and each segment is brought into main storage from disk as required. This allows much larger programs to be executed on a smaller computer.

OS/MVT

On larger 360 systems, from a 512K model 50 to a 1024K model 75, OS/MVT is used. The basic difference between MFT and MVT is the way storage space is managed. MVT uses *dynamic allocation* rather than fixed partitions. This means that the storage space required for a program is allocated when the job is initiated instead of pre-allocated as when partitions are used. Otherwise, many of the system functions in OS/MVT are handled in exactly the same way as in OS/MFT.

Figure 1-17 shows a storage map for MVT on a 512K system. As in MFT, the supervisor permanently occupies the lowest address area

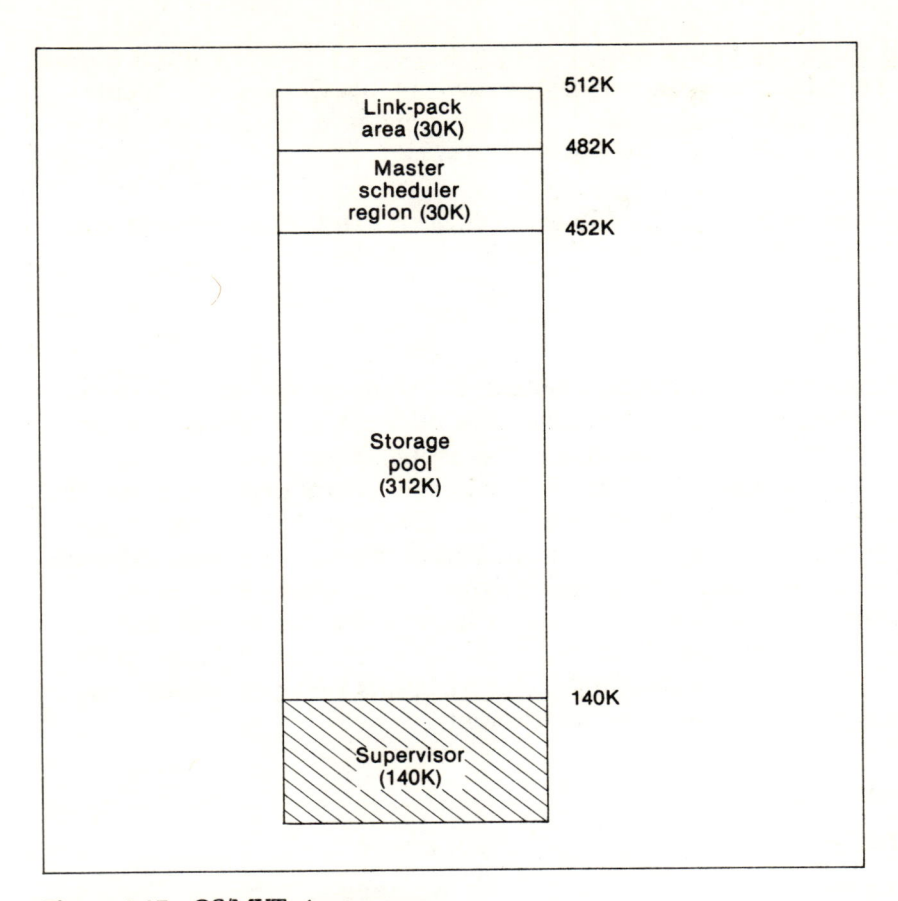

```
                    512K
    Link-pack
    area (30K)
                    482K
    Master
    scheduler
    region (30K)
                    452K




    Storage
    pool
    (312K)




                    140K
    Supervisor
    (140K)
```

Figure 1-17 OS/MVT storage map

of storage. (Notice that the MVT supervisor requires significantly more storage than in MFT.) Then, at the highest end of storage, two additional permanent areas are reserved. First, the *link-pack area* is allocated space to make heavily used I/O or other system subprograms permanently resident in storage and available for sharing. Second, the master scheduler is assigned a permanent area so that it will always be available to the operator. All the rest of storage is treated as a "pool" of space, available for dynamic allocation to programs.

The operations of MVT are very much like MFT: a reader/interpreter task is started to read the input stream and place jobs in the input queue. Then, one or more initiator tasks are started to begin execution of the jobs in the queue. Next, however, instead of assigning jobs to specific partitions according to job class as in MFT, the MVT initiator requests a program area called a *region* from the supervisor. The size of this region can be specified by job-control language statements or it will default to the region size indicated by the job class. If there isn't enough storage for the next job in the input queue, the job scheduler temporarily bypasses this job. A smaller job can then be run while waiting for sufficient storage to become available for the larger job.

OS/VS2 and OS/MVS   OS/VS2 and OS/MVS are virtual storage versions of MVT. They will be covered in chapter 6.

DISCUSSION

Quite frankly, there is nothing simple about an operating system and its functions. Many of the functions are difficult to visualize or comprehend; and the programs of the operating system often take many man-years to develop. So if you're having difficulty understanding the functions I've just described, take heart. Continue to the next topic and go on through chapters 2 and 3. Then, after you've been exposed to the elements of the job-control language and after you've seen how they direct the functions of the operating system, come back and reread the parts of this chapter you don't understand. I think you'll develop a better understanding of the concepts and terminology by seeing them applied in an active context.

Terminology

software
operating system
OS
stacked-job processing
library
system-residence device
supervisor program
job-control card
job-control statement
job-control language
JCL
job deck
job-scheduler program
reader/interpreter
initiator/terminator
output writer
input queue
output queue
master-scheduler program
multiprogramming
job class
priority
spooling program
spooling
virtual storage
real storage
language translator
object program
loader program
linkage-editor program
load module
object module

subprogram
sort/merge program
utility program
data-management services
OS/MFT
OS/MVT

partition
I/O-bound
dynamic allocation
link-pack area
region

Objectives

1. Describe the effect of stacked-job processing.
2. Briefly describe the function of each of these facilities of OS:
    a. supervisor
    b. job scheduler
    c. master scheduler
    d. multiprogramming
    e. storage space management
    f. CPU time management
    g. I/O device management
    h. spooling
    i. virtual storage
    j. language translators
    k. loader program
    l. linkage editor
    m. sort/merge program
    n. utility programs
    o. data-management services
3. Name the five basic versions of OS.
4. Describe the major difference between OS/MFT and OS/MVT.

TOPIC 3 Data-Management Services

As I said in topic 2, OS helps the programmer to reduce program coding and extensive manual file keeping by providing *data-management services* for file handling. These services are activated by the code in a source program or by options coded in job-control language. For example, if you're a COBOL programmer, you can code the block size for an output file in your source program. Then, when the program is compiled and run, the appropriate data-management service will be called into action, so the output file will be properly blocked when written. On the other hand, you can code BLOCK CONTAINS 0 RECORDS for the file in your program and then assign a proper blocking factor in your JCL to run the program. In that case, the JCL will activate the data-management service so the file will be properly blocked.

The services provided can be divided into these general categories: (1) data set storage control; (2) cataloging; (3) generation processing; (4) space allocation; (5) security; (6) I/O routines; and (7) error processing. You have to be aware of these functions before you can understand the reason for coding many of the JCL operands that will be presented in the following chapters.

Before we start, though, you should know that in OS terminology files are called *data sets*. Thus, the terms "file" and "data set" are used interchangeably throughout the rest of this book.

Data set storage control

The service called *data set storage control* is the cornerstone of data-management services. This function, through which all files are accessed, consists of a number of subfunctions. Among the OS facilities managed by this group of subfunctions are data set labeling, data control block generation, data set organization, and access method processing.

Data set labels On the System/360-370, a storage entity such as a reel of tape, a disk pack, or a drum is called a *volume* and may contain a portion of a file, a complete file, or multiple files. To identify the files on a volume, data set labels are used.

The format of the data set label and the information it provides depends on the type of file. Magnetic tape files can be labeled with either standard or non-standard (user-defined) labels, or they can be unlabeled. A file with standard labels has one label area preceding the data records and one following the records. These label areas contain information such as the file name, the date the file was created, the date after which it can be destroyed, and the number of blocks of data in the file.

As for direct-access files, they always have standard labels. But instead of being physically adjacent to the individual files, the labels for all the files in a disk pack are stored together in a special data set called the *volume table of contents*, or *VTOC* (pronounced VEE-tock).

In other words, each disk volume has a VTOC that contains the identifying information for all the files on that volume. Each label in the VTOC gives the file name, the file's physical characteristics (block length, record length, etc.), and its location on the disk.

In addition to data set labels, every tape and disk volume has a label area that contains a *volume serial number* to identify the entire volume. In chapter 2, you'll learn how to code these in your JCL. Then, in chapter 3, you'll learn how to use the LABEL parameter of OS JCL if you want to provide information for the data set label for a file.

Data control block When a program opens a file, OS creates a *data control block* (*DCB*) for the file based on information taken from the program statements and the data set label for the file. Each DCB is a table in storage that is used by various routines for controlling I/O operations. To increase its flexibility, OS allows certain data set information to be supplied at execution time by the DCB parameter in the JCL rather than by the processing program itself. This makes it possible for a file to exist in various forms and still be processed by the same programs. You'll be introduced to the DCB parameter and the values that can be coded in it in chapter 2. Then, in the chapters that follow, you'll learn about DCB values that are specific to certain applications.

Data set organization Data is organized in one of many ways in the System/360-370. This book will deal with five such organizations: (1) physical sequential, (2) indexed sequential, (3) direct, (4) partitioned, and (5) virtual.

As you learned in topic 1, physical sequential organization means that the records are written in processing sequence, one after the other. As a result, when a program reads the file, the records always appear in the same order. To process a record in the middle of the file, you have to read all of the preceding records. Tape files are always sequential; direct-access files may be sequential.

Indexed sequential and direct organizations allow you to store and retrieve records from a direct-access volume randomly. These organizations will be covered in depth in chapter 4. Partitioned organization allows several sequential files to be kept as one file in a library. This concept is presented in chapter 5. Virtual storage organization is only available on virtual storage machines. It provides many of the features of physical sequential, indexed sequential, and direct organization. Virtual storage organization is covered in chapter 6.

Access method The *access method* of a file is the method OS uses to store and retrieve records on the volume. The access method you use depends on the program and the organization of the data. If you're an assembler language programmer, you can select, to a certain degree, the type of access method you want to use; for high-level language programmers, the selection is automatic.

Access method is derived from the data set organization and the *access technique*. Although there are several techniques for teleprocessing, remote terminal message control, and other specialized file handling situations, we'll only be discussing the two major techniques: queued and basic. *Queued access technique* causes all of the automatic I/O routines of OS data-management services (described later in this topic) to be applied to the file; *basic access technique* allows you to control your own I/O processing. The common access methods are queued sequential access method (QSAM), queued indexed sequential access method (QISAM), basic sequential access method (BSAM), basic indexed sequential access method (BISAM), basic partitioned access method (BPAM), and basic direct access method (BDAM).

Cataloging

In job-control language, you can tell OS to *catalog* a file for you through the cataloging function of OS data-management services. When a file is cataloged, its name along with other information like the volume identification and file address are stored in a special system file called the *data set catalog*. When you want to access the file, you can specify just the name of the file and OS will find the file by looking up the name in the catalog.

You can also keep a file without cataloging it. In this case, if you want to access the file, you have to provide the data set name, the volume identification, and other attributes of the file. You'll learn how to control the cataloging of a file in chapter 2.

Generation processing

Generation processing allows you to refer to a cyclical data set in relation to the current version. To illustrate, consider figure 1-18. Here, the master file named MASTFILE is read into an update program where input data is added and a new master file is written out. When the next update period rolls around, the new master file created here will be the old master file that is read as input. Since data set names must be unique in the system, and since we may want to keep the old version of the master file even after it has been replaced by the new master, OS provides us with a generation processing service.

The generation processing function of data-management services keeps track of the current version of a file and allows you to code data set names with a relative generation number as part of the name. In the example in figure 1-18, then, the old master file would be referred to as MASTFILE(0) and the new master file would be referred to as MASTFILE(+ 1). Last month's file would be MASTFILE(– 1). Thus, the update program that reads the old master and creates the new master will read MASTFILE(0) and write out MASTFILE(+ 1). When the program ends, the new master just created automatically becomes MASTFILE(0); MASTFILE(0) becomes MASTFILE(– 1); MASTFILE(– 1) becomes MASTFILE(– 2); and so on. We'll cover this concept in more detail in chapter 3, but for now, I just want you to grasp the general idea of *generation data sets*.

Space allocation

The allocation of direct-access space is an important function of OS data-management services. It lets you specify how much space your file will need by coding a parameter in job-control language. OS then searches the volume to find that amount of space in segments until it gathers enough to allocate to your file. This saves you from having to find areas of disk space large enough to hold your file. In chapter 2, you'll see how to code the SPACE parameter to allocate direct-access space to your file.

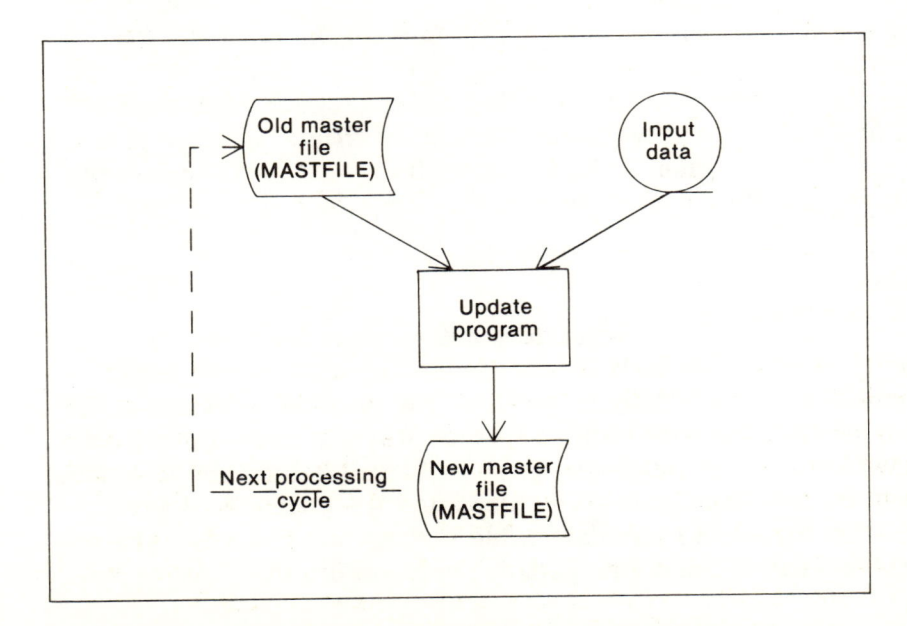

Figure 1-18 Using the generation processing function of OS data-management services

Security

OS data-management services provide *security* for sensitive files by allowing you to set *passwords* in data set labels. In this way, only those people and programs that have the proper password can read the data. In chapter 3, you'll see how to use passwords to protect your files.

I/O routines

OS data-management services provide *I/O routines* to read data from a device, write data onto a device, translate data from one recording format to another, block and unblock records, and process data set labels. This frees you to process your application programs without concern for how the data is eventually transferred. These routines are called by instructions that are coded by the assembler-language programmer or generated by the compiler of a high-level language. In your program, you simply execute an input or output instruction and OS does the rest. It finds the proper place on the volume, starts the input/output mechanism, and actually transfers the data (blocked or unblocked) to or from the recording medium.

Error processing

Error processing is provided by OS data-management services either through standard routines, optional error handling procedures, or by allowing you to process your own error routines. As a result, you needn't concern yourself with checking an input or output operation to determine if it was properly handled. OS will check each read and write to analyze its validity. If something goes wrong, whether it is a bad device, a bad volume, or bad data in the file, OS will initiate the proper error handling routine to minimize the effect of the error.

Discussion

This introduction to OS data-management services has been necessarily brief as this book is not intended as a course in data management. For you to fully understand the internal workings of OS and its many facilities will require further study in areas not covered here. However, for our purposes, you should understand the functions performed by data-management services and the terminology presented in this topic. As I have indicated throughout this topic, you will learn how to control these functions in the chapters that follow.

An Introduction to the System/360-370 and Its Operating System

Terminology

data-management services	access method
data set	access technique
data set storage control	queued access technique
volume	basic access technique
data set label	catalog
volume table of contents	data set catalog
VTOC	generation data set
volume serial number	security
data control block	password
DCB	I/O routine

Objective

Describe the intent of the seven categories of OS data-management services that follow:

a. data set storage control
b. cataloging
c. generation processing
d. space allocation
e. security
f. input/output routines
g. error processing

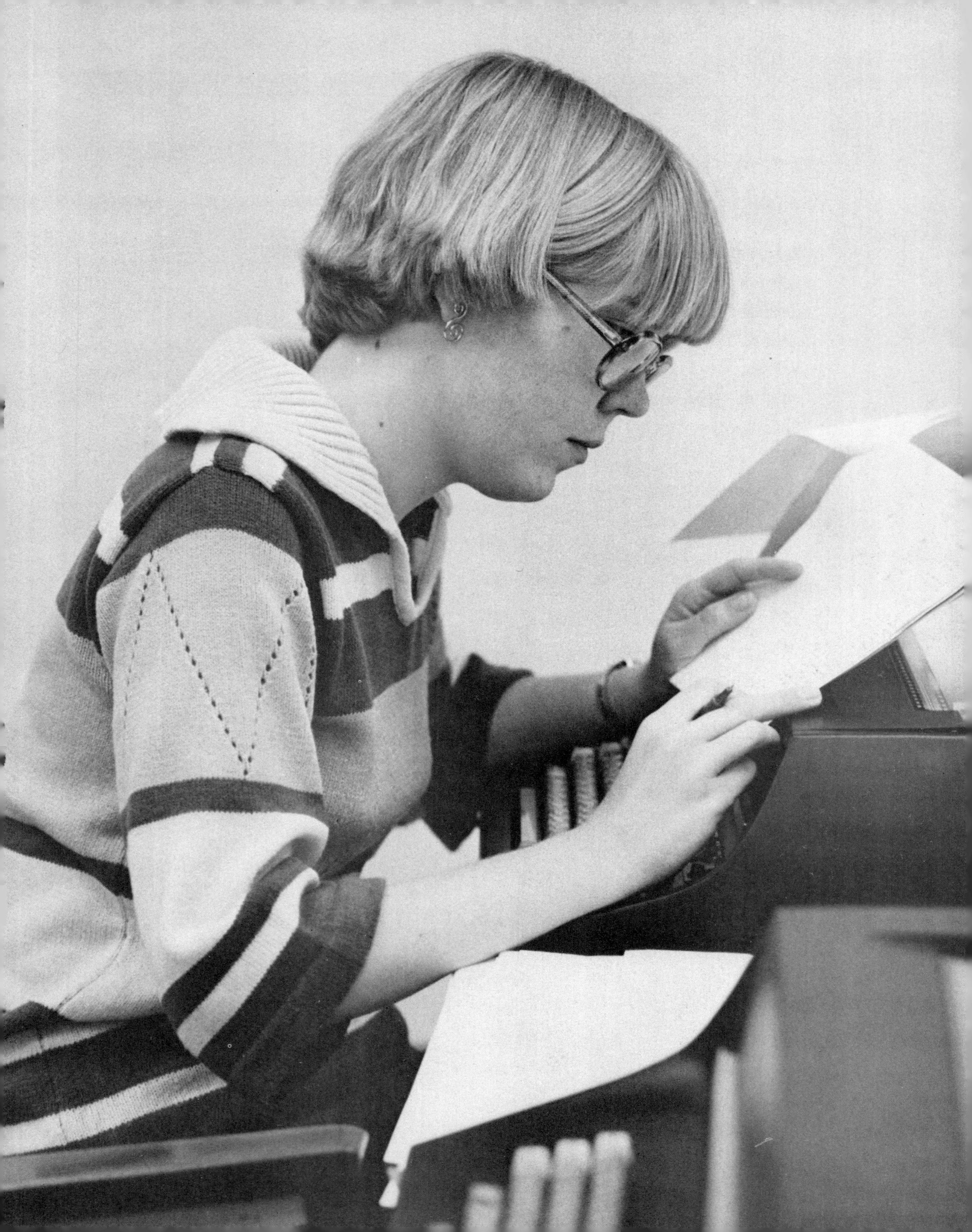

PART 2

The Core Content

This part presents the critical material of your OS JCL training. Once you have mastered it, you will be able to code the JCL you need to run a wide variety of jobs. What's more, you'll find it relatively easy to build on this **core content** by learning the additional JCL you need for certain applications and types of files. As a result, you should be prepared to put more effort into the mastery of the material in this part than you will put into subsequent parts of your JCL training.

2

Job-Control Language:
A Basic Subset

As you learned in chapter 1, OS is a collection of programs intended to make efficient use of IBM System/360-370 computer resources. Job-control language (JCL) is your means of communicating with OS. Through a series of control statements in 80-column card format, you use JCL to tell OS your job requirements.

This chapter covers the major statements of the language; others will be introduced in later chapters in conjunction with more advanced functions of the operating system. In topic 1, you'll be introduced to the general coding rules and suggested coding standards for OS JCL. In topic 2, you will find the syntax for the basic parameters of each of the major control statements. Then, in topic 3, you'll see the JCL statements applied to real situations. You'll also get a chance to write the JCL to solve real data processing problems.

TOPIC 1   Coding Rules and Standards

If you have experience in a programming language such as COBOL, FORTRAN, PL/I, or assembler language, you know that you can read and write data records, manipulate data fields, and control the flow of your program by coding certain instructions in that language. JCL is a different kind of language that doesn't allow input or output, manipulation of data, or control of program flow. Instead, it's a collection of job specifications given to the operating system. Through JCL, you tell OS what your job requires in terms of computer resources and OS services. The information you give to OS is classified into three categories: (1) information about the job as a whole and its relationship to other jobs currently in the system; (2) information about each program in the job; and (3) information about each file the programs in the job will read and write.

To OS, a *job* is a collection of one or more related job steps; a *job step* is the execution of one program. Each job step may access several files. In later sections of this chapter, you'll see that the JOB statement is used to provide job information, the EXEC statement is used to provide job step information, and the DD (Data Definition) statement is used to provide information about the input and output files.

CONTROL STATEMENT FORMAT

Job-control language statements are read into the system as 80-character records. This length allows JCL statements to be read as punched card input, although they may be read from any type of input device including magnetic tape, disk, and keyboard terminals.

The first two positions of a JCL statement must be // (slash-slash). This identifies the statement to the reader/interpreter as a JCL statement and distinguishes it from other data that may be in the input stream. The delimiter statement (to be described later) is the only exception to this rule. For it, you must code /* (slash-asterisk) in the first two positions. Positions 3 through 71 contain the name, operation, operand, and comments fields. These four fields will be discussed individually in a moment. Position 72 can be used as a continuation indicator if you must continue a control statement from one line to the next. Finally, positions 73 through 80 can be used for identification or sequence numbers. In actual practice, these last eight columns are usually left blank with two exceptions: (1) when the JCL is maintained in decks of cards that may be dropped (so they have to be put back into sequence manually); and (2) when the JCL is cataloged in procedure libraries and sequence numbers are required to update individual records. In both of these cases, sequence numbers are keyed into positions 73 through 80.

The *name field* is used to identify the name of a job, job step, or file. It is optional on most statement formats, but if coded, it is placed immediately after the slash-slash with no intervening spaces. If coded, the name field must contain from one to eight letters, numerals, or the special characters #, @, and $ (known as *national characters*). The first character of the name field must be an alphabetic or national character. Figure 2-1 shows some valid and invalid name field examples.

The *operation field* of a control statement specifies the type of operation. For example, JOB is the operation of a job statement, EXEC is the operation of an execute statement, and DD is the operation of a data definition statement. It must follow the name field with at least one separating space. If the name field is omitted, the operation field must be the first field after the //, with at least one separating space.

The *operand field* is the one to which most of this book refers. It is within this field that the actual specifications are made by means of parameters coded in free form, separated by commas. Some of the parameters are *key-word parameters*. In other words, some parameters take the form:

```
UNIT=SYSDA
```

where the reader/interpreter recognizes the key word UNIT and associates the value SYSDA with the word. On the other hand, some parameters or subparameters are *positional* and take this form:

```
DISP=(OLD,CATLG,DELETE)
```

In this case, the position of the value within a boundary is significant to its meaning. If you want to let one of the values default to a system-defined value, you would code it like this:

```
DISP=(OLD,,DELETE)
```

The two commas together indicate the absence of the second value. If you want to include only the first value, the boundaries and commas are not required, as in this example:

```
DISP=OLD
```

```
Valid name fields:

//PAYFILE
//EDITPROG
//UPDATE
//$NUMCALC

Invalid name fields:

//107RPT        Name begins with a numeric character
//UDATERPTS     More than eight characters
//DATA/IN       Illegal character: /
//  RPT1        Space between the // and the name
```

Figure 2-1 Valid and invalid name fields

In this case, the reader/interpreter would assume that OLD is the first value, and since there are no commas following, it would assume default values for the remaining parameters.

The *comments field* is optional and may contain any information you feel will help to document the system. Later, you'll be introduced to the comment statement. It is used to document large areas of JCL coding, while the comments field on each statement is useful for documenting one or two lines of JCL coding.

Continuing job-control statements

If a JCL statement will not fit in columns 3 through 71, or if you want to divide the parameters onto more than one line, you may continue the statement on the next line. To do this, first find a convenient, logical place to break off between two parameters or subparameters. Second, code a comma to indicate that another parameter or subparameter follows. Then, continue coding the statement on the next line.

Figure 2-2 shows examples of continuation lines. The first example shows how to continue operand parameters, and the second example shows how to continue statements with a comments field. Notice that a non-blank character must be coded in column 72 in order to continue a comments field. This continuation character is optional when continuing operand fields. All JCL continuation parameters must begin before column 17, or they will be treated as comments.

SUGGESTIONS FOR JCL STANDARDS

Presented here are some practical suggestions for a standard method of coding JCL. They are not required by the syntax of the language

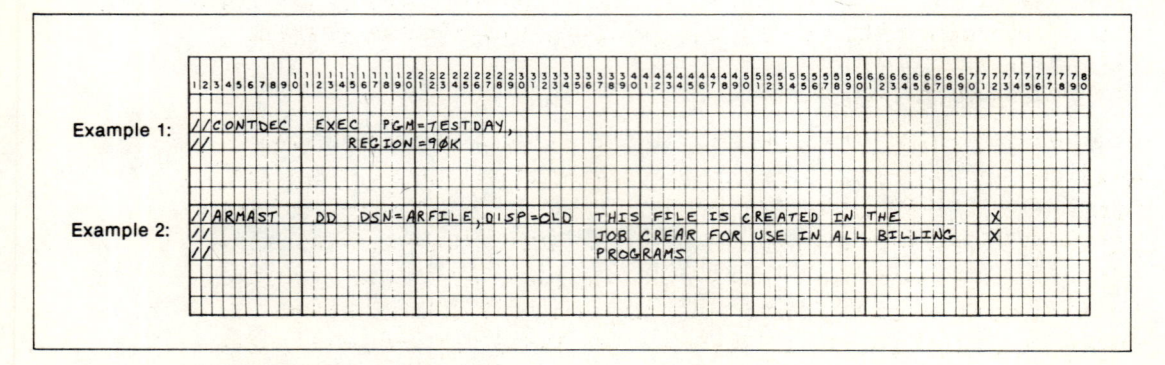

Example 1:
```
//CONTDEC  EXEC  PGM=TESTDAY,
//              REGION=90K
```

Example 2:
```
//ARMAST    DD  DSN=ARFILE,DISP=OLD  THIS FILE IS CREATED IN THE    X
//                                   JOB CREAR FOR USE IN ALL BILLING X
//                                   PROGRAMS
```

Figure 2-2 Continuing job-control statements

and if you don't want to use them, you don't have to. However, JCL is a language that can be difficult to read (especially in a long listing interspersed with JCL messages). As a result, these standards, or similar ones, are in use in many programming departments in industry to make JCL easier to read and easier to modify.

Use one parameter per line

Code only one parameter per line where possible. This will improve readability, especially in a large job. In addition, if only one parameter value in a statement needs to be changed, only that one parameter must be rekeyed. For example, consider the following JCL statement describing a file. The statement is written in the traditional free form style. (Don't concern yourself with the meaning of the parameters at this time; I'll cover them in topic 2. Just look at the structure of the statement.)

```
//GLEDGER  DD  DSN=MMA.GENLEDG,DISP=(NEW,KEEP,DELETE),
//  UNIT=SYSDA,VOL=SER=USER20,
//  SPACE=(CYL,(1,1),RLSE),DCB=(LRECL=95,BLKSIZE=4750),
//  RECFM=FB)
```

If for some reason any of the parameters must be changed (let's say that SPACE must be increased), the entire line will have to be re-entered. And with my luck, I'll get the SPACE parameter right and mess up the DCB parameter.

In contrast, if you code one parameter on a line, the above example will look like this:

```
//GLEDGER    DD    DSN=MMA.GENLEDG,
//                 DISP=(NEW,KEEP,DELETE)
//                 UNIT=SYSDA,
//                 VOL=SER=USER20,
//                 SPACE=(CYL,(1,1),RLSE),
//                 DCB=(LRECL=95,BLKSIZE=4750,RECFM=FB)
```

Now, any one of the parameters can easily be changed, and the alignment of the parameters makes the statement much easier to read.

Use consistent indentation

In a long list of JCL, consistent indentation makes reading the list much easier. My suggested standard is that you begin all operation fields (JOB, EXEC, DD) in column 12 followed by two spaces and one parameter. This will allow a name field of eight characters in length to precede the operation. If there are additional parameters, continue the statement to the next line by coding a comma after the first parameter. On the continuation line, code the next parameter in column 15. If a list of *subparameters* must be continued, begin the continuation in column 16.

You may find a way of indentation you like better than this, and if so, use it. The point I am making is that you should be consistent so that it becomes easy for anyone to read the JCL you have written.

Use meaningful names

If the first step of your job is to execute the edit program, don't call it STEP1; call it EDIT or some other name that lets you know, without looking at other documentation, what each step is doing. Similarly, if that program uses a payroll file as input, don't call the file INFILE; call it PAYFILE or some other meaningful name. I guarantee this will save you time and headaches later on.

Use constant sequences

Whenever a list of identical parameters appears more than one time in your JCL, code it in the same sequence each time. A good example of this is the DD statement. It usually contains the same parameters every time (only the values change). So if you code the parameters in the same sequence every time, it's easy to spot the parameters you are looking for. Since I haven't covered the DD statement yet, it would be premature to list the order I recommend; I'll cover that in the section on the DD statement later in this chapter.

Place code at the lowest level possible

When I present the JOB statement and the EXEC statement in topic 2, you'll see that you have the option of coding certain information either at the job level or at the job step level. For example, you can set a time limit for the entire job, or for each job step; you may specify the amount of main storage required by the entire job or the amount required by each job step.

To decide where to place code like this, I suggest you follow the principles of top-down system design. In brief, this means you should code a parameter at the EXEC, or job step level, whenever possible. This provides more flexibility in your system and makes each job step more of an independent module that can be removed or modified without changing parameters on the JOB statement. The rule of thumb, then, is to code the least amount of information on the JOB statement as possible, and as much as is needed on the EXEC statement.

EXAMPLE OF SUGGESTED STANDARDS

Figure 2-3 shows the traditional method of coding JCL with no indentation and more than one parameter per line. Figure 2-4 shows a JCL

Job Control Language: A Basic Subset 53

```
//ARSTMTS   JOB   HE66YFNH,'W. CLARY'
//EXTRACT1 EXEC  PGM=AGEDSEL,REGION=120K,PARM=010980
//STEPLIB   DD   DSN=MMA.USERLIB,DISP=SHR
//ACCTREC   DD   DSN=ARMAST,DISP=OLD
//AGEDACCT  DD   DSN=&&AGEDACCT,DISP=(NEW,PASS),UNIT=SYSDA,
//    SPACE=(TRK,(10,1),RLSE),DCB=(LRECL=120,BLKSIZE=2400,RECFM=FB)
//DELSTMT  EXEC  PGM=ARSTMTS,REGION=60K
//STEPLIB   DD   DSN=MMA.USERLIB,DISP=SHR
//AGEDACCT  DD   DSN=&&AGEDACCT,DISP=(OLD,DELETE)
//STMTS     DD   SYSOUT=A,DCB=BLKSIZE=133
//
```

Figure 2-3 Unstructured JCL list

```
//ARSTMTS   JOB   HE66YFNH,
//                'W. CLARY'
//EXTRACT1 EXEC  PGM=AGEDSEL,
//                REGION=120K,
//                PARM=010980
//STEPLIB   DD   DSN=MMA.USERLIB,
//                DISP=SHR
//ACCTREC   DD   DSN=ARMAST,
//                DISP=OLD
//AGEDACCT  DD   DSN=&&AGEDACCT,
//                DISP=(NEW,PASS),
//                UNIT=SYSDA,
//                SPACE=(TRK,(10,1),RLSE),
//                DCB=(LRECL=120,BLKSIZE=2400,RECFM=FB)
//DELSTMTS EXEC  PGM=ARSTMTS,
//                REGION=60K
//STEPLIB   DD   DSN=MMA.USERLIB,
//                DISP=SHR
//AGEDACCT  DD   DSN=&&AGEDACCT,
//                DISP=(OLD,DELETE)
//STMTS     DD   SYSOUT=A,
//                DCB=BLKSIZE=133
//
```

Figure 2-4 Structured JCL list

list with the standards observed. You can see the difference in this short example. Can you imagine the difference in a listing with 300 to 400 JCL statements? The standardized listing will be longer, but it will be much easier to interpret when you have to read it. As a result, it will be much easier to modify.

Terminology

job

job step

name field

national character

operation field

operand field

key-word parameter

positional parameter

comments field

Objectives

1. Describe the JCL statement format.
2. Explain the purpose of the name, operation, operand, and comments fields on a JCL statement.
3. Explain the reasons for using a standard method of coding JCL statements.

TOPIC 2   The Syntax of the Language

In this topic, you'll be introduced to the JCL elements that make up the basic subset of the language. I'll show you the elementary parameters of the JOB, EXEC, and DD statements. In addition, you'll see the comment, delimiter, and null statements. Together, these elements represent the core content of the language, and you'll find that they comprise about 90 percent of the JCL you'll use to process any job on the IBM System/360-370.

THE JOB STATEMENT

The JOB statement identifies the beginning of a job to the reader/interpreter and gives a name to that job. This *job name* is used by OS to communicate with the operator concerning the job. For example, if one of the steps in your job calls for a magnetic tape, OS will instruct the operator to mount that tape on a drive. It will also tell him the tape is for your job.

Another purpose of the JOB statement is to relate a computer run to an accounting procedure. Then, the computer time for a job can be charged to the department or company responsible for the job. For this reason, a job run for the engineering department of a company will usually have a different account number than a job run for the personnel department. In the examples throughout this book, I have used the *accounting information* required by the system on which the examples were tested. If you wish to copy the examples so they will run on your system, you may have to modify the accounting information to conform to your installation standards.

Figure 2-5 shows the composite statement structure (or skeleton) of the JOB statement. You should refer to it as you learn to code the JOB statement. The examples in figure 2-6 illustrate how acceptable values are coded in the JOB statement.

Accounting-information and programmer-name parameters

The first two parameters after the word JOB are accounting information and programmer name. They are positional parameters and must be coded in this order. In the examples in figure 2-6, the accounting information is HE66YFNH. This identifies my account on the System/370 I used for testing all of the JCL examples in this book.

Following the accounting information is programmer name. Notice in example 1 of figure 2-6 that the programmer name is 'MMA-LOWE'. If the name contains special characters, such as the dash, apostrophes are required. If the name contains no special characters except for the period, no apostrophes are required, as shown in example 2. If you wish to code embedded spaces in the name as shown in example 3, the apostrophes are required. In addition, if the programmer name contains an apostrophe as part of the name, like O'Reilly, you must code two consecutive apostrophes as shown in example 4. In a case like this, you may enclose the name in parentheses as shown, or you may use apostrophes as in the other examples.

The CLASS and PRTY parameters

In chapter 1, you learned that OS applies CPU cycles to programs in a way that makes use of as many cycles as possible. You also saw

```
//jobname   JOB  accounting-information,
                 programmer-name,
                 CLASS=job-class,
                 PRTY=priority-number,
                 MSGCLASS=message-class,
                 MSGLEVEL=(statements,messages),
                 REGION=region-sizeK
```

Figure 2-5 JOB statement skeleton

```
Example 1

//PROJECT1 JOB   HE66YFNH,
//              'MMA-LOWE',
//              CLASS=N,
//              MSGLEVEL=1

Example 2

//PROJECT2 JOB   HE66YFNH,
//              A.D.CLARY,
//              CLASS=D,
//              PRTY=5,
//              MSGCLASS=E,
//              MSGLEVEL=(0,0),
//              REGION=150K

Example 3

//PROJECT3 JOB   HE66YFNH,
//              'PAT MARTIN',
//              REGION=90K

Example 4

//PROJECT4 JOB   HE66YFNH,
//              (O''REILLY),
//              CLASS=D
```

Figure 2-6   JOB statement examples

that effective management of CPU time meant distributing the cycles to the most important jobs first and to the least important jobs last. It is the class (CLASS) and priority (PRTY) parameters of the JOB statement that tell OS into which category your program falls.

These two parameters are examples of installation-dependent requirements. Technically, CLASS can be any letter from A to O; however, in actual practice, the installation sets certain CLASS codes for the execution of certain types of jobs. For example, an installation could have a standard that says you may only use CLASS = A if your job uses no magnetic tape, writes less than 10,000 lines of printed output, and uses no more than 20 seconds of CPU time.

Similarly, PRTY may be any number from 1 to 13, but in actual practice the use of PRTY is established by the policy of the installation. In many cases, PRTY is omitted and the distribution of CPU cycles is determined by job class only. As a result, jobs in similar classes get equal priority scheduling.

The MSGCLASS parameter

As your job is executing, OS puts out *system messages* to tell you what happened in each step. For example, it tells you whether a file was kept or deleted after a job step was finished; how long the step took to execute; whether the step was abnormally terminated; and other information that will help you to analyze the results of your computer run. Figure 2-7 shows an example of system messages.

The message-class parameter (MSGCLASS) is associated with an output writer that, in turn, is associated with a specific output device. This enables you to route the system messages to a specific printer or other output device. If you omit MSGCLASS, the installation default will apply. Some installations use MSGCLASS to separate system messages from the output of the application programs, while others let the default values take effect so system messages come before the applications output.

The MSGLEVEL parameter

This parameter tells OS which messages you want printed. The format of the parameter is:

```
MSGLEVEL=(statements,messages)
```

where statements refers to your coded JCL statements and messages refers to the system output messages generated by OS. Since you may not want the JCL or messages printed every time you run the job, especially after the system goes into production, you can tell OS not to print them. Figure 2-8 shows the valid values and their meanings.

If you don't code the MSGLEVEL parameter, the installation default will apply. On the system I am using, the default for

```
IEF236I ALLOC. FOR MMASRAT   COB
IEF237I 375    ALLOCATED TO SYSUT1
IEF237I 37A    ALLOCATED TO SYSUT2
IEF237I 37B    ALLOCATED TO SYSUT3
IEF237I 375    ALLOCATED TO SYSUT4
IEF237I 37A    ALLOCATED TO SYSLIN
IEF142I - STEP WAS EXECUTED - COND CODE 0004
IEF285I    SYS80100.T132743.RF108.MMASRAT.SYSUT1      DELETED
IEF285I    VOL SER NOS= VSAM06.
IEF285I    SYS80100.T132743.RF108.MMASRAT.SYSUT2      DELETED
IEF285I    VOL SER NOS= PUB001.
IEF285I    SYS80100.T132743.RF108.MMASRAT.SYSUT3      DELETED
IEF285I    VOL SER NOS= PUB002.
IEF285I    SYS80100.T132743.RF108.MMASRAT.SYSUT4      DELETED
IEF285I    VOL SER NOS= VSAM06.
IEF285I    SYS80100.T132743.RF108.MMASRAT.LOADSET     PASSED
IEF285I    VOL SER NOS= PUB001.
IEF373I STEP /COB     /START 80100.1327
IEF374I STEP /COB     /STOP  80100.1328 CPU    0MIN 03.25SEC STOR VIRT 64K
```

Figure 2-7 OS system messages

```
MSGLEVEL=(statements,messages)

statements      0 = Print only the JOB statement
                1 = Print all JCL statements including statements from
                    cataloged procedures (covered in chapter 5)
                2 = Print only the input JCL (excluding cataloged procedures)

messages        0 = Print system messages only if the job abnormally
                    terminates
                1 = Print all system messages every time
```

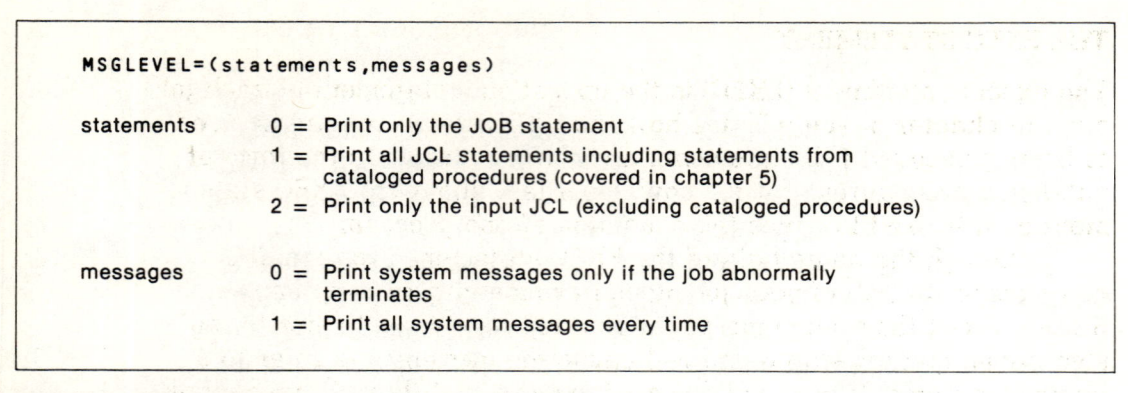

Figure 2-8 Valid MSGLEVEL values and their meanings

MSGLEVEL is (1,1). This means that if I want to see all of the JCL and all of the system messages each time the job is run, I just omit the parameter as shown in examples 3 and 4 of figure 2-6. If I want to see the system messages, but not the JCL, I will code MSGLEVEL = 0. Since there is no comma, I don't need the parentheses and OS knows I am referring to the first value in a positional string; for the second value, the system will default to 1. In example 2 of figure 2-6, I used MSGLEVEL = (0,0) to tell OS that I want to see (1) only the JOB statement and (2) the system messages only if the job abnormally terminates.

The REGION parameter

If your system is operated under MVT, you can specify the amount of main storage to be allocated to your job by coding the REGION parameter. In other words, you can override default values regarding the maximum amount of main storage allocated to your program, as in this example:

```
//ACCTJOB   JOB   HE66YFNH,
                 'WAYNE CLARY',
                 REGION=180K
```

Note that the amount of storage is specified in number of *Ks* (K = 1024 bytes). The number you code should be an even number not to exceed 16383. However, if you code an odd number, OS will assume the next higher even number.

If you code the REGION parameter on the JOB statement, you set that size for the entire job. If you code it on the EXEC statement, it is set for that step only. It is therefore wise to code the REGION parameter at the job step level, not in the JOB statement.

THE EXEC STATEMENT

The execute statement (EXEC) is the operational statement of each job step. In chapter 5, you will see how the EXEC statement can be used to bring pre-coded JCL statements into the job stream in the form of cataloged procedures. But for now, we'll talk about the EXEC statement as it is used to cause the execution of one program.

Although the name field of the EXEC statement is optional, I recommend that all of your job steps have meaningful *step names*. Since most of the system messages you will receive will refer to the step name, a blank step name will cause the messages to refer to a blank step name. If your job has six job steps and they all have blank step names, a message referring to a blank step name will be meaningless.

Figure 2-9 shows the statement skeleton for the EXEC statement. As with the JOB statement skeleton, you'll want to refer to it while learning to code the EXEC statement. Figure 2-10 gives coding examples for the EXEC statement.

The PGM parameter

The EXEC statement identifies the program to be executed in each step. Example 1 of figure 2-10 causes the execution of a program named EDITPAY; example 2 causes the execution of a program named ADCOST; example 3 causes the execution of a program named PAYUPDT; example 4 causes the execution of a program named ENG001; and example 5 causes the execution of a program named PRODCOST. These programs must be in load module form. That is, they must be object programs that have been link-edited and are now ready to be executed by the computer.

The PARM parameter

If your program requires data that can only be obtained at run time, you can send it that data by coding a PARM parameter in the EXEC statement. If, for example, your program requires a date, you can place that date into the PARM parameter and your program can

```
//stepname     EXEC  PGM=program-name,
                    PARM=program-parameters,
                    REGION=region-sizeK
```

Figure 2-9 EXEC statement skeleton

```
Example 1

    //REDCTR    EXEC   PGM=EDITPAY,
    //                 PARM=MOD

Example 2

    //SORTTRAN  EXEC   PGM=ADCOST,
    //                 PARM=(JANUARY 12, 1980),
    //                 REGION=100K

Example 3

    //UPDATE    EXEC   PGM=PAYUPDT,
    //                 PARM=(017,019,'+022'),
    //                 REGION=90K

Example 4

    //PRODRSL   EXEC   PGM=ENG001,
    //                 REGION=100K

Example 5

    //ACCTSTP   EXEC   PGM=PRODCOST
```

Figure 2-10 EXEC statement examples

receive it. Of course, the program must be expecting the data and have provisions for receiving it. In COBOL, this is accomplished by coding a Linkage Section where the data is defined and coding the USING option in the Procedure Division header. When the program is executed, the information is transferred to the definition area of the Linkage Section. The same facility is available in PL/I and assembler language.

Example 1 of figure 2-10 shows a PARM of MOD being sent to the program. Example 2 shows a PARM of JANUARY 12, 1980. Since this PARM contains a special character (the comma) and embedded spaces, it is enclosed in parentheses. Example 3 shows some numbers being sent to the program. In this case, one of the values contains a special character (the plus sign) as a significant part of its value. As a result, it is enclosed in apostrophes. Then, since there are commas in the PARM as separators, parentheses are coded around the entire field.

The REGION parameter

If your system is operated under MVT, you can specify the amount of main storage to be allocated to the job step. By coding the REGION parameter, you override default values regarding the maximum amount of main storage allocated to your program, as in this example:

```
//PROJCOST EXEC  PGM=PROJ001,
//                REGION=150K
```

Here again, as in the REGION parameter of the JOB statement, the amount of storage is requested in number of Ks (K = 1024 bytes), and the number you code should be an even number not to exceed 16383. Again, if you code an odd number, OS will assume the next higher even number. Examples 2, 3, and 4 of figure 2-10 use the REGION parameter.

THE DD STATEMENT

Since the purpose of data processing is normally to take raw or unprocessed data, modify it, rearrange it, and give results in the form of output, every program should require some form of input and output data. As a result, after each EXEC statement, you must define the characteristics of the data required by the program. This is done with the data definition (DD) statement. One DD statement is coded for each file used by the program. Each DD statement tells OS the name, status, disposition, location, space requirements, and characteristics of the file.

Figure 2-11 illustrates the DD statement skeleton for you to use while learning to code the parameters. Presented in this section are

```
Format 1:

//ddname    DD   DSN=data-set-name,
                 DISP=(status,normal-disposition,abnormal-disposition),
                 UNIT=device-name or group-name,
                 VOL=SER=volume-serial-number,
                 SPACE=(unit-of-measure(primary, secondary),RLSE),
                 DCB=(LRECL=logical-record-length,BLKSIZE=block-size,
                   RECFM=record-format)

Format 2:

//ddname    DD   *
or
//ddname    DD   DATA

Format 3:

//ddname    DD   SYSOUT=sysout-class
```

Figure 2-11 DD statement skeleton

the basic parameters and subparameters needed to process jobs with sequential files. In chapter 3 and throughout the rest of this book, you'll learn about other DD statement parameters and how to use them in specific applications.

Naming a file (DSNAME)

As you learned in chapter 1, in IBM terminology a file is called a *data set* and each data set must have a unique *data set name*. It may be coded DSN = name or DSNAME = name in the DD statement. The name you give to a data set must be unique on a volume. In other words, you may have identically named files on two separate volumes, but not on the same volume. The name must consist of from one to eight alphabetic, numeric, or national characters, and the first character must be alphabetic or national. OS uses the data set name for all references to the file.

The DD statement that refers to the data set has a name also. It is called the *ddname*. In your processing program, you assign a file name to a ddname that is associated with a data set name. To illustrate, look at figure 2-12. In the first example, you see a portion of a COBOL program—the SELECT statement for a file called PARTFILE. It is assigned to a DD statement named PARTS. This DD

```
Example 1: COBOL
    Source code:  SELECT PARTFILE   ASSIGN TO UT-S-PARTS.
    JCL:          //PARTS     DD   DSN=PTABLE,

Example 2: FORTRAN
    Source code:  READ    (5,100) X,Y,Z
    JCL:          //FT05F001 DD   DSN=PTABLE,

Example 3: PL/I
    Source code:  OPEN FILE(PARTS) INPUT;
    JCL:          //PARTS     DD   DSN=PTABLE,

Example 4: Assembler
    Source code:  PARTFILE   DCB  DDNAME=PARTS,...file description...
    JCL:          //PARTS     DD   DSN=PTABLE,
```

Figure 2-12 The relationship between the source program and the DD statement

statement defines the data set named PTABLE. So the file OS knows as PTABLE will be processed by the COBOL program as PARTFILE.

The second example shows this same relationship between a FORTRAN program and the data set. Note that in FORTRAN, the assignment is implied by coding a device code in an input/output statement. The third example shows the assignment of a file in PL/I. Finally, the fourth example shows this relationship between an assembler program and a file defined in a DD statement.

If a file is to be a *temporary file* (meaning you don't intend to save it when the job is completed), you can identify it as such by coding two ampersands (&&) preceding the data set name like this:

```
DSN=&&TEMPFILE
```

To illustrate the use of temporary data sets, consider a job that reads input data in one job step, sorts it in the next, and prints it in the last step. In this case, you could use a temporary file to pass the input data to the sort step and another temporary file to pass the sorted data to the print step. I'll show you some examples of temporary files later in this chapter.

Status and disposition of the file (DISP)

The disposition parameter (DISP) is composed of three positional subparameters: status, normal disposition, and abnormal disposition. The first subparameter, *status*, tells OS whether the file is: a new file being created in this job step (NEW); an existing file to which you want exclusive access (OLD); an existing file you want to access while others may also access it (SHR); or an existing file you want to add records to (MOD).

The second subparameter is *normal disposition*. It tells OS what to do with the file if the job step completes normally. The values you may code are KEEP, CATLG, DELETE, UNCATLG, and PASS.

The third subparameter, *abnormal disposition*, tells OS what to do with the file if the job step abnormally terminates. The values you may code are identical to the values of normal disposition except that PASS is not a valid value.

Figure 2-13 presents a table of valid DISP parameter values. Note the default values. If status is coded as OLD, SHR, or MOD, the default value for normal disposition is KEEP. If status is NEW, the second subparameter (normal disposition) must be coded since there is no default value. The third subparameter (abnormal disposition) will always default to the value you code for normal disposition. If status is not coded, it will default to NEW. For example, if DISP=(,PASS) is coded, the status is NEW.

Status	Normal disposition	Abnormal disposition
<u>NEW</u>	<u>KEEP</u> CATLG PASS DELETE	KEEP CATLG DELETE
OLD SHR MOD	<u>KEEP</u> CATLG PASS DELETE UNCATLG	KEEP CATLG DELETE UNCATLG

Note: Default values are underlined. The abnormal disposition defaults to the value coded for the normal disposition.

Figure 2-13 Valid DISP parameter values and default values

Now let's discuss the meaning of each of the DISP parameter values in detail.

Status values When you code NEW in the first subparameter of the DISP parameter, you are telling OS that you are creating a new file on the volume you specify. As a result, if OS finds a file on that volume with the same name as the one you gave your file, it will give you an error message to the effect that there is a duplicate file on the volume.

When you code OLD in the first subparameter of the DISP parameter, you are telling OS that there is a file on the volume with the name you specified in the data set name field. If OS can't find a file by that name, it will give you a JCL error message that says the file was not found. If you specified only data set name and disposition for a file (no VOLUME parameter), thinking that the file was cataloged when it really wasn't, you will get this same message. A disposition status of OLD also tells OS that you want exclusive control over the file. In other words, if another job tries to access the same file, it will have to wait until your job finishes before it can be executed.

When you code SHR as the first subparameter, you are telling OS that the file exists on the volume, but you don't want exclusive control over it (SHR means share, so more than one program can have access to the file concurrently). If OS can't find the file, you'll receive the same JCL error message mentioned previously. You should code SHR when accessing a file of general interest, such as a program library, unless you are updating that file.

When you code MOD, you are telling OS that you want to write on an existing file. If OS can't find the file on the volume you specify, you'll get the data-set-not-found message. If OS finds the file on the volume, it will pass over all the records of the file and prepare the file for processing at the end of the previous data. Then, when you perform an output operation in your program, the new records will be added at the end of the existing records.

Disposition values KEEP tells OS to save the file and make it available for later retrieval, but not to keep track of where the file is kept. As a result, a request to retrieve a file that was kept in this manner must provide OS with the data set name, the type of hardware unit, and the volume serial number where the file resides. In other words, the programmer keeps track of the unit and volume information concerning the file. This type of disposition is required for ISAM files that are created using more than one DD statement (this is discussed in chapter 4). In addition, if you want several files to have the same name, each residing on a different volume, you would code KEEP as the disposition.

CATLG tells OS to save the file and enter its name into a *catalog* for future requests. In the catalog, OS keeps the name, the type of hardware unit, the volume serial number, and the characteristics of the file. As a result, when a subsequent request is made for the file, only the data set name and disposition will be required. OS will find the data set name in the catalog that will refer it to the correct volume where the file resides. The difference between KEEP and CATLG is that a "kept" file is merely preserved for later access, while a "cataloged" file is not only preserved, but its name is added to a catalog for easy retrieval without the JCL programmer having to specify the location of the file.

DELETE tells OS to remove all references to the file and make it unavailable for future requests. This includes removal from the catalog if it was previously cataloged. A request to retrieve a file that has been deleted will result in a JCL error stating that the file was not found.

UNCATLG tells OS that the file was previously cataloged and now its name is to be removed from the catalog, but the file itself is not to be deleted. As a result, future requests for the file must specify the data set name, type of hardware unit, and volume serial number just as though it had been kept and not cataloged. The difference between DELETE and UNCATLG is that when you uncatalog a file, it is removed from the catalog but not deleted; but when you delete a file, it is deleted and also uncataloged.

PASS tells OS to keep the file temporarily until a subsequent job step uses it and gives it a final disposition. If no final disposition is given, or if no subsequent job step requests the file, it will be deleted at the completion of the job. To access a passed file in a later job step, you only need to code the data set name and the disposition (status is OLD). Note in figure 2-13 that PASS can only be coded for the normal disposition subparameter; it is not valid for abnormal disposition.

DISP examples Figure 2-14 shows some examples of the DISP parameter. Let's review them to summarize the features of this parameter.

Example 1 shows the disposition of a file that is being created in this job step. If the job completes normally, the file is to be saved for later reference. If the job abnormally ends, it will be deleted.

Example 2 illustrates the disposition of a temporary file that is to be passed to some later job step. The comma preceding PASS indicates that the first subparameter has been omitted. When this occurs, OS will assume the default value of NEW.

Example 3 shows a file that is NEW (the omitted first subparameter). It is to be cataloged if the step runs normally or deleted if the step fails.

Example 4 shows an old file. Since the second and third subparameters are omitted, there is no need for parentheses; the default value for both omitted subparameters is KEEP.

```
Example 1
    //              DISP=(NEW,KEEP,DELETE)
Example 2
    //              DISP=(,PASS)
Example 3
    //              DISP=(,CATLG,DELETE)
Example 4
    //              DISP=OLD
Example 5
    //              DISP=SHR
Example 6
    //              DISP=MOD
```

Figure 2-14 Examples of the DISP parameter

Example 5 illustrates the use of DISP = SHR. Remember that this option makes the file available to your job step and also allows other jobs to have concurrent access to the same file. One restriction is placed on the use of DISP = SHR: if you specify DISP = SHR for a file in one job step, all other references to that file in the same job must also specify SHR. Again, the default value for the second and third subparameters is KEEP.

Example 6 shows the use of DISP = MOD. This status tells OS that you want to extend an existing sequential file. By doing this, you can add records to the end of a file without reading the old data. For example, suppose daily transactions are to be summarized into a weekly transaction history file. In this case, you can write the daily transactions onto the weekly summary file with DISP = MOD each day. Your program treats the file as if it were an ordinary output file.

The location of the file (UNIT and VOLUME)

If you're creating an output file, you must tell OS where to put it; if you're accessing an existing file that hasn't been cataloged, you have to tell OS where it resides. The UNIT parameter tells OS what kind of hardware device the file is to be placed on or retrieved from. The VOLUME parameter tells OS the specific serial number of the volume the file is to be placed on or retrieved from.

The UNIT parameter You may specify the unit in one of three ways. First, you can code a unit address identifying a particular input/output device. However, this method is not recommended since it can interfere with the automatic functions of OS. So it's not covered in this book.

Second, you can specify the unit number of the device—for instance, 3330, 2314, 3350, and so forth. Although you'll see examples presented in this manner throughout this book, keep in mind that many installations don't allow you to specify actual device types. Check with your installation to find out what its standards are.

Third (and most common), you can code a *group name* that includes all devices of a particular kind. Group names are given to categories of devices at system generation time by the installation. Usually, names such as DISKA, TAPE, DRUM, SYSDA, and MICR are used to indicate the group of associated devices in that category. Here again, check with your installation to determine the proper group names for the devices you want to use.

Figure 2-15 shows examples of the UNIT parameter. Example 1 shows the UNIT parameter requesting a system direct-access device. Example 2 shows the file being assigned to a 2400 series magnetic

```
Example 1
    //              UNIT=SYSDA
Example 2
    //              UNIT=2400
Example 3
    //              UNIT=TAPE
Example 4
    //              UNIT=3330
Example 5
    //              UNIT=DISKA
```

Figure 2-15 Examples of the UNIT parameter

tape unit. Example 3 shows the file being assigned to the installation's standard magnetic tape unit. Example 4 shows a file assigned to a 3330 disk unit. Example 5 shows a file assigned to a disk device category.

The VOLUME parameter   There are several subparameters of the VOLUME parameter, but only one will be covered in this chapter. It is the most common one, the SER subparameter. It may be coded VOLUME = SER = serial number or VOL = SER = serial number, where serial number identifies a certain storage volume. This parameter is used to assign an output file to a specific storage volume or to tell OS the volume serial number of the storage volume where an uncataloged input file resides. This storage volume may be a disk pack, a tape reel, a drum, or some other unique storage entity.

Figure 2-16 shows some examples of the VOLUME parameter. The VOLUME parameter is not required for output files when you don't care what specific volume OS places the file on. The UNIT parameter will identify the type, and OS will choose the volume from that category.

Allocating space to a file (SPACE)

When your job requests a direct-access device to place a new file on, you must tell OS how much direct-access space is to be allocated to that file. To do this, you code the SPACE parameter on the DD statement. There are four basic subparameters of the SPACE parameter: unit of measure, primary quantity, secondary quantity, and the release (RLSE) option. These are positional subparameters, so they

Job Control Language: A Basic Subset   69

```
Example 1
        //              VOL=SER=017342
Example 2
        //              VOL=SER=USER12
Example 3
        //              VOL=SER=D00103
Example 4
        //              VOL=SER=LIB113
```

Figure 2-16   Examples of the VOLUME parameter

don't need key word identifiers. Other subparameters of the SPACE parameter are presented in chapters 3 and 9.

Unit of measure   You may allocate space for a file in cylinders, tracks, or blocks of data. Figure 2-17 shows examples of each unit of measure. Examples 1 and 4 show the allocation in cylinders. Examples 2 and 5 show the allocation in tracks. Examples 3 and 6 show the allocation in blocks of data: 960-byte blocks in example 3 and 1400-byte blocks in example 6.

Primary and secondary allocations   As a general rule, the second subparameter (*primary allocation*) should be the amount of space you think the file will require. In example 1 of figure 2-17, the file should take one cylinder; in example 2, the file should take five tracks; in example 3, the file should take three blocks of 960 bytes; and so on.

However, estimates can be wrong and file sizes do change. As a result, the *secondary allocation* allows for extensions or *extents* to the primary allocation. Then, if the primary allocation of space isn't large enough for the file, the secondary allocation is made. If this still isn't enough space for the file, the secondary allocation is repeated until 16 secondary extents have been added to the file space. After that, if there still isn't enough space for the file, the job will abnormally terminate.

In example 1, if one cylinder cannot hold the file, another cylinder will be allocated. If that isn't enough space for the entire file, another cylinder will be added, and so on until 16 such secondary allocations of one cylinder have been made. So the total possible allocation for the file in example 1 is 17 cylinders.

Similarly, in example 2, if the file cannot be stored in the primary allocation of five tracks, additional tracks will be allocated, two at a time, until a total of 16 two-track areas have been added to

```
Example 1
    //              SPACE=(CYL,(1,1),RLSE)
Example 2
    //              SPACE=(TRK,(5,2),RLSE)
Example 3
    //              SPACE=(960,(3,3),RLSE)
Example 4
    //              SPACE=(CYL,(10,2))
Example 5
    //              SPACE=(TRK,5,RLSE)
Example 6
    //              SPACE=(1400,10)
```

Figure 2-17 Examples of the SPACE parameter

the primary amount. So the total possible allocation for this file is 37 tracks.

The same holds true when the allocation is made in blocks of data. Example 3 shows a primary allocation of three blocks of 960 bytes. If the file is larger than this area, space to hold three more blocks of data is allocated until a total of 16 secondary extents are allocated. So the total capacity of the file illustrated in example 3 is 51 blocks of 960 bytes.

Notice that if both the primary and secondary allocations are coded, they must be enclosed in parentheses. If the secondary allocation is omitted, as in examples 5 and 6, this set of parentheses isn't required.

RLSE option Direct-access space is a system resource, just as CPU time is. As a result, the amount of disk or drum space your files use is a factor in calculating the cost of your application. It is therefore wise to use any available means to reduce the amount of unused direct-access space attached to your files. The RLSE option provides a way to do this. It tells OS to make any unused space in the file area available for use by other jobs. In other words, after the completion of a job step that allocated and used direct-access space, OS is to deallocate any space that isn't used by the records in the file. For instance, example 2 in figure 2-17 shows a space request for five tracks of primary storage, and up to 16 additional extents of two tracks. Suppose, then, that after the job step was completed, the actual number of tracks required by the file was only two. The RLSE option would tell OS to release the extra three tracks of primary storage back to the system resource pool.

If RLSE isn't coded, the blank space at the end of a file will remain with that file, unavailable for other jobs. As a result, the cost of that additional space is added to the cost of storing your file. Notice in examples 4 and 6 that the RLSE option is not coded. In this case, you close the parentheses directly behind the primary and secondary allocation.

Describing the characteristics of a file (DCB)

The data control block (DCB) parameter provides the information used by OS to perform some of its data management services. Certain subparameters of the DCB are required for almost every file; others are optional depending on the access method and the application. In this section, I'll discuss the three basic subparameters required for all files: logical record length (LRECL), block size (BLKSIZE), and record format (RECFM).

The data control block represents a table of information about the file you are using in your program. The entries in this table come from three sources: (1) your program, (2) your JCL, and (3) OS default values. As a result, although I said that LRECL, BLKSIZE, and RECFM must be entered for all files, you don't necessarily have to code them in your JCL each time.

RECFM tells OS the record format of the file. Figure 2-18 lists the acceptable values for this subparameter. You probably won't use

A	Records with ASA control characters
B	Blocked records
D	Variable length ASCII records
F	Fixed length records
G	Teleprocessing message data
M	Records with machine code control characters
R	Teleprocessing message data
S	Standard blocks of fixed length records or records that may span blocks of variable length records
T	Records that may be written on overflow tracks
U	Undefined length records
V	Variable length records

The most common record formats are: F, FB, V, and VB

Figure 2-18 Values you may code for record format (RECFM)

most of these values because they refer to special types of data. The codes you are likely to use are F, FB, V, and VB.

LRECL is the logical record length of the records in the file. If the records are variable length, blocked or unblocked, the record length is the largest record size in the file. Variable records must be identified by a four-byte control field before each record, so the logical record length is equal to the longest record length plus four bytes.

The BLKSIZE subparameter tells OS the size of a block of records in the file. It must be a multiple of the record length. For variable-length records, it must also include an extra four bytes. These four bytes precede each block and tell OS the number of records in the block.

Figure 2-19 shows examples of the DCB parameter and its three basic subparameters. Example 1 illustrates the DCB of a file of 80-character records, 12 records per block (960 bytes), with a record format of fixed blocked (FB). Example 2 shows a variable record-length file (RECFM = VB) with the longest record containing 140 bytes and the average block containing 1400 bytes. Notice that the example shows a LRECL of 144 and a BLKSIZE of 1444. Remember, that's because four leading bytes are added to each variable-length record to tell OS the record length, and another four leading bytes are added to the block to tell OS the number of records in the block.

Example 3 illustrates that no parentheses are required when only one subparameter is coded. The program using this file probably requested zero records per block as a programming option. This is frequently done to allow block sizes to be set when the program is executed. As a result, you don't have to recompile the program should the blocking factor change from run to run.

The DCB parameter is usually coded for output files only. Since OS keeps this DCB information with the file, there is no need to specify DCB information in the JCL when the file is accessed by other programs as input. OS assumes that if no DCB information is coded, it already exists in the DCB table I mentioned earlier.

```
Example 1
    //           DCB=(LRECL=80,BLKSIZE=960,RECFM=FB)
Example 2
    //           DCB=(LRECL=144,BLKSIZE=1444,RECFM=VB)
Example 3
    //           DCB=BLKSIZE=133
```

Figure 2-19 Examples of the DCB parameter

Other DD statement formats

If you look back at figure 2-11, you'll notice there are two alternate formats for the DD statement. These are used when a job requires certain types of files.

Format 2 in figure 2-11 is used for an input file that is part of the input stream; that is, a file that is coded right along with your JCL. For example, if your JCL is punched into cards and you have an input file of punched cards, the input file would be placed right after the appropriate DD statement in the JCL deck. The DD * is used for files that don't include any JCL statements; the DD DATA statement is used for input files that contain JCL statements. You'll learn more about how and when to use the * and DATA operands in the chapters that follow.

The DD statement in format 3 of figure 2-11 is used to direct an output file to a particular printing or punching device. The sysout-class determines which device is to be used. In many installations, SYSOUT = A is the standard printing class and SYSOUT = B is the standard punching class. Other values coded for SYSOUT data sets can request offline printers, plotters, magnetic character printers, and other devices not assumed to be the installation's standard output device.

DD statement examples

Figure 2-20 shows examples of DD statements that use the basic parameters I've just explained. Let's run through them briefly so you can see what they do and how they function together.

Example 1 is a DD statement named PERSFILE. That's the name used by the program to refer to the file. The data set name is PERS001, the name OS uses to refer to the file. The disposition of the file is as follows: it is a new file created in this job step (first subparameter); it is to be kept if the job step runs normally (second subparameter); and it is to be deleted if the job step abnormally terminates (third subparameter). The file is to be placed on a SYSDA (SYStem Direct Access) device (UNIT), and the volume serial number (VOL = SER) is D00103. OS is to allocate space (the SPACE parameter) on that volume as follows: reserve five cylinders to begin with, but if that is not enough, increase the amount by five more cylinders each time more space is required until 16 increments or extents have been allocated; if there is any unused space, release it (RLSE). The subparameters of the data control block are these: the logical record length (LRECL) is 90 bytes, the block size (BLKSIZE) is 3600 bytes, and the record format (RECFM) is fixed and blocked (FB).

Example 2 shows a DD statement named PRJMAST defining a file named PROJMAS. The disposition is OLD, meaning the file already

74 Chapter 2

```
Example 1

    //PERSFILE DD   DSN=PERS001,
    //              DISP=(NEW,KEEP,DELETE),
    //              UNIT=SYSDA,
    //              VOL=SER=D00103,
    //              SPACE=(CYL,(5,5),RLSE),
    //              DCB=(LRECL=90,BLKSIZE=3600,RECFM=FB)

Example 2

    //PRJMAST  DD   DSN=PROJMAS,
    //              DISP=OLD,
    //              UNIT=3330,
    //              VOL=SER=D00102

Example 3

    //PAYFILE  DD   DSN=PAYFILE,
    //              DISP=(NEW,CATLG,DELETE),
    //              UNIT=3330,
    //              VOL=SER=D00103,
    //              SPACE=(TRK,(1,1),RLSE),
    //              DCB=(LRECL=80,BLKSIZE=3600,RECFM=FB)

Example 4

    //PAYFILE  DD   DSN=PAYFILE,
    //              DISP=OLD

Example 5

    //STEPLIB  DD   DSN=MMA.PRIVLIB,
    //              DISP=SHR

Example 6

    //CARDSIN  DD   *
                   data records
    /*

Example 7

    //JCLDATA  DD   DATA
                   data records
    /*

Example 8

    //RPT101   DD   SYSOUT=A

Example 9

    //RPT102   DD   SYSOUT=A,
    //              DCB=BLKSIZE=133
```

Figure 2-20 Examples of the DD statement

exists. It resides on a 3330 disk pack named D00102. Notice that no space or DCB information is required because it is an input file (it already exists and OS kept this information when the file was created).

Example 3 shows a DD statement named PAYFILE that defines a file by the same name. The disposition is (NEW,CATLG,DELETE), meaning: the file is being created; if the job step runs normally, it is to be cataloged; if the job step fails, it is to be deleted. This file is to be placed on a 3330 disk pack named D00103. One track of initial space and 16 single-track extensions are to be reserved, and any space not required by the file is to be released back to the system. The DCB information completes the description of the file.

Examples 4 and 5 show how to retrieve a file that has been cataloged. Example 4 shows the statement to retrieve the file described in example 3. Notice that only the DSN and DISP parameters are required. As you can see, cataloging a file makes it easy to retrieve. Example 5 shows the DD statement to retrieve another cataloged file, this time with the disposition of SHR. Remember, you should code SHR when accessing a file of general interest such as a library. Then, others don't have to wait for your job to complete before using the file. Notice here that the DSN is a little different than those we've seen before. You'll learn how and when to use two-part names like this in chapter 3.

Examples 6 and 7 show methods of entering data in the input stream. The DD statements follow format 2 of figure 2-11. Notice the /* after the data records. This is the delimiter statement marking the end of the input stream. The delimiter statement will be covered in more detail later in this topic.

Examples 8 and 9 are DD statements for print files (format 3 of figure 2-11). Both statements send the output to SYSOUT class A. As I mentioned before, SYSOUT = A is the standard printing class in many installations. The statement illustrated in example 9 gives a DCB parameter with a BLKSIZE subparameter. This is required when a program gives the block size for a file as zero records per block.

Looking back over the examples in figure 2-20, you should notice that the parameters are coded in the same order for each DD statement. This is not required, but as I mentioned in topic 1 of this chapter, it makes it easier to read the JCL. The sequence I use when coding the parameters of the DD statement is the one given in figure 2-11.

Special ddnames

Just as your application program needs DD statements to link a file description to the actual file in a storage volume, OS sometimes needs DD statements for special input/output functions. Four of these ddnames you'll use are: JOBLIB, STEPLIB, SYSABEND, and SYSUDUMP.

The JOBLIB and STEPLIB statements are similar in function. They each define a private program library where programs for the job or step are to be found. If the programs are not found in that library, or if neither JOBLIB nor STEPLIB is coded, OS expects to find the program in the system library (SYS1.LINKLIB).

JOBLIB, when coded, must be the first statement following the JOB statement. It makes a program library available to all steps within the job. STEPLIB, when coded, must be the first statement following the EXEC statement. It makes a program library available to that step only. If both JOBLIB and STEPLIB are coded, the library defined by the STEPLIB statement is searched first, then the system library is searched; in other words, JOBLIB is ignored. A typical STEPLIB statement is shown in example 5 of figure 2-20.

SYSABEND and SYSUDUMP can be placed in your JCL to cause a memory dump to print if your job should abnormally terminate. The one you use is determined by the kind of dump you want. SYSABEND causes a dump of the operating system nucleus and the processing program. SYSUDUMP causes only that portion of memory containing the processing program to be dumped. Under normal conditions, you shouldn't need the system nucleus printed (it's usually used to find system problems). So you will normally use the SYSUDUMP DD statement to obtain a dump in case of abnormal termination. Examples of SYSABEND and SYSUDUMP follow:

```
//SYSABEND  DD   SYSOUT=A

//SYSUDUMP  DD   SYSOUT=A
```

In addition to these four special ddnames, each program of OS may also require ddnames such as SYSOUT, SYSPRINT, SYSIN, SYSLMOD, SYSUT, and SORTWK. These ddnames will be covered as required in the chapters dealing with the service programs and utilities of OS.

THE COMMENT STATEMENT

When you want to include comments in your JCL coding, you may write a *comment statement*. Comments can be useful to clarify an abstruse procedure, or, as blank areas between job steps or DD statements, they can make the JCL listing easier to read. The comments field in a JCL statement can be used to discuss or clarify a single JCL statement, while a comment statement can be used to explain larger sections of JCL coding.

To code the comment statement, place //* in the first three positions of the statement and put your comment data in positions 4 through 80. There is no need to continue a comment statement; if you need more space for your comment, simply follow the first comment statement with another and continue your narrative, as in this example:

```
//* THIS JOB STEP SORTS ACCOUNTS RECEIVABLE RECORDS
//* FOR INPUT TO THE MONTHLY BILLING PROGRAM.
```

THE DELIMITER STATEMENT

The *delimiter statement* is used to mark the end of data in the input stream. When you have a file to be read in on cards or in the same input stream as your JCL, you code a DD * or DD DATA statement to indicate that data follows. After the data, you place a delimiter statement in the input stream to mark the end of the data. A delimiter statement consists of /* in the first two positions of the record.

When using the DD * statement to read data, the delimiter is optional. Since OS will assume end-of-data when it encounters the next JCL statement (// in positions 1 and 2), the delimiter isn't necessary. However, when using the DD DATA statement to introduce data into the input stream, you must code the delimiter statement since this method of data definition treats everything (including JCL statements) as data. As a result, if you don't use a delimiter statement, all of the JCL following the DD DATA statement, including other jobs in the input stream, will be treated as data.

Here are two examples of the delimiter statement:

```
//SSICARD   DD   *
     data
/*
```

and

```
//JCLDATA   DD   DATA
     data
/*
```

In the first example, the delimiter statement is optional; in the second, its omission will cause problems.

THE NULL STATEMENT

As OS reads jobs, it knows where a job begins and ends by recognizing JOB statements. As a result, when it encounters a JOB statement, it places the preceding job into the input queue. But what about the last job in the input stream? If your job is the last job in the input stream, OS has no way of knowing that your job is completely read in. It may assume that the card reader ran out of input cards and the operator has not yet reloaded the hopper. And what happens if the job that follows yours has an invalid JOB statement? In that case, OS would include that entire job as part of yours, including the JCL error caused by the faulty JOB statement.

The best way to prevent these things from happening is to code a *null statement* at the end of every job. The null statement indicates end-of-job to the reader/interpreter. It's optional, and at many installations the computer operator places a null statement at the end of a batch of jobs to be read in. Additionally, some input devices generate a null statement at the end of input. Nevertheless, it doesn't hurt anything to put a null statement at the end of every job. This guarantees that OS will recognize your job as a complete unit. To code the null statement, place // in the first two positions and leave the rest of the statement blank.

Terminology

job name	normal disposition
accounting information	abnormal disposition
system message	catalog
K	group name
step name	primary allocation
data set	secondary allocation
data set name	extent
ddname	comment statement
temporary file	delimiter statement
status	null statement

Objective

Given a JCL listing, be able to identify and describe the function of the JOB, EXEC, DD, delimiter, comment, and null statements.

Problems

Referring to the JCL listing in figure 2-21, answer the following questions.

1. How many job steps are there in this job?
2. What program library do the programs reside in?
3. Was the file PERSMAST kept or cataloged when it was created?
4. What is the last statement in the listing called?

```
//PERSSEL   JOB  HE66YFNH,
//               'W. CLARY'
//SELPROG   EXEC PGM=SELPERS
//STEPLIB   DD   DSN=MMA.USERLIB,
//               DISP=SHR
//PERSFILE  DD   DSN=PERSMAST,
//               DISP=OLD
//PERSCAT   DD   DSN=&&PERSTEMP,
//               DISP=(NEW,PASS),
//               UNIT=SYSDA,
//               SPACE=(CYL,(1,1),RLSE),
//               DCB=(LRECL=100,BLKSIZE=1000,RECFM=FB)
//PRTPERS   EXEC PGM=PERSRPT1
//STEPLIB   DD   DSN=MMA.USERLIB,
//               DISP=SHR
//TEMPFILE  DD   DSN=&&PERSTEMP,
//               DISP=(OLD,DELETE)
//PERSRPT   DD   SYSOUT=A,
//               DCB=BLKSIZE=133
//
```

Figure 2-21 A sample job in OS JCL

Solutions

1. There are two job steps (EXEC statements) in the job.
2. The STEPLIB DD statements identify the program library as MMA.USERLIB.
3. It was cataloged. If it had only been kept, I would have had to tell OS the UNIT and VOLUME where it resides.
4. It is the null statement.

TOPIC 3 Examples of Job Streams

In this topic, I'll present two systems and we'll walk through the JCL step by step and line by line. You'll notice that these are not typical textbook examples. I've attempted to make them as close to "real-world" examples as possible. The first system is a payroll edit-update system and the second is a report extract for an accounts-receivable system.

THE EDIT-UPDATE SYSTEM

Figure 2-22 illustrates the system flowchart for an edit-update system that reads card input transactions, edits them, and then uses them to update a master file. The notation used in the system flowchart describes the programs and files in terms of their functions and gives their names in parentheses.

The payroll input data is copied from cards to disk by the program CARDDISK. Then, the second program, PAYEDIT, edits the data against a table file read into storage from magnetic tape. It prints an error report showing invalid data and writes the valid data onto another disk file. The third program, PAYUPD, is the update program that reads the valid data passed from the edit program, matches it with a master file, updates the matched master records, prints an update report, copies the old master records to tape, and writes the updated master records onto disk. Since data set names must be unique, the name of the output master file is different from the input master file. (In chapter 3, a technique for circumventing this problem is presented.) Then the last program, IEHPROGM (an IBM utility), renames the updated master file to the name of the old master file that was deleted in the previous step. The next time this job is run, this new master will be read in as the old master and still another new master will be created.

The JCL statements for the job

Figure 2-23 shows the JCL to execute the system just described. Let's walk through it statement by statement.

1. The job name I gave to the system is PAYROLL; the accounting information gives my account number to the operating system's accounting routines; and there's my name in the programmer name parameter.

2. The first step is the card-to-disk operation. I gave this step the name CDDISK. The EXEC statement causes the execution of the program named CARDDISK.

3. The STEPLIB DD statement tells OS that the CARDDISK program is in the private program library called MMA.USERLIB. STEPLIB only refers to the step in which it is located. Since all the STEPLIB statements in this job refer to the same library, I could have omitted them and included a JOBLIB DD statement instead. The DISP for MMA.USERLIB is SHR, so other programs can have access to it while this job is running.

4. RAWDATA is the ddname of the output disk file. The data set name is &&RAWDATA; the ampersands indicate that it is a tem-

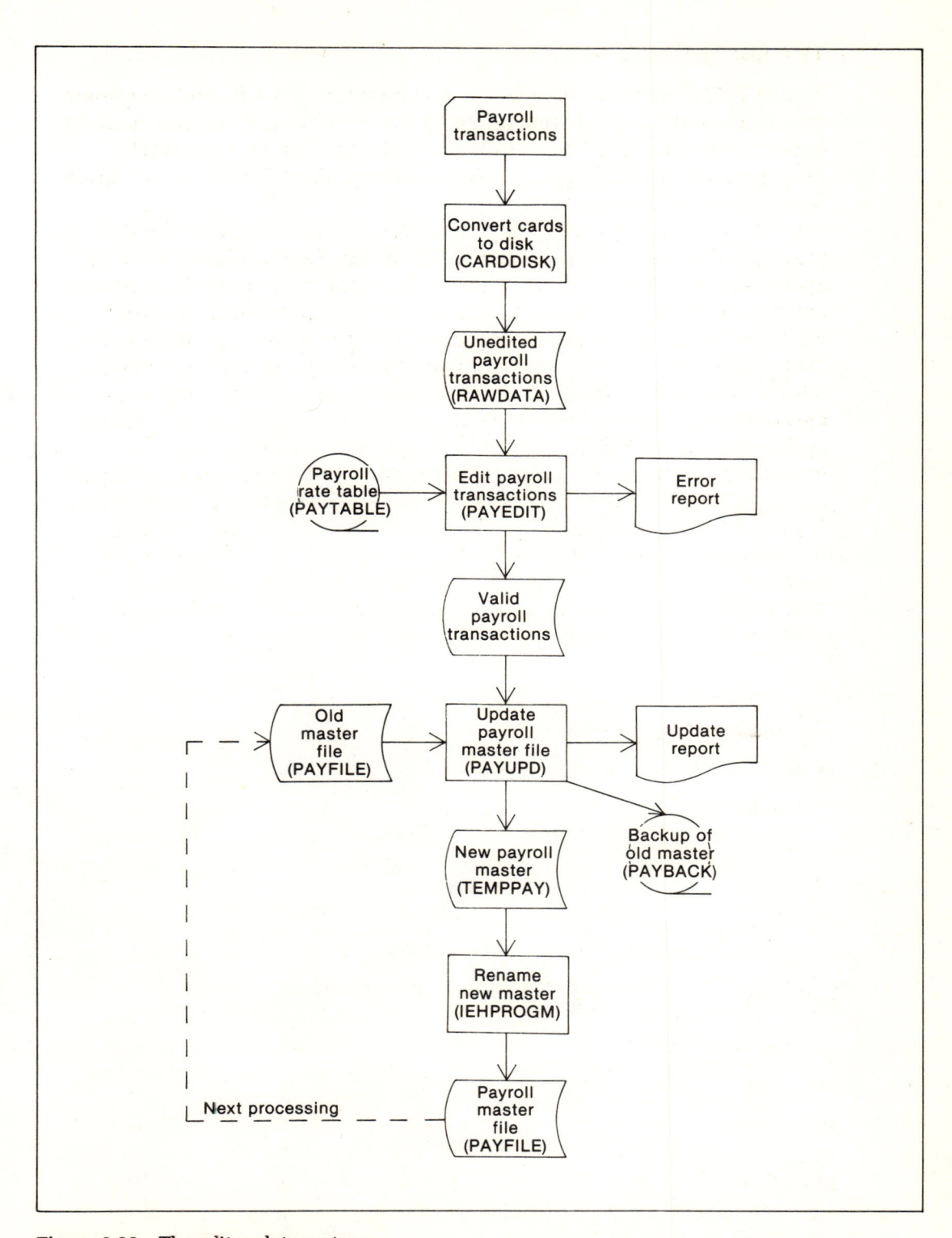

Figure 2-22 The edit-update system

Chapter 2

```
 1 //PAYROLL  JOB   HE66YFNH,
   //              'W. CLARY'
 2 //CDDISK   EXEC  PGM=CARDDISK
 3 //STEPLIB  DD    DSN=MMA.USERLIB,
   //              DISP=SHR
 4 //RAWDATA  DD    DSN=&&RAWDATA,
   //              DISP=(NEW,PASS),
   //              UNIT=SYSDA,
   //              SPACE=(CYL,(2,1),RLSE),
   //              DCB=(LRECL=80,BLKSIZE=960,RECFM=FB)
 5 //PAYCARDS DD    *
             data cards
 6 /*
 7 //EDIT     EXEC  PGM=PAYEDIT,
   //              PARM=010280
   //STEPLIB  DD    DSN=MMA.USERLIB,
   //              DISP=SHR
 8 //RAWDATA  DD    DSN=&&RAWDATA,
   //              DISP=(OLD,DELETE)
 9 //PAYTAB   DD    DSN=PAYTABLE,
   //              DISP=OLD,
   //              UNIT=TAPE
10 //ERRPT    DD    SYSOUT=A,
   //              DCB=BLKSIZE=133
11 //GOODDATA DD    DSN=&&GOODFILE,
   //              DISP=(NEW,PASS),
   //              UNIT=SYSDA,
   //              SPACE=(CYL,(2,1),RLSE),
   //              DCB=(LRECL=80,BLKSIZE=960,RECFM=FB)
12 //UPDATE   EXEC  PGM=PAYUPD,
   //              REGION=150K
   //STEPLIB  DD    DSN=MMA.USERLIB,
   //              DISP=SHR
13 //UPDINPUT DD    DSN=&&GOODFILE,
   //              DISP=(OLD,DELETE)
14 //OLDMAST  DD    DSN=PAYFILE,
   //              DISP=(OLD,DELETE,KEEP)
15 //NEWMAST  DD    DSN=TEMPPAY,
   //              DISP=(NEW,CATLG,DELETE),
   //              UNIT=3330,
   //              VOL=SER=D00103,
   //              SPACE=(CYL,(10,5),RLSE),
   //              DCB=(LRECL=140,BLKSIZE=1400,RECFM=FB)
16 //MASTBU   DD    DSN=PAYBACK,
   //              DISP=(NEW,KEEP,KEEP),
   //              UNIT=TAPE,
   //              DCB=(LRECL=140,BLKSIZE=1400,RECFM=FB)
17 //UPRPT    DD    SYSOUT=A,
   //              DCB=BLKSIZE=133
18 //RENAME   EXEC  PGM=IEHPROGM
18 //SYSPRINT DD    SYSOUT=A
18 //DD1      DD    UNIT=3330,
   //              VOL=SER=D00103
18 //SYSIN    DD    *
             IEHPROGM control statements
19 /*
20 //
```

Figure 2-23 JCL for the edit-update system

porary file, as does the disposition of (NEW,PASS). I want the file to be placed on a system direct-access device (no particular volume). I requested two cylinders of primary space with up to 16 secondary one-cylinder extents if the primary allocation isn't enough. The leftover space is to be released to the system. The DCB information I provided is record length of 80, block size of 960 (12 records), and record format of fixed blocked.

5. PAYCARDS is the DD statement for the data cards that follow it. The DD * tells OS that data follows in the input stream.

6. The delimiter statement marks the end of data in the input stream.

7. The second job step is the edit program PAYEDIT. The PARM is used to pass information to the processing program.

8. The data set passed by the first step (&&RAWDATA) is now input to the second step. As a result, the status is OLD. Since the file is no longer required after the step is executed, normal disposition is DELETE.

9. The payroll table file, PAYTABLE, is input from magnetic tape. The file was previously cataloged, so only the name and disposition are required, though I coded the UNIT value too.

10. ERRPT is the DD statement that defines the error report. Since the program specified a block size of zero records, the DCB parameter sets the block size at one record (133 characters) per block.

11. The valid data from the edit program is passed as a temporary data set (&&GOODFILE) to the update program.

12. The UPDATE step executes the program, PAYUPD; notice that the region size has been set to 150K.

13. The valid data from the edit is read as input and deleted when the step is completed.

14. The old master file (DSN = PAYFILE) is an input file (status is OLD). It is deleted if the step completes normally, but it is kept if the step abnormally terminates.

15. The new master is put out as DSN = TEMPPAY. Although that name might suggest a temporary file, it is cataloged if the step executes normally. (The name is temporary, but the file is not. Later, the name will be changed.) It is to be placed on a 3330 disk unit named D00103, with 10 cylinders of primary space and up to 16 secondary extents of five cylinders each. The record length is 140, the block size is 1400, and the record format is fixed blocked.

16. The old master file is copied during processing to a tape file for backup. The file is named PAYBACK, and it is kept but not cataloged.
17. UPRPT is the DD statement defining the update report. The DCB parameter sets the block size to 133 bytes.
18. RENAME is the name of the step that executes an IBM utility program (IEHPROGM) to rename the new master to PAYFILE and change the catalog entry accordingly. The three DD statements that follow are all associated with the utility. (See chapter 7 for a complete discussion of the IEHPROGM utility.)
19. The delimiter statement marks the end of data that is required by the utility in the input stream.
20. The null statement marks the end of the job.

THE REPORT-EXTRACT SYSTEM

Figure 2-24 illustrates a report-extract system, again using the basic elements of JCL we have covered so far. The extract program (SELACCTS) reads two files, extracts data from them to be used later in reports, and sends a file composed of selected records to the next step. The next program, ARRPT1, reads the file of selected records and produces three reports. The sort program takes the same temporary file and sorts it into the required sequence. The last program, ARRPT2, reads the sorted file and produces three more reports.

The JCL statements for the job

Figure 2-25 lists the JCL to execute the system just described. By now, you should have a reasonable understanding of the basic elements of JCL and the way the parameters work together. So here, I'll just highlight the main features of this job.

1. The job name is CISEXT.
2. EXTRACT is the first step. It causes a program named SELACCTS to be executed. PARM is used to pass information to the program.
3. ACCTREC and CUST are the DD statements for the two input files.
4. SELRECS is the temporary data set containing selected records to be passed to the first report program and to the sort program.
5. REPORT1 is the EXEC statement to execute the program ARRPT1. It requires 100K of storage.

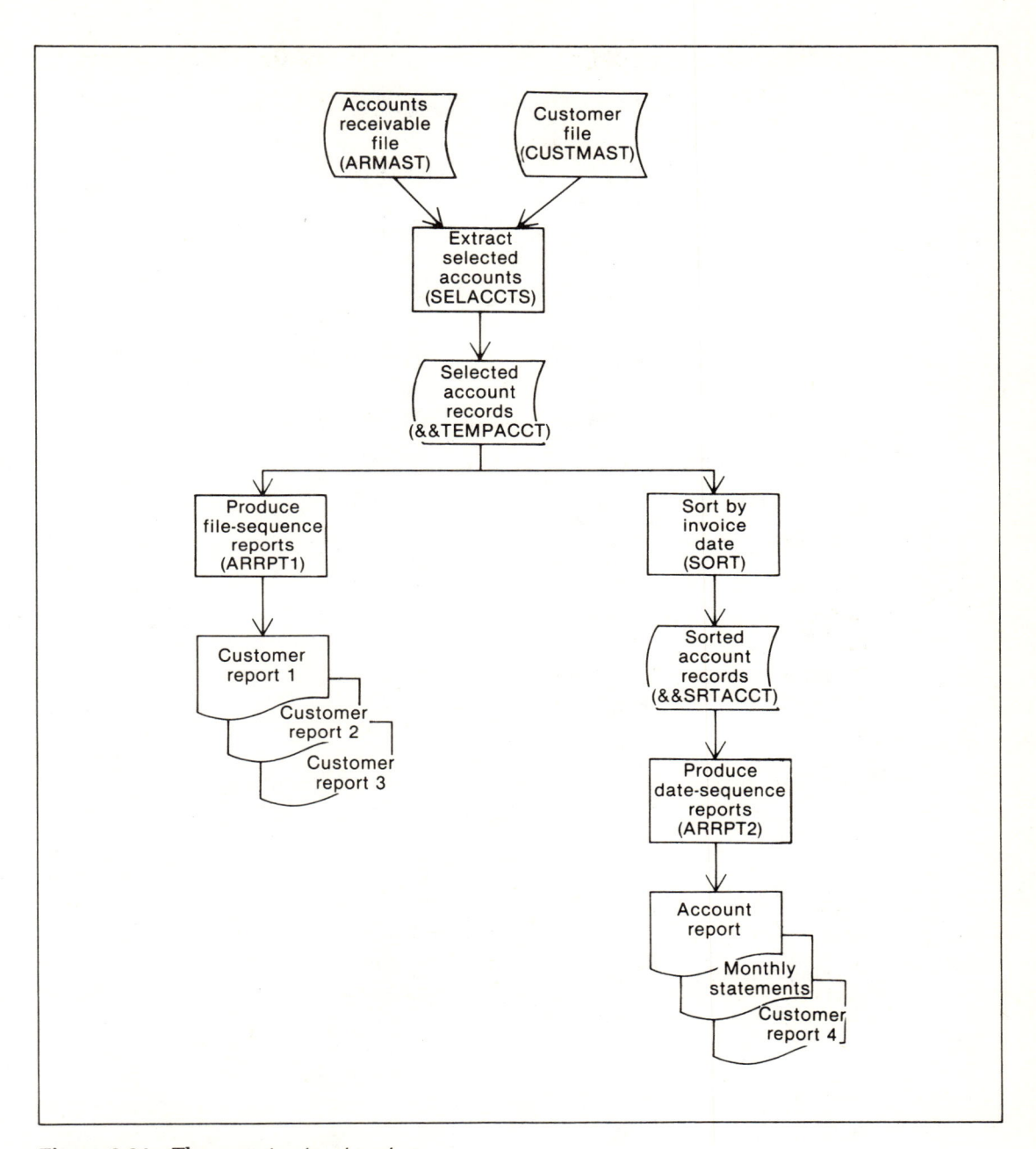

Figure 2-24 The report-extract system

6. SELRECS is the ddname for the temporary file passed from the extract program to this program.
7. CUSTRP1, CUSTRP2, and CUSTRP3 are the DD statements that define the reports. All are print files with block sizes of 133 characters (one print line per block).

```
 1 //CISEXT    JOB   HE66YFNH,
   //                'W. CLARY'
 2 //EXTRACT   EXEC  PGM=SELACCTS,
   //                PARM=013180
   //STEPLIB   DD    DSN=MMA.USERLIB,
   //                DISP=SHR
 3 //ACCTREC   DD    DSN=ARMAST,
   //                DISP=OLD
 3 //CUST      DD    DSN=CUSTMAST,
   //                DISP=OLD
 4 //SELRECS   DD    DSN=&&TEMPACCT,
   //                DISP=(NEW,PASS),
   //                UNIT=SYSDA,
   //                SPACE=(LRECL=165,BLKSIZE=1650,RECFM=FB)
 5 //REPORT1   EXEC  PGM=ARRPT1,
   //                REGION=100K
   //STEPLIB   DD    DSN=MMA.USERLIB,
   //                DISP=SHR
 6 //SELRECS   DD    DSN=&&TEMPACCT,
   //                DISP=(OLD,PASS)
 7 //CUSTRP1   DD    SYSOUT=A,
   //                DCB=BLKSIZE=133
 7 //CUSTRP2   DD    SYSOUT=A,
   //                DCB=BLKSIZE=133
 7 //CUSTRP3   DD    SYSOUT=A,
   //                DCB=BLKSIZE=133
 8 //ACCTSORT  EXEC  PGM=SORT,
   //                REGION=100K
 9 //SORTLIB   DD    DSN=SYS1.SORTLIB,
   //                DISP=SHR
10 //SORTIN    DD    DSN=&&TEMPACCT,
   //                DISP=(OLD,DELETE)
11 //SORTOUT   DD    DSN=&&SRTACCT,
   //                DISP=(NEW,PASS),
   //                UNIT=SYSDA,
   //                SPACE=(1650,(3,1),RLSE),
   //                DCB=(LRECL=165,BLKSIZE=1650,RECFM=FB)
12 //SYSIN     DD    *
                    sort control statements
   /*
13 //SORTWK01  DD    UNIT=SYSDA,
   //                SPACE=(CYL,5)
13 //SORTWK02  DD    UNIT=SYSDA,
   //                SPACE=(CYL,5)
13 //SORTWK03  DD    UNIT=SYSDA,
   //                SPACE=(CYL,5)
14 //REPORT2   EXEC  PGM=ARRPT2,
   //                REGION=90K
   //STEPLIB   DD    DSN=MMA.USERLIB,
   //                DISP=SHR
15 //SRTACCT   DD    DSN=&&SRTACCT,
   //                DISP=(OLD,DELETE)
16 //ACCTRPT   DD    SYSOUT=A,
   //                DCB=BLKSIZE=133
16 //STMTS     DD    SYSOUT=A,
   //                DCB=BLKSIZE=75
16 //CUSTRP4   DD    SYSOUT=A,
   //                DCB=BLKSIZE=133
   //
```

Figure 2-25 JCL for the report-extract system

8. ACCTSORT is the EXEC statement to execute the sort program. The DD statements that follow in this job step are all required by the sort program and are described briefly below. (See chapter 7 for a full discussion of the IBM-supplied OS sort/merge program.)

9. SORTLIB is a special DD statement similar to JOBLIB and STEPLIB. It tells OS where the sort program's related support modules are located. In this case, the sort modules reside in a library named SYS1.SORTLIB.

10. SORTIN is the temporary data set passed from previous steps.

11. SORTOUT is the ddname of the temporary file containing the sorted records. It is passed to the next step.

12. SYSIN is the DD statement defining the sort control statements in the input stream.

13. SORTWK01, SORTWK02, and SORTWK03 are work files used by the sort program. They are temporary files, used only in this step, and define areas on any system direct-access device. As a result, they are coded with only the UNIT and SPACE parameters.

14. REPORT2 is the EXEC statement to execute the second report program, ARRPT2.

15. SRTACCT is the DD statement defining the sorted records passed from the sort.

16. ACCTRPT, STMTS, and CUSTRP4 are DD statements defining the last three reports.

Objective

Given a system flowchart and job specifications, write the JCL to execute the system.

Problem

Using the system flowchart and specifications in figure 2-26, write the JCL to execute the system.

Solution

Figure 2-27 is an acceptable solution.

System flowchart

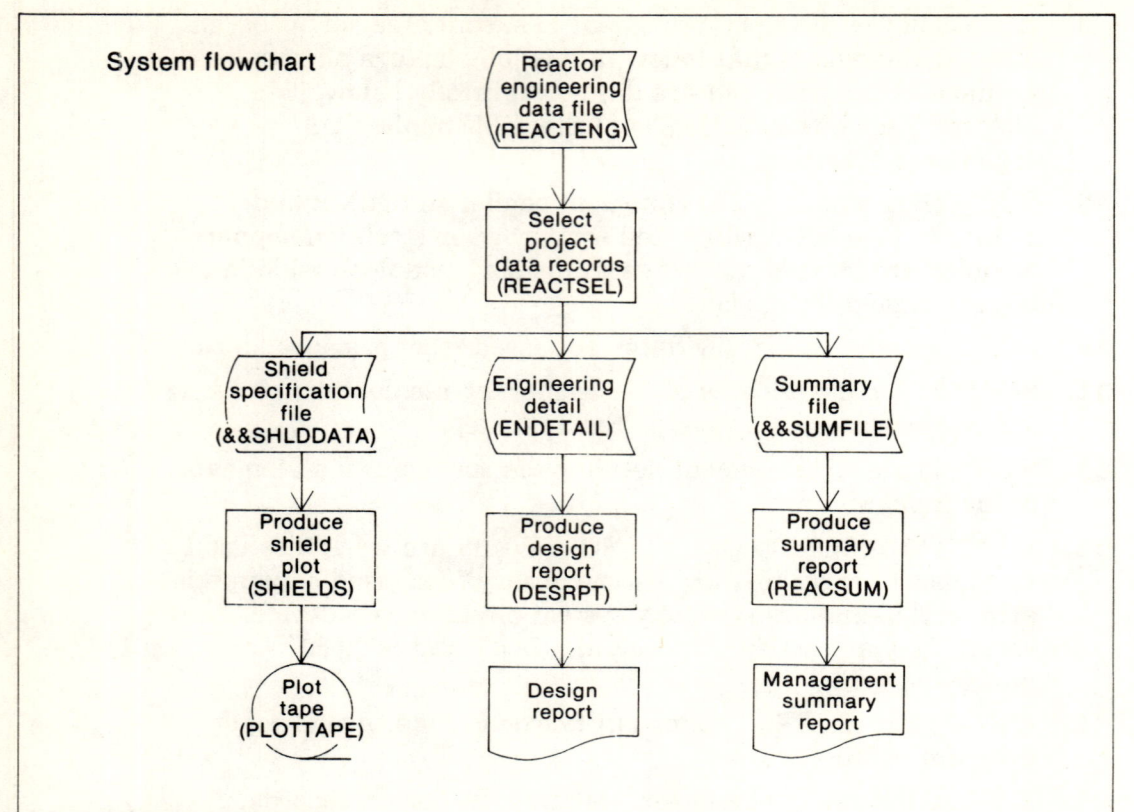

```
              Reactor
            engineering
             data file
            (REACTENG)
                 │
                 ▼
              Select
              project
           data records
            (REACTSEL)
         ┌───────┼───────┐
         ▼       ▼       ▼
      Shield  Engineering Summary
   specification  detail    file
       file    (ENDETAIL) (&&SUMFILE)
   (&&SHLDDATA)
         │       │        │
         ▼       ▼        ▼
      Produce  Produce  Produce
       shield   design  summary
        plot    report   report
      (SHIELDS) (DESRPT) (REACSUM)
         │       │        │
         ▼       ▼        ▼
        Plot   Design  Management
        tape   report   summary
      (PLOTTAPE)         report
```

Specifications

Programs: All programs reside in MMA.USERLIB.

    REACTSEL requires 100K of main storage.

    SHIELDS requires 200K of main storage. Pass it a PARM of +0009612.

    DESRPT requires 120K of main storage.

    REACSUM requires 72K of main storage.

Files:

    REACTENG is cataloged.

    &&SHLDDATA has 195-character fixed-length records with 10 records in each block. It requires about 10 cylinders on a system direct-access device.

    ENDETAIL has the same DCB as &&SHLDDATA. It requires about 22 blocks of space on a system direct-access device named D00103. If the job step runs OK, keep the file; if the job step fails, delete it.

    &&SUMFILE has the same DCB as &&SHLDDATA. It requires about 5 tracks of disk space.

    PLOTTAPE is to be cataloged on group name TAPE. If the job fails, delete it. The records are 60 bytes in length, unblocked.

    The two reports have 133-character records; both programs specify zero records per block.

Figure 2-26 System flowchart and specifications for an engineering application

```
//REACTOR   JOB  HE66YFNH,
//               'W. CLARY'
//SELECT    EXEC PGM=REACTSEL,
//               REGION=100K
//STEPLIB   DD   DSN=MMA.USERLIB,
//               DISP=SHR
//REACMAS   DD   DSN=REACTENG,
//               DISP=OLD
//SHIELD    DD   DSN=&&SHLDDATA,
//               DISP=(NEW,PASS),
//               UNIT=SYSDA,
//               SPACE=(CYL,(10,2),RLSE),
//               DCB=(LRECL=195,BLKSIZE=1950,RECFM=FB)
//ENGDET    DD   DSN=ENDETAIL,
//               DISP=(NEW,KEEP,DELETE),
//               UNIT=SYSDA,
//               VOL=SER=D00103,
//               SPACE=(1950,(22,4),RLSE),
//               DCB=(LRECL=195,BLKSIZE=1950,RECFM=FB)
//SUMFILE   DD   DSN=&&SUMFILE,
//               DISP=(NEW,PASS),
//               UNIT=SYSDA,
//               SPACE=(TRK,(5,1),RLSE),
//               DCB=(LRECL=195,BLKSIZE=1950,RECFM=FB)
//SHIELDPL  EXEC PGM=SHIELDS,
//               PARM='+0009612',
//               REGION=200K
//STEPLIB   DD   DSN=MMA.USERLIB,
//               DISP=SHR
//SHIELD    DD   DSN=&&SHLDDATA,
//               DISP=(OLD,DELETE)
//PLOTSHLD  DD   DSN=PLOTTAPE,
//               DISP=(NEW,CATLG,DELETE),
//               UNIT=TAPE,
//               DCB=(LRECL=60,RECFM=F)
//ENGDETL   EXEC PGM=DESRPT,
//               REGION=120K
//STEPLIB   DD   DSN=MMA.USERLIB,
//               DISP=SHR
//ENGDET    DD   DSN=ENDETAIL,
//               DISP=OLD,
//               UNIT=SYSDA,
//               VOL=SER=D00103
//DESRPT    DD   SYSOUT=A,
//               DCB=BLKSIZE=133
//SUMRPT    EXEC PGM=REACSUM,
//               REGION=72K
//STEPLIB   DD   DSN=MMA.USERLIB,
//               DISP=SHR
//SUMFILE   DD   DSN=&&SUMFILE,
//               DISP=(OLD,DELETE)
//MGTRPT    DD   SYSOUT=A,
//               DCB=BLKSIZE=133
//
```

Figure 2-27 JCL for the engineering application

...INVALID SAL...

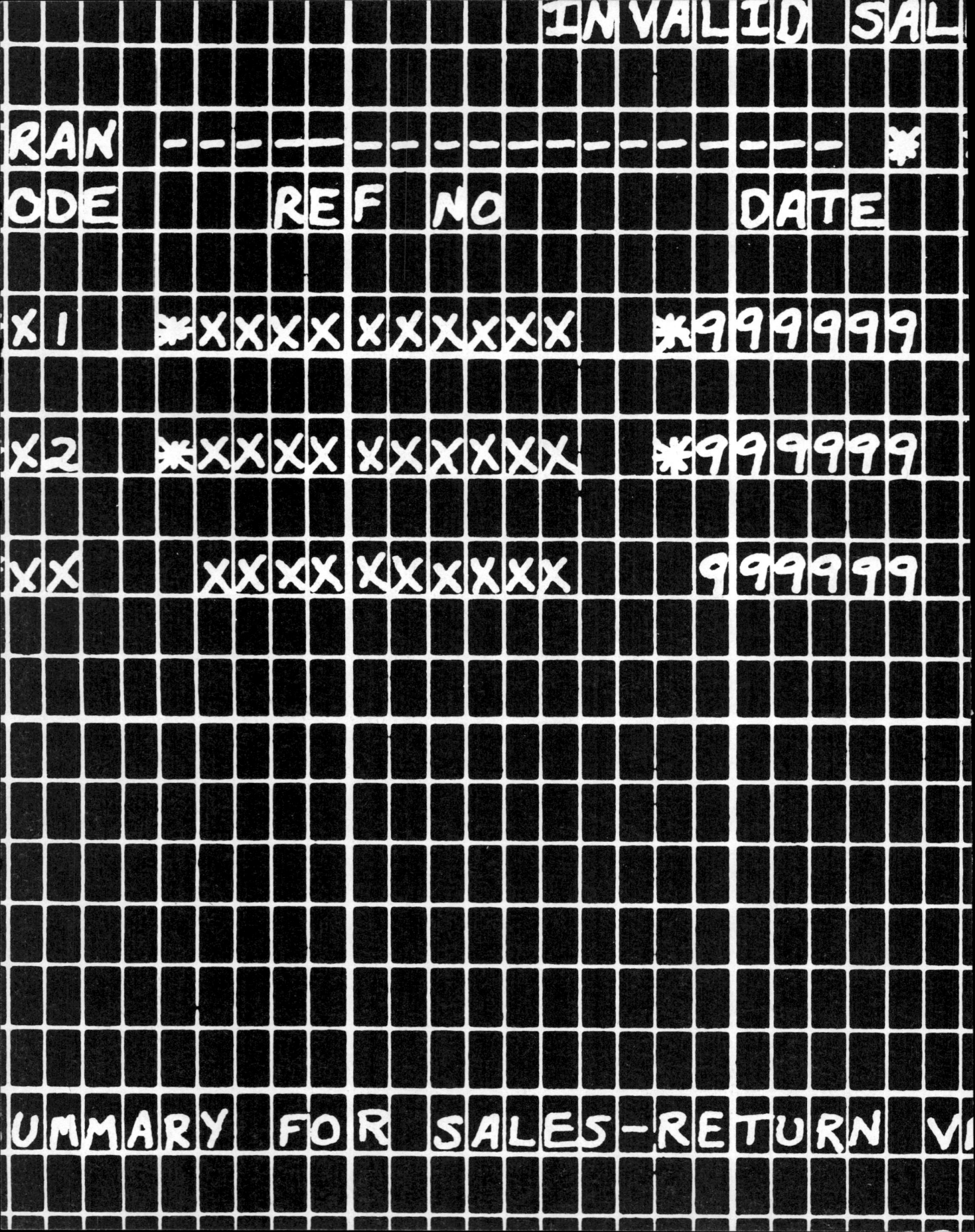

...RAN -------------------- *
...ODE   REF NO   DATE

X1   *XXXX XXXXXX   *999999

X2   *XXXX XXXXXX   *999999

XX   XXXX XXXXXX   999999

...UMMARY FOR SALES-RETURN V...

3

Expanding the Basic Subset: Advanced JCL

Now that you've been exposed to the basics of OS JCL, I'll present some advanced concepts. The flexibility of OS JCL becomes evident as you realize that it offers several ways to accomplish the same thing. It also provides you with the ability to perform many processing functions that most of us, as applications programmers, never have to concern ourselves with. Some people say the weakness of OS JCL is its flexibility. They feel that you have to wade through the options you don't need in order to understand those you do need.

This chapter introduces some of the more advanced techniques and options of OS JCL that I think you *will* find useful in your day-to-day work. Topic 1 presents techniques to (1) reduce the amount of actual coding, (2) qualify data set names, (3) group two or more files together as one file with one ddname, and (4) create and maintain generations of data sets. Topic 2 covers advanced JCL parameters of the JOB, EXEC, and DD statements.

TOPIC 1 JCL Coding Techniques

This topic shows you different ways to code some of the parameters already presented. Although they are more advanced in concept than the techniques presented in chapter 2, you'll use some of them when coding even the simplest jobs. The elements I'll cover here are backward references, qualified data set names, concatenated files, and generation data sets.

BACKWARD REFERENCES

As you looked over the examples in chapter 2 and solved the problems at the end of topics 2 and 3, you probably noticed some repetition of certain parameters. For example, several times the DCB information for one file was identical to the DCB information for other files in the same job. By coding a *backward reference* (sometimes called a *referback*), you can cause OS to copy a parameter from a preceding JCL statement. As a result, you can reduce the amount of coding you have to do, which in turn reduces the chance of coding errors.

The referback facility applies to the PGM parameter of the EXEC statement and the DSN, VOLUME, and DCB parameters of the DD statement. The general form of a backward reference is shown in figure 3-1. When a referback is used in the VOLUME parameter, however, it requires a slightly different form. Instead of coding VOL = SER as you were shown in chapter 2, you code VOL = REF followed by the general form of figure 3-1. Here's an example:

```
VOL=REF=*.PRODFILE
```

Figure 3-2 shows a JCL listing using backward references. The numbered JCL statements all pertain to this subject, so let's look at them individually.

1. ORDPROC1 is the first step of the job. It executes the program named ORDER01.
2. TEMPORD1 is the DD statement for a temporary file passed to later steps.
3. The volume serial number of TEMPORD1 is D00103.
4. The DCB for TEMPORD1 is given.
5. TEMPORD2 is another temporary file passed to later steps.
6. The volume serial number for TEMPORD2 is to be the same as TEMPORD1. Notice the referback that is used here. Since the DD statement for TEMPORD1 is in the same job step, the backward reference only has to specify the ddname.
7. The DCB for TEMPORD2 is to be the same as TEMPORD1. Here again, I used a referback instead of coding the DCB.
8. RPTIN in the job step ORDRPT1 is the first temporary file passed by the first step. Instead of giving the name in the DSN parameter, I used the referback to cause OS to use the same name. Notice that the referback must include the stepname as well as the ddname.
9. The same is true for RPTIN of step ORDRPT2: I used the referback instead of coding the data set name.

EXEC statement PGM parameter:

Format	Use
`PGM=*.stepname`	To refer to a step not in a cataloged procedure
`PGM=*.stepname.procstepname`	To refer to a step in a cataloged procedure

DD statement parameters:

Format	Use
`parameter=*.ddname`	If the ddname is within the same job step
`parameter=*.stepname.ddname`	If the ddname is within an earlier job step
`parameter=*.stepname.procstepname.ddname`	If the ddname is within a cataloged procedure called by an earlier job step

Note: Cataloged procedures are covered in chapter 5.

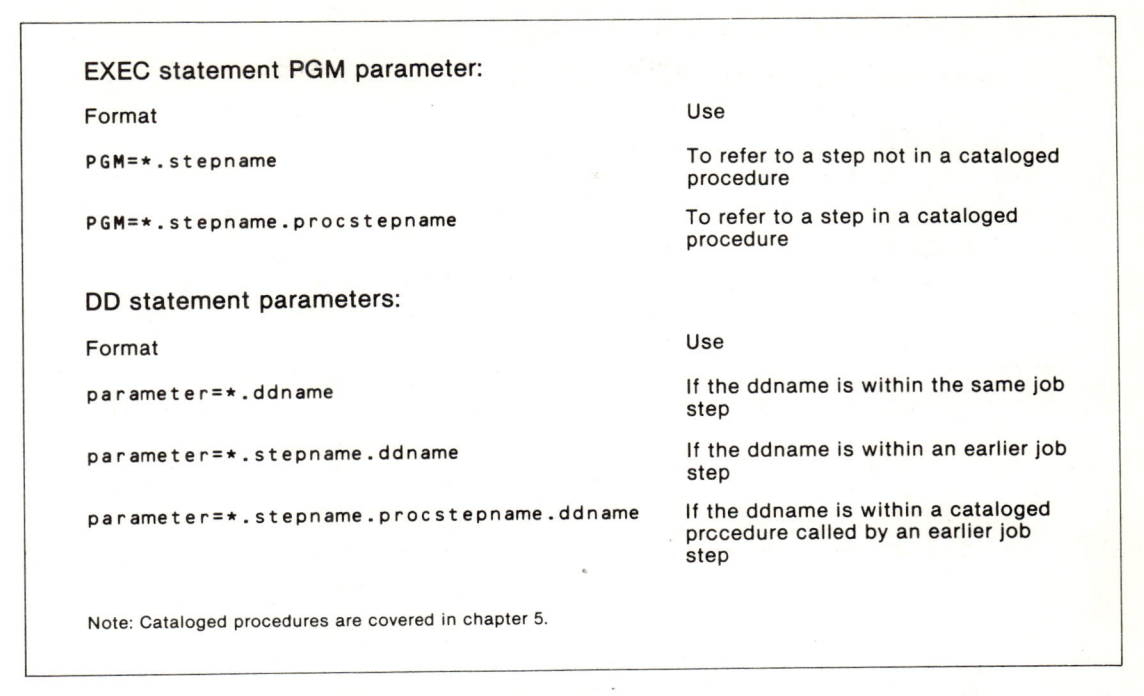

Figure 3-1   General form of the backward reference

Although it's not shown in this example, you can also code a referback for the PGM parameter. For example, if the job executed the ORDER01 program twice, the second EXEC statement for it could be written like this:

```
//ORDPROC2  EXEC    PGM=*.ORDPROC1
```

When using a referback, be sure that the stepnames are unique. Otherwise, OS won't know which step you are referring to. I'll be using referbacks throughout the remainder of this book, so you'll see plenty of examples by the time you've finished this course.

QUALIFIED NAMES

You've already seen examples of qualified names in chapter 2. Remember the DSN I used in the STEPLIB DD statement in some of the examples? It was MMA.USERLIB—two simple names joined by a period. And that's what a *qualified name* is, two or more simple names of eight or fewer characters joined by periods. This facility is useful in a large organization or a multi-user environment where the possibility of assigning duplicate file names is high.

In a qualified name, the first (leftmost) simple name is a *high-level qualifier*, or *index*. The second simple name indicates the next-

```
  //ORDERENT JOB  HE66YFNH,
  //              'W. CLARY'
1 //ORDPROC1 EXEC  PGM=ORDER01
  //STEPLIB  DD   DSN=MMA.USERLIB,
  //              DISP=SHR
  //ORDERMAS DD   DSN=ORDMST,
  //              DISP=OLD
2 //TEMPORD1 DD   DSN=&&TEMPORD1,
  //              DISP=(NEW,PASS),
  //              UNIT=SYSDA,
3 //              VOL=SER=D00103,
  //              SPACE=(CYL,(1,1),RLSE),
4 //              DCB=(LRECL=190,BLKSIZE=3800,RECFM=FB)
5 //TEMPORD2 DD   DSN=&&TEMPORD2,
  //              DISP=(NEW,PASS),
6 //              VOL=REF=*.TEMPORD1,
  //              SPACE=(CYL,(1,1),RLSE),
7 //              DCB=*.TEMPORD1
  //ORDRPT1  EXEC  PGM=ORDR001
  //STEPLIB  DD   DSN=MMA.USERLIB,
  //              DISP=SHR
8 //RPTIN    DD   DSN=*.ORDPROC1.TEMPORD1,
  //              DISP=(OLD,DELETE)
  //RPTOUT   DD   SYSOUT=A
  //ORDRPT2  EXEC  PGM=ORDR002
  //STEPLIB  DD   DSN=MMA.USERLIB,
  //              DISP=SHR
9 //RPTIN    DD   DSN=*.ORDPROC1.TEMPORD2,
  //              DISP=(OLD,DELETE)
  //RPTOUT   DD   SYSOUT=A
  //
```

Figure 3-2 JCL using backward references

level qualifier or index within the first-named level. The third simple name indicates the next-level qualifier within the second-named level, and so on. Figure 3-3 shows how this indexing works.

In this example, three companies are sharing one computer. To eliminate the possibility of duplicate file names, each company is assigned a high-level index mnemonic to identify its own files. When I code DSN = MMA.USERLIB in a DD statement, OS first uses the high-level qualifier and finds MMA. This points to the secondary index A. The entry in the secondary index labeled USERLIB points to the direct-access device and location where the file resides, as shown at the bottom of the figure.

Now suppose I work for the accounting department of the General Development Construction Company (GDC). Also suppose that our departments need unique file qualifiers as shown in figure 3-3. If I need to access a tax calculation file associated with the accounting

Expanding the Basic Subset: Advanced JCL

High level

Name	Pointer
MMA	A
PAY	B
GDC	C

To second level index →

Second level

Index	Name	File location or pointer
A	USERLIB	d
	COPYLIB	l
	PAYPROG	k
	BANKLIB	p

To direct-access device ↓

Index	Name	File location or pointer
B	PAYPROG	n
	COPYLIB	b
	PAYLIB	j
	PROCLIB	c

To direct-access device ↓

Index	Name	File location or pointer
C	PAY	1
	ACCT	2
	ENG	3

To third level index →

Third level

Index	Name	File location
1	PAYPROG	e
	DEDUCT	a
	TAXCALC	i

To direct-access device ↓

Index	Name	File location
2	GENLEDG	h
	TAXCALC	g

To direct-access device ↓

Index	Name	File location
3	COPYLIB	f
	CONSTRCT	m
	BUILD	o

To direct-access device ↓

Direct-access device

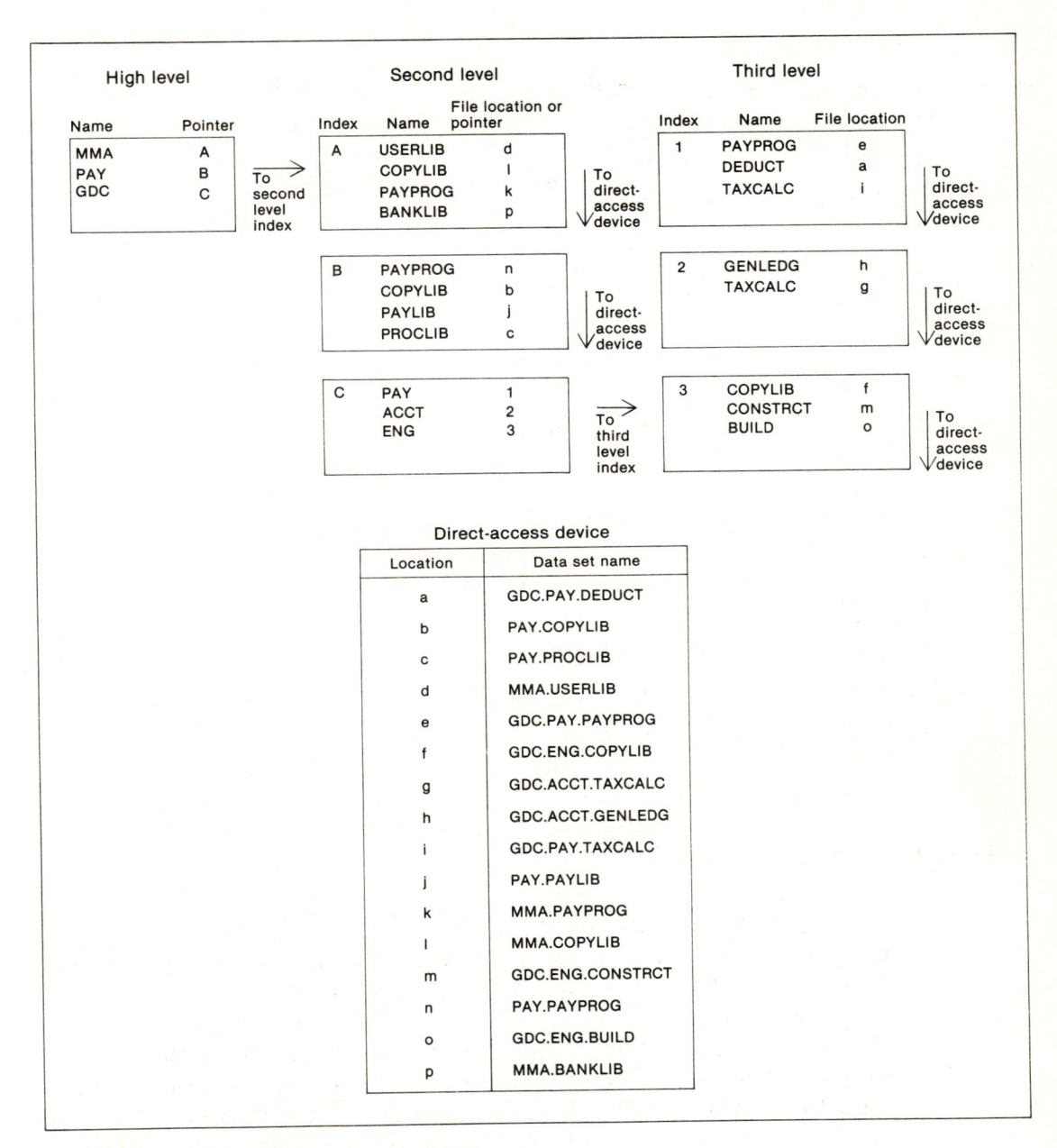

Location	Data set name
a	GDC.PAY.DEDUCT
b	PAY.COPYLIB
c	PAY.PROCLIB
d	MMA.USERLIB
e	GDC.PAY.PAYPROG
f	GDC.ENG.COPYLIB
g	GDC.ACCT.TAXCALC
h	GDC.ACCT.GENLEDG
i	GDC.PAY.TAXCALC
j	PAY.PAYLIB
k	MMA.PAYPROG
l	MMA.COPYLIB
m	GDC.ENG.CONSTRCT
n	PAY.PAYPROG
o	GDC.ENG.BUILD
p	MMA.BANKLIB

Figure 3-3 The indexing used for qualified names

department (notice that there are two files at the third level named TAXCALC), I code it like this: GDC.ACCT.TAXCALC. The high-level qualifier (GDC) points to the secondary index C. The entry for ACCT then points to the third-level index 2. Finally, the TAXCALC entry in the third-level index points to the location of the file.

CONCATENATING FILES

The word *concatenate* means to link or chain together, and that's what you do when you concatenate files: you link them together so they appear to OS as one file. To illustrate, suppose you have a program that reads 80-character records from both cards and magnetic tape. You can concatenate the two files like this:

```
//INRECS    DD   DSN=TAPEREC,
//               DISP=OLD
//          DD   *
            data cards
/*
```

To concatenate files, you code the first DD statement just as you normally would if it were the only file to be read. Then, you code the next DD statement directly after it in the input stream, but you don't code a ddname for it. You can concatenate up to 255 sequential files or up to 16 partitioned files in this way. (Partitioned files are introduced in chapter 5.) As a general rule, all of the files you concatenate must have the same characteristics in the DCB.

GENERATION DATA SETS

Many data processing applications are cyclical. In other words, they consist of new input data that is combined with an existing master file to form a new master file. The new master file then replaces the old master file for the next cycle. An example of this is the typical update job shown in figure 3-4. Input data is used to update an old master file (September) to create a new master file (October).

If we number the master files relative to one another before executing the update program, September would be 0, August would be −1 and July would be −2. After executing the update program, the October file is 0, the September file is −1, August is −2, July is −3, and so forth. In other words, each time the system is processed, the relative position of the old master file is changed.

Sometimes it is necessary to retain these old master files in their relative position for backup, special processing, statistics, audit trails, or some other reason. To do this, the *generation data set* facility of OS applies a *generation number* to each file as it is created. This identifies the chronological sequence of the generations. The format of the generation number is GnnnnnV00, where Gnnnnn is the chronological sequence number of the generation and V00 is the *version number* of that generation.

When you create a new generation data set, OS adds 1 to the sequence number and appends it to the file name like this:

```
filename.GnnnnnV00
```

Expanding the Basic Subset: Advanced JCL 97

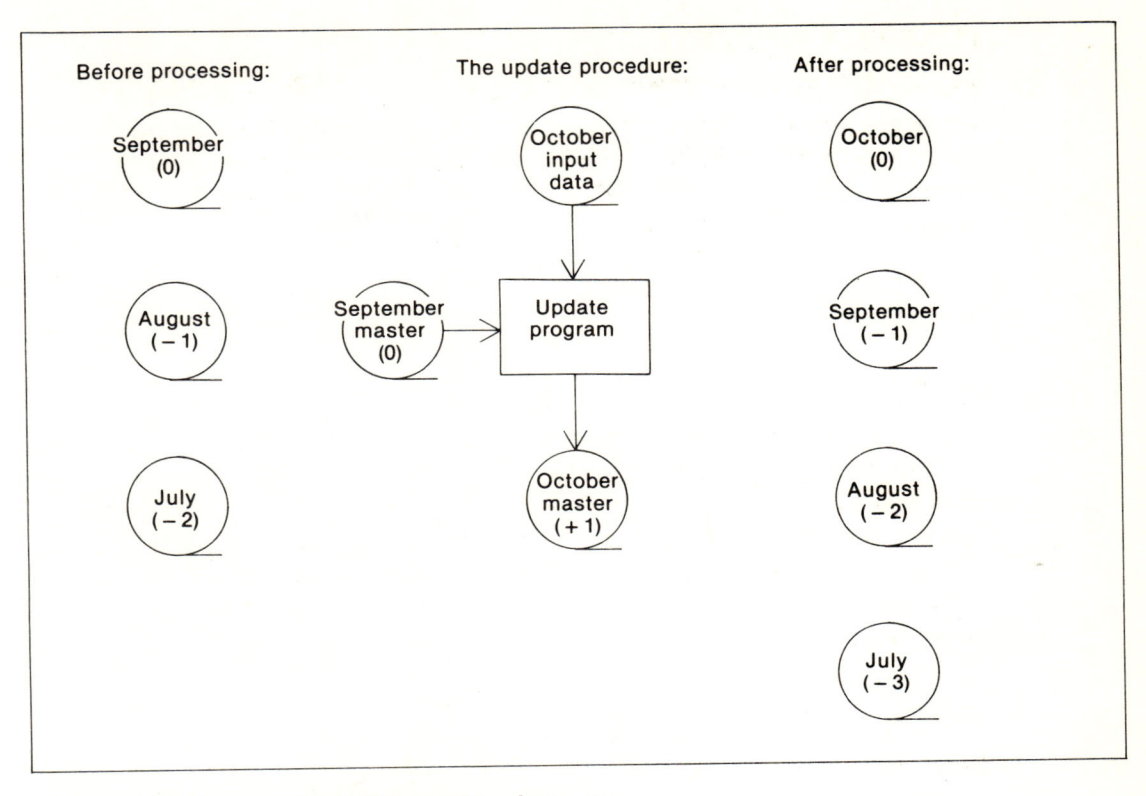

Figure 3-4 Relative position of generation data sets

OS doesn't update the version number; that's for you to use. If, for example, you want to change the data in a generation but don't want the generation number to be updated, you may write a file with the proper generation number setting the version number to V01.

To illustrate the concept of generation numbers, consider figure 3-5. It shows a system before and after creating a new generation master file. Before processing, the current master file is generation 12. After processing, the current master file is generation 13. So if you need to access the first previous master file, you must refer to generation 12 of the master file; if you need the second previous master file, you must refer to generation 11; and so forth.

In JCL, you refer to generations by their position relative to the current generation by coding a *relative generation number* in parentheses after the name in the DSN parameter. To refer to the current generation, code the DSN parameter like this: DSN = filename(0); to create a new generation, code the DSN parameter like this: DSN = filename(+ 1); to create a second generation in the same job, code the second DSN parameter like this: DSN = filename(+ 2).

Figure 3-6 shows a job using generation data sets. It reads input records from a data set in the job stream; updates the old master file,

Chapter 3

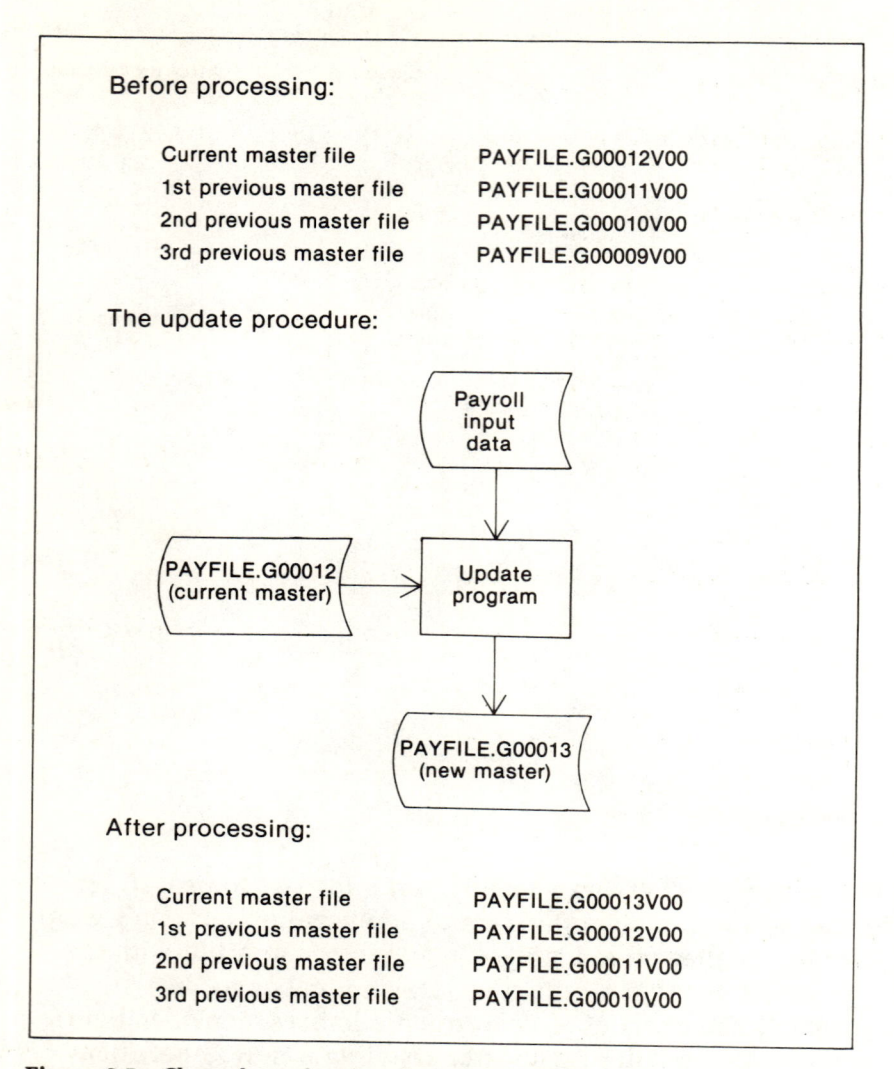

```
Before processing:

    Current master file          PAYFILE.G00012V00
    1st previous master file     PAYFILE.G00011V00
    2nd previous master file     PAYFILE.G00010V00
    3rd previous master file     PAYFILE.G00009V00

The update procedure:

              ┌──────────────┐
              │   Payroll    │
              │    input     │
              │    data      │
              └──────┬───────┘
                     │
                     ▼
  ┌─────────────┐  ┌─────────┐
  │PAYFILE.G00012│─▶│ Update  │
  │(current      │  │ program │
  │ master)      │  └────┬────┘
  └─────────────┘       │
                         ▼
                  ┌──────────────┐
                  │PAYFILE.G00013│
                  │(new master)  │
                  └──────────────┘

After processing:

    Current master file          PAYFILE.G00013V00
    1st previous master file     PAYFILE.G00012V00
    2nd previous master file     PAYFILE.G00011V00
    3rd previous master file     PAYFILE.G00010V00
```

Figure 3-5 Chronological order of generation data sets

PNTFILE(0); and writes out the new master, PNTFILE(+ 1). If, for some reason, you must rerun this job using the master file as it existed before the update, you would code it as shown in figure 3-7, with the old master as PNTFILE(− 1) and the new master file as PNTFILE(+ 1).

The relative generation numbers are updated after the completion of the job. As a result, any step that refers to a generation created in preceding steps must refer to it in relation to the generation that was current when the job began. In other words, if the first step of a job creates a new master (+ 1), and the next step is to print records from that file, it must be referred to as (+ 1) in that step also.

```
//PNTJOB     JOB   HE66YFNH,
//                 'W. CLARY'
//PNTSTEP   EXEC   PGM=PNTUPDT
//STEPLIB   DD     DSN=MMA.USERLIB,
//                 DISP=SHR
//JRDATA    DD     *
                   input records
/*
//PNTOLD    DD     DSN=PNTFILE(0),
//                 DISP=OLD
//PNTNEW    DD     DSN=PNTFILE(+1),
//                 DISP=(NEW,CATLG),
//                 UNIT=3330,
//                 VOL=SER=D00103,
//                 SPACE=(CYL,(12,2),RLSE),
//                 DCB=(MODLDSCB,LRECL=90,BLKSIZE=900,RECFM=FB)
//
```

Figure 3-6 Typical update system using generation data sets

```
//PNTRERUN  JOB   HE66YFNH,
//                'W. CLARY'
//PNTSTEP   EXEC  PGM=PNTUPDT
//STEPLIB   DD    DSN=MMA.USERLIB,
//                DISP=SHR
//JRDATA    DD    *
                  input records
/*
//PNTOLD    DD    DSN=PNTFILE(-1),
//                DISP=OLD
//PNTNEW    DD    DSN=PNTFILE(+1),
//                DISP=(NEW,CATLG),
//                UNIT=3330,
//                VOL=SER=D00103,
//                SPACE=(CYL,(12,2),RLSE),
//                DCB=(MODLDSCB,LRECL=90,BLKSIZE=900,RECFM=FB)
//
```

Figure 3-7 JCL to rerun a job using a previous generation of the master file

However, if there are two separate jobs to do this, one to create the new master and one to print it, the second job would refer to the master file as (0). Figure 3-8 may help to clarify this. The first example shows one job with two steps. The first step creates a new generation and the second refers to that new generation. The second example shows two jobs to do exactly the same thing, only this time the relative generation numbers have been updated at the completion of the first job, so the second job must refer to the updated relative generation number.

Example 1: A single job with two steps

```
//ELAPJOB  JOB   HE66YFNH,
//              'W. CLARY'
//ELAPSTEP EXEC  PGM=ELAPSE
//STEPLIB  DD    DSN=MMA.USERLIB,
//               DISP=SHR
//CTIME    DD    *
                 input data
/*
//ELMASTIN DD    DSN=ELAPFILE(0),
//               DISP=OLD
//ELMASTOT DD    DSN=ELAPFILE(+1),
//               DISP=(NEW,CATLG),
//               UNIT=SYSDA,
//               SPACE=(TRK,(1,1),RLSE),
//               DCB=(MODLDSCB,LRECL=80,BLKSIZE=960,RECFM=FB)
//RPTSTEP  EXEC  PGM=ELRPT
//STEPLIB  DD    DSN=MMA.USERLIB,
//               DISP=SHR
//ELMAST   DD    DSN=ELAPFILE(+1),
//               DISP=OLD
//ELRPT1   DD    SYSOUT=A
//
```

Example 2: Two separate jobs

```
//ELAPJOB1 JOB   HE66YFNH,
//              'W. CLARY'
//ELAPSTEP EXEC  PGM=ELAPSE
//STEPLIB  DD    MMA.USERLIB,
//               DISP=SHR
//CTIME    DD    *
                 input data
/*
//ELMASTIN DD    DSN=ELAPFILE(0),
//               DISP=OLD
//ELMASTOT DD    DSN=ELAPFILE(+1),
//               DISP=(NEW,CATLG),
//               UNIT=SYSDA,
//               SPACE=(TRK,(1,1),RLSE),
//               DCB=(MODLDSCB,LRECL=80,BLKSIZE=960,RECFM=FB)
//
//ELAPJOB2 JOB   HE66YFNH,
//              'W. CLARY'
//RPTSTEP  EXEC  PGM=ELRPT
//STEPLIB  DD    DSN=MMA.USERLIB,
//               DISP=SHR
//ELMAST   DD    DSN=ELAPFILE(0),
//               DISP=OLD
//ELRPT1   DD    SYSOUT=A
//
```

Figure 3-8 JCL illustrating that generation numbers are updated at the end of a job, not at the end of a job step

Before you can create and use generation data sets, there are two items that must be present in the system. One is a model data set control block; the other is a generation data group index.

Using a model data set control block A *model data set control block (DSCB)* is a special, cataloged data set that is used to hold data control block (DCB) information. Usually, it is an empty data set because each programmer who uses it for a generation data set will want to supply the unique DCB information that applies to his file. So any information the DSCB contains will be overridden by the DCB parameter in the programmer's JCL.

At any rate, OS requires that you specify a pre-existing DSCB in the first subparameter of a DCB for a generation data set. If you look back at figures 3-6, 3-7, and 3-8, you'll see I used a DSCB named MODLDSCB. The other DCB subparameters are coded as usual. You'll have to find out the name of the model DSCB on your system so you can use it when you code a DCB for a generation data set.

If your installation doesn't have a model DSCB set up, you can create one by coding a DD statement like this:

```
//         DD   DSN=MODLDSCB,
//              DISP=(NEW,CATLG),
//              UNIT=SYSDA,
//              VOL=SER=system-residence-volume
//              SPACE=(TRK,0),
//              DCB=(LRECL=80,BLKSIZE=160,RECFM=FB)
```

Then, when you create a new generation, you code the data set name (in this case, MODLDSCB) as the first subparameter in the DCB, followed by the characteristics of the file as you learned in chapter 2. Check with your installation, though, before you create your own model DSCB. If one already exists, your installation standards may not allow you to set up one of your own.

Building a generation data group index A *generation data group index* contains (1) the name of the generation data set you're going to create, (2) the number of generations you want to keep of that data set, and (3) instructions on what to do once that number of generations has been reached. To build the index, you have to execute a utility program named IEHPROGM. You'll learn all about this utility in chapter 7. But for now, I'll just show you what to code to build the index, without explaining why you code each statement.

Figure 3-9 shows the complete job you need to execute to create the index. The underlined values are those you can change depending on your system and how you want the generations to be defined. The

```
//EXIX     JOB  HE66YFNH,
//              'W. CLARY'
//EXPROG   EXEC PGM=IEHPROGM
//SYSPRINT DD   SYSOUT=A
//VOL1     DD   DISP=OLD,
//              UNIT=DISKA,
//              VOL=SER=CATLG2
//SYSIN    DD   *
  BLDG    INDEX=PAYMAST,ENTRIES=5,DELETE
/*
```

Figure 3-9 Creating a generation data group index

UNIT and VOLUME parameters specify the system-residence pack. INDEX identifies the name of the generation data group you are defining. Instead of PAYMAST, of course, you code the name of your file. The file name may be qualified as you learned earlier in this topic. ENTRIES identifies the number of generations you want to keep. This may be any number from 1 to 255. DELETE tells the program that when the index is full (in this case, when five generations already exist) and a new generation is created, the earliest generation of the file is to be deleted. As a result, in this example, the five most recent generations are always available. As an alternative to DELETE, you can specify EMPTY, which will delete *all* generations when the index overflows. At that point, only the most recent generation will exist.

Terminology

backward reference
referback
qualified name
high-level qualifier
index
concatenate
generation data set

generation number
version number
relative generation number
model data set control block
DSCB
generation data group index

Objectives

1. Given reference material, code the JCL to refer back to the values coded in PGM, DSN, VOLUME, and DCB parameters in the current job step, previous job steps, and procedures called by a previous job step.

2. Given reference material, code the JCL to concatenate two or more files with the same file characteristics.
3. Given reference material, code the JCL to create a generation data group index.
4. Given reference material, code the JCL to create and use generation data sets.

Problems

1. (Objective 1) Code a DCB parameter to refer back to a previous DD statement defined in a previous job step named UP1. The previous ddname is UPFILE.
2. (Objective 2) Code the DD statements to concatenate four files: PTINPUTA, PTINPUTB, PTINPUTC, and a card file. The first three files are cataloged on tape or direct-access volumes; the card file is to be entered through the input stream. Give the concatenated file the ddname of INGROUP.
3. (Objective 3) Code the JCL and utility control statements to create a generation data group index for a file named GENLED. It is to reside on a DISKA volume named CATLG2. The number of generations to be retained is ten. When the index is full, the earliest generation is to be deleted.
4. (Objective 4) Fill in the missing parameters in the JCL list shown in figure 3-10.

```
//TRUJOB    JOB   HE66YFNH,
//                'W. CLARY'
//EXTRU     EXEC  PGM=TRUNEV
//STEPLIB   DD    DSN=MMA.USERLIB,
//                DISP=SHR
//TRUDATA   DD    *
           input data
/*
//TRUFILE1  DD    DSN=[        ],              Current generation of MASTFILE
//                DISP=OLD
//TRUFILE2  DD    DSN=[        ],              New generation of MASTFILE
//                DISP=(NEW,CATLG),
//                UNIT=3330,
//                SPACE=(1300,(10,4),RLSE),
//                DCB=(MODLDSCB,LRECL=1300,BLKSIZE=1300,RECFM=F)
//RPTTRU    EXEC  PGM=TRPT001
//STEPLIB   DD    DSN=MMA.USERLIB,
//                DISP=SHR
//TRUFILE   DD    DSN=[        ],              Generation created in previous step
//                DISP=OLD
//TRURPT    DD    SYSOUT=A
//
```

Figure 3-10 Problem 4: Fill in the missing parameters

```
//EXUT      EXEC  PGM=IEHPROGM
//SYSPRINT  DD    SYSOUT=A
//VOL1      DD    DISP=OLD,
//                UNIT=DISKA,
//                VOL=SER=CATLG2
//SYSIN     DD    *
   BLDG           INDEX=GENLED,ENTRIES=10,DELETE
/*
```

Figure 3-11 Creating a generation data group index

Solutions

1. `//                  DCB=*.UP1.UPFILE`

2. ```
   //INGROUP  DD   DSN=PTINPUTA,
   //              DISP=OLD
   //         DD   DSN=PTINPUTB,
   //              DISP=OLD
   //         DD   DSN=PTINPUTC,
   //              DISP=OLD
   //         DD   *
                   card file
   /*
   ```

3. Figure 3-11 is an acceptable solution.

4. a. MASTFILE(0)

   b. MASTFILE(+1)

   c. MASTFILE(+1)

TOPIC 2   Advanced JCL Parameters

In this topic, I'll show you several new parameters to add to the basic subset. I'll also show you some additional subparameters to expand the parameters you learned about in chapter 2. I separated this group of parameters and subparameters from the basic subset because the functions they serve are specific to certain applications or because they provide optional, alternate ways to accomplish the things you learned to do in chapter 2.

THE JOB STATEMENT

The additional JOB statement parameters to be presented in this topic will give you more control over your jobs. If an error is detected by a
   ```

program in one of your job steps, you can tell OS to bypass the rest of the steps in the job; you can set a time limit for a job; and you can tell OS to hold (not execute) a job until told to release it. Figure 3-12 shows the expanded JOB statement skeleton.

The COND parameter

There are times when a job step will execute to normal completion, but some condition (such as invalid data) is discovered by the program that may adversely affect subsequent job steps. In such cases, you can use the condition (COND) parameter to tell OS to bypass subsequent job steps if a code of a certain value is passed from the program.

The code passed from the program is called a *return code*. There are two types of return codes: operating system return codes and user return codes. Operating system return codes are generated by OS and its service programs. They give indications of the success or failure of the job step. For example, the language translators send a return code of 0000 if no errors were detected in the source code and a return code of 0004 through 0016 if errors were detected. The value of the return code is a reflection of the severity of the error encountered.

User return codes are passed from your application program. You can use the return code to communicate between programs. For example, if you have a job that edits (validates) data in one step and updates a master file in the next step, the edit program can pass a return code to indicate whether or not the data is acceptable. It could pass a return code of 0000 if the data is all valid, or 0004 if some of the data is invalid. Then, you could code a COND parameter on the JOB statement that says, in effect, if 4 is less than or equal to the

```
//jobname   JOB   accounting-information,
                 programmer-name,
                 CLASS=job-class,
                 PRTY=priority-number,
                 MSGCLASS=message-class,
                 MSGLEVEL=(statements,messages),
                 REGION=region-sizeK,
                 COND=(number,relational-operator),
                 TIME=(minutes,seconds),
                 TYPRUN=HOLD
```

Figure 3-12 Expanded JOB statement skeleton

return code issued by any step in the job, do *not* execute subsequent job steps. In other words, if the condition described in a COND parameter is true, all subsequent job steps are bypassed.

Figure 3-13 shows the JCL required for this edit-update job using the COND parameter. COND=(4,LE) means that if 4 is less than or equal to any return code, the remaining steps will be bypassed. In our example, this means that if all the data were good, the return code of 0000 passed by the edit program would not satisfy the condition. As a result, the update step would be executed (not bypassed). If some of the input records were invalid, a return code of 0004 would be issued, thus satisfying the condition and the update step would be bypassed.

The relational operators for the COND parameter and their meanings are as follows:

- GT Greater than
- GE Greater than or equal to
- LT Less than
- LE Less than or equal to
- EQ Equal to
- NE Not equal to

Figure 3-14 shows examples of some of these operators. Example 1 says: if 8 is greater than any return code, bypass all subsequent job steps. Examples 2 and 3 illustrate that you can combine more than one condition in the parameter. In fact, you can code up to eight conditions in one COND parameter. Example 2 says: if 16 is less than any return code, or if 4 is greater than or equal to any return code, bypass all subsequent job steps. Example 3 shows three conditions. It

```
//EDUP      JOB   HE66YFNH,
//                'W. CLARY',
//                COND=(4,LE)
//EDIT      EXEC  PGM=EDPGM
       .
       .
       .
//UPDATE    EXEC  PGM=UPPGM
       .
       .
//
```

Figure 3-13 Using the COND parameter in the JOB statement

Example no.	JCL code	Meaning Bypass subsequent job steps if...
1	// COND=(8,GT)	8 is greater than the return code
2	// COND=((16,LT),(4,GE))	16 is less than the return code or 4 is greater than or equal to the return code
3	// COND=((0,EQ),(37,LE),(8,LE))	(1) 0 is equal to the return code, (2) 37 is less than or equal to the return code, or (3) 8 is less than or equal to the return code

Figure 3-14 Examples of the COND parameter of the JOB statement

says: if 0 is equal to, 37 is less than or equal to, or 8 is less than or equal to any return code, bypass subsequent job steps.

As with other JOB statement parameters, COND can also be coded on the EXEC statement. If you code it on the JOB statement and the condition is true, all job steps following the one issuing the return code will be bypassed. If you code it on the EXEC statement and the condition is true, only the step executed by that EXEC statement will be bypassed.

The TIME parameter

Each installation has a pre-defined time limit for CPU usage. When your job exceeds the time limit, it will be terminated. To extend or reduce the installation time limit, you code the TIME parameter.

The format of the TIME parameter is:

    TIME=(minutes,seconds)

This tells OS the number of minutes and seconds the job is to be allowed to run.

Figure 3-15 shows examples of the TIME parameter. Example 1 illustrates a time limit of 3 minutes 30 seconds. Example 2 shows a time limit of 17 minutes. Example 3 shows a time limit of 25 seconds. Example 4 illustrates the TIME parameter to eliminate timing (there are 1440 minutes in 24 hours).

The time limit can also be specified for each job step by coding it on the EXEC statement. If you code it on both the JOB statement and the EXEC statement, the time limit specified on the JOB statement takes precedence. In other words, if you specify ten minutes on the

Example no.	JCL code		Meaning

1	`//PRJOB`
	`//`
	`//`
		`JOB   HE66YFNH,`
		`      'W. CLARY',`
		`      TIME=(3,30)`
			3 minutes, 30 seconds

2	`//`	`TIME=17`	17 minutes
3	`//`	`TIME=(,25)`	25 seconds
4	`//`	`TIME=1440`	Unlimited (24 hours)

Figure 3-15 Examples of the TIME parameter of the JOB statement

EXEC statement, but the execution of previous job steps has left only five minutes remaining of the time limit specified on the JOB statement, then the step can only use those five minutes. If it takes more, the job will be abnormally terminated.

The TYPRUN parameter

You can cause a job to be placed in a hold status by coding TYPRUN = HOLD on the JOB statement. Then, the job will not be initiated until the operator (or in some cases, a special release program) releases it. The purpose of this parameter is to allow you to submit a job before you are ready to have it executed. Of course, the operator must know what conditions must be met for the job to be released.

To illustrate, suppose you want to compile a program in one job and then execute the compiled program in another job. To do this, you can submit both jobs at the same time with TYPRUN = HOLD on the second JOB statement, like this:

```
//UPJOB    JOB  HE66YFNH,
//              'W. CLARY',
//              TYPRUN=HOLD
```

Then, you can tell the operator to release the held job when the compile job is finished.

In a small shop, or in a remote batch processing environment where you can read and release the job yourself, this technique may be fine, but in a large organization, operator intervention should be kept to a minimum. As a result, the use of this parameter is often prohibited or limited. And in actual practice, it may be wiser to wait for the results of the first job before entering the second job.

On the other hand, some installations have a program you can execute to release held jobs. To use this feature, you include the release program as the last step of the first job. By coding a COND parameter to test the success of the first job, you can cause the second job to be released only if the first job ran satisfactorily. At any rate, if you want to use the TYPRUN = HOLD parameter, check with your installation first to find out (1) if it's allowed and (2) if there's a release program you can use so there won't be any need for operator intervention.

THE EXEC STATEMENT

The two new parameters of the EXEC statement are COND and TIME. They are similar to the COND and TIME parameters just presented for the JOB statement. Figure 3-16 shows the expanded skeleton for the EXEC statement.

The COND parameter

Although the COND parameter of the EXEC statement is similar to the COND parameter of the JOB statement, it has additional capabilities not present in the JOB statement version. Here, you can not only specify the conditions under which the job step may *not* be executed, but also special cases when the step should be executed. By coding the COND parameter on the EXEC statement, you can cause a step to be executed even if a previous job step abnormally terminates. (Usually when a step fails, all subsequent steps are bypassed.) You can also cause a step to be executed *only* if a previous step fails.

Figure 3-17 shows examples of the EXEC statement with COND parameters. The EXEC statement in example 1 contains a COND parameter causing the step to be bypassed if any preceding step issues a return code greater than 0007. Example 2 shows a COND parameter that will cause this step to be bypassed if the step named

```
//stepname EXEC   PGM=program-name,
                  PARM=program-parameters,
                  REGION=region-sizeK,
                  COND=(number,relational-operator),
                       =(number,relational-operator,stepname),
                       =(number,relational-operator,stepname.procstepname),
                       =EVEN,
                       =ONLY,
                  TIME=(minutes,seconds)
```

Figure 3-16 Expanded EXEC statement skeleton

Example no.	JCL code	Meaning Bypass this step if...
1	`//PAYSTEP   EXEC  PGM=PAYPROG,` `//                COND=(7,LT)`	7 is less than any return code
2	`//                COND=(4,GE,EDSTEP)`	4 is greater than or equal to the return code from EDSTEP
3	`//                COND=(20,LT,UPSTEP.RPGEN)`	20 is less than the return code from the procedure step RPGEN called by UPSTEP
4	`//                COND=((16,LT,INSTEP),(8,GE,PROJ1))`	16 is less than the return code from INSTEP or 8 is greater than or equal to the return code from PROJ1
5	`//                COND=((16,LE),(6,EQ,ACCTUP.UPPROG))`	16 is less than or equal to any return code or 6 is equal to the return code from the procedure step UPPROG called by ACCTUP
6	`//                COND=((9,LT),EVEN)`	9 is less than any return code; otherwise, execute the step even if a previous step was abnormally terminated
7	`//                COND=((8,LE,PROD1),ONLY)`	8 is less than or equal to the return code from PROD1; otherwise, execute the program only if a previous step was abnormally terminated
8	`//                COND=EVEN`	Execute this step regardless of the outcome of other steps
9	`//                COND=ONLY`	Execute this step only if a previous step was abnormally terminated

Figure 3-17 Examples of the COND parameter of the EXEC statement

EDSTEP issues a return code of 0004 or less. Example 3 causes the step to be bypassed if the return code generated by a step in a cataloged procedure (RPGEN) called by a previous job step (UPSTEP) is greater than 0020. (Cataloged procedures are covered in chapter 5.)

Up to eight conditions may be coded in a COND parameter. Example 4 shows two conditions that will cause the step to be bypassed: if 16 is less than the return code issued by the step named INSTEP, or if 8 is greater than or equal to the return code issued by the step named PROJ1. The conditions may be mixed as in example 5. It shows a step that is to be bypassed if *any* previous job step issued a return code of 0016 or greater, or if the procedure step named UPPROG that was executed by a job step named ACCTUP issued a return code of 0006.

Example 6 shows the use of the EVEN option. In this case, the step is bypassed if 9 is less than any return code; otherwise, it is to be executed. *Even* if one of the other steps abnormally terminates, as long as no return code greater than 9 is issued, the step will be executed. Example 7 is similar in that it is to be executed *only* if a previous job step abnormally terminates. However, if 8 is less than or equal to the return code issued by the step named PROD1, even though a previous job step abnormally terminates, the step will be bypassed. In other words, when EVEN or ONLY is coded with other conditions, those other conditions have priority.

Example 8 shows the COND parameter that will cause the step to be executed no matter what happens to previous steps. It will execute if all job steps run normally; and because EVEN is coded, it will run if one or more preceding steps are abnormally terminated. In contrast, example 9 shows a step that will *only* be executed if one of the preceding job steps fails.

EVEN and ONLY are mutually exclusive, so they must not be coded in the same COND parameter. They are counted when limiting the number of conditions to eight. In other words, you can code seven conditions plus an EVEN or ONLY, or you can code eight conditions without an EVEN or ONLY.

The TIME parameter

The TIME parameter on the EXEC statement is identical to the TIME parameter on the JOB statement. However, it causes the installation standard time limit to be increased or decreased at the job-step level rather than the job level. The format is:

```
TIME=(minutes,seconds)
```

If you code the TIME parameter on both the JOB statement and the EXEC statement, the time limit specified on the JOB statement takes precedence. In other words, the sum of the time limits for the steps cannot exceed the time limit for the job.

THE DD STATEMENT

The DD statement is the most flexible of all the JCL statements. It allows you to define a file in any format that can be stored within the System/360-370. To accomplish this, there are more than 20 parameters that may be coded for the DD statement. Some of these parameters have many subparameters, and others have more than one format. Not all of these will be covered in this book. Instead, in this chapter, I'll show you a "professional subset" of the language by explaining the parameters shown in the statement skeleton in figure 3-18. This material will be all that you'll need to solve normal data processing problems. Then, in chapter 9, I'll show you a number of additional DD statement operands you can use if you want more control over the storage and handling of certain files.

```
Format 1:
//ddname    DD    DUMMY,
                  DSN=filename,
                     =NULLFILE,
                  DISP=(status,normal-disposition,abnormal-disposition),
                  UNIT=(device,unit-count),
                  VOL=SER/REF=serial-number/ddname/dsname,
                  SPACE=(unit-of-measure,
                         (primary,secondary,directory/index),
                         RLSE,
                         CONTIG,
                         ROUND),
                  LABEL=(sequence,format,password,IN/OUT,expiration),
                  DCB=(LRECL=logical-record-length,
                       BLKSIZE=blocksize,
                       RECFM=record-format,
                       OPTCD=option-codes)
Format 2:
//ddname    DD    *       or    //ddname    DD    DATA
Format 3:
//ddname    DD    SYSOUT=(sysout-class,program-name,form-id),
                  OUTLIM=output-limit
```

Figure 3-18 Expanded DD statement skeleton

The DUMMY parameter and DSN = NULLFILE option

You can cause OS to simulate the presence of a file, whether or not that file is actually available to the system. To do this, you code DUMMY or DSN = NULLFILE on the DD statement. As a result, you can test portions of a program that read or write the file without actually affecting the file. When a program reads a file associated with DUMMY or DSN = NULLFILE, OS will pass an end-of-file indicator to your program. When a program writes to a file associated with one of these options, no data is transferred.

Additionally, you can code other parameters on the DD statement along with DUMMY or DSN = NULLFILE, and they will be edited for JCL syntax. To illustrate, suppose you have written a program that requires several input and output files and you are ready to test it module by module. You can code DUMMY or DSN = NULLFILE on the DD statements associated with the input and output modules so they will be tested without affecting your real data files. If your program specifies zero records per block, you must code the DCB parameter with the BLKSIZE parameter. When you are ready to use real data for your testing, simply remove the DUMMY or DSN = NULLFILE parameter and execute the job, reading and writing the real file.

Figure 3-19 shows examples of the DD DUMMY parameter and the DSN = NULLFILE option. Example 1 illustrates the simplest form of the DUMMY parameter. In this case, DCB information was provided by the program and no syntax checking was required. Example 2 shows a DUMMY parameter with the DCB information provided (the program may have specified zero block size). Example 3 shows a DUMMY parameter and other parameters coded for syntax-checking. Example 4 shows the use of the DSN = NULLFILE option.

The UNIT parameter

As you learned in chapter 2, the UNIT parameter is used to tell OS what kind of device to make available for reading or writing a file. If the file requires more than one volume, you can request that more than one device be assigned to it by coding the unit-count subparameter, shown in the UNIT format in figure 3-20. There are two ways to code this value. First, you can code a number. This will cause OS to assign that number of units to the file (the number of volumes may be greater than the number of units you assign). For example, this UNIT parameter:

```
UNIT=(SYSDA,3)
```

```
Example 1
    //PAYIN    DD   DUMMY

Example 2
    //PROJDATA DD   DUMMY,
    //              DCB=BLKSIZE=190

Example 3
    //OVERREC  DD   DUMMY,
    //              DSN=OVERHIST,
    //              DISP=(NEW,CATLG,KEEP),
    //              UNIT=SYSDA,
    //              VOL=SER=D00102,
    //              SPACE=(95,(6,3),RLSE),
    //              DCB=(LRECL=95,BLKSIZE=95,RECFM=F)

Example 4
    //ALTFILE  DD   DSN=NULLFILE,
    //              DISP=OLD,
    //              DCB=BLKSIZE=4000
```

Figure 3-19 Examples of the DUMMY parameter and NULLFILE option to simulate the presence of a file

```
         ┌unit-address┐  ┌,unit-count┐
UNIT=( ──┤device-type ├──┤           ├── )
         └group-name  ┘  └,P         ┘
```

unit-address	The channel, control unit, and unit number of a particular device. This method of assigning devices is not covered in this book.
device-type	The name of a type of device such as 2400, 3330, 1403.
group-name	A name assigned to a group of device types logically relating them. For example, SYSDA (system direct access) for disk and drum devices.
unit-count	The number of devices to be assigned to this data set.
P	Parallel mounting: use one device for each volume serial number coded in the VOLUME parameter.

Figure 3-20 Format of the UNIT parameter

would cause three disk devices to be assigned to the file. Second, you can code a P for *parallel mounting*. This will cause OS to assign one device for every volume serial number coded on the VOLUME parameter. In other words, in a UNIT parameter like this:

```
UNIT=(SYSDA,P)
```

the number of disk devices assigned to the file would depend on what was coded in the VOLUME parameter. (You'll learn how to code multiple volumes in the VOLUME parameter in just a moment.)

If you omit the unit-count subparameter and code more than one volume serial number in the VOLUME parameter, all of the volumes will be processed sequentially on the one device. The operator will be required to mount and demount the volumes when your program requests them.

The VOLUME parameter

In chapter 2, you learned how to code a volume serial number in the VOLUME parameter. Using the expanded format shown in figure 3-21, you can code more than one number or you can refer back to a previous VOLUME parameter. Figure 3-22 shows examples of both types of VOLUME parameters. Since the UNIT and VOLUME operands always work together, I've included UNIT values along with the VOLUME values in the examples.

Examples 1 through 4 show how the VOLUME operand should be coded for a single file that resides on more than one volume. As you

$$\left\{\begin{matrix} \text{VOLUME} \\ \text{VOL} \end{matrix}\right\} = \left\{\begin{matrix} \text{SER}=(\text{ser1},\text{ser2}...) \\ \text{REF}=\text{DSNAME} \\ \quad =*.\text{reference} \end{matrix}\right\}$$

SER = ser1,ser2   Tells OS the serial numbers of the volumes containing the data set for input, or the serial numbers of the volumes to put the output data set on.

REF = dsname or reference   Tells OS to copy volume information from the cataloged data set referenced by dsname or from the DD statement referenced by *.reference. Reference may be: *.ddname, indicating a DD statement within the same job step; *.stepname.ddname, indicating a DD statement in a previous job step; or *.stepname.procstepname.ddname, indicating a DD statement in a procedure called by a previous job step.

Figure 3-21   Format of the VOLUME parameter

can see, there are three volume serial numbers coded. In each case, the data set starts on volume 0123, continues on volume 9074, and ends on volume 0972.

In example 1, the UNIT parameter specifies that three disk devices be used for the file. Since there are three volumes given in the VOLUME parameter, this means that all three volumes will be mounted at the same time. Example 2 shows another way to produce the same result. Here, the P (for parallel mounting) causes one device to be allocated for every serial number listed in the VOLUME parameter. As a result, examples 1 and 2 are identical in effect.

On the other hand, example 3 shows multiple devices, but there are more volumes than devices. The first two volumes are mounted when the job step begins. Then, when the first volume has been processed, the operator will demount it and mount the third volume on that device while the program is processing the second volume.

Similarly, example 4 shows how multiple volumes are allocated to one device. In this case, when the portion of the file residing on one volume is completely read in, the operator will demount it and mount the next volume of the file.

The REF subparameter is used to refer to a previously defined volume. In topic 1 of this chapter, you saw how it could be used to refer to a ddname in the current job step, a previous job step, or a cataloged procedure called by a previous job step. In addition, you can refer directly to the volume information of a cataloged data set by coding VOL = REF = dsname (data set name). Examples 5 and 6 in figure 3-22 illustrate both these options. Example 5 shows a reference to a previous DD statement VOLUME parameter in the current job

```
Example 1
        //              UNIT=(2400,3),
        //              VOL=SER=(0123,9074,0972)
Example 2
        //              UNIT=(2400,P),
        //              VOL=SER=(0123,9074,0972)
Example 3
        //              UNIT=(2400,2),
        //              VOL=SER=(0123,9074,0972)
Example 4
        //              UNIT=2400,
        //              VOL=SER=(0123,9074,0972)
Example 5
        //              UNIT=DISKA,
        //              VOL=REF=*.OUT1
Example 6
        //              UNIT=DISKA,
        //              VOL=REF=PAYDATA
```

Figure 3-22 Examples of the UNIT and VOLUME parameters

step; example 6 shows a reference to a cataloged data set named PAYDATA.

The SPACE parameter

Figure 3-23 gives you a more complete format of the SPACE parameter than the one we used in chapter 2. I've already discussed the unit of measure, primary and secondary allocation, and the RLSE option. Now, I'll explain (1) the directory/index allocation, (2) the CONTIG option for formatting the allocated area, and (3) a method of allocating entire cylinders when the unit of measure is blocks of data.

The *directory* or *index allocation* subparameter tells OS how much space is to be allocated to a directory or index. These terms will be defined in chapters 4 and 5; for now, I just want you to know that if a file is partitioned, it must have a directory, and if it is indexed sequential, it must have an index.

If the file is partitioned, the number you code after the secondary allocation subparameter reserves the number of 256-byte records to be contained in the directory. In chapter 5, I'll discuss partitioned data sets and cover the purpose and characteristics of the directory.

$$\text{SPACE}=(\begin{Bmatrix}\text{TRK}\\\text{CYL}\\\text{block-length}\end{Bmatrix},(\text{primary},\text{secondary})\begin{Bmatrix},\text{directory}\\,\text{index}\end{Bmatrix}),\text{RLSE},\text{CONTIG},\text{ROUND})$$

TRK	Allocate space in tracks
CYL	Allocate space in cylinders
block-length	Allocate space in blocks of data
primary	Number of tracks, cylinders, or blocks to allocate to the file as a primary allocation
secondary	Number of tracks, cylinders, or blocks to allocate to the file as a secondary allocation; up to 16 extents will be added to the amount specified in primary
directory	Number of 256-character records to be contained in the partitioned data set directory
index	Number of cylinders to be allocated for the index of an indexed sequential file
RLSE	Tells OS to release unused space back to the system after the file has been closed
CONTIG	Allocate space in contiguous area
ROUND	Allocation in number of blocks should be rounded to whole cylinders

Figure 3-23 Format of the SPACE parameter

If the file is indexed sequential, the number you code indicates the number of cylinders to be allocated to the index. Secondary allocation is not allowed for indexed sequential files, so you code the primary allocation followed by two commas, then the index allocation. There is also another way to allocate space for the index. Both methods will be discussed in chapter 4 on indexed sequential file handling.

The CONTIG subparameter has to do with the format of the space allocated for the file. It says you want the space to be allocated in a contiguous (continuous) block. For a three-cylinder file, for instance, this means that instead of using one available cylinder in one area of the disk, another cylinder in another area, and the third cylinder in still another area, an area of three adjacent cylinders is to be assigned. The advantage of having a file in this format is that the read/write access mechanism doesn't have to move as far to access records in the file, so I/O speeds are faster. If the system can't find enough contiguous space for the file, the job is terminated.

The third feature of the SPACE parameter is a method of allocating whole cylinders to the file even though the allocation is requested in blocks. Usually, this method is used to allow for file expansion within the same cylinders. Here again, the benefit is efficiency—if the data is wholly contained on a definite group of cylinders, the movement of the access mechanism is reduced, resulting in a faster I/O rate. To allocate space in this manner, you code the ROUND option in the SPACE parameter.

Figure 3-24 provides examples of the SPACE parameter with the extended features. Example 1 shows the file allocation in tracks: five in the primary value and two in the secondary value. It also specifies that one 256-byte record is to be contained in the directory of this partitioned data set. (I know this third allocation value is for a directory and not an index because there is a secondary space allocation—a feature not allowed for indexed sequential files.) The primary area is to be one contiguous block of space on the direct-access volume.

Example 2 shows the SPACE parameter of a file that can use 20 cylinders of primary space. This may be either a partitioned data set or an indexed sequential data set. The directory contains two 256-byte directory records or the index is allocated two cylinders. The RLSE option causes unused space to be released when the file is closed.

Example 3 shows the allocation in blocks of data with the ROUND option coded. This option allows the data to start at the beginning of a cylinder and end at the end of a cylinder.

The LABEL parameter

There are several conditions that require the use of the LABEL parameter: (1) when the file has non-standard labels; (2) when the file is not the first file on a tape volume; (3) when you want the file to be password protected; and (4) when you want to set a retention period

```
Example 1
    //              SPACE=(TRK,(5,2,1),,CONTIG)
Example 2
    //              SPACE=(CYL,(20,,2),RLSE)
Example 3
    //              SPACE=(960,5,,,ROUND)
```

Figure 3-24   Examples of the SPACE parameter

for the file. Normally, the LABEL parameter is associated with magnetic tape since the data set labels for direct-access volumes are always standard and are automatically generated and verified. However, if you want to request a retention period or password protection for a direct-access file, you can code the LABEL parameter for it.

Figure 3-25 shows the format of the LABEL parameter and the meaning of each of its subparameters. All of the subparameters except the last one (EXPDT or RETPD) are positional and must be coded in the sequence shown in the format. Any of the subparameters may be omitted: if the sequence number isn't coded, the file is assumed to be the first one on the volume; if the label-type subparameter isn't coded, the file has standard labels; if the password subparameter isn't coded, the file is *not* password protected; if the IN/OUT values are omitted, the file can be used for either input or

```
LABEL=(data-set-sequence-number {,SL / ,SUL / ,AL / ,AUL / ,NSL / ,NL / ,BLP / ,LTM} {,PASSWORD / ,NOPWREAD} {,IN / ,OUT} {,EXPDT=yyddd / ,RETPD=days})
```

data-set-sequence-number	Relative position of the file on a tape volume
SL	Standard labels
SUL	Standard IBM and user labels
AL	ANS labels
AUL	ANS and user labels
NSL	Non-standard labels
NL	No labels
BLP	Bypass label processing
LTM	Bypass leading tapemark for DOS tape
PASSWORD	Password required to read, write, or delete
NOPWREAD	Password required to write or delete
IN	Input only
OUT	Output only
EXPDT = yyddd	Expiration date is two-position year and three-position Julian day
RETPD = days	Retention period is three-position number of days

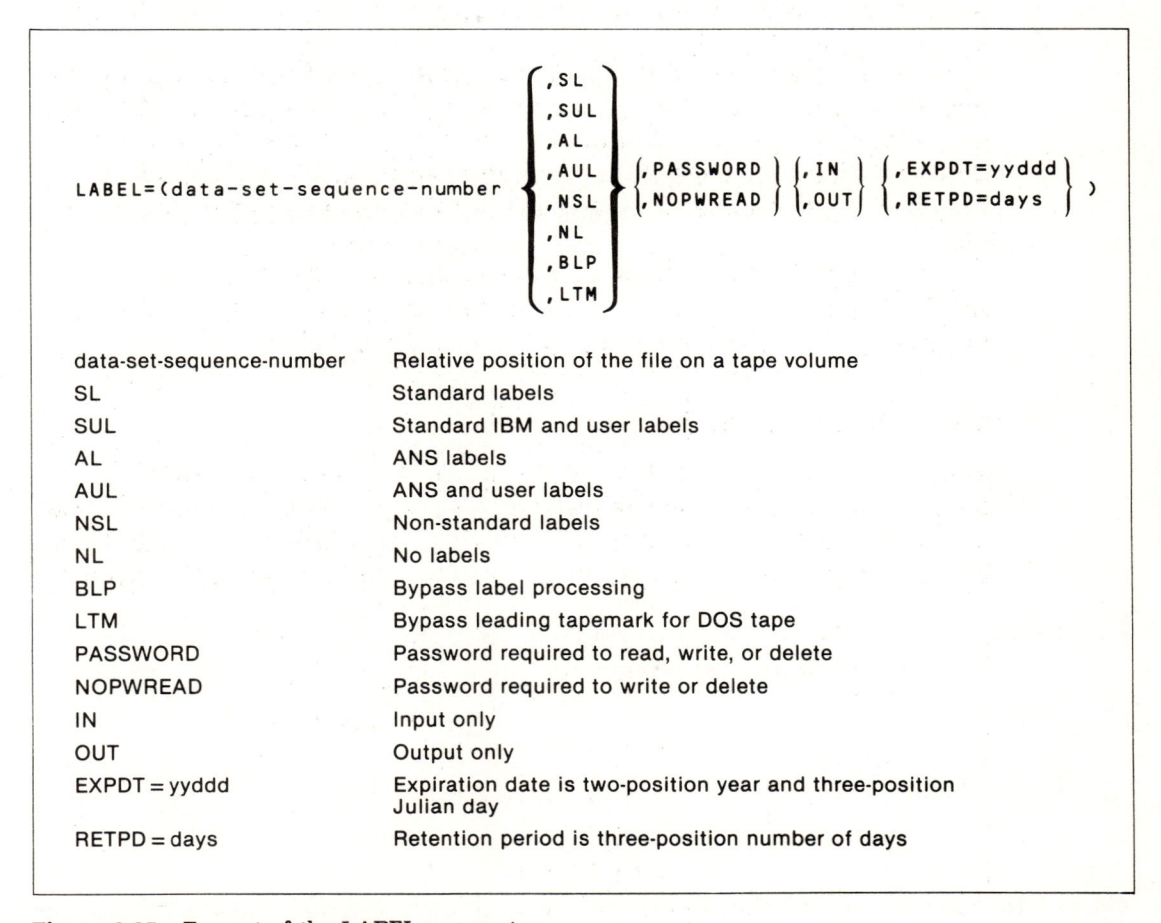

Figure 3-25 Format of the LABEL parameter

output; and if the date subparameter is omitted, the file is kept for the installation's standard retention period.

Figure 3-26 shows examples of the LABEL parameter. Example 1 illustrates a LABEL parameter for a file that is the second file on the volume. It contains ANS labels, it is password protected, it is to be used for input only, and it is to be kept until December 31, 1981. *Password protection* means that when the file is opened by the program, the operator has to supply the proper password or the file will not be made available to the program.

Example 2 shows the LABEL parameter for a file that is the first on the volume. It contains standard IBM labels, it is password protected for writing, it is to be used for output only in this job step, and it is to be kept for 180 days.

Example 3 shows a LABEL parameter for a file that is the first on the volume. It contains standard labels but no password protection, it may be used for input or output in this job step, and it is to be kept for the standard installation retention period.

Example 4 shows a LABEL parameter for a file that is also the first on the volume. It contains standard labels but no password protection, it may be used for input or output in this job step, and it has an expiration date of April 29, 1981.

Example 5 shows the LABEL parameter for a file that is the first file on the volume. It has standard labels and password protection for both reading and writing. It may be used for input or output in this job step, and it is to be kept for the standard retention period. This

```
Example 1
    //              LABEL=(2,AL,PASSWORD,IN,EXPDT=81365)
Example 2
    //              LABEL=(,,NOPWREAD,OUT,RETPD=180)
Example 3
    //              LABEL=1
Example 4
    //              LABEL=EXPDT=81120
Example 5
    //              LABEL=(,,PASSWORD)
Example 6
    //              LABEL=(,NL)
```

Figure 3-26 Examples of the LABEL parameter

example illustrates the form to use when applying password protection to direct-access files.

Example 6 shows a LABEL parameter for a file with no labels. In this case, OS will position the tape at the beginning of the data without checking for labels.

The DCB parameter

We discussed the three basic subparameters of the DCB (LRECL, BLKSIZE, and RECFM) in chapter 2. There are 35 other DCB subparameters; I've omitted some of those entirely from this book (the ones I don't think you'll ever need to use), while I've introduced others in subsequent chapters as they are needed for certain types of jobs. For now, then, the only other DCB parameter you need to be familiar with is OPTCD.

OPTCD can be used to tell OS to perform certain processing options or to give additional information about a file. Each option in the OPTCD subparameter is represented by a single alphabetic character. The options can be coded in any sequence, with no spaces or commas separating them. Figure 3-27 is a list of OPTCD options with descriptions of their functions.

You should be aware that only certain options can be selected for each access method. Figure 3-28 is a list of valid options for specific access methods. The underlined options are the ones you're most likely to use. You'll get a better feel for the OPTCD operand when you use it for indexed and direct files in chapter 4.

The SYSOUT parameter

There are two additional subparameters of the SYSOUT parameter we didn't cover in chapter 2: program name and form identification. The complete format of SYSOUT is:

```
SYSOUT=(sysout-class,program-name,form-id)
```

Program-name is the name of the program that writes to the SYSOUT file. It is optional and is usually omitted. Form-id is a one- to four-character name of a special form to be mounted in the printer. When the file is printed by the spooling program, the operator will be instructed to mount the form in the printer. Here's an example:

```
//PAYCHECK DD   SYSOUT=(C,,PCHK)
```

The name PCHK causes OS to tell the operator to mount the special form with that name in the printer associated with SYSOUT class C before the output can be printed.

OPTCD = A		Actual device addresses are given in read and write instructions
	B	End of file marks on tape are to be disregarded
	C	If the file is BPAM, BSAM, or QSAM, chained scheduling is to be used. If the file is TCAM, a segment location indicator is used.
	E	Extended block search for a block or available space. LIMCT must also be coded. (LIMCT, another DCB parameter, is covered in chapter 4.)
	F	Feedback may be requested in read and write instructions
	H	For optical readers, this value requests a hopper empty exit; for DOS tape files, it causes OS to bypass checkpoint errors
	I	Use independent overflow areas for overflow records
	L	Delete all records with all binary ones in the first byte
	M	Create a master index when required. NTM must also be coded. (NTM, another DCB parameter, is covered in chapter 4.)
	O	Online correction for optical readers
	Q	Translate ASCII input to EBCDIC or EBCDIC output to ASCII. (Alternatively, you can code AL or AUL in the LABEL parameter to accomplish the same thing.)
	R	If the file is BDAM, actual device addresses are given in read and write instructions. If the file is QISAM, it tells OS to keep reorganization data.
	T	A user totalling facility is to be used
	U	Allow error analysis of data checks on 1403 printer with the universal character set feature. If the file is ISAM, full track indexing is to be used. If the file is TCAM, it specifies that a word area is to be treated as a message.
	W	If the file is not a TCAM file, perform a validity check on a direct-access device for every write instruction executed. If the file is TCAM, the name of each message is to be placed in the work area.
	Y	Use cylinder overflow for overflow records
	Z	If the file is on tape, use a short version of the error processing procedure. If the file is ISAM, use search direct.

Figure 3-27 Complete list of OPTCD values

The OUTLIM parameter

The OUTLIM parameter allows you to set a limit on the number of print or punch records written using the SYSOUT parameter. For example, if you want no more than 2000 lines of print for a report, you code:

```
//XRPT       DD  SYSOUT=A,
//               OUTLIM=2000
```

```
BDAM  (Basic Direct-Access Method):
A  R  E  F  W

BSAM  (Basic Sequential Access Method):
B  C  H  Q  T  U  W  Z

BISAM  (Basic Indexed Sequential Access Method):
L

QSAM  (Queued Sequential Access Method):
B  C  O  Q  T  U  Z

QISAM  (Queued Indexed Sequential Access Method):
I  L  M  R  U  W  Y

Note: Underlined values indicate common usage.
```

Figure 3-28 OPTCD values you can code in conjunction with the major access methods

If the report is more than 2000 lines long, the job will end, although you'll receive the 2000 lines of printed output. By using the OUTLIM parameter, you can increase or decrease the installation standard limit for printed or punched output.

DISCUSSION

You've now been exposed to a "professional subset" of OS job-control language. If you feel somewhat confused about the purpose or application of some of the information presented so far, take heart—the rest of the book is downhill. I intentionally skimmed over some of the material in this chapter since to present a parameter completely requires not only the definitions and formats, but also the situations that require its use. As a result, as we progress through the remaining chapters, you'll see how each parameter of JCL helps to establish a complete set of characteristics about a job, job step, or file.

One thing you should be aware of at this point is that some of the parameters and subparameters presented thus far are used under the direction of installation standards. So before attempting to experiment, be sure to check the standards regulating your OS shop so you don't violate them.

Chapter 3

Terminology

return code

parallel mounting

directory allocation

index allocation

password protection

Objective

Given reference material and job specifications, code any of the parameters presented in this topic.

Problems

1. Code a DCB parameter for a file that consists of fixed-length records, each 120 characters long, blocked 10 records per block. The parameter should tell OS to perform a validity check on each write instruction for the file.
2. Code the JCL to execute the job shown in figure 3-29.

Solutions

1. `DCB=(LRECL=120,BLKSIZE=1200,RECFM=FB,OPTCD=W)`
2. Figure 3-30 is an acceptable solution. Be aware, though, that there are several different ways to code some of the parameters. For example, the COND parameter in the second EXEC statement could include the previous step name, so it would be COND=(8,LE,BUILD); the SYSOUT parameter in the last DD statement doesn't have to specify the program name, so it could be SYSOUT=(C,,PER1); and so on.

System flowchart

```
   Payroll
   master
    file
  (PAYFILE)
      |
      v
   Build
  personnel
    file
  (PERS000)
      |
      v
  Personnel
    file
  (PERSFILE)
      |
      v
   Process
  personnel
    file
  (PERS001)
      |
      v
  Personnel
   report
```

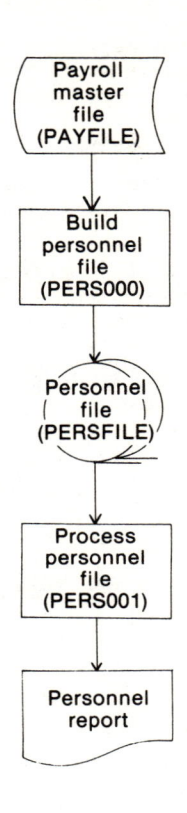

Specifications

Programs:

PERS000 requires 100K of main storage. PERS001 requires 120K of main storage. Both programs reside on a library named YOU.PROGLIB. If PERS000 issues a return code greater than 8, PERS001 is to be bypassed.

Files:

PAYFILE is cataloged on a direct-access volume. PERSFILE is to be placed on two 2400 series magnetic tape volumes. It has standard labels and is to be kept for 180 days if the step runs normally, or deleted if the step fails. The DCB for PERSFILE is: LRECL = 100, BLKSIZE = 4800, RECFM = FB.

Report:

The report is to be printed with SYSOUT class C on a special form named PER1. Its block size is 133 bytes.

Figure 3-29 System flowchart and specifications for the personnel file application

```
//BLDJOB    JOB   HE66YFNH,
//                'W. CLARY'
//BUILD     EXEC  PGM=PERS000,
//                REGION=100K
//STEPLIB   DD    DSN=YOU.PROGLIB,
//                DISP=SHR
//PAYMAST   DD    DSN=PAYFILE,
//                DISP=OLD
//PERSO     DD    DSN=PERSFILE,
//                DISP=(NEW,KEEP,DELETE),
//                UNIT=(2400,2),
//                VOL=(,,,2),
//                LABEL=(,SL,,,RETPD=180),
//                DCB=(LRECL=100,BLKSIZE=4800,RECFM=FB)
//PROCESS   EXEC  PGM=PERS001,
//                COND=(8,LE),
//                REGION=120K
//STEPLIB   DD    DSN=YOU.PROGLIB,
//                DISP=SHR
//PERSI     DD    DSN=*.PERSO,
//                DISP=OLD
//RPT1      DD    SYSOUT=(C,PERS001,PER1),
//                DCB=BLKSIZE=133
//
```

Figure 3-30 JCL for the personnel application

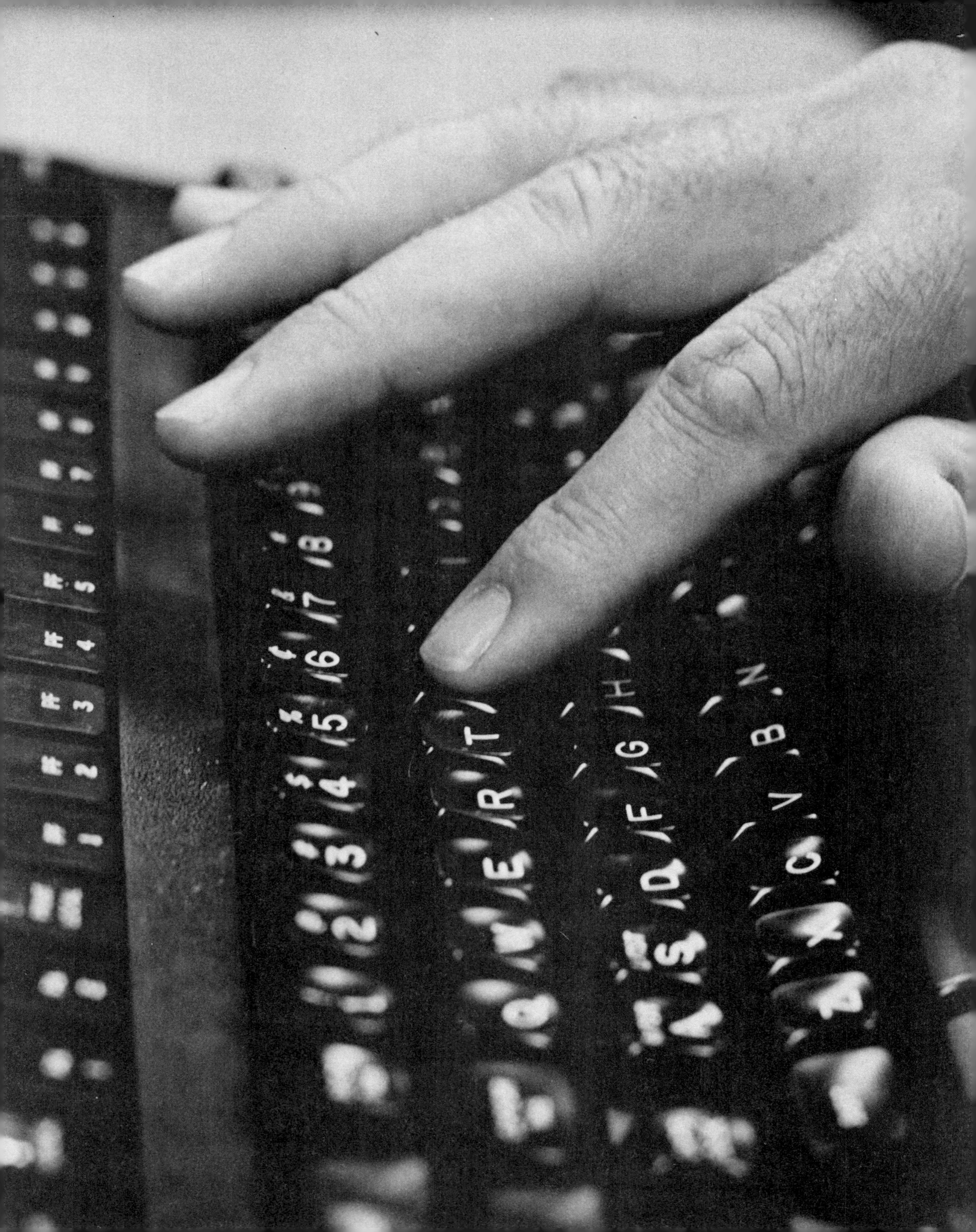

PART 3

OS JCL for Specific Applications

This part presents the OS JCL you will need to run certain types of jobs or to use certain types of files. So after you have mastered the material in part 2, you can go on to any chapter in this part. You don't have to read these chapters in any particular sequence, and you can skip any chapters that you aren't interested in. If, for example, you want to know how to compile a COBOL program, you can go directly to topic 1 of chapter 8 on the language translators. I would suggest, though, that you read over chapter 5 before too long, since libraries and procedures are referred to in several other chapters. And unless you're very interested in the advanced file handling capabilities of the DD statement or you're working with software packages that have unusual or complex DD statement parameters, I'd suggest you skip chapter 9 entirely.

structure (DO-WHILE)

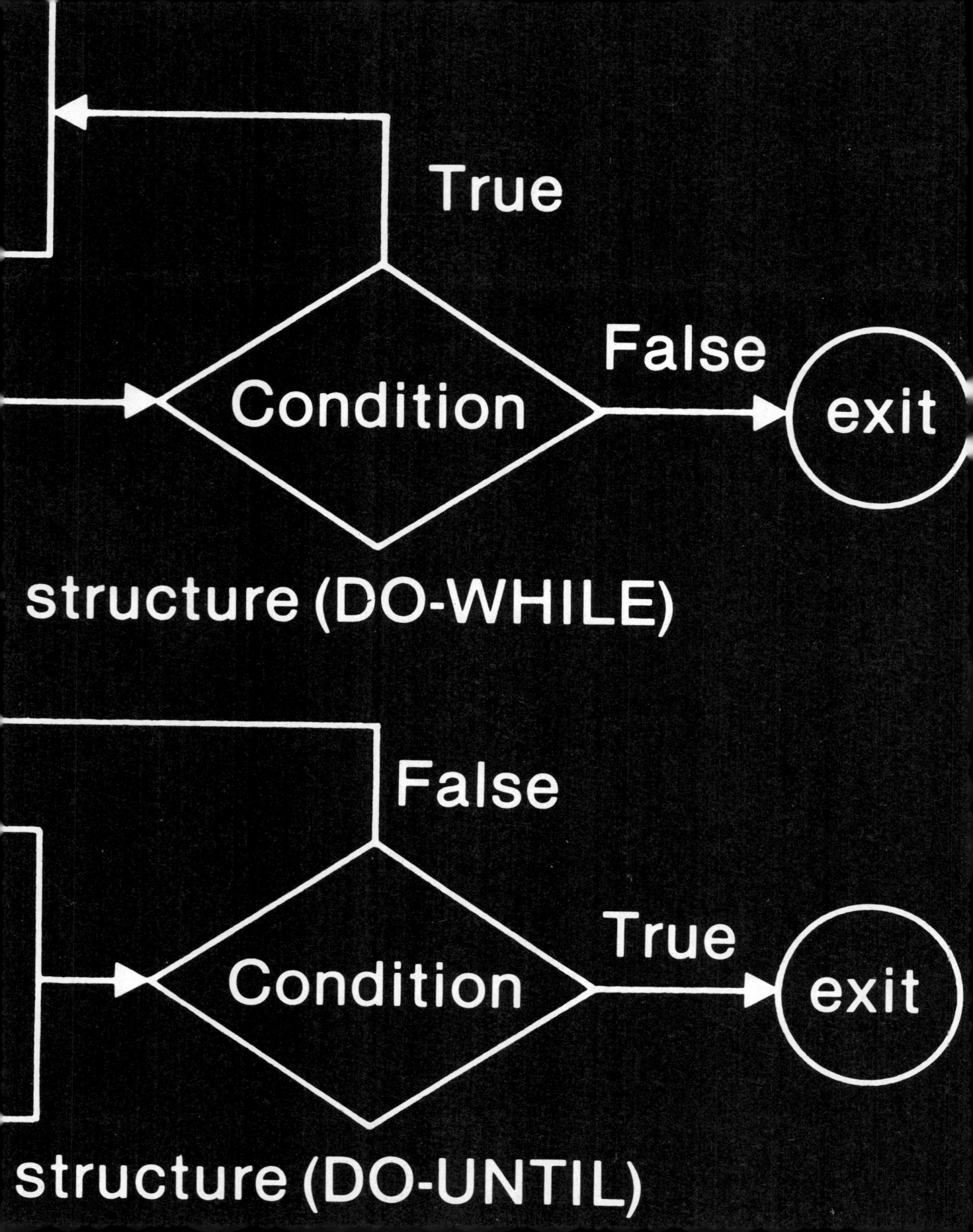

structure (DO-UNTIL)

4

Advanced File Handling

When you design a data processing system, one of the most important decisions you'll make will be to determine the type of file organization to use for direct-access files. The decisions you reach will usually be derived from answers to questions like these:

How many records will the file contain?

How often will the file be updated?

What will be the average number of records updated in one job?

Can this file be processed sequentially?

Are random extracts likely?

Although I can't tell you the organization you should use because I don't know the requirements of your system, I'll show you how to code the JCL for indexed sequential, direct, and relative file handling, and I'll give you examples of systems that use these file organizations. Then, you can relate them to your own data processing requirements. Topic 1 covers indexed sequential file handling, and topic 2 covers direct and relative file handling.

TOPIC 1 Indexed Sequential Files

All of the examples up to this point have shown JCL as it applies to physical sequential files. This method of creating and retrieving records in a file has its advantages, such as efficient usage of direct-access storage space, but it also has disadvantages in that it has many of the limitations of a tape file. For example, to update a physical sequential file, all of the records of the file must be read, rather than just those affected by transactions; and the entire file must be rewritten to insert a record into the file.

The *Indexed Sequential Access Method (ISAM)* is designed to allow both sequential and *random processing*. (Random processing means that records are not processed in any particular sequence.) Using ISAM, the records in the file are stored on the direct-access device so they can be read sequentially, but indexes are kept so any record in the file can be read randomly by looking up its location in the indexes. If records are added to the file, an additional disk area called an overflow area is used; this makes it unnecessary to rewrite the entire file as you would have to do with a physical sequential file. When a record is stored in the overflow area, the indexes are changed accordingly so all the records can still be processed in sequence according to their *key fields*. For example, in an ISAM customer file, the key would probably be the customer number. So the records could be processed sequentially in customer-number order as well as randomly by customer-number lookup.

INDEXES

The indexes for an ISAM file are kept in three levels: a master index, a cylinder index, and track indexes. The master index is optional and is normally used only for very large files. Let me skip over it for now and I'll come back to it.

The *cylinder index* is used to determine what cylinder a record is located in. To illustrate, suppose a file of customer records is stored in cylinders 11-15 of a disk pack and the cylinder index is kept on the first track of cylinder 10. Since there are five cylinders used in the file, there will be five records in the cylinder index. Each record will contain (1) a record key value and (2) the cylinder that contains the records with that key and records with lower keys. For example, a cylinder index for the customer file might contain the following data:

Key	Cylinder
1949	11
3241	12
5972	13
7566	14
9840	15

To find the record for customer 6500, OS will search the cylinder index until a higher or equal key is found. By searching this cylinder index, it will find that the record with key 6500 is located in cylinder 14.

Here's where the optional *master index* comes in. When a file is large and occupies many cylinders, the cylinder index may get to the point where it takes up more than one or two tracks. Since it is searched sequentially, the amount of time required to find a higher or equal key might be excessive. In such cases, you can elect to use a master index. By searching the master index first, OS can go directly to the proper track of the cylinder index instead of searching it from the beginning. The need for a master index depends on the amount of disk space a file will occupy. This is influenced by key length, record length, the number of records in the file, and the blocking factor.

In actual practice, a master index is seldom used. If one is used, it is likely to be found in the same cylinder as the cylinder index. For instance, track zero of cylinder 10 might contain the master index, and tracks one through three might contain the cylinder index.

Once the cylinder index has directed OS to the proper cylinder for record 6500 (in this case, cylinder 14), OS must find the proper track. The same search technique is used to search the *track index* of cylinder 14 for a higher or equal key. A track index is found on the first track of each cylinder of the file. These index records indicate the highest customer record contained on each track of the cylinder. For example, the track index for cylinder 14 might contain the following data:

Key	Track	Key	Track	Key	Track
6198	2	6609	8	7119	14
6258	3	6701	9	7200	15
6322	4	6813	10	7303	16
6398	5	6893	11	7471	17
6449	6	6979	12	7566	18
6570	7	7053	13		

By searching this index, OS can determine that record 6500 is on track seven of the cylinder. Once OS has determined the track number, it can find a record by searching for a key equal to the control number in the record—in this case, customer 6500. If you wonder why the track index in this example only shows 17 tracks (tracks 2-18), remember that the first track is used for the track index. As for the remaining two tracks, read on.

OVERFLOW AREAS

The 19th and 20th tracks of the cylinder comprise the *cylinder overflow area*. The number of tracks assigned to the overflow area is based on the number of records likely to be added to a cylinder. An indexed sequential file can also have a *general*, or *independent*, *overflow area*. This area, usually located at the end of a file, consists of one or more cylinders reserved for additions to the file. For instance, cylinder 16 might be the independent overflow area for the file just described.

To determine whether a file should have cylinder overflow areas, an independent overflow area, or both, the programmer or systems analyst must determine how additions are likely to be grouped. If no additions will ever be made to the file, both cylinder and independent overflow areas can be omitted. If the additions are likely to be spread evenly throughout the file, it is probably best to assign from one to three tracks per cylinder for overflow and allocate a small independent overflow area. On the other hand, if the additions will be bunched in small ranges of the record keys, it is more efficient to have no cylinder overflow area and have all the additions go into the independent overflow area.

An indexed sequential file, then, is made up of six areas on the disk: (1) the optional master index, (2) the cylinder index, (3) track indexes, (4) the prime data area, (5) cylinder overflow tracks, and (6) the independent overflow area. Figure 4-1 illustrates an indexed sequential file on a 2314 disk device with all six types of areas. (On a 3330 device, only 19 tracks would be used for the file; the 20th is reserved for system use.)

REORGANIZATION

Since extra searching is required for records in the overflow area, indexed sequential files should be *reorganized* periodically so all records are returned to the prime data area tracks. To do this, you can execute a utility program, IEBISAM, to copy the indexed sequential file and convert it to physical sequential organization and then

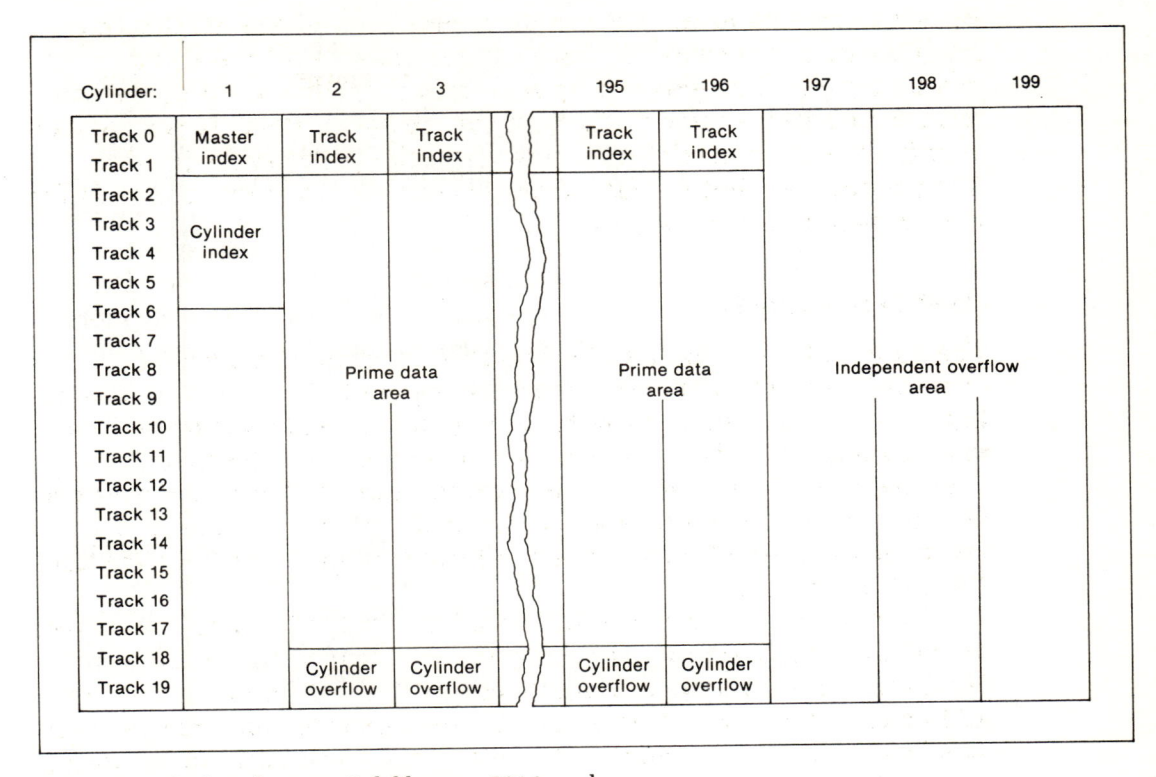

Figure 4-1 Indexed sequential file on a 2314 pack

reload the sequential file back as indexed sequential. I'll show you how to do that in chapter 7.

Alternatively, you can write your own program to copy the indexed sequential file out and read it back in. The result of this process is that as the records are written out sequentially, the overflow records are placed in their proper sequential position with other data records. Then, when the sequential file is loaded as an indexed sequential file, all the records will be in the prime data area, and the overflow areas will once again be empty until more records are added to the file.

CREATING ISAM FILES

To define an ISAM file, you may code from one to three DD statements: (1) one for the master and cylinder indexes identified by coding DSN = dsname(INDEX); (2) one for the prime area identified by coding DSN = dsname(PRIME); and (3) one for the independent overflow area identified by coding DSN = dsname(OVFLOW). The DD statements for the index and overflow areas are optional, but if they are coded, they must appear in the proper sequence—INDEX, PRIME, OVFLOW—as shown in figure 4-2. If they're omitted, the file will have an *embedded index* and an *embedded overflow area*. That means the cylinder index area and the independent overflow area will be contained in the disk space allocated to the prime data area.

To create an indexed sequential file, you must code DD statement parameters that reflect the requirements of your devices, space, and file characteristics. There are some special rules and considerations that govern the use of these parameters, so let's take a look at them. Then, we'll look at figure 4-2 in more detail, and I'll show you some other examples of ISAM-creation JCL.

The DSNAME parameter

As I just said, you can use from one to three DD statements to define the ISAM file. If you use only one, it must define the prime area and it can be coded with or without the area name (PRIME). In other words, you can use one DD statement to define an ISAM file named IFILE with the index and overflow areas embedded in the prime area by coding either DSN = IFILE(PRIME) or DSN = IFILE.

```
//CACCT     DD   DSN=CUSTACCT(INDEX),
//               DISP=(NEW,KEEP),
//               UNIT=3330,
//               VOL=SER=D00102,
//               SPACE=(CYL,3,,CONTIG),
//               DCB=(LRECL=100,RECFM=F,DSORG=IS,
//               KEYLEN=6,RKP=3,CYLOFL=3,OPTCD=YI)
//          DD   DSN=CUSTACCT(PRIME),
//               DISP=(NEW,KEEP),
//               UNIT=3330,
//               VOL=SER=D00103,
//               SPACE=(CYL,20,,CONTIG),
//               DCB=*.CACCT
//          DD   DSN=CUSTACCT(OVFLOW),
//               DISP=(NEW,KEEP),
//               UNIT=3330,
//               VOL=SER=D00103,
//               SPACE=(CYL,10,,CONTIG),
//               DCB=*.CACCT
```

Figure 4-2 ISAM file defined with three DD statements

Advanced File Handling

The DISP parameter

Whether you use one, two, or three DD statements to define the ISAM file, you can code the DISP parameter in one of two ways. You can code DISP=(NEW,KEEP) to tell OS to keep the file as a new area on disk; or you can code DISP=OLD to tell OS you are recreating the file in the same area as the old file. This will overlay the old file with the records of the new file.

If you want to catalog or pass an ISAM file, you must define the file with only one DD statement. However, if you define the file with more than one DD statement, you can catalog it by executing a utility program named IEHPROGM. To do this, the DD statements must all refer to the same device type. Since that function of IEHPROGM is not covered in detail in this book, my examples of cataloging ISAM files will use only one DD statement and DISP=(NEW,CATLG).

The VOLUME parameter

You must code the VOLUME parameter on the DD statement if (1) you want the file to reside on a specific volume or (2) the prime data area is to reside on multiple volumes. Be aware, though, that it's only the prime data area that can be on multiple volumes. The index and overflow area must each be defined on a single volume. As a result, if the index or overflow area is embedded in the prime area, the prime area *cannot* reside on multiple volumes. If the index and overflow areas are not embedded (they have their own DD statements), they may or may not reside on the same volume as the prime area.

The UNIT parameter

The UNIT parameter for an ISAM file must specify a direct-access device type. In addition, if the VOLUME parameter specifies more than one volume, the UNIT parameter must specify a corresponding number of devices. This is required since the file can be accessed randomly, and, as a result, the entire file must be available at the same time. To do this, you can either code the same number of devices on the UNIT parameter as there are volumes or you can code a P in the unit-count subparameter to indicate parallel mounting. For example, if you code the VOLUME parameter like this:

```
//              VOLUME=SER=(0123,0972,9074)
```

then you can code the UNIT parameter like this:

```
//              UNIT=(SYSDA,3)
```

or like this:

```
//                        UNIT=(SYSDA,P)
```

The SPACE parameter

When requesting space for an ISAM file, the unit of measure must be CYL for whole cylinders. The primary quantity tells OS how many cylinders to allocate. If the prime area requires more than one volume, the primary quantity tells OS to reserve that many cylinders on each volume.

As I mentioned in chapter 3, the index subparameter of the SPACE parameter tells OS how many cylinders of the prime area are to be allocated to the index. This subparameter is used when the index DD statement is omitted and you want to define the size of the embedded index.

You can code CONTIG in the SPACE parameter to cause OS to allocate the space in a contiguous block. In fact, this is usually done to speed up the I/O operations of random accessing. You cannot code the secondary allocation, RLSE, or ROUND subparameters.

The LABEL parameter

You can code the LABEL parameter to request password protection or to specify the retention period (or expiration date) for an ISAM file. See the description and examples in chapter 3.

The DCB parameter

If more than one DD statement is used to define an ISAM file, the DCB parameter must be identical in each one. As a result, it's a good idea to code a referback for this parameter in the second and third statements. Then there's no chance of a coding error that would cause your job to abend.

There are a number of DCB subparameters used for ISAM files that we haven't discussed yet. As a result, figure 4-3 gives an expanded format of the DCB parameter.

LRECL Remember that if the records in a file are variable length, blocked or unblocked, LRECL is the largest record size in the file. Since variable records must be identified by a four-byte control field before each record, the logical record length is equal to the longest record length plus four bytes.

BLKSIZE Again, a couple of reminders. First, the BLKSIZE subparameter must be a multiple of the record length. Second, for

Advanced File Handling   139

```
DCB=(LRECL=logical-record-length,
     BLKSIZE=block-size,
     RECFM=record-format,
     DSORG=data-set-organization,
     KEYLEN=key-length,
     RKP=relative-key-position,
     CYLOFL=cylinder-overflow-size,
     NTM=number-of-tracks-for-a-master-index,
     OPTCD=option-codes)
```

record-format	F = fixed; FB = fixed blocked; V = variable; VB = variable blocked
data-set-organization	PS = physical sequential; IS = ISAM
key-length	Number indicating the key length in bytes
relative-key-position	Number indicating the starting position of the record key relative to the beginning of the record
cylinder-overflow-size	Number of tracks on each cylinder of the prime data area to be used for overflow records from that cylinder
number-of-tracks-for-a-master-index	Number of tracks to be used with a master index; OPTCD must specify M
option-codes	The characters that can be used for ISAM files are I, L, M, R, U, W, and Y:

I	Use an independent overflow area for overflow records
L	Delete records having all binary ones in the first byte
M	Create a master index; NTM must also be used
R	Place reorganization criteria in the DCB
U	Use the full-track-index-write option
W	Do a validity check on all write operations
Y	Use cylinder overflow areas for overflow records

Figure 4-3 Expanded format of the DCB parameter

variable-length records, it must also include four bytes for the block-length prefix.

RECFM As you already know, RECFM tells OS the record format of the file. For ISAM files, the record format can be fixed, fixed blocked, variable, or variable blocked. The corresponding codes are F, FB, V, and VB.

DSORG Even if all the DCB information for the ISAM file (block size, record length, record format, etc.) is provided by the program, you must still code, as a minimum, the subparameter for data set organization (DSORG). The default value for DSORG is PS (physical sequential), so that's why we didn't need to code it for the files in chapters 2 and 3. The DSORG value that identifies an ISAM file is DSORG = IS.

KEYLEN KEYLEN indicates the length, in bytes, of the record key. In other words, if the key is a five-byte customer number, you will code KEYLEN = 5.

CYLOFL CYLOFL defines the number of tracks on each cylinder of the prime data area to be used to hold overflow records from other tracks on that cylinder. For example, if you code CYLOFL = 3, then three tracks of every cylinder allocated to the prime area will be reserved for overflow records. If you never add a record to the segment of the file contained in a particular cylinder, the last three tracks of that cylinder will always be empty. On the other hand, if you fill the cylinder overflow area and then add more records to that segment of the file, the additional overflow records will be placed in the independent overflow area (if you defined one with an OVFLOW DD statement). If you don't code an OVFLOW DD statement in this situation, the job will be abnormally terminated.

NTM NTM, when coded in conjunction with the OPTCD = M subparameter, tells OS to create and use a master index when the cylinder index becomes larger than a specified number of tracks. For example, if you code NTM = 5, when the cylinder index uses up five tracks, a master index will be created to index the cylinder index. Remember that the master index points to the cylinder index; the cylinder index points to the track index; and the track index points to the track containing the record.

OPTCD OPTCD, as you will recall from chapter 3, instructs OS to perform several somewhat unrelated functions. The codes that may be coded for ISAM files are I, L, M, R, U, W, and Y.

If you code OPTCD = I, OS will place overflow records in the independent overflow area defined with the third DD statement (the OVFLOW DD statement). If you don't code this value, OS will first try to place the record in the cylinder overflow area, and, if that is full, it will place the record in the independent overflow area. If you code the OPTCD = I, you must also code the OVFLOW DD statement.

OPTCD = L tells OS to delete records that have a *delete character* (a one-byte field containing all binary ones) in the first position of the record. When you want to delete a record, you write a program that places the delete character in that position of the record and rewrites the record onto the disk. But the record is not actually deleted until it is processed by a job that contains OPTCD = L.

OPTCD = M, when used in conjunction with NTM, tells OS to use a master index. If you code one, you must code both of these subparameters.

OPTCD = R tells OS to keep track of the status of cylinder overflow areas. This status information is stored with the file's data control block for use in reorganizing the file.

OPTCD = U causes OS to use the *full-track-index-write option*. Only fixed-length records are eligible for this option that causes the track index entries to be accumulated in core until enough entries are collected to fill one track. Then, the accumulated index entries are written out as one block. If you don't use this option, each index entry will be written out as the prime area record is written. When you're creating a file, using the full-track-index-write option can definitely improve the efficiency of the job.

OPTCD = W causes a write validity check to be performed for every output operation performed on the file. It is especially useful when an installation is experiencing trouble with one or more direct-access devices.

OPTCD = Y tells OS to use the cylinder overflow area to write overflow records. It is used in conjunction with the CYLOFL subparameter.

RKP RKP tells OS the relative starting position of the record key in each record. The first byte of a record is position 0. Coding RKP = 0 or omitting this subparameter can result in several conditions, depending on the record format:

1. If the records are fixed blocked, coding RKP = 0 or omitting the subparameter tells OS that the key begins in the first position of each record. So you can't use the first position as a delete code. And you can't code OPTCD = L for the file. This may be acceptable if you don't intend to delete any marked records or if you're willing to write your own routines to delete them.

2. If the records are fixed unblocked, OS doesn't care about the RKP value; it knows where to find the key. This is because fixed unblocked records are stored differently than fixed blocked

records. As a result, the first byte of the record can be used for a delete code.

3. If the records are variable-length, RKP must be coded and it must be greater than 3 to allow for the necessary four-byte control field. As a result, the delete code for variable-length records is in the fifth record position. So if you code RKP = 4 for a variable file, you can't use the delete code option, regardless of the file's blocking characteristics.

Using three DD statements for an ISAM file

Now let's look back at figure 4-2. It defines an ISAM file using all three DD statements. The first DD statement defines an area of three contiguous cylinders to be used for the cylinder index. It is to be placed on a disk pack named D00102. The DCB parameter tells OS that: the records are 100 bytes in length, fixed and unblocked; the data set organization is indexed sequential; the record key is six bytes long, starting in the fourth position of the record; and both a cylinder overflow area of three tracks at the end of each cylinder and an independent overflow area will be used for overflow records. Since NTM and OPTCD = M are omitted, there is no master index for this file.

The second DD statement defines the prime data area. It is an area of 20 contiguous cylinders on a 3330 disk pack named D00103. (The index and overflow areas may be placed on the same volume as the prime area, on another volume of the same type, or on a volume of a completely different device type—just as long as all three reside on direct-access devices that are online at the same time.) Since the DCBs for all three file areas must be identical, I coded a referback for the DCB parameter to copy the DCB of the index DD statement.

The third DD statement defines an independent overflow area of ten contiguous cylinders on the 3330 disk pack named D00103. Again, the DCB parameter is copied from the first DD statement in the series.

Embedded overflow areas and indexes

As I said earlier, sometimes you only need two or even one DD statement to create an ISAM file. For example, if I know that a file will have rather slow, stable growth, I will omit the third DD statement defining an independent overflow area. In other words, I'll assume that the embedded overflow area in the prime data area will suffice. Figure 4-4 defines an ISAM file like this, with DD statements for only

Advanced File Handling

```
//RECFILE   DD   DSN=ACCTREC(INDEX),
//               DISP=(NEW,KEEP),
//               UNIT=SYSDA,
//               VOL=SER=USER01,
//               SPACE=(CYL,1,,CONTIG),
//               DCB=(LRECL=90,RECFM=F,DSORG=IS,KEYLEN=9,
//               CYLOFL=1,OPTCD=Y)
//          DD   DSN=ACCTREC(PRIME),
//               DISP=(NEW,KEEP),
//               VOL=REF=*.RECFILE,
//               SPACE=(CYL,5,,CONTIG),
//               DCB=*.RECFILE
```

Figure 4-4 ISAM file defined with INDEX and PRIME DD statements—overflow area is embedded in the prime area

the index and prime areas. In the DCB parameter, I specified an overflow area of one track should be reserved at the end of each prime data cylinder for file additions (CYLOFL = 1 and OPTCD = Y). Also, since I wanted the index and prime areas to reside on the same volume, I coded the VOL = REF referback on the prime area DD statement.

Similarly, if a file is small—say only five cylinders of prime data space—an embedded index may be satisfactory. So I can omit the index DD statement and define the file with only the prime and overflow DD statements, as shown in figure 4-5. Here, the index value is coded in the SPACE parameter of the prime DD statement, so an area of two cylinders will be allocated for the index. These two cylinders are allocated in addition to the 12 cylinders specified in the primary allocation.

A third alternative is to define the ISAM file with a prime DD statement alone, as in figure 4-6. In this case, the index and overflow areas are both embedded in the prime area. Notice that the index, CYLOFL, and OPTCD = Y subparameters are all coded.

The point is you must do some analysis of your file and its potential growth before you can decide how many DD statements are sufficient to define it. If a file will be extended erratically, with many records added in concentrated areas, you should code a DD statement for the independent overflow area, because an embedded overflow area may not be able to contain the growth records in those isolated areas. Likewise, you should code an index DD statement to contain the cylinder index if (1) it's possible that an embedded index will become filled or (2) the file is a large one.

```
//INDDATA  DD   DSN=INDUS1(PRIME),
//              DISP=(NEW,KEEP),
//              UNIT=SYSDA,
//              VOL=SER=USER25,
//              SPACE=(CYL,(12,,2),,CONTIG),
//              DCB=(LRECL=100,BLKSIZE=1000,RECFM=FB,DSORG=IS,
//              KEYLEN=4,RKP=2,OPTCD=I)
//         DD   DSN=INDUS1(OVFLOW),
//              DISP=(NEW,KEEP),
//              VOL=REF=*.INDDATA,
//              SPACE=(CYL,2,,CONTIG),
//              DCB=*.INDDATA
```

Figure 4-5 ISAM file defined with PRIME and OVFLOW DD statements—index area is embedded in the prime area

RETRIEVING ISAM FILES

To access an ISAM file that already exists, you may also specify from one to three DD statements. You can use only one DD statement to access the file (1) if the file was created with one DD statement, (2) if it was created with more than one DD statement but all three areas reside on the same volume, or (3) if it is cataloged.

The DD statement parameters you may code when retrieving an ISAM file are DSN, DISP, UNIT, VOLUME, and DCB. If the file is cataloged or passed from a previous job step, you only need to code DSN, DISP, and DCB. The DSN and DCB parameters can be coded as referbacks if the file is used in a previous job step.

Figure 4-7 shows examples of DD statements used to access ISAM files. Notice that the DCB parameter is coded for all of the examples because DSORG is required.

Example 1 shows the DD statement to retrieve a cataloged ISAM file. Besides the DCB parameter, only the DSN and DISP parameters are required.

Example 2 shows the DD statement to retrieve an ISAM file that was kept but not cataloged. It may have been created with one, two, or three DD statements, but all three areas of the file reside on the same volume. As a result, only one DD statement is required to retrieve it.

Example 3 illustrates the DD statements required to retrieve a file where the three areas of the file don't reside on the same volume. Since the area name (INDEX, PRIME, and OVFLOW) is not coded (it's not required for retrieving ISAM files), we can't tell by looking at the JCL whether it's the index area or the overflow area or both that

Advanced File Handling   **145**

```
//PRG2FILE DD   DSN=PRG2,
//              DISP=(NEW,CATLG),
//              UNIT=SYSDA,
//              VOL=SER=USER01,
//              SPACE=(CYL,(15,,2),,CONTIG),
//              DCB=(LRECL=45,BLKSIZE=1800,RECFM=FB,DSORG=IS,
//              KEYLEN=4,RKP=3,CYLOFL=3,OPTCD=Y)
```

Figure 4-6 ISAM file defined with only PRIME DD statement—index and overflow areas are embedded in the prime area

```
Example 1
    //ELFILE   DD   DSN=ELEMENTS,
    //              DISP=OLD,
    //              DCB=DSORG=IS
Example 2
    //INVFILE  DD   DSN=INVMAST,
    //              DISP=OLD,
    //              UNIT=3330,
    //              VOL=SER=D00103,
    //              DCB=DSORG=IS
Example 3
    //CUSTFILE DD   DSN=CUSTOMER,
    //              DISP=OLD,
    //              UNIT=2314,
    //              VOL=SER=USER01,
    //              DCB=DSORG=IS
    //         DD   DSN=CUSTOMER,
    //              DISP=OLD,
    //              UNIT=3330,
    //              VOL=SER=D00103,
    //              DCB=DSORG=IS
Example 4
    //PARTS    DD   DSN=PARTFILE,
    //              DISP=MOD,
    //              UNIT=SYSDA,
    //              VOL=SER=D00103,
    //              DCB=DSORG=IS
```

Figure 4-7 Retrieving ISAM files

reside on a different volume from the prime area. We would have to look at the JCL that created the file in order to tell which areas were actually separated.

Example 4 is the DD statement to extend an ISAM file sequentially. This method is sometimes used to load several different portions of the file at different times. The disposition status of MOD tells OS to position the file past the last record. Then, as the program writes records sequentially, they are placed in sequence on the file. When using this method, all of the keys to be added must be greater than the last record key on the existing file. The records are placed in the prime area just as though this job was a continuation of the original load program.

AN EXAMPLE OF ISAM FILE HANDLING

To illustrate one application of ISAM file handling, suppose order records are to be used to prepare invoices. In an application like this, data is required from customer master records and item master records. Although this could be done using sequential files for both master files, it is often done using an ISAM file for one or both master files.

Figure 4-8 shows a system flowchart for this application. Here, the customer file is sequential and the item file is indexed sequential. Invoices are created by reading the order records and customer records in customer-key sequence and the item records on a random basis by item-number key.

Figure 4-9 shows the JCL for two jobs related to figure 4-8. The first job reads a sequential item file and converts it to an indexed sequential file. (This would normally be done only once in the life of the application.) The second job, then, reflects the processing of the system chart in figure 4-8. Notice that there is one DD statement for

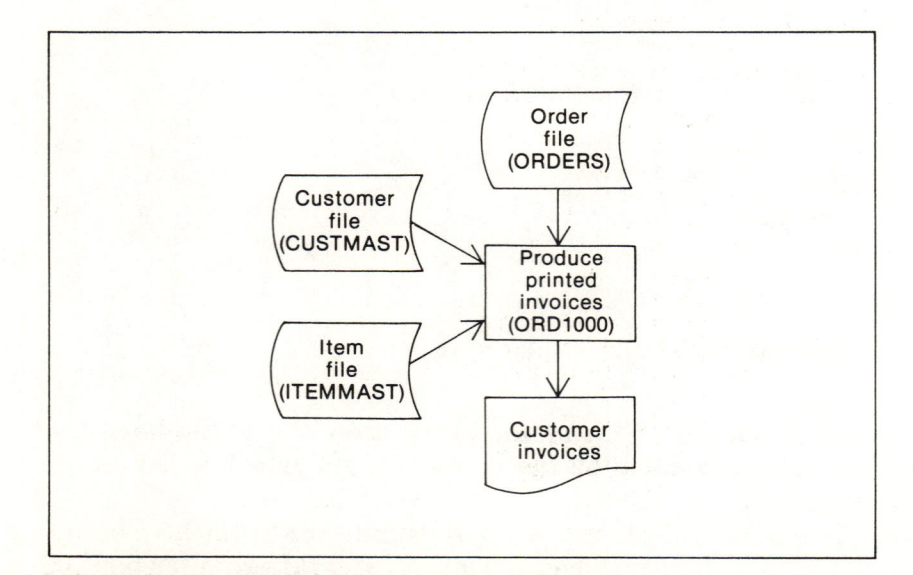

Figure 4-8 System flowchart for the prepare-invoices job

Advanced File Handling

First job:

```
//BLDISAM  JOB   HE66YFNH,
//              'W. CLARY'
//BLDSTEP  EXEC  PGM=BLDITEM
//STEPLIB  DD    DSN=MMA.USERLIB,
//               DISP=SHR
//OLDITEM  DD    DSN=ITEMFILE,
//               DISP=OLD
//NEWITEM  DD    DSN=ITEMMAST(INDEX),
//               DISP=(NEW,KEEP),
//               UNIT=DISKA,
//               VOL=SER=LIB111,
//               SPACE=(CYL,1,,CONTIG),
//               DCB=(LRECL=190,BLKSIZE=1900,RECFM=FB,DSORG=IS)
//         DD    DSN=ITEMMAST(PRIME),
//               DISP=(NEW,KEEP),
//               UNIT=DISKA,
//               VOL=SER=LIB112,
//               SPACE=(CYL,5,,CONTIG),
//               DCB=*.NEWITEM
//         DD    DSN=ITEMMAST(OVFLOW),
//               DISP=(NEW,KEEP),
//               UNIT=DISKA,
//               VOL=REF=*.NEWITEM,
//               SPACE=(CYL,2,,CONTIG),
//               DCB=*.NEWITEM
//
```

Second job:

```
//PUTINV   JOB   HE66YFNH,
//              'W. CLARY'
//PRODINV  EXEC  PGM=ORD1000
//STEPLIB  DD    DSN=MMA.USERLIB,
//               DISP=SHR
//ORDER    DD    DSN=ORDERS,
//               DISP=OLD
//CUST     DD    DSN=CUSTMAST,
//               DISP=OLD
//ITEM     DD    DSN=ITEMMAST,
//               DISP=OLD,
//               UNIT=DISKA,
//               VOL=SER=LIB111,
//               DCB=DSORG=IS
//         DD    DSN=ITEMMAST,
//               DISP=OLD,
//               UNIT=DISKA,
//               VOL=SER=LIB112,
//               DCB=DSORG=IS
//
```

Figure 4-9 Creating and processing an ISAM item master file

each ISAM area (INDEX, PRIME, and OVFLOW) when the ISAM file is created in the first job. In the second job, only two DD statements are used because the index and overflow areas both reside on the same volume, LIB111.

DISCUSSION

Indexed sequential files offer the major advantages of both sequential and random processing. Of course, this flexibility is paid for in processing speed. When processed sequentially, an indexed sequential file is likely to be slower than a physical sequential file because of the extra searches for records in the overflow areas. Similarly, when processed randomly, an indexed sequential file will be slower than a direct file (introduced in the next topic) because of the extra searches for the index records. Nevertheless, ISAM files are the most widely used form of random-access file handling, since direct file handling is more difficult to program. As more and more installations are installing System 370s with virtual storage, the more flexible Virtual Storage Access Method (VSAM) is becoming the standard method of random access. VSAM will be covered in detail in chapter 6.

Terminology

Indexed Sequential Access Method	general overflow area
ISAM	independent overflow area
random processing	reorganizing a file
key field	embedded index
cylinder index	embedded overflow area
master index	delete character
track index	full-track-index-write option
cylinder overflow area	

Objective

Given reference material, code the JCL statements to load and access an indexed sequential file.

Problems

1. Using the information provided in figure 4-10, write the JCL to load the ISAM file from tape.

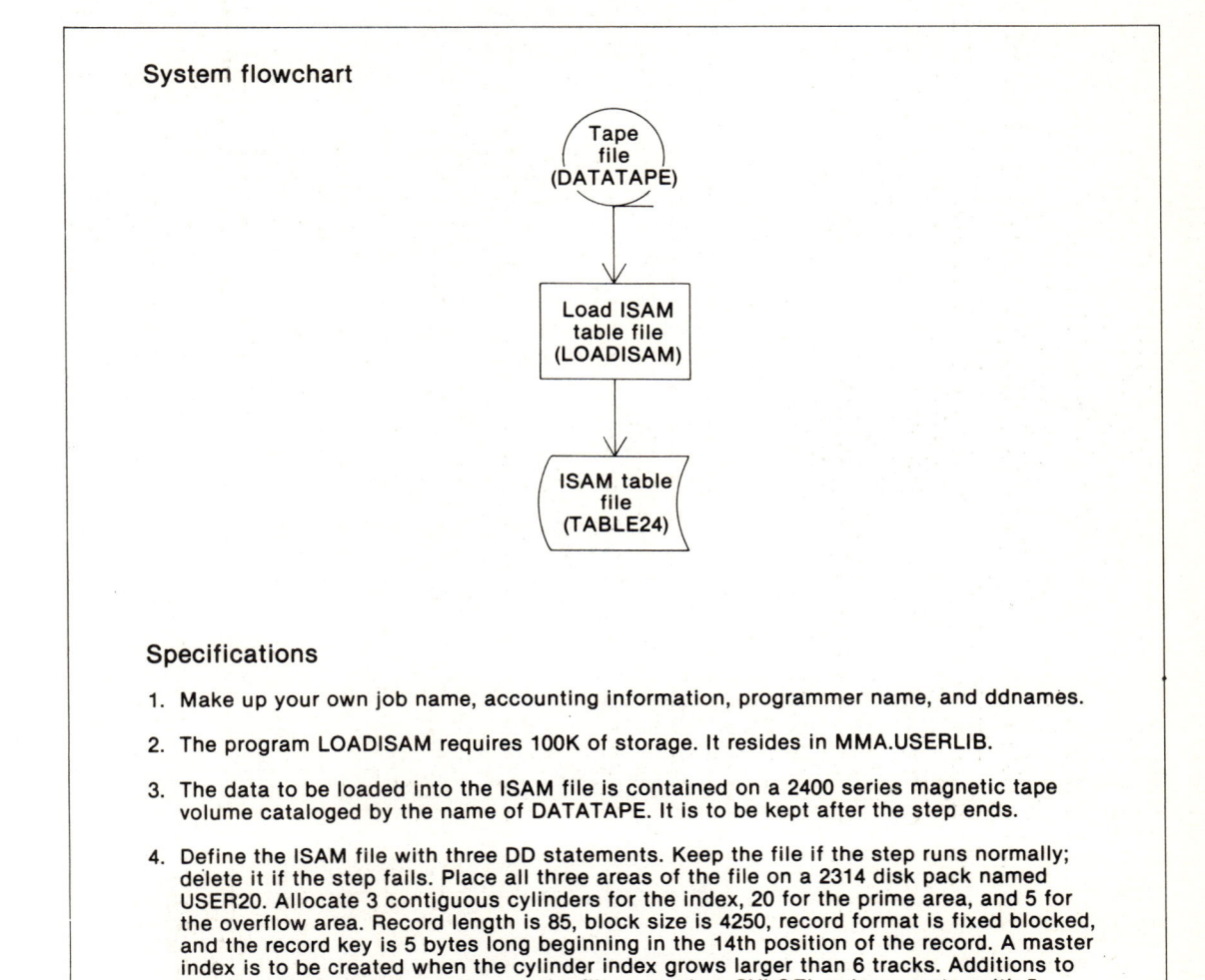

System flowchart

```
        Tape
        file
     (DATATAPE)
          |
          v
     Load ISAM
     table file
     (LOADISAM)
          |
          v
     ISAM table
        file
      (TABLE24)
```

Specifications

1. Make up your own job name, accounting information, programmer name, and ddnames.

2. The program LOADISAM requires 100K of storage. It resides in MMA.USERLIB.

3. The data to be loaded into the ISAM file is contained on a 2400 series magnetic tape volume cataloged by the name of DATATAPE. It is to be kept after the step ends.

4. Define the ISAM file with three DD statements. Keep the file if the step runs normally; delete it if the step fails. Place all three areas of the file on a 2314 disk pack named USER20. Allocate 3 contiguous cylinders for the index, 20 for the prime area, and 5 for the overflow area. Record length is 85, block size is 4250, record format is fixed blocked, and the record key is 5 bytes long beginning in the 14th position of the record. A master index is to be created when the cylinder index grows larger than 6 tracks. Additions to the file will be spread evenly over the file, so code a CYLOFL subparameter with 5 tracks allocated to it. The option code should indicate both cylinder overflow and independent overflow, and it should request a master index.

Figure 4-10 System flowchart and specifications for creating an ISAM file

2. Write the DD statements necessary to access the ISAM file created in your solution to problem 1.

Solutions

1. Figure 4-11 is an acceptable solution.
2. Figure 4-12 is an acceptable solution.

```
//LOADJOB  JOB  HE66YFNH,
//             'W. CLARY'
//LOADSTEP EXEC PGM=LOADISAM,
//             REGION=100K
//STEPLIB  DD   DSN=MMA.USERLIB,
//             DISP=SHR
//TAPEIN   DD   DSN=DATATAPE,
//             DISP=OLD
//ISAMOUT  DD   DSN=TABLE24(INDEX),
//             DISP=(NEW,KEEP,DELETE),
//             UNIT=2314,
//             VOL=SER=USER20,
//             SPACE=(CYL,3,,CONTIG),
//             DCB=(LRECL=85,BLKSIZE=4250,RECFM=FB,DSORG=IS,
//             KEYLEN=5,RKP=13,CYLOFL=5,NTM=6,OPTCD=YIM)
//         DD   DSN=TABLE24(PRIME),
//             DISP=(NEW,KEEP,DELETE),
//             VOL=REF=*.ISAMOUT,
//             SPACE=(CYL,20,,CONTIG),
//             DCB=*.ISAMOUT
//         DD   DSN=TABLE24(OVFLOW),
//             DISP=(NEW,KEEP,DELETE),
//             VOL=REF=*.ISAMOUT,
//             SPACE=(CYL,5,,CONTIG),
//             DCB=*.ISAMOUT
//
```

Figure 4-11 Creating an ISAM file

```
//ISAMTAB  DD   DSN=TABLE24,
//             DISP=OLD,
//             UNIT=2314,
//             VOL=SER=USER20,
//             DCB=DSORG=IS
```

Figure 4-12 Retrieving an ISAM file

TOPIC 2 Direct Files

Because of the complexities of direct file processing, both in coding and in concept, direct file organization is used infrequently. Nonetheless, there are certain file handling problems and situations that direct organization is well-suited for. I can't single out any one or two processing patterns as the most common for direct organization since direct files are used in so many different ways. Instead, this topic presents the JCL coding elements related to direct file processing and illustrates them in a couple of real-life situations. With this background, I hope you'll be able to apply the elements to any direct file problem you may face. Before we get into the JCL, though, let me explain the concept of direct file organization.

DIRECT FILE CONCEPTS

Like indexed sequential files, direct files allow both sequential and random access to records; but unlike ISAM files, they need no indexes. *Direct files* are created and accessed in your programs by means of the disk address of the record. The program can pass the disk address to OS in any one of three formats: physical address, relative track address, or relative block address.

The first format, *physical address*, is an eight-byte format that contains a cylinder number, track number, and record number of the desired record. To use this type of direct file, you must be thoroughly familiar with the physical device on which the file will reside. That's because you have to convert a record key to the cylinder and track number where the record resides. The method used to translate the record key to the address of the record on the disk is called a *randomizing routine*. You can study the programming manuals for your computer language to learn how to use randomizing routines to convert a record key to a physical disk address.

The second format, *relative track address*, is a three-byte format that contains the track number relative to the first track of the file. Although you don't have to know the actual addressing scheme of the physical device used for the file, you must still be familiar with the storage capacities of each track. In this format, you give OS the relative track number where the record resides and OS searches for the record key on that track. Randomizing routines are used to convert the record key to a track identity for creating and accessing records using this format.

The third format, *relative block address*, is a three-byte format that contains the block number relative to the first block in the file. (Since direct files always contain one record per block, the terms *relative block number* and *relative record number* are used interchangeably.) This is the most common form of direct file organization used with high-level languages such as COBOL and PL/I, and it's sometimes referred to as *relative file* organization. As each record is written, it is given the next sequential record number; to retrieve a record randomly, the relative record number is used as a search key to the record.

JCL FOR DIRECT AND RELATIVE FILE PROCESSING

Even though the programming considerations for direct and relative file processing may be complex, you'll be pleasantly surprised to find that the JCL requirements for these files are simple. Figure 4-13 shows examples of DD statements to create and retrieve direct and relative files. Do the parameters look familiar? They should, because except for the DCB parameter, they are identical to DD statements to create and access physical sequential files. As a result, this discussion will be directed primarily towards DCB subparameters.

```
Example 1
     //DATABLE   DD   DSN=FORMTAB,
     //               DISP=(NEW,CATLG),
     //               UNIT=3330,
     //               VOL=SER=D00103,
     //               SPACE=(CYL,3),
     //               DCB=DSORG=DA
Example 2
     //REFILE    DD   DSN=RECFILE1,
     //               DISP=OLD
Example 3
     //FORTFILE  DD   DSN=FORTFILE,
     //               DISP=(NEW,KEEP),
     //               UNIT=SYSDA,
     //               VOL=SER=USER20,
     //               SPACE=(TRK,(5,2),RLSE,CONTIG),
     //               DCB=(BLKSIZE=45,RECFM=F,DSORG=DA,
     //                KEYLEN=5,LIMCT=2,OPTCD=E)
```

Figure 4-13 Creating and retrieving direct and relative files

DCB subparameters for direct and relative files

Figure 4-14 lists the DCB subparameters most commonly used with direct files. Although you are familiar with most of them, there are certain aspects unique to direct file operations that require explanation.

BLKSIZE The block size is equal to the logical record length for fixed-length records because direct files are always unblocked. While most direct files are fixed length, they can be variable length, and if so, the block size specification must equal the record length of the longest record plus the four-byte block length prefix.

BUFNO Sometimes you may want to specify the number of I/O areas, or buffers, used for a direct file. Suppose, for example, that one of your programs requires a great deal of I/O and must work very fast. By specifying more than the two buffers normally assigned to a file, you can significantly increase the efficiency of your program. In a case like this, you could code BUFNO = n, where n is the number of buffers you want to use. Usually, though, you'll specify the number of buffers in your program when you don't want the OS default value to apply.

BUFL Direct files can be processed in assembler language using dynamically acquired buffers, meaning the buffers are assigned when the file is opened. When dynamic buffering is used, it must be specified in the assembler language program and the BUFL subparameter must be included in the JCL to tell OS what length buffer is required. BUFL has the format BUFL = n, where n is the buffer length. Although there are other cases in which you can use BUFL, in general the buffer length is provided by the program or automatically supplied by OS.

DSORG Although the program creating a direct or relative file treats it as a sequential file, the DSORG in the DCB parameter of the DD statement must be DA. The result of this combination allows the file to be created sequentially and accessed either sequentially or randomly. After the file has been created, you needn't specify the DSORG to retrieve the file.

KEYLEN If the file is to be in physical address or relative track address format, this subparameter must be coded in the DCB of the file-creation step. It specifies the length of the key field. When accessing an existing direct file, this subparameter is usually omitted since the key length has been recorded in the data set label on the disk.

Keyword	Create	Retrieve and update	Remarks
BLKSIZE	X		Number of data bytes for fixed-length records. Include a 4-byte block-length prefix for variable-length records.
BUFNO	X	X	Number of buffers to be used for file when neither OS default nor program-provided value applies.
BUFL	X	X	Specific buffer length if dynamic buffering is requested in assembler language program.
DSORG	X		DA
KEYLEN	X		Only required for physical address or relative track address format.
LIMCT	X	X	If extended search is requested (OPTCD = E), this specifies the number of blocks (if relative block format used) or the number of tracks to be searched.
OPTCD	X	X	One or more of the following codes can be used: A = physical disk address format E = extended search R = relative block disk address format W = write-verification If neither A nor R is coded, relative track address format is assumed.
RECFM	X		F = fixed-length V = variable-length

Figure 4-14 DCB parameters for direct-access files

LIMCT For certain types of I/O operations, you can request an extended search (OPTCD = E). This means that the I/O module will search for the requested record beyond the track addressed in the disk address provided by your program. If relative track addressing is used, LIMCT specifies the number of tracks to be searched beyond the starting point. If relative block addressing is used, LIMCT specifies the number of blocks to be searched beyond the starting point.

OPTCD This subparameter serves as a catchall for specifying several unrelated options that can be selected for direct file processing. First, the type of disk address format to be used is indicated here: A for physical address format; R for relative block format; and the absence of both A and R for relative track format. Extended search is requested if the option code list includes E (and must be accompanied by the LIMCT subparameter). Option code W may be coded to request a validity check on write operations.

RECFM Direct files are always unblocked, so this subparameter is always coded either F or V (fixed-length or variable-length).

Examples of DD statements

Now let's look again at the examples in figure 4-13. Example 1 illustrates the DD statement to create a direct file. The file is new, and it is to be cataloged upon successful completion of the job step. It is to be placed in three cylinders of a 3330 disk pack named D00103. The DCB information was provided by the processing program, so all I need for a DCB parameter is the data set organization (DSORG = DA).

Example 2 shows a DD statement to retrieve a direct or relative file. By looking at this DD statement, we can't tell whether the program is going to read the file sequentially or randomly. The file was cataloged by a previous job or job step, so all that's required is the DSN and DISP parameters.

Example 3 shows a DD statement with a more complex DCB parameter. The block size (and record length) is 45 bytes and the record format is F for fixed. If the record format was V, the block size would have to be four bytes longer than the record length to accommodate the control information associated with variable-length records. The data set organization is direct access (DSORG = DA), the key length is five bytes (KEYLEN = 5), the number of tracks to search for a record is limited by LIMCT to two tracks, and the OPTCD option selected is E. If OPTCD = RE had been coded, this would be a relative file.

EXAMPLES OF DIRECT FILE PROCESSING

A department/account file

A certain manufacturing company has all of its factory labor reported by the manufacturing department in which the work is done. At one point in the processing of this data, however, it is necessary to assign the labor costs to general-ledger accounts. Unfortunately, the table that relates the department number to the account number is too big—about 125 entries and 1000 bytes—to be loaded into core storage with some of the programs that use it. On the other hand, an indexed sequential file to allow random lookup of account number using department number as key would be very inefficient due to the multiple searches and reads of index records for such a small number of data records.

A direct file with physical or relative track addressing is a good solution to this problem. The key can be department number (four bytes) and the rest of the record can contain the account number (also four bytes). Since a 2314 track can hold 48 of these short records, the entire file will fit on three tracks with room for up to 144 departments. Then, by specifying the extended search option and setting the disk address to the first track of the file, all three tracks of the file can be searched for a particular key by using just one read instruction.

The job shown in figure 4-15 creates this department/account file using card records that relate each department number to one general-ledger account number. Look first at the DCB for the department/account file. The BLKSIZE and KEYLEN subparameters reflect the record length and key length of the records to be created, and DSORG specifies direct-access organization. Since I want to use a read-by-key technique with the extended search option to locate the record for a department, the OPTCD and LIMCT are coded like this: the OPTCD subparameter requests the extended search option (E); the LIMCT subparameter specifies how many tracks will be searched during the extended search. I used the value 3 in the LIMCT subparameter so all three tracks will be searched, and thus every record in the file will be searched even if the file contains the maximum number of records.

In the job shown in figure 4-16, the direct file created in figure 4-15 is coded as an old file to be used as input. Since it was cataloged previously, I don't need to code the DCB; the information was given during creation and now resides on the data set label.

```
//DEPACC    JOB  HE66YFNH,
//               'W. CLARY'
//CARDDISK EXEC  PGM=LOAD01
//STEPLIB   DD   DSN=MMA.USERLIB,
//                DISP=SHR
//TABCARDS  DD   *
           card file
/*
//DEPTACCT DD   DSN=DAFILE,
//              DISP=(NEW,CATLG),
//              UNIT=2314,
//              VOL=SER=USER01,
//              SPACE=(8,144,,CONTIG),
//              DCB=(BLKSIZE=8,RECFM=F,DSORG=DA,KEYLEN=4,
//               LIMCT=3,OPTCD=E)
//
```

Figure 4-15 Creating a direct department/account file to be read by relative track addressing

```
//LABOR    JOB  HE66YFNH,
//              'W. CLARY'
//LABUPD  EXEC  PGM=LABORDIS
//STEPLIB  DD   DSN=MMA.USERLIB,
//               DISP=SHR
//DEPTACCT DD   DSN=DAFILE,
//               DISP=OLD
//LABCOST  DD   DSN=LABMAST,
//               DISP=OLD
//LABRPT   DD   SYSOUT=A
//
```

Figure 4-16 Retrieving the department/account file

A customer file

This next example illustrates the use of relative file processing. A technical publisher did business by direct mail and had a large customer history file. Although many customers were repeat business, the majority of the customers were people who had purchased one book. As a result, no simple customer number could be generated that would make easy access to the records of the customer history file possible.

The solution was to generate a relative file of customers, and to print the relative record number on the mailing labels of advertisements sent to the customers. Then, when the orders or address changes came in with the mailing label still affixed, a data entry operator could key in the relative record number to access a customer's master record.

Figure 4-17 shows the system charts to:

1. Load the initial customer file. Remember that relative files must be created sequentially and that you must allocate all the space you will ever need when you create the file. In this case, the load program pads the end of the file with enough dummy records to contain the insertions for a given period; then the entire file will be recreated with more dummy records.
2. Produce mailing labels. The records are read sequentially into a program containing sort linkage (COBOL sort/merge feature) so they can be sorted by zip code, and the mailing labels are printed.

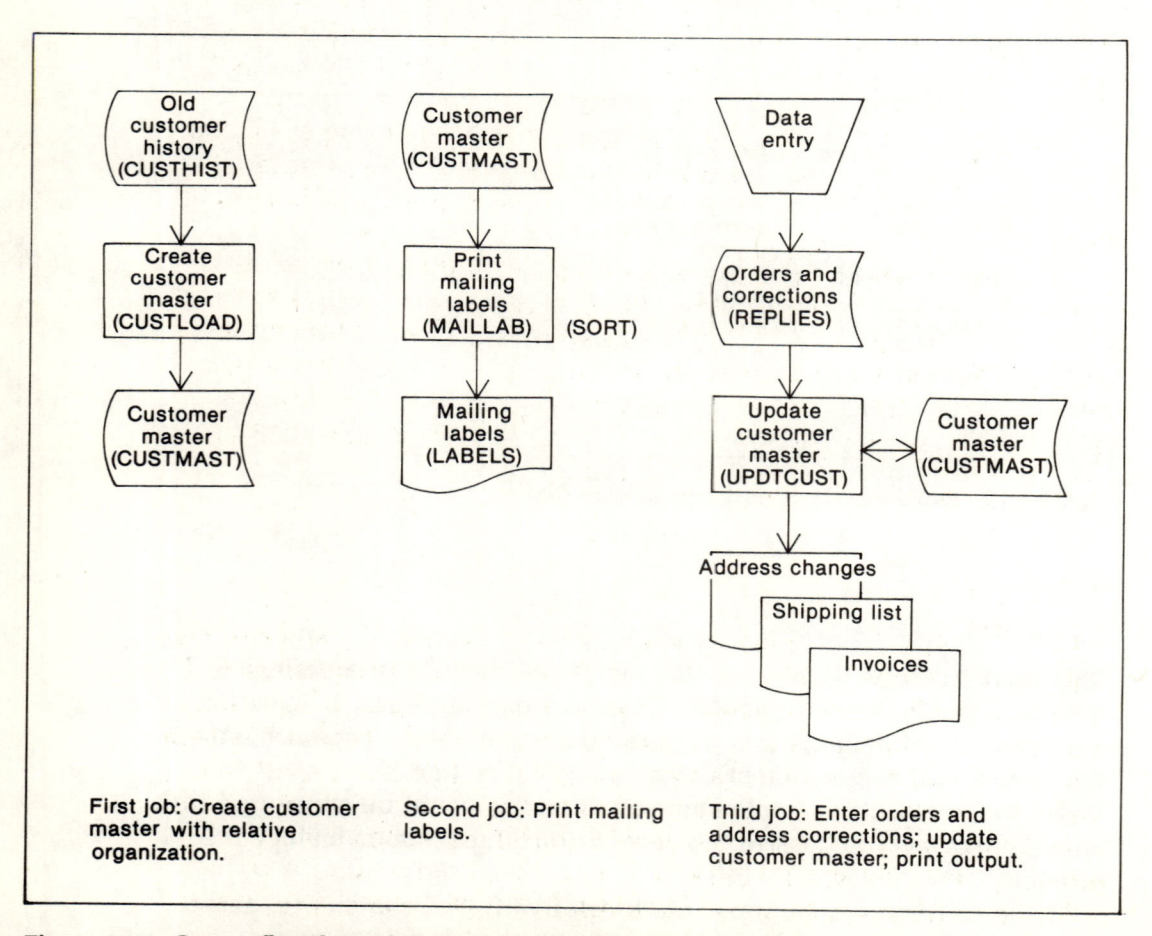

Figure 4-17 System flowcharts for creating and using a relative file

3. Enter orders and address corrections. The data entry transactions that contain the relative record number from the address label are read. The relative record number is then used to randomly access the proper customer master. (This could be done with an online update but I've shown it as a batch process for simplicity.)

As before, the JCL to process this system doesn't reflect the complexity of the programs it executes. Figure 4-18 lists the JCL to execute the load function, the mailing label function, and the update function.

In the first job, the program named CUSTLOAD reads the old customer history file sequentially and writes the new customer master file sequentially. The first relative record number is 00000 and is incremented by 1 with each write. The relative customer master file is written and cataloged on the 3330 pack named D00103, and it initially requests 10 contiguous cylinders of disk space with 16 10-cylinder secondary entents. The record length is 105 bytes, fixed-unblocked. The organization is direct access, and OPTCD = R tells OS to use relative block (record) addressing.

The second job executes a program to read the customer master file sequentially, sort the records in zip code order, and print mailing labels. The DD statement for the labels identifies a special form to be mounted.

Finally, in the last job, the program named UPDTCUST reads a transaction from the transaction file (REPLIES); randomly reads the CUSTMAST file using the relative record number as the key; updates the master record and rewrites it; and produces invoices, a shipping list, and the address correction register. Once again, the DD statement for the relative file could be referring to a physical sequential file, for there's no difference in the JCL.

DISCUSSION

As you can see, direct file processing is easy enough to handle in JCL, but the programming considerations related to direct file processing are not so easy. Look up direct file processing in the programming manual of the language you use and you'll see what I mean. Although almost all programming languages will allow you to work on direct files, most applications actually using direct files are programmed in assembler language. This is not to say that there aren't some good applications programmed in COBOL and PL/I; it's just that working with direct files in a compiler language becomes more cumbersome than most problem-oriented programmers want to fool with.

Job 1: Create customer master

```
//GENER     JOB  HE66YFNH,
//               'W. CLARY'
//CUSTGEN   EXEC PGM=CUSTLOAD
//STEPLIB   DD   DSN=MMA.USERLIB,
//               DISP=SHR
//OLDCUST   DD   DSN=CUSTHIST,
//               DISP=OLD
//NEWCUST   DD   DSN=CUSTMAST,
//               DISP=(NEW,CATLG),
//               UNIT=3330,
//               VOL=SER=D00103,
//               SPACE=(CYL,(10,10),,CONTIG),
//-              DCB=(BLKSIZE=105,RECFM=F,DSORG=DA,OPTCD=R)
//
```

Job 2: Print mailing labels

```
//PLABEL    JOB  HE66YFNH,
//               'W. CLARY'
//PRTLAB    EXEC PGM=MAILLAB
//STEPLIB   DD   DSN=MMA.USERLIB,
//               DISP=SHR
//CUSTFILE  DD   DSN=CUSTMAST,
//               DISP=OLD
//SORTWK01  DD   UNIT=SYSDA,
//               SPACE=(CYL,5,,CONTIG)
//SORTWK02  DD   UNIT=SYSDA,
//               SPACE=(CYL,5,,CONTIG)
//SORTWK03  DD   UNIT=SYSDA,
//               SPACE=(CYL,5,,CONTIG)
//LABELS    DD   SYSOUT=(A,,3UPL)
//
```

Job 3: Update customer master

```
//UPCSTJOB  JOB  HE66YFNH,
//               'W. CLARY'
//UPCUST    EXEC PGM=UPDTCUST
//STEPLIB   DD   DSN=MMA.USERLIB,
//               DISP=SHR
//INDATA    DD   DSN=REPLIES,
//               DISP=OLD
//CUSTFILE  DD   DSN=CUSTMAST,
//               DISP=OLD
//INVOICES  DD   SYSOUT=(A,,INVC),
//               DCB=BLKSIZE=90
//SHIPLIST  DD   SYSOUT=A,
//               DCB=BLKSIZE=133
//ADDCHG    DD   SYSOUT=A,
//               DCB=BLKSIZE=133
//
```

Figure 4-18 Creating and retrieving a customer file to be read by relative record addressing

Advanced File Handling   **161**

In general, there are two reasons why direct files aren't popular. First, it is usually difficult to develop an efficient randomizing routine for reducing the record key to a track address or physical address. Second, the programmer must code file-maintenance routines that keep track of available space when records are added to or deleted from a file. Since these routines can be very complex, direct files are just plain tough to use.

Terminology

direct file
physical address
randomizing routine
relative track address

relative block address
relative block number
relative record number
relative file

Objective

Given reference material, write the JCL statements to load and retrieve a direct-access file.

Problems

1. Write a DD statement to create and catalog a file with the following characteristics: (1) the ddname is DATABLE and the data set name is TABLE1; (2) the file should be placed on a system direct-access device named R00273; (3) 14 contiguous tracks should be allocated with 3 tracks for each secondary extent; (4) the block size is 27 bytes, the key is 6 bytes long, and the record format is fixed; (5) the program specifies dynamic buffering and the buffer length will be 540 bytes; (6) the records should be accessed by relative record addresses; and (7) the extended search option should *not* be used.

2. Write a DD statement to retrieve the file defined by your solution to problem 1.

Solutions

1. Figure 4-19 is an acceptable solution.
2. ```
//DAFILE   DD   DSN=TABLE1,
//   DISP=OLD
```
```

```
//DATABLE   DD  DSN=TABLE1,
//              DISP=(NEW,CATLG),
//              UNIT=SYSDA,
//              VOL=SER=R00273,
//              SPACE=(TRK,(14,3),,CONTIG),
//              DCB=(BLKSIZE=27,RECFM=F,DSORG=DA,BUFL=540,
//               KEYLEN=6,OPTCD=R)
```

Figure 4-19 Creating a relative file

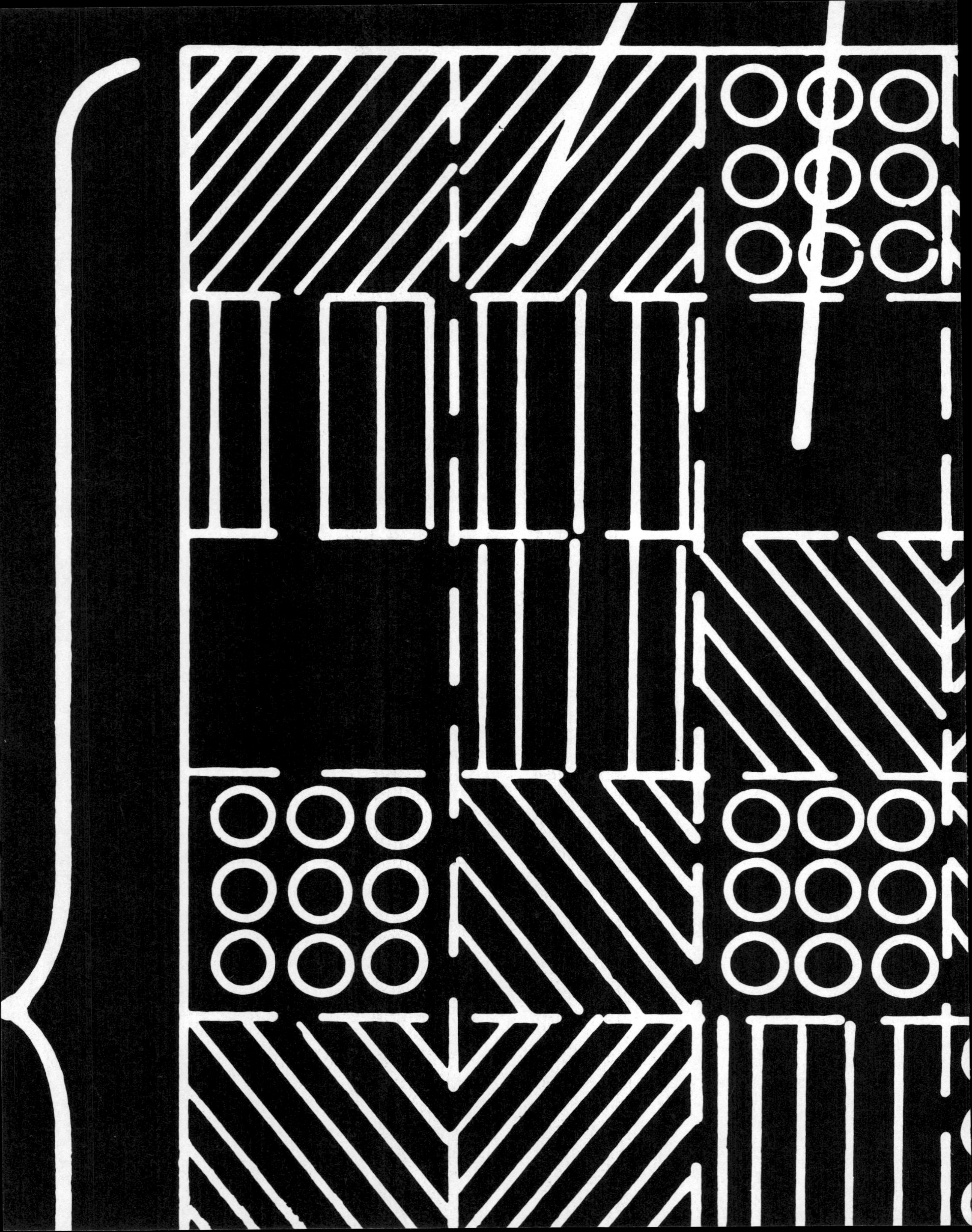

5

Libraries and Procedures

This chapter introduces the concept of JCL *procedures*—that is, precoded segments of JCL that can be included into your job stream as it is executed. To understand how this concept works, you need to learn about libraries since the procedures you will write and use may be stored in a special type of library. As a result, topic 1 provides the conceptual background you need on libraries, and topic 2 shows you how to create, test, and use JCL procedures.

TOPIC 1 Libraries

In general, there are four kinds of *libraries* used in an OS shop: source, procedure, object, and load libraries. A *source library* is made up of source programs or segments of programs to be compiled. A *procedure library* consists of cataloged procedures such as the procedures you use to compile source programs. In the next topic you'll learn how to create, test, modify, and use procedures. An *object library* consists of object program modules created by the compilers or assembler. Before these object modules can be executed, however, they must be link-edited by either the loader program or the linkage-editor program. This type of library is used to hold often-used, separately-compiled subroutines that are called from a main program. Finally, a *load library* consists of object program modules that have already been link-edited. They are therefore ready to execute directly from the library without further preparation. The file named MMA.USERLIB that we've used throughout this book as a STEPLIB is a load library.

In contrast to simpler operating systems like DOS, an OS system usually has several different source, object, and load libraries. In a typical installation, for example, there are a number of *system libraries*. These are permanent libraries containing source statements, object modules, and load modules likely to be used by all groups within an EDP department. In addition, there may be one or more *user library* of each type. For instance, various application and system programming groups may each have one or more source, object, or load libraries. (There is usually only one procedure library for an installation, although it is possible to have more than one.)

The libraries of OS are direct-access data sets that consist of a *directory* followed by a number of sequential files called *members*. The directory is simply a table of the names of all members in the data set plus the starting address of each member. Each member consists of one or more blocks of data organized sequentially. The entire library is referred to as a *partitioned data set* (or *PDS*), and it is usually cataloged.

CREATING AND MODIFYING PARTITIONED DATA SETS

There are three ways in which you can create and modify partitioned data sets. First, you can write your own routines in assembler language. Although OS includes assembler language macro instructions to do this, few user programs are written to process partitioned data sets. For this reason, the JCL to process user-written PDS maintenance will not be covered in this book.

The second way to create and modify partitioned data sets is to code linkage-editor statements when you compile and link a program. The output of the compiler is read into the linkage-editor program where it is placed into a load library. This method of PDS maintenance is presented in chapter 8 on the language translators.

The third way to process partitioned data sets is to execute OS utility programs that are designed for that purpose. The utility programs that apply to partitioned data sets in particular are IEBUPDTE, IEHPROGM, IEBCOPY, IEHMOVE, and IEBPTPCH. Although this book is not intended to teach utility programs, I have included examples of some of these utilities in chapter 7. For the purposes of this chapter, I will discuss briefly the IEBUPDTE utility program. It represents the most common method of creating and maintaining source and procedure libraries in an OS system.

Creating a partitioned data set

Figure 5-1 shows a job that creates a PDS. The EXEC statement causes the IEBUPDTE program to be executed. It contains a PARM parameter with the value NEW. This tells the program that there is no old data set as input and that a new data set is to be created.

SYSPRINT is the ddname of the output message file used by the utility. This DD statement causes a listing to be printed that tells you if the partitioned data set was created or modified correctly. I'll show you several examples in a few moments.

SYSUT2 is the ddname of the output data set (the new partitioned data set). Note the SPACE parameter: it contains an entry of 5 in the directory allocation subparameter. If you'll recall the discussion of the SPACE parameter from chapter 3, you'll remember that this subparameter tells OS how many 256-byte directory blocks to use for a PDS. Also note that the DSORG subparameter specifies PO for partitioned organization.

SYSIN defines the input file of control statements for the utility. All OS utility programs require control information to direct specific

```
//LIBCREAT JOB  HE66YFNH,
//              'W. CLARY'
//CREATE   EXEC PGM=IEBUPDTE,
//              PARM=NEW
//SYSPRINT DD   SYSOUT=A
//SYSUT2   DD   DSN=MMA.EXAMPLIB,
//              DISP=(NEW,CATLG),
//              UNIT=3330,
//              VOL=SER=D00102,
//              SPACE=(TRK,(120,,5)),
//              DCB=(LRECL=80,BLKSIZE=80,RECFM=FB,DSORG=PO)
//SYSIN    DD   *
./ ADD    NAME=EXAMP1,LEVEL=00,SOURCE=0,LIST=ALL
./ NUMBER NEW1=100,INCR=10
  GET LIST (R,T);
  DO WHILE (R>T);
    R = R * 4;
    SUMRY = R + T;
    PUT LIST (SUMRY);
  END;
./ ENDUP
/*
//
```

Figure 5-1 Creating a library with the IEBUPDTE utility program

optional functions. The first two positions of a utility control statement contain ./ (period-slash) to distinguish them from the JCL statements and data in the input stream. In figure 5-1, the control statements are ADD, NUMBER, and ENDUP.

The ADD statement tells the utility to add a new member to the library (in this case, the first member). NAME gives the name of the member. LEVEL indicates the version of the member to use; for our purposes, I'll always use LEVEL = 00 to create a member and LEVEL = 01 to update an existing member. SOURCE tells the utility program where the input data for the member is to be found: SOURCE = 0 tells the IEBUPDTE program that the data to add or change a member is in the input stream, while SOURCE = 1 indicates that the data is to be supplied from some other source. For our purposes, I'll always use SOURCE = 0. LIST = ALL requests a listing of the updated member.

The NUMBER statement tells IEBUPDTE to sequentially number the records. NEW1 gives the number of the first record in the member. INCR gives the incremental value to be added to each sequence number for every record of the member. In the example, the records are to be sequentially numbered from 100 by 10 (100, 110, 120, and so on). This allows for space to insert records later. The numbers assigned by the NUMBER statement are placed in columns 73-80 of the source records and are important when you have to change the contents of the member. You'll see examples of this in just a moment.

The ENDUP statement indicates the end of the control statements for the program. It is required for all runs of the IEBUPDTE program, and follows all other utility control statements and data for members of the partitioned data set being created or modified. The /* statement marks the end of the utility control statement input.

Once this job is executed, the system will have a new partitioned data set named MMA.EXAMPLIB. This data set will consist of one member, EXAMP1, that will contain the six records shown between the NUMBER and ENDUP statements in the figure. These six records will be numbered 00000100, 00000110, 00000120, 00000130, 00000140, and 00000150. The sequence number will be in positions 73-80 of each record.

Adding a member to a partitioned data set

Figure 5-2 shows a job to add two members to the library created in figure 5-1. The EXEC statement causes IEBUPDTE to be executed with PARM = MOD, telling OS that the input partitioned data set is to be modified and written out to the new partitioned data set.

```
//LIBADD    JOB  HE66YFNH,
//               'W. CLARY'
//UPSTEP    EXEC PGM=IEBUPDTE,
//               PARM=MOD
//SYSPRINT  DD   SYSOUT=A
//SYSUT1    DD   DSN=MMA.EXAMPLIB,
//               DISP=OLD
//SYSUT2    DD   DSN=MMA.EXAMPLIB,
//               DISP=OLD
//SYSIN     DD   *
./ ADD     NAME=EXAMP2,LEVEL=00,SOURCE=0,LIST=ALL
./ NUMBER  NEW1=100,INCR=10
       IDENTIFICATION DIVISION.
      *
       PROGRAM-ID.  PULLNMAN.
      *
       ENVIRNOMENT DIVISION.
      *
       CONFIGURATION SECTION.
      *
       SOURCE-COMPUTER.  IBM-370.
       OBJECT-COMPUTER.  IBM-370.
      *
./ ADD     NAME=EXAMP3,LEVEL=00,SOURCE=0,LIST=ALL
./ NUMBER  NEW1=100,INCR=10
PARTSCAN   START 0
BEGIN      SAVE  (14,12)
           BALR  3,0
           USING *,3
           ST    13,SAVE+4
           LA    13,SAVE
./ ENDUP
/*
//
```

Figure 5-2 Adding members to a library with IEBUPDTE

SYSUT1 is the ddname of the old partitioned data set and SYSUT2 is the name of the new partitioned data set. You'll notice that they both refer to the same data set name in this case. The result is that the file is updated in the area already allocated on disk. SYSIN defines the input members and the control statements: ADD, NUMBER, and ENDUP. These statements are similar to those used when creating the library, so you shouldn't have any trouble with them.

Modifying a member of a partitioned data set

To make corrections or change a partitioned data set, you can use the same JCL you used to add members to an existing partitioned data set (such as that shown in figure 5-2). In fact, you can add members and modify others in the same job step. Figure 5-3 shows a job to change records of the second member in our example library (EXAMP2). Although I've coded a SYSUT2 DD statement for this job, it's not required when you are only modifying members and use the UPDATE = INPLACE option. I always code it so I can use the same JCL to add members, change members, or both.

The CHANGE statement identifies the member, requests a listing of all records in the updated member, and requests that the update take place in the space already allocated to the member. In the example, the first data statement in the input stream will replace the record with sequence number 120; the second data statement will replace the record with sequence number 140. If I wanted to insert a new record, I couldn't use the UPDATE = INPLACE option because more space would be required.

The NUMBER statement causes the member to be renumbered after the changes are made. Again, as in figures 5-1 and 5-2, the sequence numbers will start with 100 and increase by tens. SEQ1 = ALL means that all the records in the member are to be renumbered. Since the changes made to the member are just simple replacements, the NUMBER statement could be omitted entirely; the original sequence numbers would still apply.

Suppose now that I want to make some further changes to EXAMP2—changes that require inserting and deleting some records. Then, I can use a JCL setup like the one in figure 5-4. Here, two new

```
//LIBMOD    JOB  HE66YFNH,
//               'W. CLARY'
//MODLIB    EXEC PGM=IEBUPDTE,
//               PARM=MOD
//SYSPRINT  DD   SYSOUT=A
//SYSUT1    DD   DSN=MMA.EXAMPLIB,
//               DISP=OLD
//SYSUT2    DD   DSN=MMA.EXAMPLIB,
//               DISP=OLD
//SYSIN     DD   *
./ CHANGE   NAME=EXAMP2,LIST=ALL,UPDATE=INPLACE
./ NUMBER   SEQ1=ALL,NEW1=100,INCR=10
       PROGRAM-ID.  PULLNAME.                                    00000120
       ENVIRONMENT DIVISION.                                     00000140
./ ENDUP
/*
//
```

Figure 5-3 Changing a member of a library with IEBUPDTE

Libraries and Procedures 171

The JCL:

```
//LIBMOD   JOB  HE66YFNH,
//              'W. CLARY'
//MODLIB   EXEC PGM=IEBUPDTE,
//              PARM=MOD
//SYSPRINT DD   SYSOUT=A
//SYSUT1   DD   DSN=MMA.EXAMPLIB,
//              DISP=OLD
//SYSUT2   DD   DSN=MMA.EXAMPLIB,
//              DISP=OLD
//SYSIN    DD   *
./ CHANGE   NAME=EXAMP2,LIST=ALL
./ NUMBER   SEQ1=ALL,NEW1=100,INCR=10
     *AUTHOR.       WAYNE CLARY.                      00000122
     *INSTALLATION.    MMA.                           00000124
./ DELETE   SEQ1=200,SEQ2=200
./ ENDUP
/*
//
```

EXAMP2 before the update:

```
      IDENTIFICATION DIVISION.                        00000100
    *                                                 00000110
      PROGRAM-ID.   PULLNAME.                         00000120
    *                                                 00000130
      ENVIRONMENT DIVISION.                           00000140
    *                                                 00000150
      CONFIGURATION SECTION.                          00000160
    *                                                 00000170
      SOURCE-COMPUTER.   IBM-370.                     00000180
      OBJECT-COMPUTER.   IBM-370.                     00000190
    *                                                 00000200
```

EXAMP2 after the update:

```
      IDENTIFICATION DIVISION.                        00000100
    *                                                 00000110
      PROGRAM-ID.   PULLNAME.                         00000120
     *AUTHOR.       WAYNE CLARY.                      00000130
     *INSTALLATION.    MMA.                           00000140
    *                                                 00000150
      ENVIRONMENT DIVISION.                           00000160
    *                                                 00000170
      CONFIGURATION SECTION.                          00000180
    *                                                 00000190
      SOURCE-COMPUTER.   IBM-370.                     00000200
      OBJECT-COMPUTER.   IBM-370.                     00000210
```

Figure 5-4 Inserting and deleting records using IEBUPDTE

records follow the NUMBER statement. They have sequence numbers 122 and 124, so they'll be inserted between records 120 and 130. Then, the DELETE statement indicates that record 200 should be deleted from the member. It does this by specifying 200 in both the SEQ1 and SEQ2 fields. If more than one record in a row were to be deleted, SEQ1 and SEQ2 would contain different values. For example, if records 160 through 200 were to be deleted, this DELETE statement would be used:

```
./ DELETE SEQ1=160,SEQ2=200
```

Notice that I couldn't use the UPDATE = INPLACE option to make these changes because the updated member won't be the same size as the old member.

Once the changes have been made, the NUMBER statement says to renumber all the records in the member, starting with 100 and numbering by tens. All the changes made are shown in the listing of EXAMP2 at the bottom of figure 5-4.

IEBUPDTE messages (the SYSPRINT file)

Figure 5-5 shows three examples of IEBUPDTE SYSPRINT listings. The first example is the listing of an IEBUPDTE execution that adds a member to the partitioned data set (the job in figure 5-1). Following the ADD and NUMBER statements is a listing of the new member along with the sequence numbers that were assigned to each statement. The messages at the end of the listing tell me that: the name EXAMP1 was not found in the name directory, so it was stored with address format TTR (TT = track number and R = record number); the highest condition code (return code) was zero; and the IEBUPDTE program ended. The second example illustrates the messages you will receive if you try to change a member that doesn't exist in the library. The messages tell me that: the member EXAM1 was not found in the name directory; this is an invalid operation; the highest condition code was 4; and the IEBUPDTE ended. The third example shows the listing for a changed member. Both the old and new records (sequence number 120) are shown on the listing for audit-trail purposes. It's a good idea to keep a file of these IEBUPDTE listings so you'll always have the most recent version of a member available, and so you can see how the member was changed.

A COMPLETE EXAMPLE

To recap what I've said in this topic and to make the concept a little clearer for you, let's build a library to hold source-program

Example 1: Adding a member

```
        SYSIN                      NEW MASTER                                IEBUPDTE LOG PAGE 0001

./ ADD    NAME=EXAMP1,LEVEL=00,SOURCE=0,LIST=ALL
./ NUMBER NEW1=100,INCR=10
                                   GET LIST (R,T);                                    00000100
                                   DO WHILE (R>T);                                    00000110
                                      R = R * 4;                                      00000120
                                      SUMRY = R + T;                                  00000130
                                      PUT LIST (SUMRY);                               00000140
                                   END;                                               00000150
./ ENDUP

IEB817I MEMBER NAME (EXAMP1  ) NOT FOUND IN NM DIRECTORY.  STOWED WITH TTR.
IEB818I HIGHEST CONDITION CODE WAS 00000000
IEB819I END OF JOB IEBUPDTE.
```

Example 2: Changing a member (member not found)

```
        SYSIN                      NEW MASTER                                IEBUPDTE LOG PAGE 0001

./ CHANGE NAME=EXAM1,LIST=ALL,UPDATE=INPLACE
./ NUMBER SEQ1=ALL,NEW1=100,INCR=10

IEB817I MEMBER NAME (EXAM1   ) NOT FOUND
IEB807I INVALID OPERATION.
IEB818I HIGHEST CONDITION CODE WAS 00000004
IEB819I END OF JOB IEBUPDTE.
```

Example 3: Changing a member

```
        SYSIN                      NEW MASTER                                IEBUPDTE LOG PAGE 0001

./ CHANGE NAME=EXAMP1,LIST=ALL,UPDATE=INPLACE
./ NUMBER SEQ1=ALL,NEW1=100,INCR=10
                                   GET LIST (R,T);                                    00000100
                                   DO WHILE (R>T);                                    00000110
                                      R = R * 4;                            *         00000120   REPLACED*
                                      R = R * 6;                            *         00000120   REPLACEMENT*
                                      SUMRY = R + T;                                  00000130
                                      PUT LIST (SUMRY);                               00000140
                                   END;                                               00000150
./ ENDUP

IEB818I HIGHEST COMPLETION CODE WAS 00000000
IEB819I END OF JOB IEBUPDTE.
```

Figure 5-5 Examples of the SYSPRINT listing from IEBUPDTE

statements. The first member will be a small portion of a COBOL program. Then, I'll add an assembler-language member. Finally, I'll correct an error I discovered in the COBOL program.

The top part of figure 5-6 shows the JCL, utility control statements, and the first member of our library. Except for some of the values in the SYSUT2 DD statement and the member itself, this JCL is just like that in figure 5-1. The bottom part of the figure shows the listed output of the SYSPRINT DD statement. In figure 5-7, the assembler-language member is added to the library, as shown in the SYSPRINT output. Finally, figure 5-8 shows the job to correct the error (a misspelled word) in the COBOL member, along with the SYSPRINT listing of the corrected result.

DISCUSSION

Libraries are used for many different functions in OS. Because source programs, object programs, and load modules are maintained in libraries, the need for program card decks is reduced, both in the development and production environment. JCL statements are kept in libraries in the form of procedures, so commonly used JCL coding can be executed without reading large quantities of control statements. And control cards for utilities and sorts are often kept in libraries so several programmers can have access to groups of control cards without having to recode them for each job.

Terminology

library	user library
source library	directory
procedure library	member
object library	partitioned data set
load library	PDS
system library	

Objectives

1. Name the four types of OS libraries and describe the typical contents of each.
2. Given job specifications, code the JCL to execute the IEBUPDTE utility program.

Libraries and Procedures

The JCL:

```
//BLDLIB  JOB  HE66YFNH,
//             'W. CLARY',
//        EXEC PGM=IEBUPDTE,
//             PARM=NEW
//SYSPRINT DD  SYSOUT=A
//SYSUT2   DD  DSN=MMA.PROGLIB,
//             DISP=(NEW,CATLG,DELETE),
//             UNIT=3330,
//             VOL=SER=D00103,
//             SPACE=(TRK,(10,2)),
//             DCB=(LRECL=80,BLKSIZE=80,RECFM=FB,DSORG=PO)
//SYSIN    DD  *
./ ADD    NAME=COBOL1,LEVEL=00,SOURCE=0,LIST=ALL
./ NUMBER NEW1=100,INCR=10
       IDENTIFICATION DIVISION.                              00000100
       PROGRAM-ID. SAMPLE1.                                  00000110
       ENVIRONMENT DIVISION.                                 00000120
       CONFIGURATION SECTION.                                00000130
       SOURCE-COMPUTER. IBM-360.                             00000140
       OBJECT-COMPUTER. IBM-360.                             00000150
./ ENDUP
/*
//
```

The SYSPRINT listing:

```
    SYSIN                              NEW MASTER                    IEBUPDTE LOG PAGE 0001

./ ADD    NAME=COBOL1,LEVEL=00,SOURCE=0,LIST=ALL
./ NUMBER NEW1=100,INCR=10
       IDENTIFICATION DIVISION.
       PROGRAM-ID. SAMPLE1.
       ENVIRONMENT DIVISION.
       CONFIGURATION SECION.
       SOURCE-COMPUTER. IBM-360.
       OBJECT-COMPUTER. IBM-360.
./ ENDUP

IEB817I MEMBER NAME (COBOL1 ) NOT FOUND IN NM DIRECTORY.  STOWED WITH TTR.
IEB818I HIGHEST CONDITION CODE WAS 00000000
IEB819I END OF JOB IEBUPDTE.
```

Figure 5-6 Creating a source-program library

176 Chapter 5

```
The JCL:

//ADDLIB   JOB  HE66YFNH,
//              'W. CLARY'
//EXUP     EXEC PGM=IEBUPDTE,
//              PARM=MOD
//SYSPRINT DD   SYSOUT=A
//SYSUT1   DD   DSN=MNA.PROGLIB,
//              DISP=OLD
//SYSUT2   DD   DSN=MMA.PROGLIB,
//              DISP=OLD
//SYSIN    DD   *
./ ADD     NAME=ASSEM1,LEVEL=00,SOURCE=0,LIST=ALL
./ NUMBER  NEW1=100,INCR=10
REORDLST START 0
BEGIN    SAVE  (14,12)
         BALR  3,0
         USING *,3
         ST    13,SAVE+4
         LA    13,SAVE
         OPEN  (CARDIN,INPUT,PRTOUT,OUTPUT)
./ ENDUP
/*
//

The SYSPRINT listing:

       SYSIN              NEW MASTER              IEBUPDTE LOG PAGE 0001

     ./ ADD    NAME=ASSEM1,LEVEL=00,SOURCE=0,LIST=ALL
     ./ NUMBER NEW1=100,INCR=10
                          REORDLST START 0                               00000100
                          BEGIN    SAVE  (14,12)                         00000110
                                   BALR  3,0                             00000120
                                   USING *,3                             00000130
                                   ST    13,SAVE+4                       00000140
                                   LA    13,SAVE                         00000150
                                   OPEN  (CARDIN,INPUT,PRTOUT,OUTPUT)    00000160
     ./ ENDUP
IEB817I MEMBER NAME (ASSEM1 ) NOT FOUND IN NM DIRECTORY. STOWED WITH TTR.
IEB818I HIGHEST CONDITION CODE WAS 00000000
IEB819I END OF JOB IEBUPDTE.
```

Figure 5-7 Adding a member to the source-program library

Libraries and Procedures

The JCL:

```
//CHGLIB   JOB  HE66YFNH,
//             'W. CLARY'
//EXUP     EXEC PGM=IEBUPDTE,
//             PARM=MOD
//SYSUT1   DD   DSN=MMA.PROGLIB,
//             DISP=OLD
//SYSUT2   DD   DSN=MMA.PROGLIB,
//             DISP=OLD
//SYSIN    DD   *
./ CHANGE NAME=COBOL1,LIST=ALL,UPDATE=INPLACE
./ NUMBER SEQ1=ALL,NEW1=100,INCR=10
       CONFIGURATION SECTION.                                00000130
./ ENDUP
/*
//
```

The SYSPRINT listing:

```
     SYSIN                          NEW MASTER              IEBUPDTE LOG PAGE 0001

./ CHANGE NAME=COBOL1,LIST=ALL,UPDATE=INPLACE
./ NUMBER SEQ1=ALL,NEW1=100,INCR=10
       IDENTIFICATION DIVISION.                                         00000100
       PROGRAM-ID. SAMPLE1.                                             00000110
       ENVIRONMENT DIVISION.                                            00000120
       CONFIGURATION SECTION.                              *            00000130  *REPLACED*
       CONFIGURATION SECTION.                              *            00000130  *REPLACEMENT*
./ ENDUP
           SOURCE-COMPUTER.  IBM-360.                                   00000140
           OBJECT-COMPUTER.  IBM-360.                                   00000150
IEB818I HIGHEST CONDITION CODE WAS 00000000
IEB819I END OF JOB IEBUPDTE.
```

Figure 5-8 Changing a member in the source-program library

Problems

1. (Objective 2) Using figures 5-1 and 5-6 as examples, code the JCL and utility control statements for creating a library of control cards. The job specifications are as follows:

   a. Catalog the partitioned data set, MYLIB, on a 2314 disk pack named USER01.

   b. Allocate five tracks for the data set with one directory block.

   c. The record length is 80 bytes, the block size is 160 bytes, and the record format is FB.

   d. Create the library with two members. The data for the first member, MYMEMB1, is:

   ```
   SORT FIELDS=(1,5,A),FORMAT=CH
   ```

   The data for the second member, MYMEMB2, is:

   ```
   SORT FIELDS=(12,9,A,40,9,A),FORMAT=CH
   ```

   In each case, the data should begin in position 2 of the record.

   e. The records in both members are to be numbered from 10 by increments of 10.

2. (Objective 2) Using figures 5-3 and 5-8 as examples, code the JCL and utility control statements for changing the first member of the library you created in problem 1. The member should consist of this record only:

   ```
   SORT FIELDS=(1,5,A,31,7,A),FORMAT=CH
   ```

Solutions

1. Figure 5-9 is an acceptable solution.
2. Figure 5-10 is an acceptable solution.

TOPIC 2 JCL Procedures

What are JCL procedures used for? Imagine this situation: you have been involved in a large system development project that is nearing completion. The programs have been written and tested individually and in combination with other programs. Now it is time to put the whole thing together as one system. As you begin to look the system over, you notice that if you make one job for each function, you will

```
//CRLIB     JOB   HE66YFNH,
//               'W. CLARY'
//EXUP      EXEC  PGM=IEBUPDTE,
//               PARM=NEW
//SYSPRINT  DD   SYSOUT=A
//SYSUT2    DD   DSN=MYLIB,
//               DISP=(NEW,CATLG),
//               UNIT=2314,
//               VOL=SER=USER01,
//               SPACE=(TRK,(5,,1)),
//               DCB=(LRECL=80,BLKSIZE=160,RECFM=FB,DSORG=PO)
//SYSIN     DD   *
./ ADD     NAME=MYMEMB1,LEVEL=00,SOURCE=0,LIST=ALL
./ NUMBER  NEW1=10,INCR=10
 SORT FIELDS=(1,5,A),FORMAT=CH
./ ADD     NAME=MYMEMB2,LEVEL=00,SOURCE=0,LIST=ALL
./ NUMBER  NEW1=10,INCR=10
 SORT FIELDS=(12,9,A,40,9,A),FORMAT=CH
./ ENDUP
/*
//
```

Figure 5-9 Creating a control-statement library

```
//CHLIB     JOB   HE66YFNH,
//               'W. CLARY'
//EXUP      EXEC  PGM=IEBUPDTE,
//               PARM=MOD
//SYSPRINT  DD   SYSOUT=A
//SYSUT1    DD   DSN=MYLIB,
//               DISP=OLD
//SYSUT2    DD   DSN=MYLIB,
//               DISP=OLD
//SYSIN     DD   *
./ CHANGE  NAME=MYMEMB1,LIST=ALL,UPDATE=INPLACE
./ NUMBER  SEQ1=ALL,NEW1=10,INCR=10
 SORT FIELDS=(1,5,A,31,7,A),FORMAT=CH                    00000010
./ ENDUP
/*
//
```

Figure 5-10 Changing a member of a control-statement library

be duplicating many job steps (some programs are executed in more than one job). In addition, since the system is a general one that can be used by different departments and programmers, you can see problems of duplicate JCL decks and the associated problems of maintaining those decks as changes to the system occur.

Using JCL procedures will reduce or eliminate these problems. By coding the JCL for an individual job or task and placing it in a procedure library, a programmer who needs to use that JCL can usually code a few JCL statements to execute a procedure that contains dozens or even hundreds of JCL statements.

EXECUTING JCL PROCEDURES

A JCL *procedure* is a group of JCL statements included in the input stream or contained in a procedure library that is executed as a result of coding the procedure name on an EXEC statement. To illustrate, consider the JCL in figure 5-11. Suppose I want to include this JCL in several jobs. One way would be to just code it each time I need it. A better way would be to code it once as a procedure, then call or *invoke* that procedure when I need it.

To invoke a procedure, you code the *procedure name* in an EXEC statement. The form to use for invoking a procedure is:

```
//stepname    EXEC    procedure-name
```

or

```
//stepname    EXEC    PROC=procedure-name
```

When OS encounters an EXEC statement like this, it replaces it with the JCL statements contained in the procedure and begins to execute them. To execute a procedure named PERS01, for example, I will code an EXEC statement like this:

```
//STEP1       EXEC    PROC=PERS01
```

Then, when OS encounters this EXEC statement in my job stream, the JCL contained in PERS01 will be executed.

```
//PERS01    PROC
//E71       EXEC   PGM=E71
//STEPLIB   DD     DSN=MMA.USERLIB,
//                 DISP=SHR
//PARTABLE  DD     DSN=E71TOL,
//                 DISP=OLD
//INVALIST  DD     SYSOUT=A,
//                 DCB=BLKSIZE=133
//          PEND
```

Figure 5-11 A sample JCL procedure

Using instream procedures

A JCL procedure included in the input stream of a job is called an *instream procedure*. It is identified by a PROC statement as the first statement of the procedure and a PEND (procedure end) statement as the last statement of the procedure. The name field in the PROC statement (the field that immediately follows the //) gives a name to the procedure. Thus, the procedure in figure 5-11 is coded as an instream procedure named PERS01.

The instream procedure must appear in the input stream before the EXEC statement that refers to it. Although an instream procedure appears only once in the input stream, it can be executed any number of times by coding EXEC statements that refer to it.

When OS encounters an instream procedure, it doesn't execute the JCL contained in it immediately. It is executed when the EXEC statement is encountered that invokes the procedure. Figure 5-12 shows a job that uses an instream procedure named STEP1A. Here, the sequence in which the programs will be executed is: PROG1, PROG2, PROGA1, and PROGA2. (I've used somewhat meaningless program names to point out the order of execution.) The EXEC statement labeled STEP3 causes the procedure STEP1A to be executed.

Why use instream procedures? Wouldn't it be just as easy to code the JCL statements in their proper order and have OS execute them as it encounters them?

```
//INEXP     JOB    HE66YFNH,
//                 'W. CLARY'
//STEP1A    PROC
//E01       EXEC   PGM=PROGA1
    .
//E02       EXEC   PGM=PROGA2
    .
//          PEND
//STEP1     EXEC   PGM=PROG1
    .
    .
//STEP2     EXEC   PGM=PROG2
    .
    .
//STEP3     EXEC   PROC=STEP1A
//
```

Figure 5-12   A job with an instream procedure

There are two cases when you should use an instream procedure. The first case is when the same set of JCL is to appear more than once in a job, but it's unlikely that that set of JCL will be required by any other job. If the procedure in figure 5-12 was to be executed several times in a job, it might look like figure 5-13, where the procedure is coded once and executed three times.

The second case when you should use an instream procedure is when testing a procedure before placing it into the procedure library. In actual practice, many programmers don't take the time to test their procedures in this manner, although if they did, it would usually save time in the long run. I recommend the use of instream procedures to test the JCL unless your system uses an input device other than a card reader and the manipulation of data is cumbersome. Cards containing the procedure are easily extracted from a job deck and can be used to insert the test procedure into the procedure library. There are also other input devices (CRT screens, for example) that allow flexible data movement so procedures can be extracted from one job stream and inserted into another. However, there are some forms of data input (key-to-tape, for example) where extracting the procedure from the job stream and inserting it into a library-maintenance job

```
//TWREXP    JOB    HE66YFNH,
//                 'W. CLARY'
//STEP1A    PROC
//E01       EXEC   PGM=PROGA1
    .
//E02       EXEC   PGM=PROGA2
    .
//          PEND
//STEP1     EXEC   PGM=PROG1
    .
    .
//STEP2     EXEC   PGM=PROG2
    .
    .
//STEP3     EXEC   PROC=STEP1A
//STEP4     EXEC   PGM=PROG4
    .
//STEP5     EXEC   PROC=STEP1A
//STEP6     EXEC   PROC=STEP1A
//
```

Figure 5-13 An instream procedure that is executed several times during the job

stream is difficult to accomplish. In this case, I suggest you place the procedure in the procedure library and test it there.

When an instream procedure is executed, you can obtain a listing of the input JCL (JCL that is not a part of the procedure) and the procedure JCL by coding a 1 as the first subparameter of the MSGLEVEL parameter on the JOB statement. (At my installation, this is the default value.) Input JCL statements are identified on the listing by the familiar // in the first positions of the statement. The procedure JCL statements are identified by these characters in the first positions of the statement:

- + + Procedure statements as they appear in the procedure (not modified)
- + / Procedure statements that you modify by overriding the statements (this is presented later in this topic)
- + + * Procedure statements other than comment statements that OS considers to be comments (this usually indicates an error)
- *** Comment statements within a procedure

Using cataloged procedures

The term *cataloged procedure* means that the procedure has been placed into a procedure library and can be executed directly by coding the procedure name on an EXEC statement. To illustrate, suppose we tested the instream procedure you saw in figure 5-12 and found it to be satisfactory. Now we want to place it into a library so we can eliminate the need to code it into every job stream that uses it.

To place the procedure into the procedure library, you execute the IEBUPDTE utility program as you learned in the preceding topic. Figure 5-14 shows an example. Notice that the PROC and PEND statements are omitted. That's because they are optional for cataloged procedures. Also notice the SYSIN DD statement. It uses the DD DATA form of instream data definition. This is required to allow JCL to be treated as data in the input stream. Remember, though, that you must code a delimiter statement (/*) after the procedure to mark the end of the procedure.

To execute the cataloged procedure, just code its name on an EXEC statement. Figure 5-15 shows the JCL to execute the same procedure that we executed as an instream procedure in figure 5-13. When executing a cataloged procedure, the JCL listing will print the input JCL with // in the first positions of the statement. The procedure

184 Chapter 5

```
//LIBUP     JOB  HE66YFNH,
//               'W. CLARY'
//UPSTEP    EXEC PGM=IEBUPDTE,
//               PARM=MOD
//SYSPRINT  DD   SYSOUT=A
//SYSUT1    DD   DSN=SYS1.PROCLIB,
//               DISP=SHR
//SYSUT2    DD   DSN=SYS1.PROCLIB,
//               DISP=SHR
//SYSIN     DD   DATA
./ ADD     NAME=STEP1A,LEVEL=00,SOURCE=0,LIST=ALL
./ NUMBER  NEW1=100,INCR=10
//E01       EXEC PGM=PROGA1
   .
   .
   .
//E02       EXEC PGM=PROGA2
   .
   .
   .
./ ENDUP
/*
//
```

Figure 5-14 Placing the tested procedure into the system procedure library


```
//CATPROC   JOB  HE66YFNH,
//               'W. CLARY'
//STEP1     EXEC PGM=PROG1
   .
   .
//STEP2     EXEC PGM=PROG2
   .
   .
//STEP3     EXEC PROC=STEP1A
XXE01       EXEC PGM=PROGA1
   .
   .
XXE02       EXEC PGM=PROGA2
   .
   .
//
```

Figure 5-15 Executing a cataloged procedure

JCL will contain these characters in the first positions of the statement:

    XX   Procedure statements as they appear in the procedure (not modified)

X/   Procedure statements that you modified by overriding the statements (this is presented later in this topic)

XX*   Procedure statements other than comment statements that OS considers to be comments (this usually indicates an error)

***   Comment statements within a procedure

MODIFYING PROCEDURES

The remainder of this topic shows you how to (1) use symbolic parameters in procedures, (2) override, add, and nullify procedure parameters, (3) add DD statements to procedures, and (4) allow for instream input in a procedure. Although I'm going to deal specifically with cataloged procedures, the same principles apply to instream procedures as well.

Using symbolic parameters

Figure 5-16 shows a procedure named EDITLOAN that executes a program named BNKEDIT1. This program reads a file of transactions, edits them for validity, and produces two output files: a disk file of valid transactions and a printout of invalid records. Let's suppose that this procedure is to be used in a number of different ways. Perhaps the same set of JCL could be used for a program named BNKEDIT2. Also suppose that you would like to be able to place the

```
//EDITLOAN PROC
//EDIT1    EXEC PGM=BNKEDIT1
//STEPLIB  DD   DSN=MMA.BANKLIB,
//              DISP=SHR
//TRANS    DD   DSN=LOANTRAN,
//              DISP=OLD
//GOOD     DD   DSN=GOODDATA,
//              DISP=(NEW,KEEP,DELETE),
//              UNIT=2314,
//              VOL=SER=USER01,
//              SPACE=(TRK,(2,1),RLSE),
//              DCB=(LRECL=80,BLKSIZE=960,RECFM=FB)
//BAD      DD   SYSOUT=A,
//              DCB=BLKSIZE=133
```

Figure 5-16   A procedure named EDITLOAN without symbolic parameters

good data file on either a 2314 or 3330 device and that the DCB information can vary from time to time. In this case, you could set up the procedure using *symbolic parameters*. Briefly, this means that you don't define those values in the procedure itself, but rather when you execute the procedure.

A symbolic parameter represents the value of a parameter and is defined by coding one ampersand (&) preceding a key word that you make up. For example, figure 5-17 shows the EDITLOAN procedure with symbolic parameters assigned to the program name, the good data file name, and to the UNIT, VOLUME, SPACE, and DCB parameters. In this case, &PROG, &NAME, &UNIT, &VOL, &SPACE, and &DCB must be replaced by valid values at execution time.

Figure 5-18 shows the JCL to execute the procedure replacing the symbolic parameters with real values. It also shows the way the procedure looks when it is actually executed. Notice that to give values to the symbolic parameters, you don't have to code the ampersand. If a replacement value contains special characters, it must be enclosed in apostrophes. For example, the SPACE and DCB symbolic parameters in figure 5-18 are enclosed in apostrophes because they contain commas and parentheses.

Assigning default values to symbolic parameters Now let's go one step further and say that although *sometimes* you want to change some of the parameters of this procedure, *most* of the time they will be executed just as shown in figure 5-16. In this case, you can assign *default values* to the parameters in the PROC statement, using the same kind of format as was used in the EXEC statement in figure

```
//EDITLOAN  PROC
//EDIT1     EXEC  PGM=&PROG
//STEPLIB   DD    DSN=MMA.BANKLIB,
//                DISP=SHR
//TRANS     DD    DSN=LOANTRAN,
//                DISP=OLD
//GOOD      DD    DSN=&NAME,
//                DISP=(NEW,KEEP,DELETE),
//                UNIT=&UNIT,
//                VOL=SER=&VOL,
//                SPACE=&SPACE,
//                DCB=&DCB
//BAD       DD    SYSOUT=A,
//                DCB=BLKSIZE=133
```

Figure 5-17 The EDITLOAN procedure with symbolic parameters

```
The EXEC statement to execute the procedure:

//EXEDIT    EXEC   PROC=EDITLOAN,
//                 PROG=BNKEDIT2,
//                 NAME=CHECKTRN,
//                 UNIT=3330,
//                 VOL=D00103,
//                 SPACE='(CYL,(1,1),RLSE)',
//                 DCB='(LRECL=80,BLKSIZE=8000,RECFM=FB)'


The procedure as it is executed:

XXEDIT1     EXEC   PGM=BNKEDIT2
XXSTEPLIB   DD     DSN=MMA.BANKLIB,
XX                 DISP=SHR
XXTRANS     DD     DSN=LOANTRAN,
XX                 DISP=OLD
XXGOOD      DD     DSN=CHECKTRN,
XX                 DISP=(NEW,KEEP,DELETE),
XX                 UNIT=3330,
XX                 VOL=SER=D00103,
XX                 SPACE=(CYL,(1,1),RLSE),
XX                 DCB=(LRECL=80,BLKSIZE=8000,RECFM=FB)
XXBAD       DD     SYSOUT=A,
XX                 DCB=BLKSIZE=133
```

Figure 5-18 Executing the EDITLOAN procedure replacing symbolic parameters with their proper values

5-18. Then, if you don't code the parameters in the EXEC statement, the default values will apply.

Figure 5-19 shows this same procedure with symbolic parameters and assigned default values. When you execute the procedure, if you code:

```
//EXEDIT    EXEC   PROC=EDITLOAN
```

with no symbolic parameters, the procedure will be executed just as shown in figure 5-16.

If you code a symbolic parameter when default values are given, only that value will change. For example, figure 5-20 shows the EXEC statement to execute the procedure in figure 5-19 changing only the UNIT and VOLUME parameters. The rest of the symbolic parameters take their values from the assigned default values.

Nullifying symbolic parameters Perhaps you want to nullify symbolic parameters. For example, if you are testing a system and you

```
//EDITLOAN PROC  PROG=BNKEDIT1,
//              NAME=GOODDATA,
//              UNIT=2314,
//              VOL=USER01,
//              SPACE='(TRK,(2,1),RLSE)',
//              DCB='(LRECL=80,BLKSIZE=960,RECFM=FB)'
//EDIT1    EXEC  PGM=&PROG
//STEPLIB  DD    DSN=MMA.BANKLIB,
//              DISP=SHR
//TRANS    DD    DSN=LOANTRAN,
//              DISP=OLD
//GOOD     DD    DSN=&NAME,
//              DISP=(NEW,KEEP,DELETE),
//              UNIT=&UNIT,
//              VOL=SER=&VOL,
//              SPACE=&SPACE,
//              DCB=&DCB
//BAD      DD    SYSOUT=A,
//              DCB=BLKSIZE=133
```

Figure 5-19 Assigning default values to the symbolic parameters in the EDITLOAN procedure

The EXEC statement to execute the procedure:

```
//EXEDIT   EXEC  PROC=EDITLOAN,
//              UNIT=3330,
//              VOL=D00103
```

The procedure as it is executed:

```
XXEDIT1    EXEC  PGM=BNKEDIT1
XXSTEPLIB  DD    DSN=MMA.BANKLIB,
XX               DISP=SHR
XXTRANS    DD    DSN=LOANTRAN,
XX               DISP=OLD
XXGOOD     DD    DSN=GOODDATA,
XX               DISP=(NEW,KEEP,DELETE),
XX               UNIT=3330,
XX               VOL=SER=D00103,
XX               SPACE=(TRK,(2,1),RLSE),
XX               DCB=(LRECL=80,BLKSIZE=960,RECFM=FB)
XXBAD      DD    SYSOUT=A,
XX               DCB=BLKSIZE=133
```

Figure 5-20 Executing the EDITLOAN procedure replacing some symbolic parameters while allowing others to default

want one of the files to be a dummy file, you could code a symbolic parameter to be replaced by either the positional parameter DUMMY (during the test) or by spaces (during production runs). Figure 5-21 shows a procedure like this. It also shows the EXEC statement to execute the procedure, replacing the symbolic parameter with the positional parameter DUMMY, and the procedure as it looks when executed. Here, it's important to note that whenever you code a symbolic parameter for a positional parameter, you should use a period for a field delimiter as shown in the NUMBERS DD statement. Then, if you nullify that symbolic parameter, the period will be deleted and will not precede another parameter. If you code a comma as a field delimiter here, the comma will remain, possibly causing a JCL error.

Notice that the replacement value in the EXEC statement calling the procedure includes a comma (to act as a field delimiter replacing the period). As a result, the value must be enclosed in apostrophes.

Figure 5-22 shows an EXEC statement to execute the same procedure, but this time with the symbolic parameter nullified. The

The procedure:

```
//CALCPROC  PROC
//CALCSTEP  EXEC   PGM=CALCPROG
//STEPLIB   DD     DSN=MMA.USERLIB,
//                 DISP=SHR
//NUMBERS   DD     &DUM.DSN=NUMFILE,
//                 DISP=OLD
//RESULTS   DD     SYSOUT=A
```

The EXEC statement to execute the procedure:

```
//EXCALC    EXEC   PROC=CALCPROC,
//                 &DUM='DUMMY,'
```

The procedure as it is executed:

```
XXCALCSTEP EXEC   PGM=CALCPROG
XXSTEPLIB  DD     DSN=MMA.USERLIB,
XX                DISP=SHR
XXNUMBERS  DD     DUMMY,DSN=NUMFILE,
XX                DISP=OLD
XXRESULTS  DD     SYSOUT=A
```

Figure 5-21 Executing a procedure replacing a symbolic parameter with DUMMY

```
The EXEC statement to execute the procedure in figure 5-21:


//EXCALC    EXEC   PROC=CALCPROC,
//                 &DUM=


The procedure as it is executed:

XXCALCSTEP  EXEC  PGM=CALCPROG
XXSTEPLIB   DD    DSN=MMA.USERLIB,
XX                DISP=SHR
XXNUMBERS   DD    DSN=NUMFILE,
XX                DISP=OLD
XXRESULTS   DD    SYSOUT=A
```

Figure 5-22 Nullifying a symbolic parameter

---

spaces after the equal sign cause the symbolic parameter to be deleted. The general form to nullify a symbolic parameter is:

```
symbolic-parameter=
```

Overriding procedure parameters

Now you know how to write procedures with symbolic parameters and how to execute those procedures replacing symbolic parameters with either execution-time values or default values. But what if you want to use a procedure that was set up without symbolic parameters, or one that doesn't contain a symbolic parameter for the value you want to change? You can still change a parameter in a procedure even when no symbolic parameter was assigned to it by coding *override statements*.

Overriding the EXEC statement in a procedure You can override parameters on EXEC statements within a procedure by coding:

```
parameter.procstepname=value
```

where parameter is the name of the parameter you want to override and procstepname is the name of the procedure step in which the EXEC statement is located. This will change the procedure EXEC statement parameter to the value you code after the equal sign.

Alternatively, you can code:

```
parameter=value
```

This form will cause differing results depending on the parameter being overridden. If the parameter is PARM, it applies only to the first procedure step. If the parameter is TIME, it applies to the entire procedure. If the parameter is any other EXEC statement parameter, it applies to every step in the procedure.

To illustrate, figure 5-23 shows a cataloged procedure with two steps. Suppose you want to execute this procedure, but you need to change the REGION on both steps to 120K, the PARM in the first step to 'MONDAY', and the COND in the second step to (4,LE,EXSTEP). A valid EXEC statement is shown in figure 5-23, along with the procedure as it will look when executed.

Overriding DD statements in a procedure You can also override DD statements contained in a procedure. To do this, you code:

```
//procstepname.ddname   DD   parameter=value
```

This will cause the parameter value coded on your override statement to replace the parameter coded on the DD statement in the procedure. A word of caution, however, is in order: the override statements modifying several DD statements must be in the same order as the DD statements appear in the procedure. In other words, if a procedure step contains DD1, DD2, and DD3 DD statements in that order and you are changing parameters on all three, the override statements in the input stream must also be in that same order (procstepname.DD1, procstepname.DD2, procstepname.DD3).

To illustrate what I've been saying, look again at figure 5-23. Let's say that you now must change the DCB on RPFILE to (LRECL=80,BLKSIZE=960,RECFM=FB) and the DISP of INRPT to (OLD,PASS). Figure 5-24 shows the EXEC statement and the DD statements to override these parameters along with the procedure as it will appear when executed.

When changing a DCB parameter, only the values you code on the override DD statement will be changed. For example, if a procedure contains a DCB parameter like this:

```
//          DCB=(LRECL=80,BLKSIZE=160,RECFM=FB)
```

and you code an override DD statement that contains this:

```
//          DCB=LRECL=160
```

192   Chapter 5

```
The procedure:

//EXTPROC   PROC
//EXSTEP    EXEC  PGM=EXTRACT,
//                REGION=100K,
//                COND=(4,LE),
//                PARM='FRIDAY'
//STEPLIB   DD    DSN=MMA.USERLIB,
//                DISP=SHR
//MAST      DD    DSN=ACCTMAST,
//                DISP=OLD
//RPFILE    DD    DSN=&&RPT1,
//                DISP=(NEW,PASS),
//                UNIT=SYSDA,
//                SPACE=(CYL,(5,2),RLSE),
//                DCB=(LRECL=100,BLKSIZE=1000,RECFM=FB)
//RPSTEP    EXEC  PGM=RPT220,
//                REGION=90K,
//                COND=(8,LE,EXSTEP)
//STEPLIB   DD    DSN=MMA.USERLIB,
//                DISP=SHR
//INRPT     DD    DSN=&&RPT1,
//                DISP=(OLD,DELETE)
//RPT01     DD    SYSOUT=A,
//                DCB=BLKSIZE=133
```

The EXEC statement to execute the procedure:

```
//EXEXT     EXEC  PROC=EXTPROC,
//                REGION=120K,
//                PARM.EXSTEP='MONDAY',
//                COND.RPSTEP=(4,LE,EXSTEP)
```

The procedure as it is executed:

```
XXEXSTEP    EXEC  PGM=EXTRACT,
XX                REGION=120K,
XX                COND=(4,LE),
XX                PARM='MONDAY'
XXSTEPLIB   DD    DSN=MMA.USERLIB,
XX                DISP=SHR
XXMAST      DD    DSN=ACCTMAST,
XX                DISP=OLD
XXRPFILE    DD    DSN=&&RPT1,
XX                DISP=(NEW,PASS),
XX                UNIT=SYSDA,
XX                SPACE=(CYL,(5,2),RLSE),
XX                DCB=(LRECL=100,BLKSIZE=1000,RECFM=FB)
XXRPSTEP    EXEC  PGM=RP220,
XX                REGION=120K,
XX                COND=(4,LE,EXSTEP)
XXSTEPLIB   DD    DSN=MMA.USERLIB,
XX                DISP=SHR
XXINRPT     DD    DSN=&&RPT1,
XX                DISP=(OLD,DELETE)
XXRPT01     DD    SYSOUT=A,
XX                DCB=BLKSIZE=133
```

Figure 5-23   Overriding the EXEC parameters in a procedure

Libraries and Procedures   193

```
The EXEC and DD statements to execute the procedure:

//EXTRACT     EXEC  PROC=EXTPROC
//EXSTEP.RPFILE  DD  DCB=(LRECL=80,BLKSIZE=960,RECFM=FB)
//RPSTEP.INRPT   DD  DISP=(OLD,PASS)

The procedure as it is executed:

XXEXSTEP    EXEC  PGM=EXTRACT,
XX                REGION=100K,
XX                COND=(4,LE),
XX                PARM='FRIDAY'
XXSTEPLIB   DD    DSN=MMA.USERLIB,
XX                DISP=SHR
XXMAST      DD    DSN=ACCTMAST,
XX                DISP=OLD
X/RPFILE    DD    DSN=&&RPT1,
X/                DISP=(NEW,PASS),
X/                UNIT=SYSDA,
X/                SPACE=(CYL,(5,2),RLSE),
X/                DCB=(LRECL=80,BLKSIZE=960,RECFM=FB)
XXRPSTEP    EXEC  PGM=RPT220,
XX                REGION=90K,
XX                COND=(8,LE,EXSTEP)
XXSTEPLIB   DD    DSN=MMA.USERLIB,
XX                DISP=SHR
X/INRPT     DD    DSN=&&RPT1,
X/                DISP=(OLD,PASS)
XXRPT01     DD    SYSOUT=A,
XX                DCB=BLKSIZE=133
```

Figure 5-24 Overriding the DD parameters in a procedure

then the procedure will be executed with the DCB looking like this:

```
//              DCB=(LRECL=160,BLKSIZE=160,RECFM=FB)
```

Adding and nullifying parameters in a procedure

Figure 5-25 shows a one-step procedure. In order to illustrate adding and nullifying parameters on the EXEC and DD statements within a procedure, suppose you want to (1) remove the COND parameter from the EXEC statement, (2) add a REGION parameter with a value of 100K, (3) remove the UNIT and VOLUME information from TABLE24, and (4) add a DCB to INTRPT with a value of BLKSIZE = 133. To do this, you would code the additional parameters just as you would if you were changing a parameter; you would code the nullified parameters the same way, but with blank values. Figure 5-25 shows the EXEC and DD statements to execute the procedure described

Chapter 5

The procedure:

```
//INTCALC   PROC
//INTSTEP   EXEC  PGM=STDCALC1,
//                COND=(4,LE)
//STEPLIB   DD    DSN=MMA.USERLIB,
//                DISP=SHR
//LOANFILE  DD    DSN=BANKLMST,
//                DISP=OLD
//TABLE24   DD    DSN=FORMTAB,
//                DISP=OLD,
//                UNIT=2400,
//                VOL=SER=0965
//INTRPT    DD    SYSOUT=A
```

The EXEC and DD statements to execute the procedure:

```
//GETINT    EXEC  PROC=INTCALC,
//                COND.INTSTEP=,
//                REGION=100K
//INTSTEP.TABLE24  DD  UNIT=,
//                VOL=
//INTSTEP.INTRPT   DD  DCB=BLKSIZE=133
```

The procedure as it is executed:

```
XXINTSTEP  EXEC  PGM=STDCALC1,
XX               REGION=100K
XXSTEPLIB  DD    DSN=MMA.USERLIB,
XX               DISP=SHR
XXLOANFILE DD    DSN=BANKLMST,
XX               DISP=OLD
X/TABLE24  DD    DSN=FORMTAB,
X/               DISP=OLD
X/INTRPT   DD    SYSOUT=A,DCB=BLKSIZE=133
```

Figure 5-25 A procedure with added and nullified parameters

along with the procedure as it appears when executed. Notice that OS automatically takes care of inserting and deleting the commas that separate parameters.

Adding a DD statement to a procedure

Looking again at figure 5-25, suppose you had to add a completely new DD statement—let's say another output file. To do this, just code the DD statement as required, as you normally would code it, and give it a ddname that follows this format:

```
//procstepname.ddname    DD    operands
```

When you use this technique, be sure to place the added DD statements after all the override DD statements.

Figure 5-26 illustrates a procedure step as written, the EXEC statement to call the procedure, and the added DD statement. Also shown is the procedure as it appears when executed.

Including input in a procedure stream

You can't code DD * or DD DATA statements in a procedure, but there is a way to include input data in the input stream. To do this, you need to learn a new DD statement parameter: DDNAME. It is coded only on DD statements in a procedure, and it refers to a DD statement in the step that calls the procedure.

To illustrate, look at figure 5-27. It shows a procedure to execute an edit program that requires data in its input stream (defined by

```
The procedure:

//RPPROC    PROC
//RPT01     EXEC  PGM=RPTPROG
//STEPLIB   DD    DSN=MMA.USERLIB,
//                DISP=SHR
//MAST      DD    DSN=CUSTFILE,
//                DISP=OLD
//RPT       DD    SYSOUT=A

The EXEC and DD statements to execute the procedure:

//EXRP        EXEC  PROC=RPPROC
//RPT01.TABLE DD    DSN=TABLE01,
//                  DISP=OLD,
//                  DCB=DSORG=IS

The procedure as it is executed:

XXRPT01    EXEC  PGM=RPTPROG
XXSTEPLIB  DD    DSN=MMA.USERLIB,
XX               DISP=SHR
XXMAST     DD    DSN=CUSTFILE,
XX               DISP=OLD
XXRPT      DD    SYSOUT=A
//TABLE    DD    DSN=TABLE01,
//               DISP=OLD,
//               DCB=DSORG=IS
```

Figure 5-26 Adding a DD statement to a procedure

The procedure:

```
//EDITPROC  PROC
//EDIT      EXEC  PGM=EDITTRAN
//STEPLIB   DD    DSN=MMA.USERLIB,
//                DISP=SHR
//DATAIN    DD    DDNAME=INTRANS
//GOODDATA  DD    DSN=&&GOODTRAN,
//                DISP=(NEW,PASS),
//                UNIT=SYSDA,
//                SPACE=(80,(100,10),RLSE),
//                DCB=(LRECL=80,BLKSIZE=80,RECFM=FB)
//BADDATA   DD    SYSOUT=A
```

The EXEC and DD statements to execute the procedure:

```
//EDIT1     EXEC  PROC=EDITPROC
//INTRANS   DD    *
                  transactions
/*
```

The procedure as it is executed:

```
XXEDIT      EXEC  PGM=EDITTRAN
XXSTEPLIB   DD    DSN=MMA.USERLIB,
XX                DISP=SHR
XXDATAIN    DD    *
                  transactions
/*
XXGOODDATA  DD    DSN=&&GOODTRAN,
XX                DISP=(NEW,PASS),
XX                UNIT=SYSDA,
XX                SPACE=(80,(100,10),RLSE),
XX                DCB=(LRECL=80,BLKSIZE=80,RECFM=FB)
XXBADDATA   DD    SYSOUT=A
```

Figure 5-27 Executing a procedure with the DDNAME parameter to refer to an instream data file

DATAIN). If this set of JCL were not a procedure, but executed in an input stream, DATAIN could be coded as:

```
//DATAIN    DD    *
```

followed by the transactions to be edited and then by a delimiter. But since it is a procedure, I have coded it like this:

```
//DATAIN    DD    DDNAME=INTRANS
```

to refer to the real input file in the step that calls the procedure. That means the execution JCL will have to include a DD statement with a ddname of INTRANS for the input file. The middle part of figure 5-27 shows this DD statement, while the last part shows the procedure as

Libraries and Procedures **197**

it will actually be executed. Notice that the DDNAME parameter causes the input data to be read in its proper place in the procedure.

GENERAL RULES GOVERNING THE USE OF PROCEDURES

There are a few rules you should be aware of when you're working with procedures:

1. Procedures cannot contain JOB, delimiter, NULL, JOBLIB, DD *, or DD DATA statements.
2. A procedure cannot execute another procedure.
3. You cannot execute a procedure in the same job that updates the procedure in the library.

A COMPLETE EXAMPLE

To help you grasp all of the new concepts and techniques presented in this chapter, I want to show you an example with many of the techniques applied. It will recap the major functions applicable to JCL procedures.

Figure 5-28 shows the system chart for the example system. This is a system for controlling a leasing operation. Lease transactions are to be read in the input stream and edited. The good transactions are used to update the lease master file and to produce two reports. However, the system applies to two similar applications with different file characteristics, one for equipment and the other for real estate. As a result, there are certain parameters in the JCL that I know will change from job to job, so I'll code them as symbolic parameters.

Figure 5-29 shows the job to place the procedure in the procedure library (SYS1.PROCLIB). Notice that the procedure name is LEASE and that it contains symbolic parameters with assigned default values. The ADD statement for IEBUPDTE specifies a new member; the NUMBER statement causes each line in the member to be sequenced from 100 by 10; and the ENDUP statement marks the end of the IEBUPDTE input.

After the IEBUPDTE job has been executed, if you want to execute the procedure with all its default values, you code:

```
//EXLEASE   EXEC   PROC=LEASE
//LSINPUT   DD    *
     transactions
/*
```

If, on the other hand, you want to change the edit program name and the lease master file name, you code:

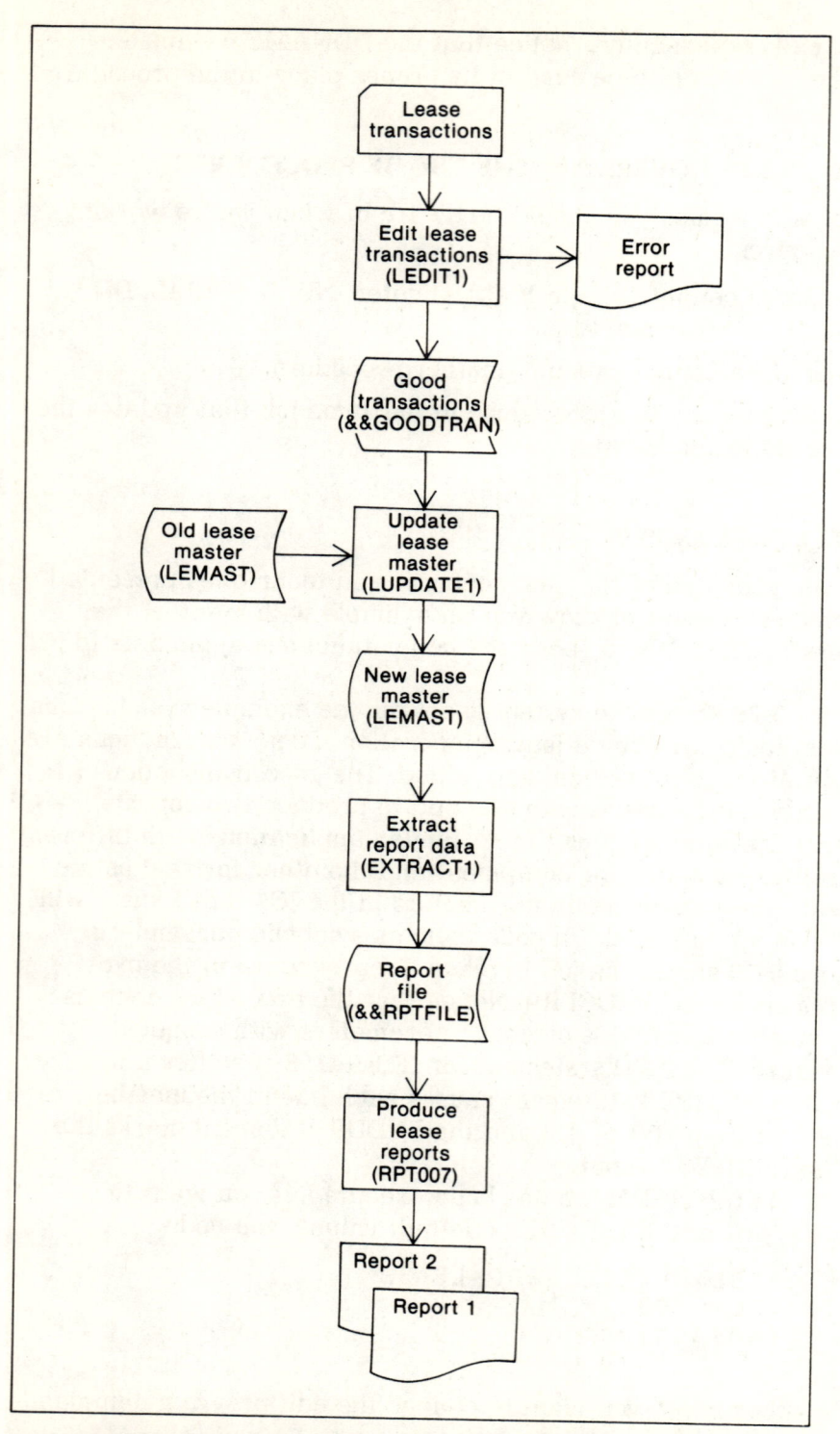

Figure 5-28 System flowchart for a job that uses cataloged procedures

```
//ADDPROC  JOB   HE66YFNH,
//               'W. CLARY'
//UPDATE   EXEC  PGM=IEBUPDTE,
//               PARM=MOD
//SYSPRINT DD    SYSOUT=A
//SYSUT1   DD    DSN=SYS1.PROCLIB,
//               DISP=SHR
//SYSUT2   DD    DSN=SYS1.PROCLIB,
//               DISP=SHR
//SYSIN    DD    DATA
./ ADD    NAME=LEASE,LEVEL=00,SOURCE=0,LIST=ALL
./ NUMBER NEW1=100,INCR=10
//LEASE    PROC  EPROG=LEDIT1,
//               UPROG=LUPDATE1,
//               MAST=LEMAST,
//               XRPT=EXTRACT1,
//               RPROG=RPT007
//LSEDIT   EXEC  PGM=&EPROG
//STEPLIB  DD    DSN=MMA.USERLIB,
//               DISP=SHR
//LSTRANS  DD    DDNAME=LSINPUT
//GOODDATA DD    DSN=&&GOODTRAN,
//               DISP=(NEW,PASS),
//               UNIT=SYSDA,
//               SPACE=(TRK,(50,20),RLSE),
//               DCB=(LRECL=80,BLKSIZE=960,RECFM=FB)
//BADDATA  DD    SYSOUT=A
//LSUPDT   EXEC  PGM=&UPROG,
//               COND=(4,LE,LSEDIT)
//STEPLIB  DD    DSN=MMA.USERLIB,
//               DISP=SHR
//LSUPTRN  DD    DSN=&&GOODTRAN,
//               DISP=(OLD,DELETE)
//OLDMAST  DD    DSN=&MAST(0),
//               DISP=OLD
//NEWMAST  DD    DSN=&MAST(+1),
//               DISP=(NEW,CATLG),
//               UNIT=2314,
//               VOL=SER=USER20,
//               SPACE=(CYL,12,,CONTIG),
//               DCB=(LRECL=60,BLKSIZE=2400,RECFM=FB)
//LSRPTEX  EXEC  PGM=&XRPT,
//               COND=(4,LE,LSEDIT)
//STEPLIB  DD    DSN=MMA.USERLIB,
//               DISP=SHR
//LSMAST   DD    DSN=&MAST(+1),
//               DISP=OLD
//RPTFILE  DD    DSN=&&RPTFILE,
//               DISP=(NEW,PASS),
//               UNIT=SYSDA,
//               SPACE=(CYL,(6,1),RLSE),
//               DCB=*.LSMAST
```

Figure 5-29 A job that places the lease procedure in the system procedure library (part 1 of 2)

```
//LSRPT     EXEC  PGM=&RPROG,
//                COND=(4,LE,LSEDIT)
//STEPLIB   DD    DSN=MMA.USERLIB,
//                DISP=SHR
//RPTDATA   DD    DSN=&&RPTFILE,
//                DISP=(OLD,DELETE)
//RPT1      DD    SYSOUT=A,
//                DCB=BLKSIZE=133
//RPT2      DD    SYSOUT=A,
//                DCB=BLKSIZE=133
./ ENDUP
/*
//
```

Figure 5-29 A job that places the lease procedure in the system procedure library (part 2 of 2)

```
//EXLEASE   EXEC  PROC=LEASE,
//                EPROG=LEDIT2,
//                MAST=LRMAST
//LSINPUT   DD    *
     transactions
/*
```

The result of this JCL is that LEDIT2, not LEDIT1, will be executed in the procedure step named LSEDIT, and the file referenced by the DD statements OLDMAST, NEWMAST, and LSMAST will be LRMAST instead of LEMAST. The other symbolic parameters will assume their assigned default values. In any event, LSINPUT defines the transaction file in the input stream that will be read by the edit program when it reads LSTRANS.

If the update program is changed to put out a report, I'll change the procedure accordingly. But to test the program before changing the procedure, I'll add a DD statement to the job stream to include the report by coding this:

```
//EXLEASE       EXEC  PROC=LEASE
//LSINPUT       DD    *
     transactions
/*
//LSUPDT.UPRPT  DD    SYSOUT=A
```

If a step that requires access to the good transaction file is to be included after the procedure, I have to change the DISP of that file in the last step that uses it. Instead of deleting it, I want OS to pass it so the added step can use it. Figure 5-30 shows how to handle this situation. After the LSINPUT file, I have to include a DD statement with the new DISP information. This statement identifies the procedure step (LSUPDT) and the ddname (LSUPTRN) of the file the new DISP applies to.

```
//EXLEASE   EXEC   PROC=LEASE
//LSINPUT   DD   *
             transactions
/*
//LSUPDT.LSUPTRN   DD   DISP=(OLD,PASS)
//NEWSTEP   EXEC   PGM=RPTGOOD
//STEPLIB   DD   DSN=MMA.USERLIB,
//              DISP=SHR
//GOODDATA DD   DSN=&&GOODTRAN,
//              DISP=(OLD,DELETE)
//RPT3      DD   SYSOUT=A,
//              DCB=BLKSIZE=133
```

Figure 5-30 Overriding parameters in the lease procedure

If I want NEWMAST to be cataloged on tape instead of a 2314 disk pack, I will code it like this:

```
//EXLEASE   EXEC   PROC=LEASE
//LSINPUT   DD   *
             transactions
/*
//LSUPDT.NEWMAST   DD   UNIT=2400
//              VOL=SER=01278,
//              SPACE=
```

This changes the UNIT and VOL values and deletes the SPACE operand entirely.

I think you have the idea by now. But before you go on, take another look at figure 5-29. I've included it in the problems for this topic.

Terminology

procedure   cataloged procedure
invoking a procedure   symbolic parameter
procedure name   default value
instream procedure   override statement

Objectives

1. Given a cataloged procedure residing on the system procedure library and job specifications, write the JCL statements to execute the procedure.

2. Given job specifications, write a procedure that includes symbolic parameters, default values, and instream data file definition.

Problems

1. (Related to objective 1) If the procedure in figure 5-29 was executed using the JCL in figure 5-31, write the procedure as it would appear when executed.

2. (Objective 1) Write the EXEC and DD statements necessary to execute the procedure in figure 5-29 using the following job specifications:

   a. Use default values for all symbolic parameters except &MAST. The value replacing &MAST should be LSFILE1.

   b. Add a DD statement to the LSUPDT step to define a report whose (1) ddname is RPT7, (2) SYSOUT class is A, and (3) block size is 133.

   c. Change the UNIT and VOLUME information for NEWMAST in the LSUPDT step to refer to a 3330 disk pack named GDC3330.

3. (Objective 2) Write a procedure that allows for different program names, file names, UNIT values, VOLUME values, and DCB values, using the following job specifications:

   a. The procedure contains one step.

   b. The program name should be a symbolic parameter with an assigned default value of GENPROG2. Use MMA.USERLIB as a STEPLIB.

   c. The input file name should be a symbolic parameter with an assigned default value of GENDATA2. The disposition of this file should be OLD.

```
//EXLEASE   EXEC   PROC=LEASE,
//                 EPROG=LEDIT5,
//                 MAST=LEASFILE,
//                 COND.LSUPDT=(8,LE,LSEDIT)
//LSINPUT   DD    *
           transactions
/*
//LSEDIT.GOODDATA    DD    DISP=(MOD,PASS),
//                SPACE=,
//                DCB=(LRECL=,BLKSIZE=,RECFM=)
//LSUPDT.LSUPRPT    DD    SYSOUT=A,
//                DCB=BLKSIZE=133
//LSRPT.RPTDATA    DD    DISP=(OLD,PASS)
```

Figure 5-31 JCL to execute the lease procedure

d. The output file is a report. Its SYSOUT class should be a symbolic parameter with an assigned default value of A. No DCB information is required.

e. Make up your own procedure, step, DD, and symbolic parameter names.

Solutions

1. Figure 5-32 is an acceptable solution.
2. Figure 5-33 is an acceptable solution.
3. Figure 5-34 is an acceptable solution. Notice that you only have to code symbolic parameters for the parameters you want to assign default values to. If you want to add other EXEC or DD information at execution time, you can code it in your execution JCL.

```
XXLSEDIT     EXEC  PGM=LEDIT5
XXSTEPLIB    DD    DSN=MMA.USERLIB,
XX                 DISP=SHR
XXLSTRANS    DD    *
             transactions
/*
X/GOODDATA   DD    DSN=&&GOODTRAN,
X/                 DISP=(MOD,PASS),
X/                 UNIT=SYSDA
XXBADDATA    DD    SYSOUT=A
XXLSUPDT     EXEC  PGM=LUPDATE1,
XX                 COND=(8,LE,LSEDIT)
XXSTEPLIB    DD    DSN=MMA.USERLIB,
XX                 DISP=SHR
XXLSUPTRN    DD    DSN=&&GOODTRAN,
XX                 DISP=(OLD,DELETE)
XXOLDMAST    DD    DSN=LEASFILE(0),
XX                 DISP=OLD
XXNEWMAST    DD    DSN=LEASFILE(+1),
XX                 DISP=(NEW,CATLG),
XX                 UNIT=2314,
XX                 VOL=SER=USER20,
XX                 SPACE=(CYL,12,,CONTIG),
XX                 DCB=(LRECL=60,BLKSIZE=2400,RECFM=FB)
X/LSUPRPT    DD    SYSOUT=A,
X/                 DCB=BLKSIZE=133
XXLSRPTEX    EXEC  PGM=EXTRACT1,
XX                 COND=(4,LE,LSEDIT)
XXSTEPLIB    DD    DSN=MMA.USERLIB,
XX                 DISP=SHR
XXLSMAST     DD    DSN=LEASFILE(+1),
XX                 DISP=OLD
XXRPTFILE    DD    DSN=&&RPTFILE,
XX                 DISP=(NEW,PASS),
XX                 UNIT=SYSDA,
XX                 SPACE=(CYL,(6,1),RLSE),
XX                 DCB=*.LSMAST
XXLSRPT      EXEC  PGM=RPT007,
XX                 COND=(4,LE,LSEDIT)
XXSTEPLIB    DD    DSN=MMA.USERLIB,
XX                 DISP=SHR
X/RPTDATA    DD    DSN=&&RPTFILE,
X/                 DISP=(OLD,PASS)
XXRPT1       DD    SYSOUT=A,
XX                 DCB=BLKSIZE=133
XXRPT2       DD    SYSOUT=A,
XX                 DCB=BLKSIZE=133
```

Figure 5-32 The lease procedure as executed by the JCL in figure 5-31

```
//EXLEASE    EXEC   PROC=LEASE,
//                  MAST=LSFILE1
//LSINPUT    DD    *
             transactions
/*
//LSUPDT.NEWMAST   DD   UNIT=3330,
//                      VOL=SER=GDC3330
//LSUPDT.RPT7   DD   SYSOUT=A,
//                   DCB=BLKSIZE=133
```
Note: The DD statements must be in this order.

Figure 5-33 Executing the lease procedure with an alternate master file, alternate DD information, and a new output file

```
//GENPROC    PROC   PROG=GENPROG2,
//                  FILE=GENDATA2,
//                  CLASS=A
//GENSTEP    EXEC   PGM=&PROG
//STEPLIB    DD     DSN=MMA.USERLIB,
//                  DISP=SHR
//GENIN      DD     DSN=&FILE,
//                  DISP=OLD
//GENRPT     DD     SYSOUT=&CLASS
```

Figure 5-34 A procedure with symbolic parameters and default values

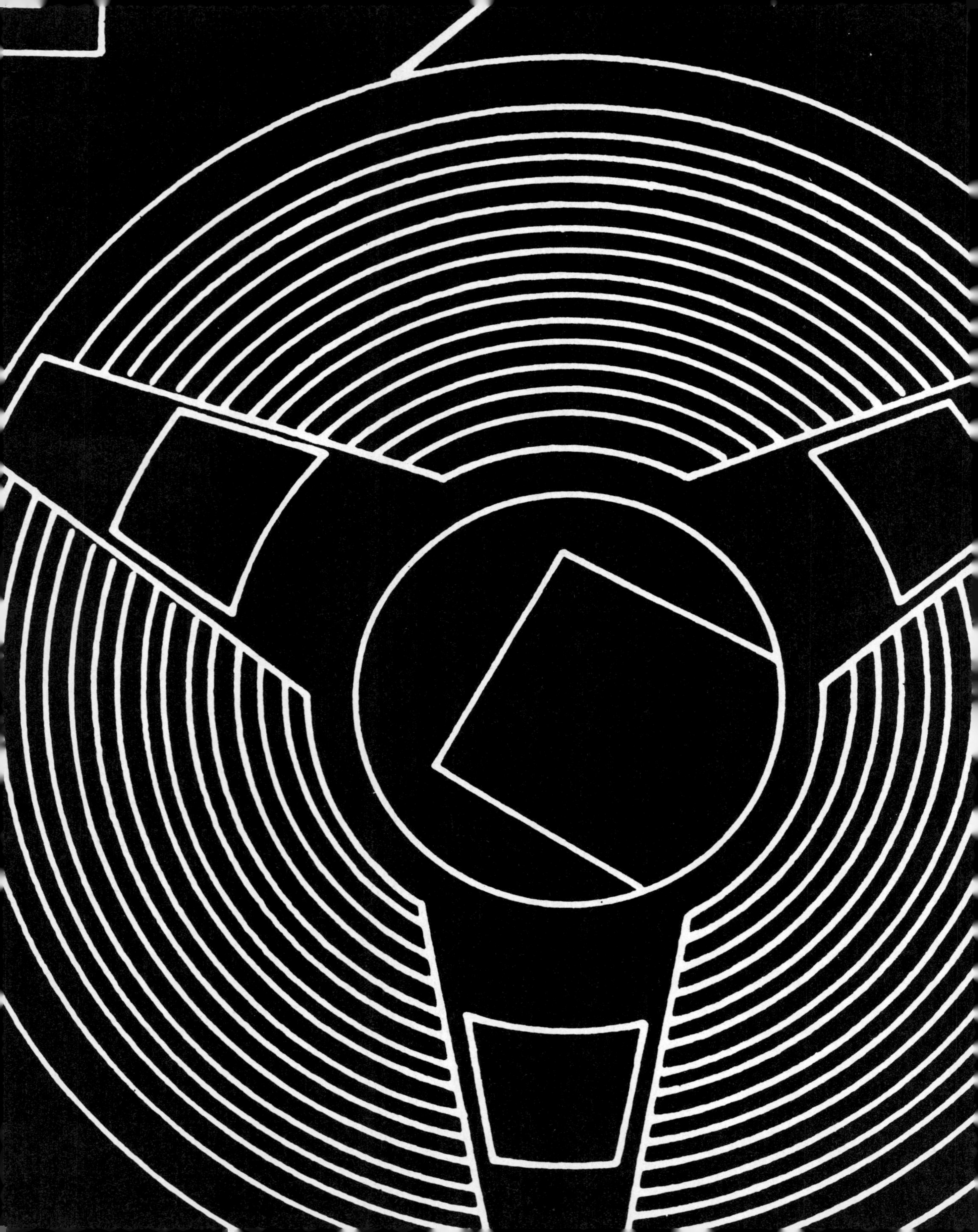

6

JCL for OS/VS Environment

If I were to present the quantity of material on OS virtual storage systems that could easily be covered, this chapter would be larger than the rest of the book. So keep in mind that this is an introductory treatment, and that almost all of the JCL you have learned applies directly to OS/VS systems. As a result, this chapter will cover the fundamentals of virtual storage systems. Topic 1 introduces the concept of virtual storage as it applies to OS/VS systems and the additional JCL parameters available. Topic 2 is a discussion of VSAM (Virtual Storage Access Method) file handling.

TOPIC 1   Conceptual Background and Additional JCL for Virtual Storage Systems

1

In chapter 1, I briefly touched on the subject of virtual storage so you would have some idea what the term meant. Now, I want to give you a more detailed explanation of how virtual storage works on the System/370. Then, I'll explain what new JCL parameters apply to virtual storage systems.

VIRTUAL STORAGE CONCEPTS

The System/370 is designed to allow the simulation of a large amount of *virtual storage* on a CPU with much less *real storage*. For example, a 2048K byte virtual storage CPU might be simulated on a CPU with only 768K bytes of actual, or real, storage. This simulation is accomplished by using disk storage as an extension of CPU storage.

During processing, only small portions of the programs being executed are actually present in real storage. The parts of the programs that aren't currently being used are stored on disk. As additional portions of programs are required, other parts that are no longer needed are written out to the disk and new ones replace them.

There are three advanced versions of OS available for use on the System/370: VS1, VS2, and MVS (where VS stands for virtual storage). However, MVS is simply a more advanced version of VS2 that allows for up to 16 processors, not just one, to be operating at the same time. The operating system can switch off between processors, so you never know where your program is actually running. For the purposes of this book, VS2 and MVS are so similar that any references to VS2 will apply to MVS as well. VS1 and VS2 are structured much like MFT and MVT, but they make use of the virtual storage features of the 370 CPUs.

OS/VS1

Figure 6-1 illustrates the relationships between simulated, or virtual, storage, and real storage in VS1. It also illustrates the terms related to IBM virtual storage. Here, real storage consists of a supervisor area plus a *page pool*. The page pool area consists of portions of the programs currently being multiprogrammed. These program portions are fixed-size blocks, 2K bytes in length, called *pages*. The 2K blocks of real storage they occupy are called *page frames*.

As a program is executed, required pages are brought into real storage from disk. If the page that was already in storage was changed during its execution, then it is written back on the disk. This shuttling of pages back and forth from CPU storage to disk storage is called *paging*, or *swapping*. The result of paging is a system that appears to the user as 512K bytes of storage containing a supervisor and several full programs being multiprogrammed.

Page and page frame management, then, is like another operating system level below the normal functions of MFT. In fact, VS1 can be thought of as virtual storage managed by MFT, with a second-level operating system that simulates the large MFT system on a smaller amount of real storage.

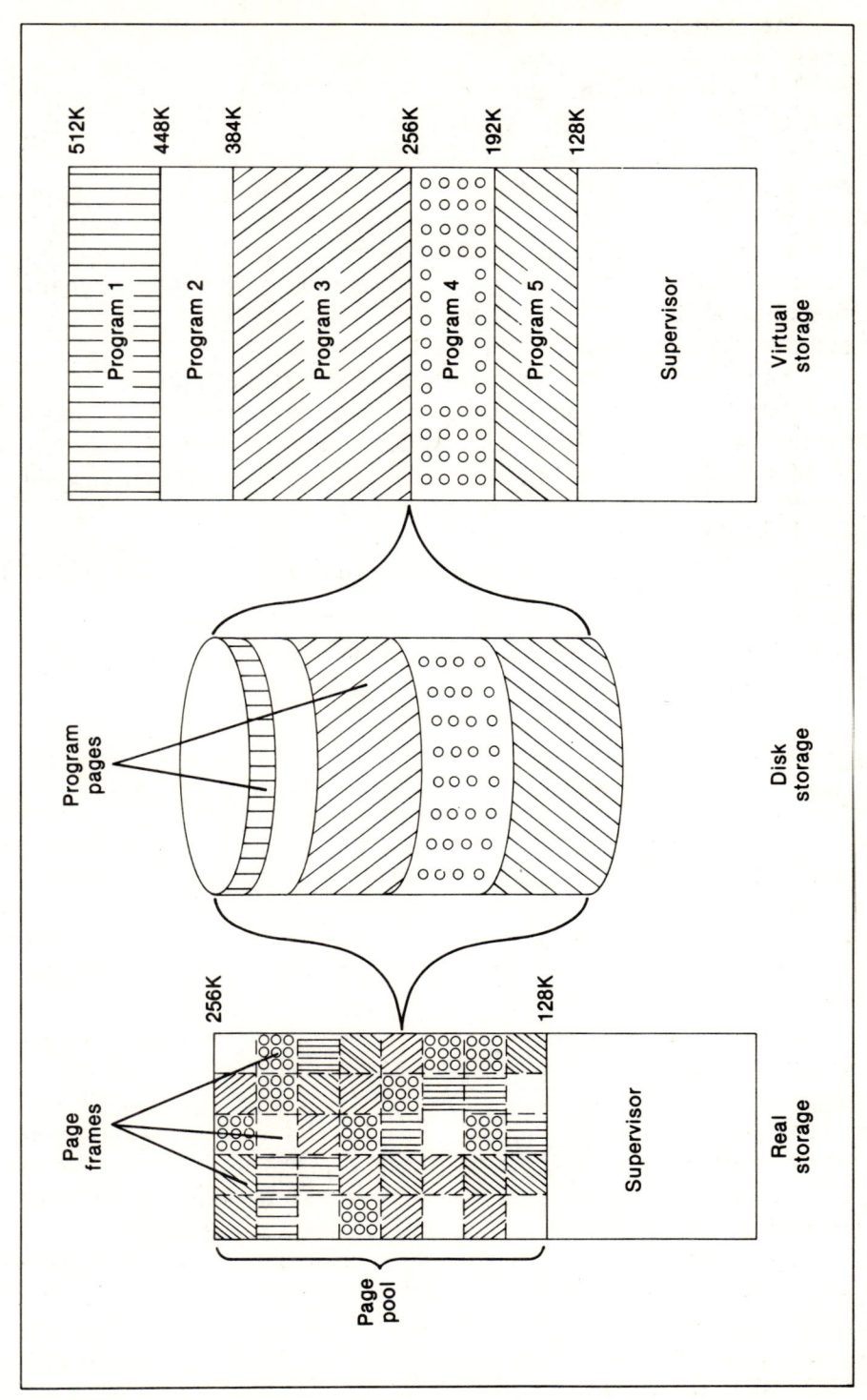

Figure 6-1 The concept of virtual storage on the System/370

That's quite a mouthful, but I think figure 6-2 will help you understand what I'm saying. It shows how a virtual storage area of 768K, used in much the same way as the MFT system, is simulated in 256K of real CPU storage through VS1. In other words, the real storage area that's shown is the physical system; the virtual storage area is how the system appears to the user. Except for the supervisor area, real storage is divided into 2K page frames to form a page pool for use in executing the programs to be run on the virtual machine. The simulated CPU storage area is divided into problem program partitions just as in MFT, plus two additional areas unique to VS1: the pageable supervisor area and the V = R area.

The *pageable supervisor area* is used just as its name implies. Since the VS1 supervisor is so large, only the most heavily used parts of it are permanently kept in the 80K supervisor area of real storage. The less frequently used parts are run in the pageable supervisor area of virtual storage. In figure 6-2, 128K is allocated for this partition. This means, of course, that only a small portion of the supervisor is likely to be present in real storage at one time. The rest of it will be stored on disk.

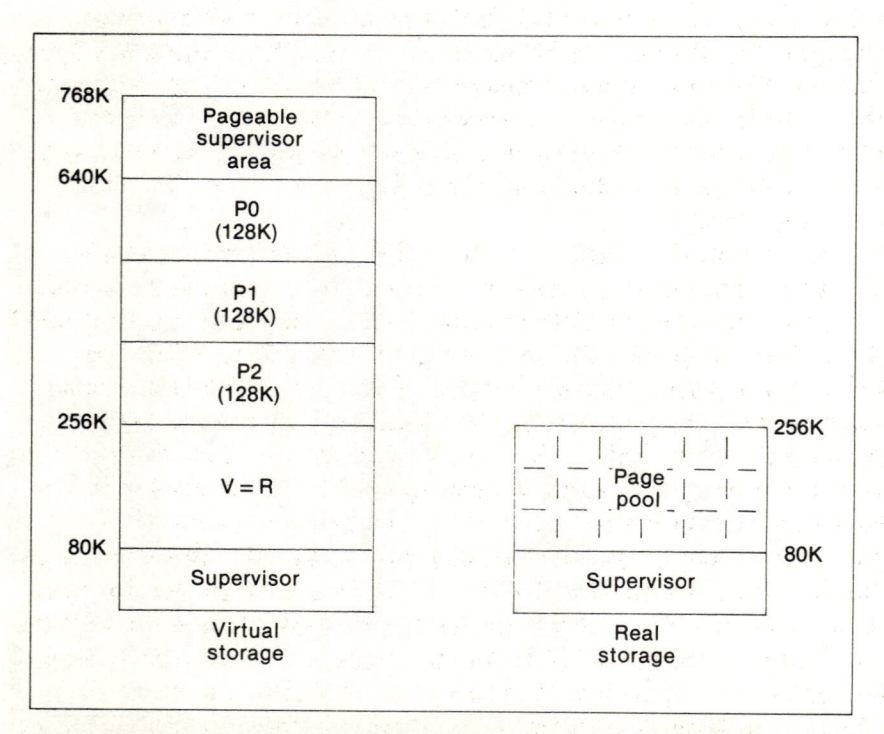

Figure 6-2 VS1 simulates a large MFT system on a much smaller system

The *V = R area* (virtual equals real) allows some programs to be assigned fixed locations in real storage. This means that the program will not be paged out to disk under any circumstances. Although it's not common to do this, it is sometimes necessary for programs that have time-dependent routines. Since many teleprocessing I/O devices require responses according to strict timing schedules, a program that monitors a teleprocessing network is a typical example. If the program was paged out to disk and then had to be paged back in again, too much time would have elapsed before the program could respond to each I/O device.

The rest of the simulated storage area is divided into partitions that are used in the same way as MFT program partitions, but there are a couple of points to note. First, because in VS1 the reader/interpreter and output writer functions are part of the pageable supervisor code, none of the problem program partitions have to be used for them. And second, the virtual storage area can be allocated only in 64K units called *segments*. Common partition sizes, then, are 64K, 128K, 192K, and 256K.

OS/VS2

Figure 6-3 is similar to figure 6-2, but it represents a VS2 system. The same relationship that exists between MFT and VS1 relates MVT to VS2. That is, VS2 is a virtual storage version of MVT. The VS2 supervisor simulates a large virtual storage area managed in the same general way as an MVT system in a smaller amount of real storage. In figure 6-3, 2752K of virtual storage is simulated on a CPU with 1024K of real storage.

You can see in the illustration how the VS2 supervisor is also divided into a permanently resident nucleus and a pageable portion. The pageable parts are combined with the routines that are normally assigned to the link-pack area in a MVT system and together they are assigned to the highest address portion of the virtual storage area. The master scheduler program is then assigned an area of virtual storage just below the link-pack area. Finally, below that, the dynamic region area is the virtual storage area available for executing problem programs. It is managed by VS2 in the same way that MVT manages its problem program storage pool. As in VS1, the V = R area is available for programs that have to be in real storage all the time.

At any moment, then, the page frames of real storage (in VS2 the pages and page frames are 4K bytes in length) will hold active pages from the pageable supervisor, the link-pack modules, the master scheduler, or problem programs in the dynamic region area. All of the inactive pages are stored on disk. When a page that's on disk is

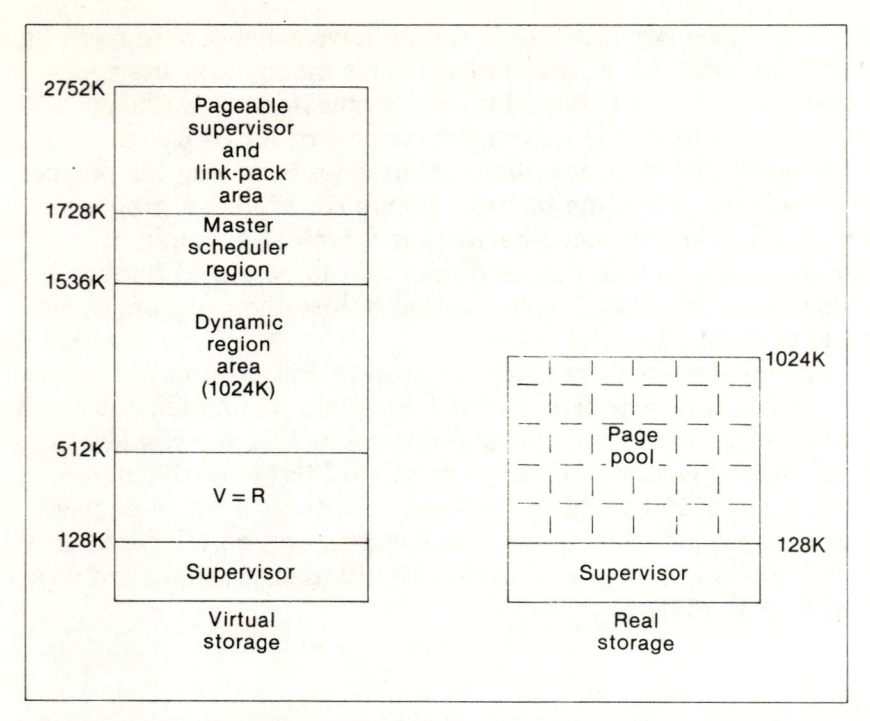

Figure 6-3 VS2 simulates a large MVT system on a much smaller system

required to execute an instruction, the supervisor swaps out to disk some page that is not currently needed and reads the required page into the real storage page frame that is now available.

Programming considerations

Obviously, to accomplish swapping and real storage management, VS1 and VS2 are much more complex than MFT or MVT. From a user's point of view, however, a VS1 or VS2 system looks like a large MFT or MVT system. As a result, using a System/370 operating under a virtual storage version of OS should present no new problems to the programmer who is competent in MFT and MVT.

WRITING JCL FOR VS SYSTEMS

Writing JCL statements for OS/VS should be no more difficult than writing the JCL for MFT or MVT that you have seen in previous portions of this book. The key is in understanding that now you not only must provide job, program, and file information, but also information about the virtual storage environment your program will operate in.

Figure 6-4 presents the formats of JCL parameters available for use with OS/VS systems. Since many OS/VS JCL parameters relate to

```
JOB and EXEC statement parameters

ADDRSP=VIRT
      =REAL

PERFORM=n      (where n is a number between 1 and 255)

DD statement parameters

FREE=CLOSE
    =END

AMP=AMORG
```

Figure 6-4 JCL formats for the OS/VS environment

modular elements of the operating system that may or may not be installed in your system, I haven't included them. I'm only going to discuss the parameters that pertain to general data processing functions.

The JOB statement

There are two additional, optional parameters you may code in the JOB statement. They are ADDRSP and PERFORM.

ADDRSP is used to tell OS/VS whether your program can be paged or not. If you code ADDRSP = REAL, your program won't be paged; it will be processed in the V = R area of the CPU. If you code ADDRSP = VIRT, or if you don't code this parameter at all, your program can be paged. Installation standards normally restrict the use of REAL to special applications.

PERFORM is used to associate the job with a performance group. Briefly, a *performance group* is a logical grouping of jobs to be run using preset priority schemes assigned by the installation to selected classifications of jobs. The format for coding this parameter is PERFORM = n, where n is a number between 1 and 255. Check with your installation to see if you should use performance groups, and if so, what the significance of the performance group number is.

Figure 6-5 shows examples of JOB statements using these new parameters. Example 1 shows a job that will run in real storage (V = R area) because it contains ADDRSP = REAL. Example 2 shows a job that will run in virtual storage (it will be paged) because it contains ADDRSP = VIRT. It will be executed with the priority scheme defined for performance group 12. Example 3 shows a job that will

```
Example 1

    //GOJOB    JOB  HE66YFNH,
    //              'W. CLARY',
    //              ADDRSP=REAL
Example 2

    //PROCCON  JOB  HE66YFNH,
    //              'W. CLARY',
    //              ADDRSP=VIRT,
    //              PERFORM=12
Example 3

    //ENTSYS   JOB  HE66YFNH,
    //              'W. CLARY'
```

Figure 6-5 Examples of JOB statements with OS/VS parameters

also be executed in virtual storage since the ADDRSP parameter is omitted.

The EXEC statement

As with most EXEC statement parameters, the two added parameters for VS systems are identical to parameters on the JOB statement: ADDRSP and PERFORM. ADDRSP tells OS/VS whether the job step can be paged or not. PERFORM causes the job step to be associated with a specific performance group. As in the JOB statement, it provides the number of a predefined performance group that indicates the priority scheme to use when allocating resources.

Figure 6-6 illustrates examples of the EXEC statement using the two new parameters. Example 1 shows the job step to be executed in the V = R area and associated with performance group 1. Example 2 shows a job to be executed in virtual storage and to be associated with performance group 9. Since the ADDRSP parameter is omitted in example 3, this job step will be executed in virtual storage. It will be associated with performance group 17.

The DD statement

Although there are more than a dozen additional parameters available to the OS/VS user for the DD statement, only two have general purpose usage: FREE and AMP. The others refer to the 3800 printing subsystem, to teleprocessing options, or to optional file security features.

FREE allows you to tell the operating system to deallocate files when they are closed, rather than at the end of the job step. Figure

```
Example 1
    //UPSTEP    EXEC    PGM=UPDATE,
    //                  ADDRSP=REAL,
    //                  PERFORM=1
Example 2
    //ENT041    EXEC    PGM=CALCGROS,
    //                  ADDRSP=VIRT,
    //                  PERFORM=9
Example 3
    //DEFN      EXEC    PGM=DEFINE,
    //                  PERFORM=17
```

Figure 6-6 Examples of EXEC statements with OS/VS parameters

```
Example 1
    //MASTROLL  DD     DSN=RMAMAST,
    //                 DISP=OLD,
    //                 FREE=END
Example 2
    //PAYFILE   DD     DSN=C12PAY,
    //                 DISP=OLD
Example 3
    //TAB01     DD     DSN=CUSTREF,
    //                 DISP=OLD,
    //                 FREE=CLOSE
```

Figure 6-7 Examples of the FREE parameter of the DD statement

6-7 shows three DD statements illustrating the use of FREE. Example 1 shows the FREE parameter with the value of END. This means the data set will be released at the end of the job step. Example 2 has the FREE parameter omitted (the default value is END), so it has the same result as example 1. Example 3 shows the FREE parameter with the value CLOSE. This lets OS/VS deallocate the file as soon as the program closes it. By coding FREE = CLOSE, that resource is available to other programs that may require the same file or unit. If a file is to be opened more than once in a program, don't code the FREE = CLOSE option.

A good time to use FREE = CLOSE is the case where your program reads an internal table from disk or tape before processing other data, and once the table is stored in your program, it is closed and never referred to again. In this case, FREE = CLOSE makes the device and file available to other programs that otherwise would have to wait until your job step completed before using them.

The AMP parameter applies to VSAM file handling, covered in the next topic. Briefly, it is used to indicate that the file is a VSAM organized file. There are two instances when you must code it. The first case is in conjunction with a DD DUMMY statement for a VSAM file; the second case is when you use an ISAM program to process a VSAM file. I'll show you examples of both uses in the next topic.

TOPIC 2 Virtual Storage Access Method (VSAM) File Handling

The *Virtual Storage Access Method* (*VSAM*) of organizing and accessing data files includes the features of physical sequential, indexed sequential, and relative file organizations. The records can be retrieved sequentially or randomly in the sequence they were loaded in (*entry-sequenced*), in a record-key sequence (*key-sequenced*), or in relative-record-number sequence (*relative-record-sequenced*). However, even though this access method is more powerful and more flexible than any other, the amount of JCL required for VSAM files is less than that required for physical sequential files. In addition to this, programs that were written to process ISAM files can be used unchanged to process VSAM files.

VSAM AND THE ACCESS METHOD SERVICES PROGRAM

Before you can understand why you don't need as much JCL for VSAM files as you do for physical sequential files, you need to know something about how VSAM files are set up. All VSAM files must be cataloged in a *master catalog* either directly or indirectly. By directly, I mean that the VSAM data set is actually referenced by the master catalog. By indirectly, I mean that the master catalog refers to a *user catalog* that in turn refers to the VSAM data set. The space required for a VSAM data set is called a *data space*; and a data set is called a *cluster*.

To catalog, allocate space for, and define a cluster, you use a special program, much like a utility program, called *Access Method Services*. That means that for VSAM files, the Access Method Services program takes on many of the normal JCL functions. As a result, the JCL required to process the file is minimal.

The coding rules for Access Method Services commands, although similar to JCL coding rules, have several differences:

1. A space or comma can be used to separate parameters.
2. Instead of an equals sign to indicate a parameter's value, each parameter name is followed immediately by the value enclosed in parentheses. Here's an example:

    NAME(MMACAT)

3. To continue a command to the next line, code a dash (-) after a parameter and continue the next parameter or function on the next line. The dash may be preceded by a space for readability. Here's an example:

    FILE(LIBAREA) -
    VOLUME(USER20)

Although there are several commands in the Access Method Services program, I will discuss only one: DEFINE. See the IBM publication *OS/VS1 Access Method Services* or *OS/VS2 Access Method Services* for a complete description of the other available commands.

DEFINING THE AREAS FOR VSAM DATA SETS

When you learned to create sequential files, everything was done with the DD statement in JCL; you used it to tell OS where to place the file, how much space to allocate to it, and what the characteristics of the file were. For VSAM files, you must tell OS/VS these things *before* you code the DD statement referring to the file. That means, before you can load a VSAM data set, there must first exist a master catalog, optionally a user catalog, a data space, and a cluster.

In VS1, the DEFINE command is used to define a master catalog; in VS2, the master catalog is defined at system generation time. In either case, since establishing the master catalog is normally done only once for an installation, I won't cover it in this book.

Most installations that use VSAM files have user catalogs and data spaces established for departments or other organizations, so you may never have to define either one. As a result, the information on defining a user catalog and a data space is presented as background so you'll know how these jobs are done. You should find out what user catalog you are to use by checking with the management of your computer installation. It is important to note that there can be only one user catalog per volume.

This leaves you with only one task to perform before you can load and use a VSAM data set: defining the cluster (the data set itself). This tells OS/VS the type of VSAM data set, the estimated number of records, and the attributes of the file.

User catalogs

User catalogs can be thought of as groups of VSAM files cataloged through the master catalog. In other words, the master catalog points to the user catalog and the user catalog points to the individual data sets. Figure 6-8 shows this relationship between the master catalog, the user catalogs, and the actual VSAM data sets. The master catalog points to a VSAM data set, a non-VSAM data set, or a user catalog. The user catalog then points to other VSAM and non-VSAM data sets. Later in this topic, I'll show you how to put non-VSAM data sets into the VSAM catalogs and how to gain access to them through the catalogs.

Defining a user catalog Figure 6-9 shows a job to create a user catalog using the Access Method Services program. The program name is IDCAMS. SYSPRINT is the name of the output message file. The ddname VOLNAME is a name given to a volume to be referred to by the DEFINE command. SYSIN defines the input to the IDCAMS program.

DEFINE is the command; USERCATALOG is the function of the command (create a user catalog). The catalog's characteristics are defined by the information enclosed in the outer pair of parentheses:

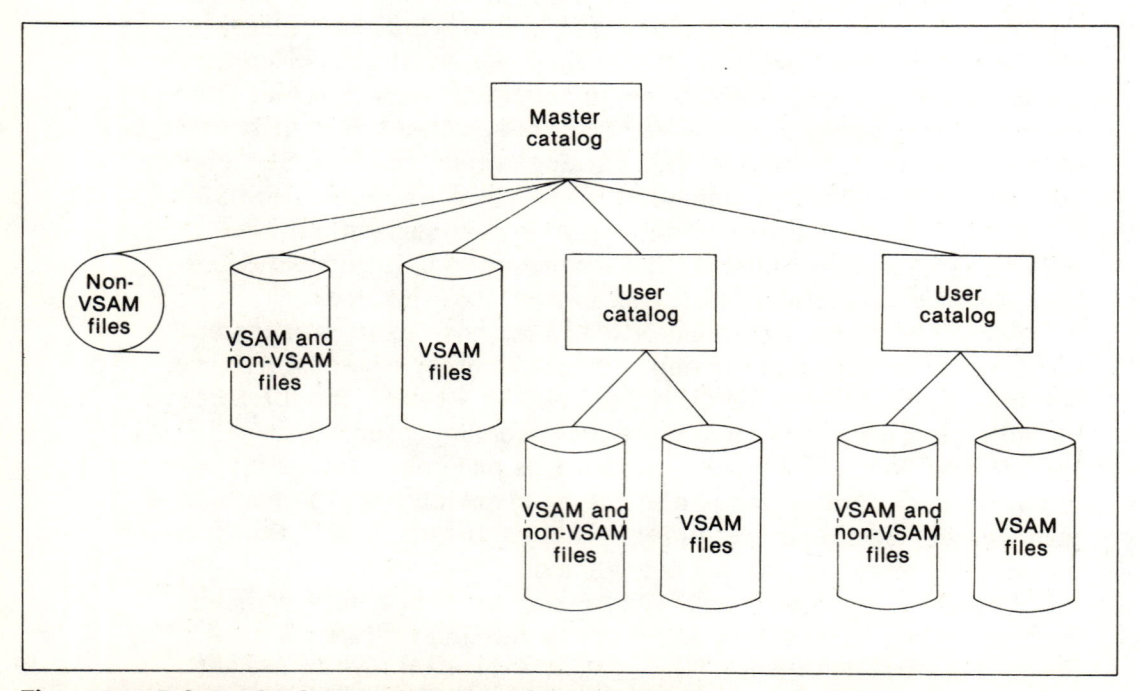

Figure 6-8 Relationship between VSAM catalogs and data sets

```
//USCAT     JOB   HE66YFNH,
//                'W. CLARY'
//CATGEN    EXEC  PGM=IDCAMS
//SYSPRINT  DD    SYSOUT=A
//VOLNAME   DD    DISP=OLD,
//                UNIT=3330,
//                VOL=SER=D00103
//SYSIN     DD    *
  DEFINE    USERCATALOG (NAME(MMACAT) -
            MASTERPW(MYPASS) -
            FILE(VOLNAME) -
            VOLUME(D00103) -
            RECORDS(100 20))
/*
```

Figure 6-9 Creating a VSAM user catalog

the name of the catalog is MMACAT; the master password is MYPASS (this password must be specified on any request to access the catalog); the catalog is to reside on the volume defined by the ddname VOLNAME; the volume serial number is D00103; and the number of records, indicating the primary and secondary space allocation for the catalog, is 100 records for the primary allocation and 20 records in each of 15 secondary extents. (Notice that for VSAM files, there are 15 extents rather than 16 as you've seen for other types of files.)

JOBCAT and STEPCAT DD statements To use a user catalog, you have to identify it to OS/VS for each job or job step. There are two special DD statements available to do this: JOBCAT and STEPCAT. The JOBCAT DD statement, if coded, must be the first statement after the JOB statement or JOBLIB statement. It tells OS/VS what user catalog to use for every step in the job. The STEPCAT DD statement, if coded, must be the first statement after the EXEC statement or STEPLIB statement. It tells OS/VS what user catalog to use for that one job step. Later, I'll show you some examples and tell you what happens if you combine the two or omit both JOBCAT and STEPCAT DD statements.

Defining a data space

Once the user catalog has been established, the next step is to define an area to hold VSAM data sets. To do this, you must tell OS/VS the volume, device type, space requirements, and catalog name required for the area. Figure 6-10 shows a job to define a data space on a

```
//DEFSP     JOB   HE66YFNH,
//                'W. CLARY'
//EXAMS     EXEC  PGM=IDCAMS
//STEPCAT   DD    DSN=MMACAT,
//                DISP=SHR
//SYSPRINT  DD    SYSOUT=A
//SPCDEF    DD    DISP=OLD,
//                UNIT=3330,
//                VOL=SER=D00103
//SYSIN     DD    *
 DEFINE      SPACE (FILE(SPCDEF) -
                   VOLUMES(D00103) -
                   CYLINDERS(20 5)) -
                   CATALOG(MMACAT/MYPASS)
/*
```

Figure 6-10 Creating a VSAM data space

3330 volume named D00103 that uses 20 cylinders of primary space and up to 15 secondary extents of 5 cylinders. Notice that this volume is identified by an earlier DD statement. Notice, too, that the function is VOLUMES, in contrast to VOLUME for a catalog. The data space is to be cataloged in the user catalog I created in the previous example (MMACAT). The master password, MYPASS, is provided by the CATALOG function of the DEFINE command. The STEPCAT DD statement identifies the user catalog.

When a data space is established on a volume, that volume can only be accessed for VSAM files through the catalog associated with the data space. In other words, the volume can only be used for VSAM files that are included in the catalog or non-VSAM files, regardless of where they are cataloged. There can be more than one data space on a volume, and space for a cluster can be allocated from any data space on the volume.

Defining a cluster

As I mentioned, a cluster is the name given to a VSAM data set. After space has been allocated on the direct-access device, you can define the cluster.

Figure 6-11 shows you how to define all three types of VSAM clusters: key-sequenced, entry-sequenced, and relative-record-sequenced. I showed the DEFINE commands alone for the entry- and relative-record-sequenced files; the rest of the JCL statements would be the same as they are for the key-sequenced file.

In all three examples, the functions of the DEFINE command are CLUSTER and CATALOG. The characteristics of the cluster are given in the CLUSTER function in the outer pair of parentheses:

Key-sequenced data set:

```
//CLUST      JOB   HE66YFNH,
//                 'W. CLARY'
//DEFN       EXEC  PGM=IDCAMS
//STEPCAT    DD    DSN=MMACAT,
//                 DISP=SHR
//SYSPRINT   DD    SYSOUT=A
//FILEAREA   DD    DISP=OLD,
//                 UNIT=3330,
//                 VOL=SER=D00103
//SYSIN      DD    *
  DEFINE     CLUSTER(NAME(MKSFILE) -
             FILE(FILEAREA) -
             VOLUMES(D00103) -
             RECORDS(100 30) -
             RECORDSIZE(90 90) -
             INDEXED -
             KEYS(5 12)) -
             CATALOG(MMACAT/MYPASS)
/*
```

Entry-sequenced data set:

```
  DEFINE     CLUSTER(NAME(MSSFILE) -
             FILE(FILEAREA) -
             VOLUMES(D00103) -
             CYLINDERS(20 10) -
             RECORDSIZE(80 80) -
             NONINDEXED) -
             CATALOG(MMACAT/MYPASS)
```

Relative-record-sequenced data set:

```
  DEFINE     CLUSTER(NAME(MRSFILE) -
             FILE(FILEAREA) -
             VOLUMES(D00103) -
             TRACKS(100 50) -
             RECORDSIZE(50 90) -
             NUMBERED) -
             CATALOG(MMACAT/MYPASS)
```

Figure 6-11 Creating VSAM data set clusters

1. NAME indicates the name of the VSAM file to be created.
2. FILE refers to the DD statement defining the device and volume where the file is to reside.
3. VOLUMES indicates the volume serial number where the file is to reside.
4. RECORDS, CYLINDERS, or TRACKS specifies the unit of measure for the primary and secondary space allocation.

5. RECORDSIZE indicates the average and maximum record length of the records in the cluster.

6. INDEXED, NONINDEXED, or NUMBERED indicates the type of VSAM data set: key-sequenced, entry-sequenced, or relative-record-sequenced.

7. KEYS is used to indicate the length and starting position of record keys in the key-sequenced data set.

The CATALOG function specifies the catalog name of the user catalog defined by the STEPCAT DD statement. Also provided is the master password required to access the catalog.

In this example, the key-sequenced VSAM file is to be accessed using only a primary key. Sometimes, though you may want to use other fields to access the records in a file. You can do this by coding additional functions in the DEFINE command. Because the use of alternate keys is beyond the scope of this book, I'm not going to cover it in any more detail. I just wanted you to be aware of it, since you may run into it in your shop.

LOADING AND UPDATING A VSAM DATA SET

Each programming language contains techniques and considerations for processing VSAM files, and these should be understood before loading or updating a VSAM file. Since this book does not teach programming, these techniques will not be covered here. I'm assuming that you know the general programming rules that apply to creating and updating VSAM data sets.

As I mentioned, the JCL is greatly simplified for processing VSAM files since several of the functions normally requested in JCL have already been provided by the Access Method Services program. After the cluster has been defined, a VSAM data set can be created or updated with the same DD statement. In other words, if I want to load data into the key-sequenced cluster I defined in figure 6-11, and later I want to update that data set, I can code this DD statement:

```
//VFILE      DD   DSN=MKSFILE,
//                DISP=OLD
```

In order to access this file, I also have to code a JOBCAT or STEPCAT DD statement for its catalog. Figure 6-12 shows some more examples of JOBCAT and STEPCAT DD statements defining user catalogs. If both JOBCAT and STEPCAT are coded, STEPCAT takes precedence over JOBCAT for the step it appears in. If neither is coded, OS/VS will attempt to locate the VSAM file in the master catalog. The job will abnormally terminate if the file is not cataloged in the master catalog.

```
Example 1
        //CREATE   JOB  HE66YFNH,
        //              'W. CLARY'
        //JOBCAT    DD   DSN=MMACAT,
        //               DISP=SHR

Example 2
        //UPJ      JOB  HE66YFNH,
        //              'W. CLARY'
        //JOBLIB    DD   DSN=MMA.USERLIB,
        //               DISP=SHR
        //JOBCAT    DD   DSN=MMACAT,
        //               DISP=SHR

Example 3
        //GORES    JOB  HE66YFNH,
        //              'W. CLARY'
        //GOEDIT   EXEC PGM=A96EDIT
        //STEPLIB   DD   DSN=MMA.USERLIB,
        //               DISP=SHR
        //STEPCAT   DD   DSN=MMACAT,
        //               DISP=SHR

Example 4
        //GENDATA  JOB  HE66YFNH,
        //              'W. CLARY'
        //JOBLIB    DD   DSN=MMA.USERLIB,
        //               DISP=SHR
        //JOBCAT    DD   DSN=MMACAT,
        //               DISP=SHR
        //EX01P    EXEC PGM=UPDATE7
        //STEPLIB   DD   DSN=MMA.USERLIB,
        //               DISP=SHR
        //STEPCAT   DD   DSN=MMACAT,
        //               DISP=SHR
```

Figure 6-12 Examples of JOBCAT and STEPCAT DD statements

The AMP parameter

As I mentioned in the last topic, there is one JCL parameter you may have occasion to use that applies only to VSAM files: the AMP parameter. Although this parameter has several subparameters, the only one you need in general practice is AMP = AMORG. This tells OS that the file is a VSAM file. The only two times it is required is when you (1) specify DUMMY for a VSAM file or (2) use an ISAM program to process a VSAM file. Here are two examples:

```
//MASTFILE  DD  DUMMY,
//              AMP=AMORG

//ISFILE    DD  DSN=PROMAST,
//              DISP=OLD,
//              AMP=AMORG
```

USING NON-VSAM FILES THROUGH VSAM CATALOGS

Although it's not necessary to catalog non-VSAM files in the master or user catalogs to access them, you may do this to use the security features of VSAM. If you place a non-VSAM file in a VSAM catalog, the password associated with that catalog is required to access the non-VSAM file. The result of placing a non-VSAM file in a master or user catalog is that an entry is created in the catalog, but no space is allocated for the file.

Figure 6-13 shows an example of placing a non-VSAM file in a VSAM user catalog. The STEPCAT DD statement identifies the user catalog. The DEFINE command defines the file: NONVSAM is the first function and identifies a file named PERSFILE residing on a 3350 disk pack named LIB113; CATALOG is the second function giving the name of the user catalog and the password associated with it.

USING ISAM PROGRAMS TO PROCESS VSAM FILES

If you have an assembler, PL/I, or COBOL program that accesses an ISAM file and that ISAM file is to be converted to a VSAM file, you may be able to continue to use the program without changing it. However, there are several restrictions on the program that must be met before you can use it to process the VSAM file. These are spelled out in the IBM publication *OS/VS Virtual Storage Access Method (VSAM) Programmer's Guide*. If your program qualifies according to the restrictions presented in that publication, all you have to do is change the JCL to refer to the VSAM file instead of the ISAM file.

Figure 6-14 shows a job step that uses an ISAM file and the same job step after the ISAM file has been converted to a VSAM key-

```
//NONVDEF   JOB   HE66YFNY,
//                'W. CLARY'
//CATSTEP   EXEC  PGM=IDCAMS
//STEPCAT   DD    DSN=MMACAT,
//                DISP=SHR
//SYSPRINT  DD    SYSOUT=A
//SYSIN     DD    *
  DEFINE   NONVSAM(NAME(PERSFILE)   -
                  DEVICETYPES(3350) -
                  VOLUMES(LIB113))  -
           CATALOG(MMACAT/MYPASS)
/*
```

Figure 6-13 Placing a non-VSAM file in a VSAM user catalog

```
A job step to process an ISAM file:

//UPSTEP    EXEC  PGM=UPDMAST
//STEPLIB   DD    DSN=MMA.USERLIB,
//                DISP=SHR
//FORIPT    DD    DSN=FORMIN,
//                DISP=OLD
//FORTAB    DD    DSN=FORMTBLE,
//                DISP=OLD,
//                DCB=DSORG=IS
//FORLST    DD    SYSOUT=A


A job step executing the same program to process a VSAM file:

//UPSTEP    EXEC  PGM=UPDMAST
//STEPLIB   DD    DSN=MMA.USERLIB,
//                DISP=SHR
//STEPCAT   DD    DSN=MMACAT,
//                DISP=SHR
//FORIPT    DD    DSN=FORMIN,
//                DISP=OLD
//FORTAB    DD    DSN=FORMTAB,
//                DISP=OLD,
//                AMP=AMORG
//FORLST    DD    SYSOUT=A
```

Figure 6-14 Executing an ISAM program to process a VSAM file

sequenced file. The STEPCAT DD statement identifies the user catalog in which the VSAM file is now cataloged. Since the same program is used unchanged to access the VSAM file, the ddname of this file must be exactly the same in both steps. In this example, the ddname is FORTAB. The DSN is different, though, because the file was given a new data set name when it was converted to a VSAM file. Notice that the AMP = AMORG parameter is coded to tell OS/VS that the file is a VSAM file even though the program is coded to process an ISAM file. This combination automatically causes an ISAM interface to be invoked that will translate between the program and the VSAM I/O module.

DISCUSSION

You may feel that I have skimmed over the information presented in this chapter and that you have only a slightly better understanding of virtual storage and VSAM files than you had when you began. I agree. However, as I pointed out in the opening paragraph of the chapter, to present a full and comprehensive discussion of the subject would take us far beyond the realm of JCL. On the other hand, if you now understand some of the terminology of IBM virtual storage, the JCL to execute programs in an OS/VS environment, and the basic steps for creating and modifying VSAM files, then you are in a better position to learn more about this area of OS, and this book has served its purpose on the subject.

Terminology

Virtual Storage Access Method	master catalog
VSAM	user catalog
entry-sequenced	data space
key-sequenced	cluster
relative-record-sequenced	Access Method Services

Objective

Given reference material, write the JCL and DEFINE command to (1) define a VSAM user catalog, (2) define a VSAM data space, (3) define a VSAM cluster, and (4) execute a program that loads and updates a VSAM file.

Problems

1. Write the JCL and DEFINE command to create a user catalog with these characteristics: (1) the name is CAT001; (2) the master password is ENTRYPW; (3) it should be placed on a 3330 disk pack named LIB111; and (4) the space should be defined in terms of records—50 in the primary portion and 15 in each secondary portion. Make up your own ddname to define the space on the volume.

2. Write the JCL and DEFINE command for a data space with these characteristics: (1) it should be located on a 3330 disk pack named LIB111; (2) the space should be allocated in tracks—120 in the primary portion and 30 in each secondary portion; and (3) the associated catalog is CAT001.

3. Write the JCL and DEFINE command to define a VSAM cluster with these characteristics: (1) the name is VSPFILE; (2) it is a key-sequenced data set with a 7-byte key beginning in the 14th position of each record; (3) it should be placed on a 3330 disk pack name LIB111; (4) it will consist of fixed-length, 100-byte records; (5) the space should be defined in terms of records—200 in the

primary portion and 20 in each secondary portion; and (6) the associated user catalog is CAT001.

4. Write the JCL to execute a program named LOADVS that resides in a user library named MMA.VSLIB. The program uses the following files:

   a. A VSAM file named VSPFILE that is cataloged in a user catalog named CAT001. The ddname of the file is VSFILE.

   b. An OLD sequential file named OLDFILE. The ddname is OLDMAST.

   c. A print file with the ddname RPTA. Its block size is 133.

Solutions

1. Figure 6-15 is an acceptable solution.
2. Figure 6-16 is an acceptable solution.
3. Figure 6-17 is an acceptable solution.
4. Figure 6-18 is an acceptable solution.

```
//USERCAT  JOB  HE66YFNH,
//              'W. CLARY'
//AMS      EXEC PGM=IDCAMS
//SYSPRINT DD   SYSOUT=A
//LIBAREA  DD   DISP=OLD,
//              UNIT=3330,
//              VOL=SER=LIB111
//SYSIN    DD   *
  DEFINE        USERCATALOG (NAME(CAT001) -
                MASTERPW(ENTRYPW) -
                FILE(LIBAREA) -
                VOLUME(LIB111) -
                RECORDS(50 15))
/*
```

Figure 6-15 Creating a VSAM user catalog

```
//DEFSP    JOB  HE66YFNH,
//              'W. CLARY'
//ANS      EXEC PGM=IDCAMS
//STEPCAT  DD   DSN=CAT001,
//              DISP=SHR
//SYSPRINT DD   SYSOUT=A
//SPCDEF   DD   DISP=OLD,
//              UNIT=3330,
//              VOL=SER=LIB111
//SYSIN    DD   *
  DEFINE   SPACE (FILE(SPCDEF) -
                 VOLUMES(LIB111) -
                 TRACKS(120 30)) -
           CATALOG(CAT001/ENTRYPW)
/*
```

Figure 6-16 Creating a VSAM data space

```
//CLUST    JOB  HE66YFNH,
//              'W. CLARY'
//DEFN     EXEC PGM=IDCAMS
//STEPCAT  DD   DSN=CAT001,
//              DISP=SHR
//SYSPRINT DD   SYSOUT=A
//FILEAREA DD   DISP=OLD,
//              UNIT=3330,
//              VOL=SER=LIB111
//SYSIN    DD   *
  DEFINE   CLUSTER (NAME(VSPFILE) -
                   FILE(FILEAREA) -
                   VOLUMES(LIB111) -
                   RECORDS(200 20) -
                   RECORDSIZE(100 100) -
                   INDEXED -
                   KEYS(7 14)) -
           CATALOG(CAT001/ENTRYPW)
/*
```

Figure 6-17 Creating a VSAM cluster

JCL for OS/VS Environment

```
//LOAD      JOB   HE66YFNH,
//                'W. CLARY'
//LOADSTEP  EXEC  PGM=LOADVS
//STEPLIB   DD    DSN=MMA.VSLIB,
//                DISP=SHR
//STEPCAT   DD    DSN=CAT001,
//                DISP=SHR
//VSFILE    DD    DSN=VSPFILE,
//                DISP=OLD
//OLDMAST   DD    DSN=OLDFILE,
//                DISP=OLD
//RPTA      DD    SYSOUT=A,
//                DCB=BLKSIZE=133
//
```

Figure 6-18 Executing a program that accesses a VSAM file

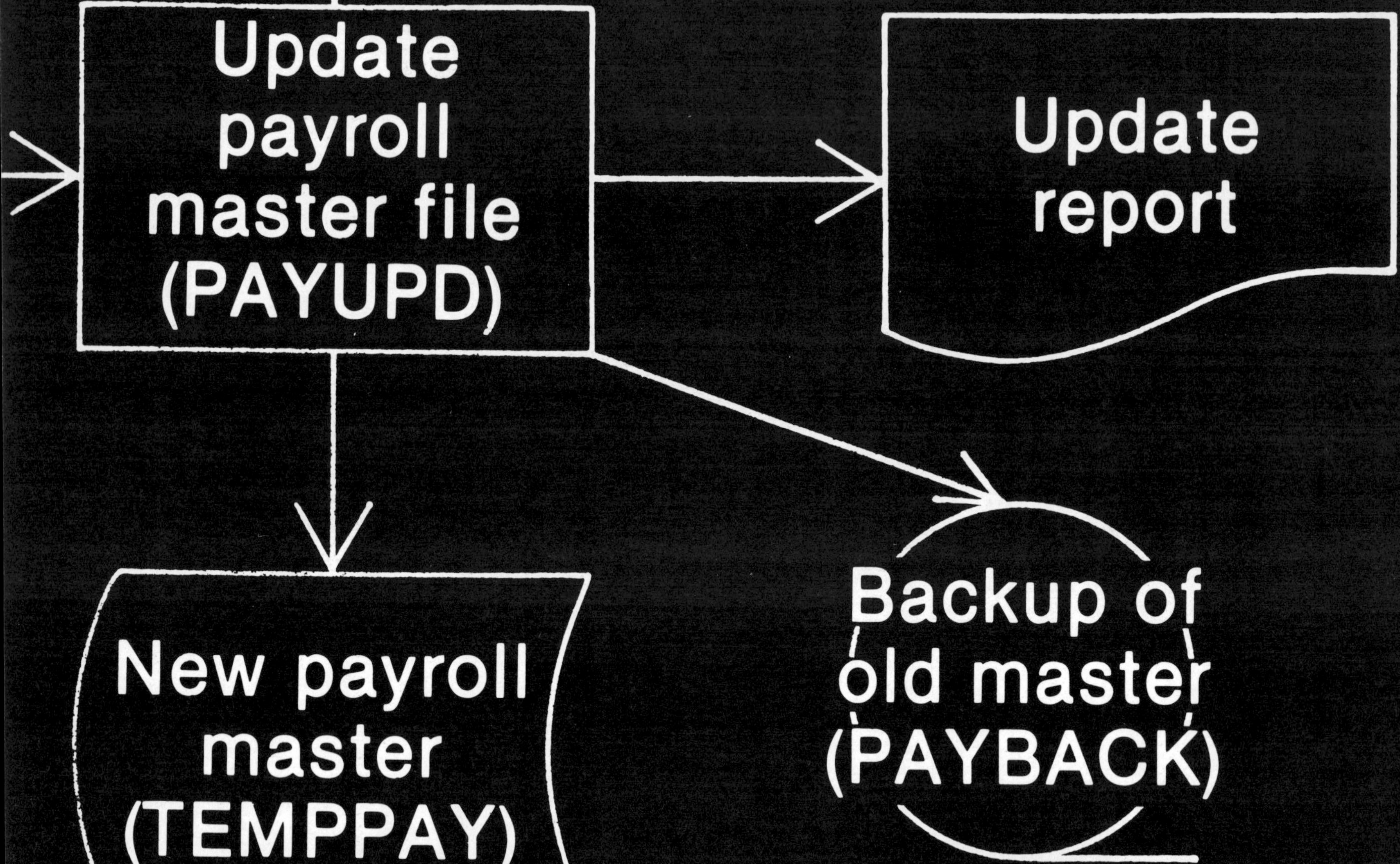
Update payroll master file (PAYUPD)
Update report
New payroll master (TEMPPAY)
Backup of old master (PAYBACK)

7

OS Utilities and the Sort/Merge Program

Several common data processing functions are required frequently in an OS installation. These functions include copying, reorganizing, compressing, sorting, merging, and changing the status of data sets. To eliminate the need for each programmer to write programs that perform these general functions, OS provides utility programs and the sort/merge program to accomplish them. You supply control information to tailor the utilities and the sort/merge program to fit your requirements. Topic 1 of this chapter presents a basic subset of OS utilities; topic 2 presents the sort/merge program.

TOPIC 1   OS Utility Programs

The purpose of OS *utility programs* is to reduce situations where several programmers write identical routines to accomplish similar tasks. Utility programs are executed and controlled by JCL statements and *utility control statements*. In the utility control statements, you tell the utility exactly what you want it to do.

CODING THE JCL TO EXECUTE UTILITIES

The JCL required to execute utility programs follows one general pattern with minor variations. As I discuss individual utilities, I'll show you the JCL required. For now, let's look at the general form so you can get an idea of the JCL needed. Figure 7-1 shows this general form.

The EXEC statement identifies the utility program by name. The PARM parameter is used with some utilities to specify additional information about this execution or to set a mode of operation. For example, in one utility PARM=NEW means that a data set is being created, while PARM=MOD means that an existing file is to be modified. No STEPLIB or JOBLIB DD statement is required since OS utility programs always reside in the system library.

SYSPRINT identifies the output message file. This is the output normally printed by the utility to let you know how the program ran. A typical SYSPRINT listing will show the utility control statements, the input data, and the final result—for example, the new or changed file.

SYSUT1 is the ddname used by many utilities for the input master file. The file attributes include a description of the input data set—DSN, DISP, UNIT, and VOLUME information along with information you normally would code if you were accessing the file with your own program. In a few utilities, the input file can have any ddname you want (you direct the utility to the input and output files with control statements). Also, sometimes the input file DD statement can be omitted. One example is when you're creating a new file.

SYSUT2 is the ddname of the output file. Here, you give all the file attributes required to create the file. If the output file already exists and you are changing or extending it, the disposition will be OLD or MOD. As with SYSUT1, some utilities let you name the DD statement for the output file anything you want.

SYSUT3 and SYSUT4 are work files or overflow files that are used by a few utilities. Usually, they will define areas on a direct-

```
//stepname EXEC   PGM=utility-name,
//               PARM=parm-value
//SYSPRINT DD    SYSOUT=A
//SYSUT1   DD    input-file-attributes
//SYSUT2   DD    output-file-attributes
//SYSUT3   DD    work-file-attributes
//SYSUT4   DD    work-file-attributes
//SYSIN    DD    {*   }
                 {DATA}
         utility control statements and input data
/*
```

Figure 7-1 General form of the JCL required for utility programs

access device but will not assign data set names (DSNs). Their disposition is usually coded (NEW,DELETE).

SYSIN identifies the input-stream data file of utility control statements. It may use DD * to introduce non-JCL data into the input stream, or it may use DD DATA to introduce JCL data (// in positions 1 and 2) into the input stream. Alternatively, it can refer to a sequential file on tape or disk or to a partitioned data set containing the control statements. In this case, instead of an asterisk or the word DATA, the DD statement gives the DSN and attributes of the required file. (One utility program, IEBISAM, doesn't require control statements since it derives its control specifications from the PARM parameter of the EXEC statement. As a result, that utility doesn't require a SYSIN DD statement.)

If the input data is in the input stream, you should code a delimiter statement to end the input-stream data file. It is required to end data streams preceded by DD DATA, but it's optional for DD *.

CODING UTILITY CONTROL STATEMENTS

Although each utility requires different control statements, all OS utility programs follow the same general coding rules for these statements. As a result, after you have learned to code a few utility programs, you will be able to learn others easily. The general coding rules are as follows:

1. Utility control statements are coded in 80-column card format. Positions 1 through 71 are used for the statement; position 72 may be used for a continuation character; and positions 73 through 80 may be used for optional identification or sequence numbers.

2. All control statements follow this format:

    ```
    label operation operand comments
    ```

    These four fields are used as follows:

    a. The label identifies the statement and, if coded, must usually begin in the first position of the statement. In actual practice, the label is usually omitted.

    b. The operation field specifies the type of control statement. It must be preceded and followed by at least one space. If the label is omitted, the operation field must begin after position 1. I usually omit the label and code the operation field in position 3.

    c. The operand field is composed of key-word parameters separated by commas. It also must be preceded and followed by at least one space. I usually begin the operand field in position 12.

d. The comments field is optional, but if you code it, it also must be preceded and followed by at least one space.
3. To continue a control statement to another line or card, you must place a non-blank character in position 72 and begin the continued statement in position 16 of the next line.

A BASIC SUBSET OF OS UTILITIES

I have selected four commonly used utility programs as the basic subset: IEBCOPY, IEBISAM, IEBPTPCH, and IEHPROGM. (Another utility, IEPUPDTE, is covered in chapter 5.) In addition, I've included a discussion on the IEFBR14 program, a special program supplied by IBM that's not technically a utility program but is used like a utility. After you learn to use these five programs, I think you'll be able to figure out how to use the others from the IBM utilities manual.

The IEBCOPY utility

The IEBCOPY utility program is used to copy partitioned data sets. (See chapter 5 for a description of partitioned data sets.) With the options available, you can create a backup copy of a library in its entirety, select members to be copied, or exclude members that are not to be copied. You can also merge two partitioned data sets together, rename certain members, and replace selected members by other data.

This program is also used to *compress* partitioned data sets. When partitioned data sets are modified—old members deleted and new members added—unused areas of disk space (not large enough to contain whole members) begin to accumulate throughout the file. When IEBCOPY copies a partitioned data set, it eliminates these unused blocks of space.

Figure 7-2 shows the formats for the IEBCOPY control statements. The COPY statement identifies the input and output files; the SELECT statement can be used to tell OS to copy only certain members of the data set; and the EXCLUDE statement can be used to tell OS *not* to copy certain members.

The bottom part of figure 7-2 shows the JCL sequence used to execute IEBCOPY. The DD statements ddname1, ddname2, and so on to ddname-n can be any names you want; one defines the output file and the others define the input files. The COPY statement tells the program which ones are input and which is output by the INDD and OUTDD parameters. For example, if my output DD statement is FILEOUT, and my input DD statement is FILEIN, then the COPY statement would be:

```
Control statement formats:

label    COPY      OUTDD=ddname1,INDD=ddname2,ddname3...

label    SELECT    MEMBER=member-name1,member-name2...

label    EXCLUDE   MEMBER=member-name1,member-name2...

JCL requirements:
EXEC
SYSPRINT
ddname1
ddname2
.
.
ddname-n
SYSUT3
SYSUT4
SYSIN
control statements
/*
```
Note: The sequence of ddname1 to ddname-n in the job stream is not important; the OUTDD and INDD parameters determine which files are input and which are output.

Figure 7-2 Control statement formats and JCL requirements for the IEBCOPY utility program

```
COPY              OUTDD=FILEOUT,INDD=FILEIN
```

If more than one file is identified in the INDD parameter, those files are copied one after another to create the output file. In other words, two or more files combine to make one file. There is no practical limit to the number of input files that may be coded.

IEBCOPY requires two work areas, so the SYSUT3 and SYSUT4 DD statements must be coded for this utility. However, the areas don't have to be very big, so in general you only need to assign one track of space to each.

Figure 7-3 shows four examples of IEBCOPY. Example 1 shows a full copy—all members of the partitioned data set named MMA.USERLIB are copied to a new partitioned data set named MMA.BACKLIB for backup. Example 2 is another full copy, but this time the data set is *compressed in place*. Notice that the input and output statements define the same file.

Examples 3 and 4 illustrate multiple input files. Example 3 shows how to copy selected members to another file. Only those members

Example 1: Copying a library

```
//COPJOB    JOB  HE66YFNH,
//               'W. CLARY'
//COPSTEP   EXEC PGM=IEBCOPY
//SYSPRINT  DD   SYSOUT=A
//INPUT1    DD   DSN=MMA.USERLIB,
//               DISP=SHR
//OUTPUT1   DD   DSN=MMA.BACKLIB,
//               DISP=(NEW,CATLG),
//               UNIT=3330,
//               VOL=SER=D00103,
//               SPACE=(CYL,(20,10,5)),
//               DCB=(LRECL=80,BLKSIZE=800,RECFM=FB,DSORG=PO)
//SYSUT3    DD   UNIT=3330,
//               SPACE=(TRK,1)
//SYSUT4    DD   UNIT=3330,
//               SPACE=(TRK,1)
//SYSIN     DD   *
   COPY     OUTDD=OUTPUT1,INDD=INPUT1
/*
//
```

Example 2: Copying a library so it's compressed in place

```
//COMPRESS  JOB  HE66YFNH,
//               'W. CLARY'
//COMP      EXEC PGM=IEBCOPY
//SYSPRINT  DD   SYSOUT=A
//INOUT     DD   DSN=MMA.BANKLIB,
//               DISP=OLD
//SYSUT3    DD   UNIT=3330,
//               SPACE=(TRK,1)
//SYSUT4    DD   UNIT=3330,
//               SPACE=(TRK,1)
//SYSIN     DD   *
   COPY     OUTDD=INOUT,INDD=INOUT
/*
//
```

Figure 7-3 Examples of the IEBCOPY utility program (part 1 of 2)

selected are copied. Notice that you don't specify which file the members come from, even though there are two input files. Example 4 shows how to exclude certain members from the copy operation. In this example, all members are copied with the exception of those named in the EXCLUDE statement.

The IEBISAM utility

The IEBISAM utility program is used to copy an indexed sequential access method (ISAM) file either to another ISAM file or to a

Example 3: Copying selected members from two data sets

```
//SELJOB    JOB   HE66YFNH,
//                'W. CLARY'
//SELSTEP   EXEC  PGM=IEBCOPY
//SYSPRINT  DD    SYSOUT=A
//OLDFILE1  DD    DSN=SRC.COPYLIB,
//                DISP=SHR
//OLDFILE2  DD    DSN=SRC.MEMBLIB,
//                DISP=SHR
//NEWFILE   DD    DSN=SRC.SELLIB,
//                DISP=(NEW,CATLG),
//                UNIT=2314,
//                VOL=SER=USER01,
//                SPACE=(800,(10,4,4)),
//                DCB=(LRECL=80,BLKSIZE=800,RECFM=FB,DSORG=PO)
//SYSUT3    DD    UNIT=SYSDA,
//                SPACE=(TRK,1)
//SYSUT4    DD    UNIT=SYSDA,
//                SPACE=(TRK,1)
//SYSIN     DD    *
   COPY     OUTDD=NEWFILE,INDD=OLDFILE1,OLDFILE2
   SELECT   MEMBER=RES01,RES12,RES92
/*
//
```

Example 4: Excluding certain members from two data sets (same JCL as in example 3)

```
//SYSIN     DD    *
   COPY     OUTDD=NEWFILE,INDD=OLDFILE1,OLDFILE2
   EXCLUDE  MEMBER=RES07,RES08,RES67,RES70
/*
```

Figure 7-3 Examples of the IEBCOPY utility program (part 2 of 2)

sequential file in an *unloaded ISAM format*. Then, it can be used to load that sequential file back into an ISAM file. This is one method commonly used to reorganize ISAM files. (See chapter 4 for more on ISAM files.)

Of the JCL shown in figure 7-1, IEBISAM uses the EXEC, SYSPRINT, SYSUT1, and SYSUT2 statements. It differs from the other utilities, though, in that it requires no control statements. It receives its direction through the PARM parameter of the EXEC statement. The valid values that can be coded in the PARM parameter are: COPY, UNLOAD, LOAD, and PRINTL. Figure 7-4 gives an example of each.

COPY causes the file defined by the SYSUT1 DD statement to be copied to the file defined by the SYSUT2 DD statement. The first example in figure 7-4 shows an ISAM-to-ISAM copy.

Example 1: Copying an ISAM file

```
//ISCOPY    JOB   HE66YFNH,
//                'W. CLARY'
//ISCSTEP   EXEC  PGM=IEBISAM,
//                PARM='COPY'
//SYSPRINT  DD    SYSOUT=A
//SYSUT1    DD    DSN=LOANMAST,
//                DISP=OLD,
//                UNIT=2314,
//                VOL=SER=USER25,
//                DCB=DSORG=IS
//SYSUT2    DD    DSN=LOANTRL(INDEX),
//                DISP=(NEW,KEEP),
//                UNIT=2314,
//                VOL=SER=USER20,
//                SPACE=(CYL,1,,CONTIG),
//                DCB=(LRECL=95,BLKSIZE=950,RECFM=FB,DSORG=IS,
//                KEYLEN=6,RKP=3,OPTCD=YI)
//          DD    DSN=LOANTRL(PRIME),
//                DISP=(NEW,KEEP),
//                VOL=REF=*.SYSUT2,
//                SPACE=(CYL,20,,CONTIG),
//                DCB=*.SYSUT2
//          DD    DSN=LOANTRL(OVFLOW),
//                DISP=(NEW,KEEP),
//                VOL=REF=*.SYSUT2,
//                SPACE=(CYL,1,,CONTIG),
//                DCB=*.SYSUT2
//
```

Example 2: Unloading an ISAM file

```
//UNLOAD    JOB   HE66YFNH,
//                'W. CLARY'
//UNLOAD    EXEC  PGM=IEBISAM,
//                PARM='UNLOAD'
//SYSPRINT  DD    SYSOUT=A
//SYSUT1    DD    DSN=ISMAST,
//                DISP=OLD,
//                DCB=DSORG=IS
//SYSUT2    DD    DSN=ISBACKUP,
//                DISP=(NEW,KEEP),
//                UNIT=2400,
//                VOL=SER=7291,
//                DCB=(LRECL=60,BLKSIZE=3600,RECFM=FB)
//
```

Figure 7-4 Examples of the IEBISAM utility program (part 1 of 2)

UNLOAD causes the ISAM file defined by SYSUT1 to be copied (unloaded) to a sequential file defined by SYSUT2. The second example shows an ISAM file being unloaded. It's important to note that an unloaded ISAM file cannot be processed using a program designed to

OS Utilities and the Sort/Merge

```
Example 3: Loading an ISAM file

//LOADJOB  JOB   HE66YFNH,
//               'W  CLARY'
//LOADSTEP EXEC  PGM=IEBISAM,
//               PARM='LOAD'
//SYSPRINT DD    SYSOUT=A
//SYSUT1   DD    DSN=ISBACKUP,
//               DISP=OLD,
//               UNIT=2400,
//               VOL=SER=7291
//SYSUT2   DD    DSN=ISMAST,
//               DISP=(NEW,CATLG),
//               UNIT=2314,
//               VOL=SER=USER01,
//               SPACE=(CYL,(10,,4),,CONTIG),
//               DCB=(LRECL=60,BLKSIZE=3600,RECFM=FB,DSORG=IS,
//                KEYLEN=6,RKP=3,CYLOFL=6,OPTCD=Y)
//

Example 4: Printing an ISAM file

//PTISAM   JOB   HE66YFNH,
//               'W. CLARY'
//PRINT    EXEC  PGM=IEBISAM,
//               PARM='PRINTL'
//SYSPRINT DD    SYSOUT=A
//SYSUT1   DD    DSN=ISMAST,
//               DISP=OLD,
//               DCB=DSORG=IS
//SYSUT2   DD    SYSOUT=A
//
```

Figure 7-4 Examples of the IEBISAM utility program (part 2 of 2)

read conventional physical sequential files since the index and overflow pointers are included in an unloaded ISAM file.

LOAD does just the opposite: it causes the sequential unloaded ISAM file defined by SYSUT1 to be loaded as an ISAM file defined by SYSUT2. The file defined by SYSUT1 must be an unloaded ISAM file. In other words, you cannot create an ISAM file from a physical sequential file using this utility. The third example in figure 7-4 shows the file previously unloaded being loaded back into an ISAM file.

PRINTL causes the ISAM file defined by SYSUT1 to be printed in hexadecimal format on the print class defined by the SYSUT2 DD statement. Example 4 shows how to print an ISAM file.

The IEBPTPCH utility

The IEBPTPCH utility program is used to print or punch sequential and partitioned data sets. The options allow you to select certain members of a partitioned data set or certain fields in the records of a sequential or partitioned data set. You can also print or punch the directory of a partitioned data set. In addition, you can edit the input for formatted printing or punching.

Figure 7-5 illustrates the control statement formats and JCL sequence used for IEBPTPCH. There are four basic control statements: PRINT, PUNCH, MEMBER and RECORD. PRINT causes the data set to be printed, and it may be qualified with MEMBER and RECORD statements (for partitioned data sets) or with RECORD statements alone (for sequential data sets). PUNCH causes the data set to be punched and may be qualified in the same manner. The MEMBER statement tells the program which member of a partitioned data set is to be printed or punched, and the RECORD statement tells the program which fields in a record are to be printed or punched.

```
Control statement formats:

label   {PRINT}   PREFORM=A or M,
        {PUNCH}   TYPORG=PS or PO,
                  TOTCONV=XE or PZ,    (or omit for alphanumeric)
                  CNTRL=n,
                  STARTAFT=n,
                  STOPAFT=n,
                  SKIP=n,
                  MAXNAME=n,
                  MAXFLDS=n,
                  INITPG=n,
                  MAXLINE=n,
                  CDSEQ=n,
                  CDINCR=n

label   MEMBER    NAME=member-name

label   RECORD    FIELD=(length,input-location,conversion,output-location)...

JCL requirements:

EXEC
SYSPRINT
SYSUT1
SYSUT2
SYSIN
```

Figure 7-5 Control statement formats and JCL requirements for the IEBPTPCH utility program

The PRINT/PUNCH parameters The PRINT and PUNCH statements have a whole list of parameters that can be coded. Let me describe them briefly.

The PREFORM parameter indicates that the data set is already formatted for printing or punching, which means the records contain a control character for line spacing or punch stacker selection. The value A stands for an ASA character, while M specifies a machine-code character. If you code PREFORM = A or M, don't code any other parameters or control statements.

TYPORG indicates the data set organization. PS is physical sequential and PO is partitioned organization. The default value is PS.

TOTCONV indicates that the data is to be converted to hexadecimal (XE) or to unpacked decimal (PZ) format. If not coded, the data will be printed in alphanumeric format.

CNTRL indicates a control character for line spacing or punch stacker selection. For a print operation, 1 is for single spacing, 2 is for double spacing, and 3 is for triple spacing. For a punch operation, 1 is for stacker 1 and 2 is for stacker 2. The default value, whether printing or punching, is 1.

STARTAFT tells the program to bypass the number of records specified before beginning to print or punch. STOPAFT tells the program to stop printing or punching when the number of records specified has been read. SKIP causes the program to print or punch every nth record as specified. This parameter is useful when sampling records from a large file.

MAXNAME is used when printing or punching partitioned data sets. It specifies the number of members to be printed or punched. It must be equal to the number of MEMBER statements following the PRINT or PUNCH statement. MAXFLDS is used when you are formatting the output. It tells the program how many individual fields you are formatting.

INITPG is for printing operations only. It sets an initial page number for the printed listing. The default value is 1. MAXLINE sets the number of lines per page. The default value is 60 lines per page.

CDSEQ sets the initial card sequence number to be punched in columns 73 through 80 of the output cards. If CDSEQ is omitted, the cards are not sequenced. CDINCR tells the program the increment to be added to the sequence number for each card. The default value is 10. Of course, these two parameters are applicable only to punching operations.

The MEMBER and RECORD statements The formats of the MEMBER and RECORD statements are pretty much self-explanatory. The MEMBER statement simply tells which members of the partitioned data set should be printed or punched. The RECORD statement specifies which fields to operate on. Each FIELD parameter in the RECORD statement tells how long the field is, where the field starts in the input record, what format the data should be converted to before it's printed (hexadecimal, unpacked decimal, or alphanumeric), and where the field should begin in the output line or card. One FIELD parameter is coded for each field to be operated on.

Some examples   Now, let's look at figure 7-6. It shows two simple examples of printing and punching, without selecting members or formatting output.

The first example shows the statements to print a sequential file (TYPORG = PS). The output is to be double-spaced (CNTRL = 2) with a maximum of 50 lines per page (MAXLINE = 50).

The second example shows the execution of IEBPTPCH to punch a partitioned data set (TYPORG = PO). The second 100 records (STARTAFT = 100, STOPAFT = 200) are to be punched with sequence numbers in positions 73 through 80. The sequence numbers will start with 00000100, and each statement will be incremented by 5 (CDSEQ = 100, CDINCR = 5).

Figure 7-7 shows two more examples of the IEBPTPCH utility. These are more complicated in that they illustrate the selection and formatting options.

```
Example 1: Printing a sequential file

//EXPT      EXEC  PGM=IEBPTPCH
//SYSPRINT  DD    SYSOUT=A
//SYSUT1    DD    DSN=PAYFILE,
//                DISP=OLD
//SYSUT2    DD    SYSOUT=A
//SYSIN     DD    *
  PRINT     TYPORG=PS,CNTRL=2,MAXLINE=50
/*

Example 2: Punching a partitioned data set

//EXPCH     EXEC  PGM=IEBPTPCH
//SYSPRINT  DD    SYSOUT=A
//SYSUT1    DD    DSN=GENFILE,
//                DISP=OLD
//SYSUT2    DD    SYSOUT=B
//SYSIN     DD    *
  PUNCH     TYPORG=PO,STARTAFT=100,STOPAFT=200,CDSEQ=100,CDINCR=5
/*
```

Figure 7-6   Examples of the IEBPTPCH utility program without selection or editing

```
Example 1: Printing three fields of each record in a sequential file

//SELPT     EXEC  PGM=IEBPTCH
//SYSPRINT  DD    SYSOUT=A
//SYSUT1    DD    DSN=LOANFILE,
//                DISP=OLD
//SYSUT2    DD    SYSOUT=A
//SYSIN     DD    *
  PRINT     TYPORG=PS,CNTRL=2,STOPAFT=500,SKIP=5,MAXFLDS=3,       X
            INITPG=10,MAXLINE=56
  RECORD    FIELD=(6,12,PZ,7),FIELD=(5,20,,16),FIELD=(30,26,,50)
/*

Example 2: Punching three members of a partitioned data set

//SELPCH    EXEC  PGM=IEBPTCH
//SYSPRINT  DD    SYSOUT=A
//SYSUT1    DD    DSN=MMA.USERLIB,
//                DISP=SHR
//SYSUT2    DD    SYSOUT=B
//SYSIN     DD    *
  PUNCH     TYPORG=PO,MAXNAME=3
  MEMBER    NAME=PAYPROG
  MEMBER    NAME=GENLED
  MEMBER    NAME=OUT24
/*
```

Figure 7-7 Examples of the IEBPTPCH utility program with selection and editing

The first example illustrates a PRINT operation with the following requirements:

1. Print every fifth record (SKIP = 5) of the first 500 records (STOPAFT = 500) in the sequential file (TYPORG = PS).

2. Begin the page numbers at 10 (INITPG = 10) with 56 lines per page (MAXLINE = 56), including the spaces between the lines—the listing is double-spaced (CNTRL = 2). Three fields will be printed in each line (MAXFLDS = 3).

3. Format the printed output line like this:

    a. Print the 6-character input field that begins in position 12 on the listing. It should start in the 7th position of the print line. Convert the packed decimal data to unpacked decimal for printing.

    b. Print the 5-character input field that begins in position 20. It should start in the 16th print position. Don't perform any data conversion (the two consecutive commas indicate that the conversion subparameter is omitted).

    c. Print the 30-character input field that begins in position 26. It should start in the 50th position of the print line. Don't perform any data conversion.

Notice that I had to code a character in column 72 of the PRINT statement so I could continue the parameter list on the next line.

The second example shows how to punch three members of a partitioned data set. Here, I am punching three object programs from my program library MMA.USERLIB. The punching specifications are:

1. Punch three members (MAXNAME = 3) of a partitioned data set (TYPORG = PO).
2. The first member is PAYPROG (NAME = PAYPROG), the second is GENLED, and the third is OUT24.

When coding several MEMBER statements, they must be in the same sequence as the members in the partitioned data set. In our example, if OUT24 is physically located before GENLED in the partitioned data set, the program will punch PAYPROG and GENLED but will have already passed over OUT24 before reading the statements that affect it. As a result, a message will be printed telling me that the program couldn't find OUT24 in the data set.

The IEHPROGM utility

The IEHPROGM utility program is used to modify system control information in the volume table of contents and in the data set label. You can use it to delete and rename members of partitioned data sets, or to delete, rename, catalog, and uncatalog data sets. Additionally, as you learned in chapter 3, you can use it to build indexes for generation data groups.

Figure 7-8 shows the formats of the control statements, plus the JCL required to execute IEHPROGM. There are five basic statements and several more advanced statements used to build and delete catalog indexes and to add and modify data set passwords. The advanced statements will be skipped in this discussion. The five basic control statements are SCRATCH, RENAME, CATLG, UNCATLG, and BLDG. (Since we covered BLDG in chapter 3, it is included here for reference only.) Figure 7-9 illustrates how to use these basic control statements.

The first example in figure 7-9 shows a SCRATCH operation. To *scratch* a data set means to remove all references to that data set from the volume table of contents of the direct-access device. After a data set is scratched, further attempts to access it are not valid. Notice in the format in figure 7-8 that you can use SCRATCH for a library member by coding the MEMBER parameter. Also notice the VOL parameter. It specifies the device as well as the serial number of the volume.

The second example shows a RENAME operation. RENAME simply changes the data set name (or member name if partitioned) to the

```
Control statement formats:

label    SCRATCH    DSNAME=file-name,
                    VOL=device=serial-number,     (Example: VOL=3330=D00103)
                    MEMBER=member-name

label    RENAME     DSNAME=old-file-name,
                    VOL=device=serial-number,
                    NEWNAME=new-file-or-member-name,
                    MEMBER=old-member-name

label    CATLG      DSNAME=file-name,
                    VOL=device=serial-number

label    UNCATLG    DSNAME=file-name

label    BLDG       INDEX=file-name,
                    ENTRIES=n,
                    DELETE

Note: The DSNAME entry must specify the fully qualified data set name of the file.
      For example, for a generation data set: PAYFILE.G00001V00.

JCL requirements:

EXEC
SYSPRINT
ddname1    (defines the permanently mounted, system-residence volume)
ddname2    (defines a mountable volume where the data set resides)
SYSIN
```

Figure 7-8 Control statement formats and JCL requirements for the IEHPROGM utility program

new name you provide in the control statements. In the example, the data set TEMPPAY is renamed PAYMAST. If a member of a partitioned data set is to be renamed, you will also code the MEMBER parameter to identify the old member name.

Example 3 shows the IEHPROGM function to catalog a file. This causes the same result as if you had coded DISP = (NEW,CATLG) when the file was created. In this case, the file GMREL was created with a disposition of (NEW,KEEP). Here, it is being cataloged. You can use this IEHPROGM function to catalog ISAM files that were created with more than one DD statement, as long as all three areas of the ISAM file reside on the same volume. (See chapter 4 for more information on ISAM files.)

Chapter 7

Example 1: Scratching a data set

```
//SCR       EXEC  PGM=IEHPROGM
//SYSPRINT  DD    SYSOUT=A
//SYS1      DD    UNIT=3330,
//                VOL=SER=SYS001
//VOL1      DD    DISP=OLD,
//                UNIT=3330,
//                VOL=SER=D00103
//SYSIN     DD    *
   SCRATCH  DSNAME=GRFILE,VOL=3330=D00103
/*
```

Example 2: Renaming a data set

```
//RENAME    EXEC  PGM=IEHPROGM
//SYSPRINT  DD    SYSOUT=A
//SYS1      DD    UNIT=3330,
//                VOL=SER=SYS001
//VOL1      DD    DISP=OLD,
//                UNIT=3330,
//                VOL=SER=D00103
//SYSIN     DD    *
   RENAME   DSNAME=TEMPPAY,VOL=3330=D00103,NEWNAME=PAYMAST
/*
```

Example 3: Cataloging a data set

```
//CAT       EXEC  PGM=IEHPROGM
//SYSPRINT  DD    SYSOUT=A
//SYS1      DD    UNIT=3330
//                VOL=SER=SYSC01
//SYS2      DD    UNIT=3330,
//                VOL=SER=D00103
//SYSIN     DD    *
   CATLG    DSNAME=GMREL,VOL=3330=D00103
/*
```

Figure 7-9 Examples of the IEHPROGM utility program (part 1 of 2)

Example 4 shows the IEHPROGM function to uncatalog a file. UNCATLG removes the file name from the catalog, but the file is still available. It's just as though you had coded DISP = (NEW,KEEP) instead of (NEW,CATLG) when the file was created. If you want to completely delete a cataloged file, you must code the SCRATCH and UNCATLG statements to remove the file name from the catalog and delete the file from the disk. If you only scratch a cataloged file, its name will still be in the catalog, but the file won't exist. This will result in a JCL error (DATA SET NOT FOUND) when you try to access it by using the catalog. The fifth example in figure 7-9 shows a SCRATCH and UNCATLG operation.

```
Example 4: Uncataloging a data set

//UNCAT     EXEC PGM=IEHPROGM
//SYSPRINT  DD   SYSOUT=A
//SYSFLE    DD   UNIT=3350,
//               VOL=SER=CAT002
//MYFILE    DD   UNIT=3350,
//               VOL=SER=LIB111
//SYSIN     DD   *
   UNCATLG  DSNAME=ROFDS
/*

Example 5: Deleting a cataloged data set

//DELETE    EXEC PGM=IEHPROGM
//SYSPRINT  DD   SYSOUT=A
//DEV1      DD   UNIT=3330,
//               VOL=SER=PUBC01
//DEV2      DD   UNIT=2314,
//               VOL=SER=USER20
//SYSIN     DD   *
   SCRATCH  DSNAME=ORGDATA,VOL=2314=USER20
   UNCATLG  DSNAME=ORGDATA
/*

Example 6: Building a generation data group index

//BLDGDG    EXEC PGM=IEHPROGM
//SYSPRINT  DD   SYSOUT=A
//CATDD     DD   UNIT=DISKA,
//               VOL=SER=SYS001
//GDG       DD   UNIT=DISKA,
//               VOL=SER=LIB114
//SYSIN     DD   *
   BLDG     INDEX=MMAMAST,ENTRIES=4,DELETE
/*
```

Figure 7-9 Examples of the IEHPROGM utility program (part 2 of 2)

The last example shows the IEHPROGM function to build a generation data group index. Refer back to chapter 3 for the description of generation data sets.

The IEFBR14 program

Although the IEFBR14 program is not considered by IBM to be a utility program, (it's not presented in the IBM utilities manual), we use it like a utility. This program is unusual in that it doesn't do anything. In fact, its name is derived from an assembler language instruction for a no-op (no operation). Then why use it if it doesn't do anything? There are several cases when you may want to run a program that works under all circumstances. I'll present two of these cases.

File manipulation First, IEFBR14 provides us with a means of coding DD statements in a job step that won't affect any data. To illustrate, consider the first example in figure 7-10. Here, the IEFBR14 program is executed, and a DD statement is coded in the job step. Even though the file referenced by that DD statement is not affected by the IEFBR14 program, OS will process the disposition of the file. In this case, the file is deleted.

The IEFBR14 program can also be used to catalog and uncatalog data sets that already exist, or to create a null file. Figure 7-10 shows examples of these other three uses. The second example catalogs a file (it was created previously with DISP=(NEW,KEEP)), the third uncatalogs a file, and the fourth creates a new file with no data. Since IEFBR14 is easier to use than IEHPROGM, many programmers use

Example 1: Deleting a data set

```
//KILLSTEP  EXEC  PGM=IEFBR14
//FILE      DD    DSN=ENGDATA,
//                DISP=(OLD,DELETE)
```

Example 2: Cataloging a data set

```
//CATSTEP   EXEC  PGM=IEFBR14
//CATF      DD    DSN=LOCREG,
//                DISP=(OLD,CATLG)
```

Example 3: Uncataloging a data set

```
//UNCSTEP   EXEC  PGM=IEFBR14
//UNCF      DD    DSN=BRONPRD
//                DISP=(OLD,UNCATLG)
```

Example 4: Building a data set

```
//BLDSTEP   EXEC  PGM=IEFBR14
//BLDFLE    DD    DSN=MRK7DATA,
//                DISP=(NEW,KEEP),
//                UNIT=DISKA,
//                VOL=SER=LIE113,
//                SPACE=(800,(5,2)),
//                DCB=(LRECL=80,BLKSIZE=800,RECFM=FB)
```

Figure 7-10 Examples of the IEFBR14 program to delete, catalog, uncatalog, and build data sets

this do-nothing program for all their file manipulations involving deleting, cataloging, and uncataloging.

Testing JCL The second use of IEFBR14 is as a dummy program for testing JCL. Since the program can't fail, the return code issued is always zero. The file disposition is accomplished just as if the program were real.

To illustrate, look at figure 7-11. It shows a job in three phases of testing. In the first phase, all three steps execute the IEFBR14 program to test the JCL for syntax errors. The master files are dummy files, so no real data is affected. In the second phase, real program names and STEPLIB DD statements replace the IEFBR14 programs. These replacements can also be done one at a time to test the system in a modular fashion. In the third phase, real files are used in place of the dummy files. The result is an orderly, controlled method of testing large job streams.

RETURN CODES

OS utilities issue return codes that can be tested in the COND parameters of your JCL. This can be useful when an abnormal situation arises and you want to bypass the execution of subsequent steps in a job. Figure 7-12 lists the return codes of the utilities presented here. A description of their meanings is also presented.

Terminology

utility program
utility control statement
compress

compress in place
unloaded ISAM format
scratch

Objectives

1. Write the JCL and utility control statements to execute IEBCOPY, IEBISAM, IEBPTPCH, and IEHPROGM.
2. Write the JCL to execute the IEFBR14 program to (1) create a null file, (2) delete a file, (3) catalog a file, and (4) uncatalog a file.

Problems

1. (Objective 1) Write the JCL to copy one partitioned data set to another, using these specifications:
   a. The old data set name is PODSFILE.

Phase 1:

```
//DM1200    JOB   HE66YFNH,
//                'W. CLARY'
//CAPSTEP   EXEC  PGM=IEFBR14
//CAPIN     DD    DUMMY
//CAPOUT    DD    DSN=CAPPRL,
//                DISP=(NEW,CATLG),
//                UNIT=DISKA,
//                VOL=SER=LIB111,
//                SPACE=(TRK,(10,2),RLSE),
//                DCB=(LRECL=90,BLKSIZE=1800,RECFM=FB)
//PRTSTEP   EXEC  PGM=IEFBR14
//CAPDATA   DD    DSN=CAPPRL,
//                DISP=OLD
//PRTLST    DD    SYSOUT=A
//STMTSTEP  EXEC  PGM=IEFBR14
//STMTMAST  DD    DUMMY
//CAPDATA   DD    DSN=CAPPRL,
//                DISP=OLD
//STMTLST   DD    SYSOUT=A
//
```

Phase 2:

```
//DM1200    JOB   HE66YFNH,
//                'W. CLARY'
//CAPSTEP   EXEC  PGM=CAPPROM
//STEPLIB   DD    DSN=MMA.USERLIB,
//                DISP=SHR
//CAPIN     DD    DUMMY
//CAPOUT    DD    DSN=CAPPRL,
//                DISP=(NEW,CATLG),
//                UNIT=DISKA,
//                VOL=SER=LIB111,
//                SPACE=(TRK,(10,2),RLSE),
//                DCB=(LRECL=90,BLKSIZE=1800,RECFM=FB)
//PRTSTEP   EXEC  PGM=CAPPRT1
//STEPLIB   DD    DSN=MMA.USERLIB,
//                DISP=SHR
//CAPDATA   DD    DSN=CAPPRL,
//                DISP=OLD
//PRTLST    DD    SYSOUT=A
//STMTSTEP  EXEC  PGM=CAPPRT2
//STEPLIB   DD    DSN=MMA.USERLIB,
//                DISP=SHR
//STMTMAST  DD    DUMMY
//CAPDATA   DD    DSN=CAPPRL,
//                DISP=OLD
//STMTLST   DD    SYSOUT=A
//
```

Figure 7-11 Testing a job stream in three phases using IEFBR14 and DUMMY files (part 1 of 2)

Phase 3:

```
//DM1200    JOB   HE66YFNH,
//                'W. CLARY'
//CAPSTEP   EXEC  PGM=CAPPROM
//STEPLIB   DD    DSN=MMA.USERLIB,
//                DISP=SHR
//CAPIN     DD    DSN=CAPMAST,
//                DISP=OLD
//CAPOUT    DD    DSN=CAPPRL,
//                DISP=(NEW,CATLG),
//                UNIT=DISKA,
//                VOL=SER=LIB111,
//                SPACE=(TRK,(10,2),RLSE),
//                DCB=(LRECL=90,BLKSIZE=1800,RECFM=FB)
//PRTSTEP   EXEC  PGM=CAPPRT1
//STEPLIB   DD    DSN=MMA.USERLIB,
//                DISP=SHR
//CAPDATA   DD    DSN=CAPPRL,
//                DISP=OLD
//PRTLST    DD    SYSOUT=A
//STMTSTEP  EXEC  PGM=CAPPRT2
//STEPLIB   DD    DSN=MMA.USERLIB,
//                DISP=SHR
//STMTMAST  DD    DSN=STMTMAST,
//                DISP=OLD
//CAPDATA   DD    DSN=CAPPRL,
//                DISP=OLD
//STMTLST   DD    SYSOUT=A
//
```

Figure 7-11 Testing a job stream in three phases using IEFBR14 and DUMMY files (part 2 of 2)

    b. The new data set name is NEWPODS.

    c. The new file should reside on a 2314 disk pack named USER20.

    d. Allocate 20 cylinders for the primary extent, 10 for the secondary extents, with 5 directory blocks.

    e. The records in the file will be fixed-length, 80 bytes long, blocked 12 to a block.

    f. Copy all members except PODS27.

    g. Catalog the new data set.

2. (Objective 1) Write the JCL to unload an ISAM file named ISMAST to a scratch tape (a 2400 series magnetic tape volume). The file is on a 3330 disk pack named D00103 and has fixed records that are 85 characters long, blocked 10 records to a block. Catalog the output tape.

Program name	Return code	Meaning
IEBCOPY	00	Program ran OK
	04	Probable error—program executed
	08	Unrecoverable error—program terminated
IEBISAM	00	Program ran OK
	12	Unrecoverable error—program terminated
IEBPTPCH	00	Program ran OK
	04	No data was found in the input data set
	08	Unrecoverable error—program terminated
	16	Unrecoverable error—program terminated
IEHPROGM	00	Program ran OK
	04	Syntax error on name field or in PARM parameter value
	08	Bad control statement—operation not performed, program executed
	12	SYSPRINT, SYSIN, or I/O error—program terminated
	16	Unrecoverable error—program terminated
IEFBR14	00	Always the return code

Figure 7-12 Return codes issued by OS utility programs

3. (Objective 1) Write the JCL to execute a utility program that will do the following:

   a. Print the first 50 records in a member of a partitioned data set named GPOLIB. The member name is SEL001.

   b. Format the output listing. It should be double-spaced, with 58 lines per page. The first page number should be 1.

4. (Objective 1) Write the JCL to scratch and uncatalog the ISAM file described in problem 2. For the permanently mounted volume, use volume serial number SYS001, a 3330 disk pack.

5. (Objective 2) Write the JCL to execute the IEFBR14 program to delete a cataloged file named UNC21.

OS Utilities and the Sort/Merge

Solutions

1. Figure 7-13 is an acceptable solution.
2. Figure 7-14 is an acceptable solution.
3. Figure 7-15 is an acceptable solution.
4. Figure 7-16 is an acceptable solution.
5. Figure 7-17 is an acceptable solution.

```
//COPY      EXEC  PGM=IEBCOPY
//SYSPRINT  DD    SYSOUT=A
//COP1      DD    DSN=PODSFILE,
//                DISP=OLD
//COP2      DD    DSN=NEWPODS,
//                DISP=(NEW,CATLG),
//                UNIT=2314,
//                VOL=SER=USER20,
//                SPACE=(CYL,(20,10,5)),
//                DCB=(LRECL=80,BLKSIZE=960,RECFM=FB,DSORG=PO)
//SYSUT3    DD    UNIT=3330,
//                SPACE=(TRK,1)
//SYSUT4    DD    UNIT=3330,
//                SPACE=(TRK,1)
//SYSIN     DD    *
   COPY     OUTDD=COP2,INDD=COP1
   EXCLUDE  MEMBER=PODS27
/*
```

Figure 7-13 Executing IEBCOPY to copy a data set

```
//UNLOAD    EXEC  PGM=IEBISAM,
//                PARM='UNLOAD'
//SYSPRINT  DD    SYSOUT=A
//SYSUT1    DD    DSN=ISMAST,
//                DISP=OLD,
//                UNIT=3330,
//                VOL=SER=DOG103,
//                DCB=DSORG=IS
//SYSUT2    DD    DSN=BACKMAST,
//                DISP=(NEW,CATLG),
//                UNIT=2400,
//                DCB=(LRECL=85,BLKSIZE=850,RECFM=FB)
```

Figure 7-14 Executing IEBISAM to unload an ISAM file

```
//P1STEP    EXEC  PGM=IEBPTPCH
//SYSPRINT  DD    SYSOUT=A
//SYSUT1    DD    DSN=GPOLIB,
//                DISP=SHR
//SYSUT2    DD    SYSOUT=A
//SYSIN     DD    *
   PRINT    TYPORG=PO,CNTRL=2,STOPAFT=50,MAXNAME=1,INITPG=1,MAXLINE=58
   MEMBER   NAME=SELC01
/*
```

Figure 7-15 Executing IEBPTPCH to print a library member

```
//SCUNC     EXEC  PGM=IEHPROGM
//SYSPRINT  DD    SYSOUT=A
//VOL1      DD    UNIT=3330,
//                VOL=SER=SYS001
//VOL2      DD    UNIT=3330,
//                VOL=SER=D00103
//SYSIN     DD    *
   SCRATCH  DSNAME=ISMAST,VOL=3330=D00103
   UNCATLG  DSNAME=ISMAST
/*
```

Figure 7-16 Executing IEHPROGM to scratch and uncatalog an ISAM file

```
//KILL      EXEC  PGM=IEFBR14
//FILE      DD    DSN=UNC21,
//                DISP=(OLD,DELETE)
```

Figure 7-17 Executing IEFBR14 to delete a file

TOPIC 2   The OS Sort/Merge Program

Since input data seldom enters a computer system in the order of the desired output, the sort/merge program is one of the most commonly used programs in existence. As a result, most computers provide sort/merge programs that are generalized so you can customize the sorting and merging to fit your specific file requirements. You provide control information, and the sort/merge adjusts itself accordingly to sort or merge the records in the sequence you specify.

There are two functions of the sort/merge operation (as the name implies). The *sort* function assumes all input records are out of sequence, and it puts them in the sequence you ask for; the *merge* function assumes that the input records are in the proper sequence, but in multiple files, so it combines them into one sequenced file. When you request the sort function, both the sort and merge may be executed, depending on the number of records in the file to be sorted. When you request the merge function, only the merge will be executed.

IBM provides the user with one of three versions of its sort/merge program, depending on the hardware installed on the system. In addition, there are software vendors who will sell you still other versions. In this topic, I'll only be discussing the JCL and sort/merge control statements for the IBM-supplied versions. However, please bear in mind throughout this discussion that there are only minor changes in the JCL when you change from the IBM sort/merge to another vendor's sort/merge package. You should check with your installation for more specific guidelines regarding the sort/merge program.

EXECUTING THE SORT/MERGE PROGRAM THROUGH JCL

The sort/merge program can be executed in one of two ways: either through JCL statements like any other program or through linkages to user-written programs in languages like COBOL, PL/I, and assembler. I'll get to the JCL for executing user-written sorts in a few minutes. In this section, though, I want to show you how to execute the sort/merge program on its own.

Sort/merge control statements

When the sort/merge program is executed through JCL, it is controlled by the JCL specifications and by *sort/merge control statements*. This is similar to the way utility programs are controlled by utility control statements. The sort/merge program reads one or more input files, and, depending on the information provided by the control statements, it sorts the records of those files, merges them together, and writes an output file in the proper sequence.

Figure 7-18 illustrates the formats of the sort/merge control statements. There are two commands (SORT and MERGE) to execute the two functions of the program. There are also other control statements that can be used to link the sort to user-written exits, but these will not be covered here.

```
Format 1:

{SORT  }
{MERGE }   FIELDS=(location,length,sequence,...),FORMAT=format

Format 2:

{SORT  }
{MERGE }   FIELDS=(location,length,format,sequence,...)
```

location	The beginning position of the field within the record
length	The number of characters in the field
sequence	Either A for ascending or D for descending
format	A two-character code for the type of data: CH for character data, BI for binary data, ZD for zoned decimal data. Use format 1 if all fields are the same type of data; use format 2 if the fields are different types of data.

Note: Position 1 of the SORT and MERGE statements must be blank.

Figure 7-18 Sort/merge control statement formats

    The purpose of the FIELDS parameter in the SORT and MERGE control statements is to tell the sort/merge program the sequence you want the output to be in. Each series of location, length, and sequence subparameters makes up a single *key field* by which the program is to be sequenced. Then, the key fields specified in the control statement make up a *control word*. Internally, the sort/merge program views the control word as a single field and uses it to control the sequencing of the file.

    To illustrate, look at figure 7-19. It shows ten unsorted records, the SORT control statement to sort those records into the desired sequence, and the result of the operation: the sorted records.

    In this example, the file is to be sorted by a control word made up of three key fields. According to the FIELDS parameter of this SORT control statement, the program is directed to (1) sort the records in ascending order according to the 6-character field that begins in position 3 of each record; (2) within that sequence, sort the records into descending order according to the 3-character field that begins in position 11; and (3) within that sequence, sort the records into ascending order according to the 3-character field that begins in position 18. In other words, the subfields of the SORT control statement indicate major to minor sequencing from left to right in the control statement.

Figure 7-19 Example of the sort operation

Unsorted records:

Position:	3-8	11-13	18-20
	012345	AAA	012
	012345	ABC	907
	011947	RB2	106
	047693	AAT	999
	142342	BBR	212
	002973	972	660
	112233	617	127
	019412	322	432
	019412	605	692
	019412	605	000

SORT statement:

```
SORT    FIELDS=(3,6,A,11,3,D,18,3,A),FORMAT=CH
```

Sorted records:

002973	972	660
011947	RB2	106
012345	ABC	907
012345	AAA	012
019412	605	000
019412	605	692
019412	322	432
047693	AAT	999
112233	617	127
142342	BBR	212

You can see the result of this sequencing in the bottom part of figure 7-19. The records are in ascending sequence according to the values in positions 3-8. For the records that have the same data in this field (012345 and 019412), the records are in descending sequence according to the values of the field in positions 11-13. Finally, for the records that still have the same value (019412 in the first field and 605 in the second field), the records are in ascending sequence according the values found in positions 18-20.

The FORMAT parameter of the SORT/MERGE control statement indicates what type of data is contained in the key fields. In this case, it's character (CH) data. You can also code BI for binary data or ZD for zoned decimal data. If the fields each contain different types of data, you would use the second SORT statement format in figure 7-18. For example, the SORT statement that follows would perform the same sequencing as that shown in figure 7-19 if the fields were different data types:

```
SORT FIELDS=(3,6,CH,A,11,3,BI,D,18,3,ZD,A)
```

This assumes that the first field is character data, the second is binary, and the third is zoned decimal.

To illustrate the use of the MERGE statement, look at figure 7-20. It shows two files, already in the desired sequence, that I want to merge into a single sequenced file. After the MERGE statement is executed, the output is in the same sequence as the input, but the two files are combined into one sequenced file. The subfields of the MERGE statement comprising the control word for the merge operation are similar to those for the sort operation, and the same rules apply.

Coding the JCL

Figure 7-21 shows the JCL statements you need in order to execute the sort/merge program. The EXEC statement causes the sort/merge program to be executed with a PARM parameter. The program name SORT is the name of the sort/merge version installed in my computer. You should check with your installation to determine the name of the program to execute. I'll explain the PARM values in just a moment.

The SORTLIB DD statement defines the library where the support modules for the sort/merge program reside. You'll have to find out the name of this library at your installation. SYSOUT defines the standard print device for sort messages.

SORTIN defines the input file to be sorted. If you are requesting a merge operation, you use SORTIN01, SORTIN02, etc., to define the two or more input files to the merge. If you are sorting more than one file, you can concatenate them into the SORTIN file like this:

```
//SORTIN    DD   DSN=INFILE1,
//               DISP=OLD
//          DD   DSN=INFILE2,
//               DISP=OLD
```

In this case, the sort program will treat INFILE1 and INFILE2 as a single file to be sorted.

```
              Input file 1:              Input file 2:
Position:     1-5      9                 1-5      9
              01234    A                 01234    B
              02694    A                 01234    E
              02694    D                 02988    A
              02988    R                 06111    T
              05617    B                 07122    R
              05617    C                 88216    A
              98999    D                 98999    A
              98999    E                 98999    Z
              99667    X                 99500    B
              99999    Z                 99999    T
```

MERGE statement:

```
    MERGE    FIELDS=(1,5,A,9,1,A),FORMAT=CH
```

Merged file:

```
    01234    A
    01234    B
    01234    E
    02694    A
    02694    D
    02988    A
    02988    R
    05617    B
    05617    C
    06611    T
    07122    R
    88216    A
    98999    A
    98999    D
    98999    E
    98999    Z
    99500    B
    99667    X
    99999    T
    99999    Z
```

Figure 7-20 Example of the merge operation

```
//EXSORT    EXEC PGM=SORT,
//               PARM=',SIZE=MAX'
//SORTLIB   DD   DSN=SYS1.SORTLIB,
//               DISP=SHR
//SYSOUT    DD   SYSOUT=A
//SORTIN    DD   DSN=UNSFILE,
//               DISP=OLD
//SORTWK01  DD   UNIT=SYSDA,
//               SPACE=(CYL,20,,CONTIG)
//SORTWK02  DD   UNIT=SYSDA,
//               SPACE=(CYL,20,,CONTIG)
//SORTWK03  DD   UNIT=SYSDA,
//               SPACE=(CYL,20,,CONTIG)
//SORTOUT   DD   DSN=STFILE,
//               DISP=(NEW,CATLG),
//               UNIT=2314,
//               VOL=SER=USER20,
//               SPACE=(1800,(10,2),RLSE),
//               DCB=(LRECL=90,BLKSIZE=1800,RECFM=FB)
//SYSIN     DD   *
  SORT          FIELDS=(2,13,A,20,1,A),FORMAT=CH
/*
```

Figure 7-21 JCL required for the sort/merge program

SORTWKnn DD statements are work areas defined on tape or direct-access volumes. The nn may be a number from 01 to 32 for tape SORTWKs or 01 to 06 for direct-access SORTWKs. Actually, tape SORTWKs are rare, so you'll usually find three to six direct-access SORTWK areas are defined. A merge-only function doesn't require work areas, so you can omit the SORTWKs from the merge JCL.

The amount of space you request for these *intermediate storage areas* is determined by record length, the number of records to be sorted, and the number of intermediate areas you define. Formulas for calculating intermediate storage requirements differ depending on the version of the sort/merge and the type of hardware installed. You should check with your installation to find how to calculate the most efficient size for these work areas on your system. And it's a good idea to use the CONTIG option in the SPACE parameter for these areas.

SORTOUT defines the output file where the sorted records are written. It can be a new file with DISP=(NEW,KEEP) or (NEW,CATLG), or it can be an extension of an old file with DISP=(MOD,KEEP).

SYSIN defines the input control statements to the sort/merge program. It can define instream data by coding DD *, or it can have a

DSN that specifies a separate file or member of a partitioned data set that contains the sort/merge control statements. In figure 7-21, a single control statement is coded instream. It says to sort the file (UNSFILE) into ascending sequence by the 13-character field starting in position 2 of each record. Within that field, the file will be sorted into ascending sequence by the character in position 20. Both fields contain character format data.

Coding PARM values for the sort/merge There are five PARM parameter options you can supply to the sort/merge in a positional list, as shown in figure 7-22. Here is a description of each, along with recommendations on using them:

1. Coding the first subparameter, which changes the sort technique, is not recommended because the sort/merge will derive an appropriate technique. It's mentioned here since it is positional, so you must code a comma to indicate its absence.

```
PARM='technique,SIZE= {XXX} ,MSG=yy, {LIST  } ,DIAG'
                     {MAX}           {NOLIST}
```

technique	Sequence distribution technique—not recommended
SIZE=	Actual main storage size or MAX for maximum available—MAX recommended
MSG=yy	The field yy can have one of these values:
	NO No messages are to be printed
	CC Print only critical messages on the system console
	CP Print only critical messages on the printer and system console
	AC Print all messages on the system console
	AP Print all messages on the printer and critical messages on the system console
	PC Print all messages on the printer and system console
	It is recommended that MSG be omitted entirely.
LIST NOLIST	LIST means print a listing of the sort/merge control statements; NOLIST means suppress the listing—LIST is recommended
DIAG	Provides a list of control statements, a module map, and a list of diagnostic messages describing the sort execution. It can also be used to generate a dump of the sort/merge main storage. This option is not recommended.

Figure 7-22 PARM values for the sort/merge EXEC statement

2. You can specify the amount of main storage to be allocated to the program by coding SIZE = core-size or SIZE = MAX. If you code SIZE = MAX, the program will calculate the available main storage and allocate it, resulting in a more efficient sort operation. I recommend that you always code SIZE = MAX.
3. You can override the options specified at your installation concerning the printing of messages by coding MSG = xx, where xx is one of the two-character codes listed in figure 7-22. I recommend that you don't override the options specified by your installation. So don't code this option.
4. The listing option can be overridden by coding either LIST or NOLIST. LIST causes all program control statements to be printed; NOLIST suppresses all printing. I recommend that you code LIST if LIST isn't your installation default.
5. The fifth option, DIAG, should never be used unless you need a detail listing of the modules of the sort/merge program. The only time you should select this option is when the sort/merge program doesn't work properly and you are reporting that to IBM or the software vendor.

Figure 7-23 gives three examples of PARM parameters. The PARM in example 1 specifies that 100,000 bytes of main storage should be used for the sort/merge program, and that no messages or sort/merge control statements should be printed. In example 2, the PARM says to use as much main storage as is available for the sort/merge run, to print critical messages on both the printer and system console, and to print a listing of the sort/merge control statements. And in example 3, the PARM simply says to use as much main storage as possible for the program. I recommend that you code all sort/merge PARMs like example 3.

```
Example 1
    //EX1       EXEC  PGM=SORT,
    //                PARM=',SIZE=100000,MSG=NO,NOLIST'
Example 2
    //EX2       EXEC  PGM=SORT,
    //                PARM=',SIZE=MAX,MSG=CP,LIST'
Example 3
    //EX3       EXEC  PGM=SORT,
    //                PARM=',SIZE=MAX'
```

Figure 7-23 Examples of PARM values for the sort/merge program

Sample jobs

Figure 7-24 shows a job to execute the sort operation. It sorts a file named TEMPCOST into the sequence specified in the SORT statement, using SORTWK01 through SORTWK03 for intermediate work areas, then writes the sorted output onto the file defined by SORTOUT (SORTCOST).

Figure 7-25 shows a job to execute a merge operation that reads three SORTIN files and merges them into one output file, HISTALL. Remember that the three input files are already in the sequence defined by the MERGE statement, and they will now be combined into the output file in that same sequence.

EXECUTING THE SORT/MERGE PROGRAM FROM A USER-WRITTEN PROGRAM

For certain applications, you may find it more convenient to code a *COBOL sort*, *PL/I sort*, or *assembler sort* instead of a *standalone sort* (one executed through JCL). That means the sort/merge program is executed because of special statements you've put in your program.

```
//SORTJOB  JOB   HE66YFNH,
//              'W. CLARY'
//SORTSTEP EXEC  PGM=SORT,
//              PARM=',SIZE=MAX'
//SORTLIB  DD    DSN=SYS1.SORTLIB,
//              DISP=SHR
//SYSOUT   DD    SYSOUT=A
//SORTIN   DD    DSN=TEMPCOST,
//              DISP=OLD
//SORTWK01 DD    UNIT=SYSDA,
//              SPACE=(CYL,10,,CONTIG)
//SORTWK02 DD    UNIT=SYSDA,
//              SPACE=(CYL,10,,CONTIG)
//SORTWK03 DD    UNIT=SYSDA,
//              SPACE=(CYL,10,,CONTIG)
//SORTOUT  DD    DSN=SORTCOST,
//              DISP=(NEW,CATLG),
//              UNIT=3330,
//              VOL=SER=D00103,
//              SPACE=(CYL,(20,10),RLSE),
//              DCB=(LRECL=65,BLKSIZE=3250,RECFM=FB)
//SYSIN    DD    *
    SORT       FIELDS=(1,7,A,21,1,A,37,6,D),FORMAT=CH
/*
//
```

Figure 7-24 Sorting a file

```
//MGJOB     JOB  HE66YFNH,
//               'W. CLARY'
//MERGSTEP  EXEC PGM=SORT,
//               PARM=',SIZE=MAX'
//SORTLIB   DD   DSN=SYS1.SORTLIB,
//               DISP=SHR
//SYSOUT    DD   SYSOUT=A
//SORTIN01  DD   DSN=PAYFREQ,
//               DISP=OLD
//SORTIN02  DD   DSN=PAYHIST,
//               DISP=OLD
//SORTIN03  DD   DSN=PAYCURR,
//               DISP=OLD
//SORTOUT   DD   DSN=HISTALL,
//               DISP=(NEW,CATLG),
//               UNIT=2314,
//               VOL=SER=USER25,
//               SPACE=(1000,(50,12),RLSE),
//               DCB=(LRECL=100,BLKSIZE=1000,RECFM=FB)
//SYSIN     DD   *
  MERGE    FIELDS=(12,5,A,27,2,D),FORMAT=CH
/*
//
```

Figure 7-25 Merging three files

Figure 7-26 shows the JCL to execute a sort from a program written in COBOL, PL/I, or assembler language. The program specified in the EXEC statement is the name of the user-written program. The DD statements are the same as if there were no sort involved, except for the SORTWK DD statements and the SORTLIB DD statement. These are coded the same as for standalone sorts. The source program specifies which of the other files is to be sorted and which is to hold the sorted records. No control statements are used because the source program gives the sort/merge specifications. Consult the programmer's guide for your language to learn the programming considerations for executing the sort/merge program from your own programs.

DISCUSSION

In this topic, I've presented a general view of the IBM sort/merge program by showing the JCL and sort/merge control statements necessary to execute any version now in use. However, as I mentioned at the beginning of this topic, there are three currently supported versions of the IBM-supplied sort/merge program and at least one major non-

```
//LANGSORT JOB  HE66YFNH,
//              'W. CLARY'
//LANGSTEP EXEC PGM=MYPROG,
//              REGION=120K
//STEPLIB  DD   DSN=MMA.USERLIB,
//              DISP=SHR
//SORTLIB  DD   DSN=SYS1.SORTLIB,
//              DISP=SHR
//LANGIN   DD   DSN=OLDFILE,
//              DISP=OLD
//SORTWK01 DD   UNIT=SYSDA,
//              SPACE=(CYL,10,,CONTIG)
//SORTWK02 DD   UNIT=SYSDA,
//              SPACE=(CYL,10,,CONTIG)
//SORTWK03 DD   UNIT=SYSDA,
//              SPACE=(CYL,10,,CONTIG)
//LANGOUT  DD   DSN=NEWFILE,
//              DISP=(NEW,CATLG),
//              UNIT=SYSDA,
//              VOL=SER=PUB001,
//              SPACE=(TRK,(90,10),RLSE),
//              DCB=(LRECL=80,BLKSIZE=800,RECFM=FB)
//
```

Figure 7-26 Executing a COBOL, PL/I, or assembler sort

IBM sort/merge package available for use on the System/360-370. (The non-IBM package I'm referring to is the Whitlow Computer Systems Inc. SYNCSORT.) As a result, some of the information presented here may not be required by the version of the sort/merge installed on your computer system, or there may be ways to increase the efficiency of the sorting and merging operation by coding the JCL in a different way than shown here. So I recommend that you study the sort/merge standards in use at your installation and pattern your sort/merge JCL and control statements after them. Then, with experience, you'll be able to code efficient sort/merge jobs.

Terminology

sort
merge
sort/merge control statement
control word
key field

intermediate storage
COBOL sort
PL/I sort
assembler sort
standalone sort

Objective

Given reference material, write the JCL and sort/merge control statements to execute the IBM-supplied OS sort/merge program to given specifications.

Problems

1. Write the JCL and sort/merge control statements to sort a file, using the following specifications:
   a. Sort on two fields: position 6 for a length of 5 in ascending sequence and position 27 for a length of 7 in descending sequence. The fields are both character data.
   b. The input file is a data set named SMA22. It is an existing cataloged data set. Its record length is 95, its block size is 1900, and its record format is FB.
   c. The output file is to reside on a 2314 disk volume named USER12. It will require enough space to hold 16 blocks of 10 records each. The record length is 95, the block size is 950, and the record format is FB. Make up your own data set name.
   d. Use three SORTWK areas on 3330 devices.
   e. Use the sort/merge program name and library name that are used in your installation.
2. Write the JCL and sort/merge control statements to merge three files, using the following specifications:
   a. Merge three cataloged input files on the 10 characters beginning in position 3 of each record in ascending sequence. The first file is named PREVCOST, the second file is named CURRCOST, and the third file is named ALTCOST.
   b. Catalog the output data set on a 3330 disk volume named PUB001. The data set name is to be TOTCOST. Allocate space in blocks of 960 characters: one block in the primary and one block in each secondary extent. The record length is 80, the block size is 960, and the record format is FB.
   c. Use the sort/merge program name and library name that are used in your installation.

Solutions

1. Figure 7-27 is an acceptable solution.
2. Figure 7-28 is an acceptable solution.

```
//STJOB     JOB  HE66YFNH,
//               'W. CLARY'
//SORT1     EXEC PGM=SORT,
//               PARM=',SIZE=MAX'
//SORTLIB   DD   DSN=SYS1.SORTLIB,
//               DISP=SHR
//SYSOUT    DD   SYSOUT=A
//SORTIN    DD   DSN=SMA22,
//               DISP=OLD
//SORTWK01  DD   UNIT=3330,
//               SPACE=(CYL,10,,CONTIG)
//SORTWK02  DD   UNIT=3330,
//               SPACE=(CYL,10,,CONTIG)
//SORTWK03  DD   UNIT=3330,
//               SPACE=(CYL,10,,CONTIG)
//SORTOUT   DD   DSN=SORTSMA,
//               DISP=(NEW,KEEP),
//               UNIT=2314,
//               VOL=SER=USER12,
//               SPACE=(950,(16,1),RLSE),
//               DCB=(LRECL=95,BLKSIZE=950,RECFM=FB)
//SYSIN     DD   *
   SORT         FIELDS=(6,5,A,27,7,D),FORMAT=CH
/*
//
```

Figure 7-27 Executing the sort operation

```
//MGJOB     JOB  HE66YFNH,
//               'W. CLARY'
//MERG      EXEC PGM=SORT,
//               PARM=',SIZE=MAX'
//SORTLIB   DD   DSN=SYS1.SORTLIB,
//               DISP=SHR
//SYSOUT    DD   SYSOUT=A
//SORTIN01  DD   DSN=PREVCOST,
//               DISP=OLD
//SORTIN02  DD   DSN=CURRCOST,
//               DISP=OLD
//SORTIN03  DD   DSN=ALTCOST,
//               DISP=OLD
//SORTOUT   DD   DSN=TOTCOST,
//               DISP=(NEW,CATLG),
//               UNIT=3330,
//               VOL=SER=PUB001,
//               SPACE=(960,(1,1),RLSE),
//               DCB=(LRECL=80,BLKSIZE=960,RECFM=FB)
//SYSIN     DD   *
   MERGE        FIELDS=(3,10,A),FORMAT=CH
/*
//
```

Figure 7-28 Executing the merge operation

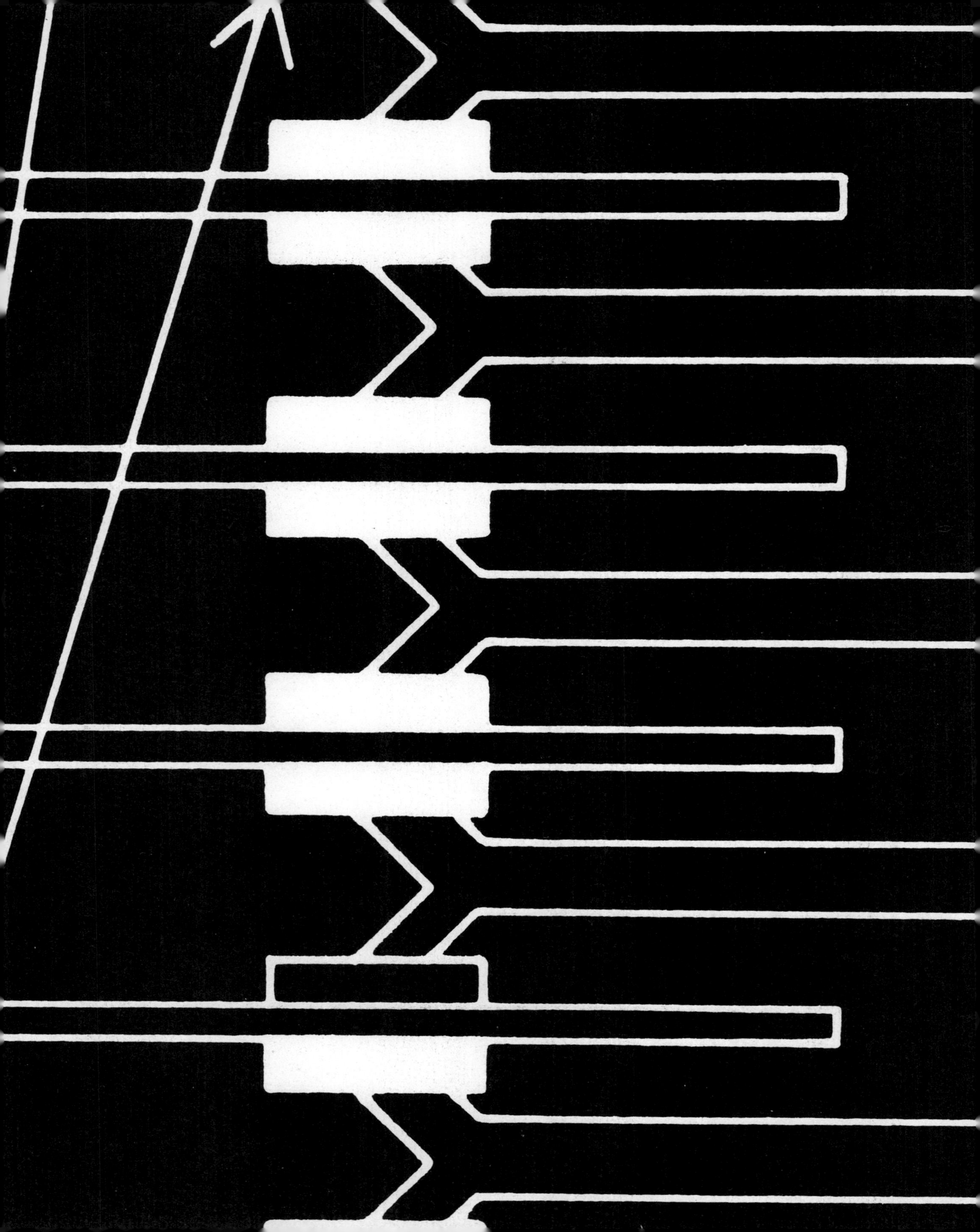

8

Language Translators and the Link-Edit Program

When you write a program in COBOL, PL/I, assembler, or FORTRAN, it must be translated into machine language and put into a format that can be executed by the computer. This chapter presents the JCL you need in order to execute the language translators and the link-edit program for this purpose. In topic 1, you'll learn how to compile your source program and execute the first level of the link-edit program (that is, to link edit a program that is not a subprogram and doesn't call a subprogram). Then, in topic 2, you'll learn how to execute the next level of the link-edit program for programs that use subprograms or are themselves subprograms.

TOPIC 1 Language Translators

As you learned in chapter 1, the *language translators* are the assemblers and compilers supplied with an operating system. With OS, multiple versions of assembler, COBOL, FORTRAN, PL/I, and RPG compilers are provided. Other compilers are also available, but they aren't widely used. The intent of the language translators is to reduce the programming time required to prepare a working object program. In this topic, I'll show you how to code the JCL for the four most commonly used translators: assembler, COBOL, FORTRAN, and PL/I.

CATALOGED PROCEDURES FOR THE LANGUAGE TRANSLATORS

Most installations have cataloged procedures to execute the compilers in a number of different ways. (Cataloged procedures are covered in chapter 5.) There are usually four cataloged procedures associated with each language translator. First, there is a procedure to *compile-only*. This usually produces a source listing and diagnostic messages where required. It can also create an *object module*. As you learned in chapter 1, although an object module consists of machine instructions, it is not executable as it is. It must be link edited to resolve relative addresses and any external references made outside the program.

Second, there is a procedure to *compile-and-link* the program. This is usually a two-step procedure: the first step compiles the program as in a compile-only procedure, and the second step prepares the object module for execution by link editing it and placing it into a load library. (You'll learn more about link editing in topic 2.) The *load module* can now be executed from the load library without further preparation. This procedure is usually used after the program has been fully tested and is ready to be placed into production.

Third, there is a procedure to *compile-and-go*. Briefly, this means that the source program is compiled, and the output of the compile is executed by another program—the loader program. This is the procedure you will normally use to test a program. After it has been tested, you can execute a compile-and-link procedure or just execute the link-edit program to place the load module into the load library for production purposes.

Fourth, there is a procedure to *compile-link-and-go*. This procedure is often used to make minor modifications to programs in production. The program is compiled, link edited, and executed in one job. It is useful when you expect the compilation to be successful, and it saves a separate link-edit operation later.

Coding PARM values for cataloged procedures

As with any cataloged procedure, you can override the values coded in the compilation procedures. The most significant values you may want to override when executing these cataloged procedures are those set by the PARM parameter. The PARM parameter specifies the *compiler options*, such as the punching of an object deck and the printing of certain diagnostic and debugging information, that are in effect during the run.

There are many options associated with the OS language translators. For example, much of the printed compiler output, such as cross-reference listings and maps, is optional. In addition, each compiler has optional debugging features and other facilities that you may want to eliminate to increase the speed of the compilation and the efficiency of the compiled program. These options can be selected or excluded by using the PARM parameter in the EXEC statement that invokes the cataloged procedure. For example, the statement:

```
//CSTEP     EXEC   PROC=COBUCG,
//                 PARM.COB='XREF,LINCNT=60'
```

will cause a cross-reference listing to be printed by the COBOL compiler and a maximum of 60 lines to be printed on each page of the compiler printed output.

Before you can start using the PARM parameter to control options, however, you must be aware that there are two previous levels at which options can be set. First, when the system is generated, the options are given default values recommended by IBM; these are adjusted to meet the requirements of the installation. These values are in effect during the compilation unless they are changed by a PARM value at another level.

The second level at which options can be set is within the procedure itself. In other words, the EXEC statement in the procedure that executes the compiler program may have its own PARM parameter to modify some of the default values. The options set by the PARM are called *procedure options*.

Now back to you, the JCL programmer. Whenever you code the PARM parameter in an EXEC PROC statement, your PARM values replace the ones in the procedure you invoke. *All* of the values of the PARM in the procedure are replaced by the values you code, whether or not they represent the same options. So if you want one or more of the procedure options to remain in effect, you must code them in your PARM; otherwise, they will revert to their default values. For example, suppose that you want to use the PARM parameter to set the LINCNT option when you execute the COBOL compile-and-go (COBUCG) procedure. Suppose, also, that one of the COBUCG procedure options is LOAD, but the default value established at system generation time is NOLOAD. If you want LOAD to be in effect, you must code it along with the LINCNT value or the NOLOAD option will be used.

To determine what the default values for a compiler are, you can compile a program with this EXEC statement for the compiler you are interested in:

```
//COMP      EXEC   PROC=compile-only-procedure
//                 PARM.compile-step-name=''
```

Since the PARM is coded, all of the procedure options will be overridden. But since there aren't any values coded between the two apostrophes, the default values will be the only ones in effect and the only ones printed on the listing of compiler options that you get as a part of your compiler output. Examples of the option listing for COBOL, PL/I, FORTRAN, and assembler language are given in figure 8-1. By studying your option listing, you'll know for sure what the default values are on your system for each compiler. To find out what the procedure options are for one of the cataloged procedures you are using, you can study the procedure JCL printed on the JCL listing. You'll see some examples in the next section.

Your only problem once you have the listings of default and procedure options is knowing what they mean and how to code them. To find out, you'll have to go to the IBM programmer's guide for the language you're working in and the version of OS you're using. The programmer's guides give a complete list of options available on each compiler.

EXAMPLES OF THE LANGUAGE TRANSLATOR PROCEDURES

In the remainder of this topic, I will discuss the cataloged procedures to execute the COBOL, PL/I, FORTRAN, and assembler compilers. You will undoubtedly notice that the statements from these cataloged procedures do not follow my suggested standards for coding JCL. I've presented them here the way they actually appear when executed so you won't be confused when you see them on your own listings. I've also used the standard method of identifying input and procedure JCL statements: the lines beginning with // are input JCL statements; the lines beginning with XX are JCL statements from the procedure; and the lines beginning with X/ are procedure statements that have been overridden by JCL statements in the input stream.

The procedures used by your installation to execute the language translators may vary slightly from the ones shown here, but they should be similar enough so you can understand them with the explanations presented. Since all of the procedures are similar, I'll show you one example of each of the four basic procedures. You'll see a FORTRAN compile-only, an assembler compile-and-link, a COBOL compile-and-go, and a PL/I compile-link-and-go. I'll also show you the JCL for executing any of the four procedures for any of the languages.

Compile-only

Figure 8-2 shows a typical FORTRAN compile-only procedure. This procedure will compile the program, produce an object module that can be punched into cards or placed into an object library (either per-

Example of COBOL compiler option listing:

```
*STATISTICS*     SOURCE RECORDS =   177    DATA DIVISION STATEMENTS =   64    PROCEDURE DIVISION STATEMENTS =   40
*OPTIONS IN EFFECT*     SIZE =  90112  BUF =    8192  LINECNT = 52  SPACE1,   FLAGW,    SEQ,   SOURCE
*OPTIONS IN EFFECT*     NODMAP, NOPMAP,  CLIST,   SUPMAP, NOXREF, NOSXREF,    LOAD,   NODECK,  APOST, NOTRUNC, NOFLOW
*OPTIONS IN EFFECT*     NOTERM, NONUM, NOBATCH, NONAME, COMPILE=01, NOSTATE,  LIB,    VERB,    ZWB,   SYST
```

Example of PL/I compiler option listing:

```
PL/I OPTIMIZING COMPILER        VERSION 1 RELEASE 3.0 PTF 69           TIME: 15.20.47      DATE: 28 MAR 80      PAGE 1

OPTIONS SPECIFIED
OBJECT,NODECK

OPTIONS USED
AGGREGATE      NOCOUNT            ATTRIBUTES(FULL)
ESD            NODECK             CHARSET(60,EBCDIC)
INSOURCE       NOFLOW             NOCOMPILE(S)
LMESSAGE       NOGONUMBER         FLAG(I)
NEST           NOGOSTMT           LINECOUNT(55)
OBJECT         NOIMPRECISE        MARGINS(2,72,0)
OFFSET         NOINCLUDE          SEQUENCE(73,80)
OPTIONS        NOINTERRUPT        SIZE(257744)
SOURCE         NOLIST             NOSYNTAX(S)
STMT           NOMACRO            XREF(FULL)
               NOMARGINI
               NONUMBER
               NOOPTIMIZE
               NOSTORAGE
               NOTERMINAL
```

Example of FORTRAN compiler option listing:

```
LEVEL 21.8 ( JUN 74 )                                          OS/360    FORTRAN H

            COMPILER OPTIONS - NAME= MAIN,OPT=00,LINECNT=58,SIZE=0000K,
                               SOURCE,EBCDIC,NOLIST,NODECK,LOAD,MORAP,NOEDIT,NOXREF
```

Example of assembler language option listing:

```
                               ASM 0201 15.05 03/28/80               ASSEMBLER DIAGNOSTICS AND STATISTICS              DATE 80.088/15.13.14       PAGE 6

NO STATEMENTS FLAGGED IN THIS ASSEMBLY
HIGHEST SEVERITY CODE WAS     0
OPTIONS FOR THIS ASSEMBLY
  ALIGN, ALOGIC, BUFSIZE(STD), NODECK, ESD, FLAG(0), LINECOUNT(55), LIST, NOMCALL, YFLAG, WORKSIZE(2097152)
  NONLOGIC, NONUMBER, OBJECT, NORENT, RLD, NOSTMT, NOLIBMAC, NOTERMINAL, NOTEST, XREF(SHORT)
  SYSPARM()
```

Figure 8-1 Examples of compiler option listings for COBOL, PL/I, FORTRAN, and assembler language

```
//FORTHC    PROC      FORTCOR=200K,
//                    BLK=1600
//FORT      EXEC      PGM=IEKAA00,PARM='MAP,NOLOAD',REGION=&FORTCOR
//SYSUDUMP  DD        SYSOUT=A
//SYSPRINT  DD        SYSOUT=A
//SYSPUNCH  DD        SYSOUT=B
//SYSLIN    DD        DSNAME=&&LOADSET,DISP=(MOD,PASS),UNIT=SYSDA,
//                    DCB=(RECFM=FB,BLKSIZE=&BLK,LRECL=80),
//                    SPACE=(1600,(400,160),,CONTIG,ROUND)
```

Figure 8-2 A typical FORTRAN compile-only procedure

manent or temporary), print a listing of the source program, and print a list of errors encountered.

FORTHC is the name of the procedure for the FORTRAN H compile-only. You should check to see which FORTRAN compiler is in use at your installation. For example, you may have the FORTRAN G compiler, in which case you should code FORTGC for the name of the procedure. The symbolic parameters, FORTCOR and BLK, are given default values in the PROC statement, so if you don't code values for them in your input JCL, the values given in the procedure will take effect.

FORT is the name of the step that executes the FORTRAN compiler. The program for this compiler (FORTRAN H) is IEKAA00, the procedure options are MAP and NOLOAD, and the REGION is the value of &FORTCOR. The program name for the FORTRAN G compiler is IEYFORT, and the procedure options are usually the same as for FORTRAN H.

SYSUDUMP is the DD statement that defines a core dump print file. If the compiler abnormally terminates (something that's very rare), this DD statement will cause a dump of the compiler program to print. If this should happen, give the dump to the systems programming staff at your installation.

SYSPRINT is the DD statement for the standard output listing that includes the source program, diagnostics, and any optional compiler output you may have requested. SYSPUNCH is the DD statement for the punch file, used when you request an object deck to be punched by coding DECK in the PARM parameter of the EXEC statement.

SYSLIN is the DD statement defining the data set where the object module will be placed. In the procedure, it's a temporary data set named &&LOADSET. If you want to save the object module for later linking and execution, you'll have to override this DD statement, giving the name of a permanent data set.

Executing the procedure   Figure 8-3 shows the JCL you will code to execute the compile-only procedure for COBOL, PL/I, FORTRAN, and assembler language. Figure 8-4 shows the effective JCL (the JCL as it is executed by the computer) for the FORTRAN compile-only. Notice that I didn't code values for the symbolic parameters. As a result, the default values in the PROC statement of the procedure are in effect. And since I didn't code any PARMs in the EXEC PROC = FORTHC statement, the procedure options are in effect.

Compile-and-link

Figure 8-5 shows a typical assembler language compile-and-link procedure. You'll notice that the first step, ASM, is similar to the FORT step shown in figure 8-2. The major difference is that the assembler

```
COBOL:

//COBCOMP EXEC   PROC=COBUC
//COB.SYSIN DD   *
       COBOL source program
/*


PL/I:

//PLICOMP EXEC   PROC=PLIXC
//PLI.SYSIN DD   *
       PL/I source program
/*


FORTRAN:

//FORTCOMP EXEC  PROC=FORTHC
//FORT.SYSIN DD  *
       FORTRAN source program
/*


Assembler language:

//ASMCOMP EXEC   PROC=ASMFC
//ASM.SYSIN DD   *
       assembler language source program
/*
```

Figure 8-3   JCL to execute the compile-only procedure for COBOL, PL/I, FORTRAN, and assembler language

```
//FORTCOMP  EXEC      PROC=FORTHC
XXFORT      EXEC      PGM=IEKAA00,PARM='MAP,NOLOAD',REGION=200K
XXSYSUDUMP  DD        SYSOUT=A
XXSYSPRINT  DD        SYSOUT=A
XXSYSPUNCH  DD        SYSOUT=B
XXSYSLIN    DD        DSNAME=&&LOADSET,DISP=(MOD,PASS),UNIT=SYSDA,
XX                    DCB=(RECFM=FB,BLKSIZE=1600,LRECL=80),
XX                    SPACE=(1600,(400,160),,CONTIG,ROUND)
//SYSIN     DD  *
     FORTRAN source program
/*
```

Figure 8-4 Effective JCL for the FORTRAN compile-only procedure

```
XXASMFCL    PROC      ASMCOR=256K,LKEDCOR=256K,DECK=NODECK,
XX          HEWL=HEWL,BLK=1600
XXASM       EXEC      PGM=IFOX00,PARM='LOAD,&DECK',REGION=&ASMCOR
XXSYSUDUMP  DD        SYSOUT=A
XXSYSPRINT  DD        SYSOUT=A
XXSYSPUNCH  DD        SYSOUT=B
XXSYSLIB    DD        DSN=SYS2.MACLIB,DISP=SHR
XX          DD        DSN=SYS1.MACLIB,DISP=SHR
XXSYSUT1    DD        SPACE=(1700,(600,100)),UNIT=SYSDA,DSN=&&SYSUT1
XXSYSUT2    DD        SPACE=(1700,(300,50)),UNIT=SYSDA,DSN=&&SYSUT2
XXSYSUT3    DD        SPACE=(1700,(300,50)),UNIT=SYSDA,DSN=&&SYSUT3
XXSYSGO     DD        DSN=&&LOADSET,DISP=(MOD,PASS),UNIT=SYSDA,
XX                    DCB=(RECFM=FB,LRECL=80,BLKSIZE=&BLK),
XX                    SPACE=(1600,(120,30),,CONTIG,ROUND)
XXLKED      EXEC      PGM=&HEWL,PARM='LIST,XREF',COND=(5,LT,ASM),
XX                    REGION=&LKEDCOR
XXSYSUDUMP  DD        SYSOUT=A
XXSYSPRINT  DD        SYSOUT=A
XXSYSUT1    DD        UNIT=SYSDA,SPACE=(1024,(120,30)),DSN=&&SYSUT1
XXSYSLMOD   DD        DSN=&&GOSET(GO),DISP=(NEW,PASS),UNIT=SYSDA,
XX                    SPACE=(1024,(300,,17),,CONTIG,ROUND)
XXSYSLIN    DD        DSN=&&LOADSET,DISP=(OLD,DELETE)
```

Figure 8-5 A typical assembler language compile-and-link procedure

requires four additional DD statements: SYSUT1 through SYSUT3 as work areas, and SYSLIB to define MACRO libraries required by the assembler. You'll also notice that the DD statement of the temporary data set created in the ASM step is called SYSGO instead of SYSLIN as you saw in the FORTRAN compile.

The second step, LKED, executes the link-edit program. The program name here is HEWL (some installations may be using a version called IEWL). The link-edit program name in this procedure is provided by a symbolic parameter so the programmer can choose HEWL or IEWL. Two PARMs, LIST and XREF, will be in effect if they're not overridden by the programmer's JCL. And this step won't be executed if the condition code from the first step is greater than 5.

The LKED step uses the object module passed from the ASM step as input (defined by the SYSLIN DD statement in the LKED step) and places the link-edited output (the load module) into a load library defined with the SYSLMOD DD statement. In the procedure, the load library is a temporary data set named &&GOSET. Here again, if you want to save the load module in a permanent load library, you'll have to override the SYSLMOD DD statement to refer to a permanent data set.

SYSUDUMP, here as in the compile step, defines the print file that will print a storage dump should the link-edit program abnormally terminate. SYSPRINT is the standard print file for link-edit messages. And SYSUT1 is a work file required by the link-edit program.

Executing the procedure Figure 8-6 shows the JCL to execute the compile-and-link procedure for COBOL, PL/I, FORTRAN, and assembler language. The LKED.SYSLMOD DD statement in each example is the override DD statement to identify a permanent load library. The name in parentheses adjacent to the data set name of the load library is the load module name. This is the name you will specify in an EXEC PGM statement to execute the program.

Figure 8-7 shows the effective JCL for the assembler language compile-and-link. Notice that the symbolic parameter default values have been applied and the SYSLMOD DD statement has been overridden.

Compile-and-go

Figure 8-8 shows a typical COBOL compile-and-go. Once again, the first step, COB, is similar to the compile steps you've seen in the previous examples. SYSUT1, SYSUT2, SYSUT3, and SYSUT4 are DD statements defining work areas required by the compiler. SYSLIB defines the COPY libraries where commonly used segments of COBOL source code are kept for inclusion in COBOL source programs as they are compiled. SYSLIN defines the data set for the object module that will be passed to the next step for execution.

The GO step is where your program is executed. However, in a compile-and-go procedure, it is executed indirectly. Remember that an object module is not executable as it is; it must be link edited before it can be executed. Notice that the name of the program executed in the second step is LOADER. LOADER uses your object module as input, link edits it into a temporary load library, and then transfers control

```
COBOL:

//COBLK     EXEC  PROC=COBUCL
//COB.SYSIN DD   *
     COBOL source program
/*
//LKED.SYSLMOD DD  DSN=MMA.USERLIB(COBPROG),
//               DISP=(OLD,KEEP)
```

PL/I:

```
//PLILK     EXEC  PROC=PLIXCL
//PLI.SYSIN DD   *
     PL/I source program
/*
//LKED.SYSLMOD DD  DSN=MMA.USERLIB(PLIPROG),
//               DISP=(OLD,KEEP)
```

FORTRAN:

```
//FORTLK    EXEC  PROC=FORTHCL
//FORT.SYSIN DD  *
     FORTRAN source program
/*
//LKED.SYSLMOD DD  DSN=MMA.USERLIB(FORTPROG),
//               DISP=(OLD,KEEP)
```

Assembler language:

```
//ASMLK     EXEC  PROC=ASMFCL
//ASM.SYSIN DD   *
     assembler language source program
/*
//LKED.SYSLMOD DD  DSN=MMA.USERLIB(ASMPROG),
//               DISP=(OLD,KEEP)
```

Figure 8-6 JCL to execute the compile-and-link procedure for COBOL, PL/I, FORTRAN, and assembler language

to it. As a result, you can think of the loader as a temporary link editor. The GO step of the procedure includes a DD statement to define the object module (SYSLIN). Also required in this step are any DD statements required for the input and output files used by your program.

Notice too that the GO step in this procedure includes a SYSLIB DD statement. You'll find SYSLIB in link-edit steps and loader steps for COBOL, PL/I, and FORTRAN. For COBOL, as shown in this example, two libraries are concatenated to provide special pre-compiled modules necessary for the program to execute. These can be I/O

Language Translators and the Link-Edit Program

```
//ASMLK     EXEC  PROC=ASMFCL
XXASM       EXEC  PGM=IFOX00,PARM='LOAD,NODECK',REGION=256K
XXSYSUDUMP  DD    SYSOUT=A
XXSYSPRINT  DD    SYSOUT=A
XXSYSPUNCH  DD    SYSOUT=B
XXSYSLIB    DD    DSN=SYS2.MACLIB,DISP=SHR
XX          DD    DSN=SYS1.MACLIB,DISP=SHR
XXSYSUT1    DD    SPACE=(1700,(600,100)),UNIT=SYSDA,DSN=&&SYSUT1
XXSYSUT2    DD    SPACE=(1700,(300,50)),UNIT=SYSDA,DSN=&&SYSUT2
XXSYSUT3    DD    SPACE=(1700,(300,50)),UNIT=SYSDA,DSN=&&SYSUT3
XXSYSGO     DD    DSN=&&LOADSET,DISP=(MOD,PASS),UNIT=SYSDA,
XX                DCB=(RECFM=FB,LRECL=80,BLKSIZE=1600),
XX                SPACE=(1600,(120,30),,CONTIG,ROUND)
//SYSIN DD  *
      assembler language source program
/*
XXLKED      EXEC  PGM=HEWL,PARM='LIST,XREF',COND=(5,LT,ASM),
XX                REGION=256K
XXSYSUDUMP  DD    SYSOUT=A
XXSYSPRINT  DD    SYSOUT=A
XXSYSUT1    DD    UNIT=SYSDA,SPACE=(1024,(120,30)),DSN=&&SYSUT1
X/SYSLMOD   DD    DSN=MMA.USERLIB(ASMPROG),
X/                DISP=(OLD,KEEP)
XXSYSLIN    DD    DSN=&&LOADSET,DISP=(OLD,DELETE)
```

Figure 8-7 Effective JCL for the assembler language compile-and-link procedure

modules, data-conversion modules, or other functional modules required by your program that are included in the load module.

Executing the procedure Figure 8-9 shows the JCL to execute the compile-and-go procedure for COBOL, PL/I, FORTRAN, and assembler language. In each case, I've assumed the source program reads an input card file and prints an output listing. So a DD statement for each file is required in the GO step.

For the COBOL, PL/I, and assembler programs, the ddnames must be the same as the ddnames in the source program. In this example, I've used the ddnames CARDFLE and PRINTFLE. In FORTRAN, however, the source program tells the system which files to use by specifying a device number that is assigned to a certain device. Then, the ddnames in the JCL follow the pattern of those in the figure, FT06F001 and FT05F001. Here, the first two numeric digits (06 and 05) refer to the I/O device. The last three digits (001) refer to the sequence number of the file on that device. In short, then, GO.FT06F001 and GO.FT05F001 for the FORTRAN run are equivalent in function to GO.PRINTFLE and GO.CARDFLE.

Figure 8-10 shows the effective JCL for the COBOL compile-and-go. Note that the object module is not saved in this execution. As a

```
XXCOBUCG    PROC    DMAP=NODMAP,PMAP=NOPMAP,SIZ=131072,BUF=8192,GOCOR=128K,
XX                  XREF=NOXREF,STATE=NOSTATE,COPY=COPYLIBT
XXCOB       EXEC    PGM=IKFCBL00,REGION=128K,
XX                  PARM='SUPMAP,&DMAP,&PMAP,SIZE=&SIZ,BUF=&BUF,&XREF,
XX                  &STATE'
XXSYSUDUMP  DD      SYSOUT=A
XXSYSPRINT  DD      SYSOUT=A
XXSYSLIB    DD      DSNAME=CTI00.COPYLIB,DISP=SHR
XX          DD      DSNAME=IMS2.&COPY,DISP=SHR
XXSYSLIN    DD      DSNAME=&&LOADSET,DISP=(MOD,PASS),UNIT=SYSDA,
XX                  DCB=(LRECL=80,BLKSIZE=800,RECFM=FB),
XX                  SPACE=(1600,(100,10),,CONTIG,ROUND)
XXSYSUT1    DD      UNIT=SYSDA,
XX                  SPACE=(1600,(600,600),,CONTIG,ROUND)
XXSYSUT2    DD      UNIT=SYSDA,
XX                  SPACE=(1600,(100,10),,CONTIG,ROUND)
XXSYSUT3    DD      UNIT=SYSDA,
XX                  SPACE=(1600,(100,10),,CONTIG,ROUND)
XXSYSUT4    DD      UNIT=SYSDA,
XX                  SPACE=(1600,(100,10),,CONTIG,ROUND)
XXGO        EXEC    PGM=LOADER,PARM='MAP,SIZE=120000',COND=(5,LT,COB),
XX                  REGION=&GOCOR
XXSYSUDUMP  DD      SYSOUT=A
XXSYSOUT    DD      SYSOUT=A
XXSYSLIB    DD      DSNAME=SYS1.COBLIB,DISP=SHR
XX          DD      DSNAME=SYS2.COBLIB,DISP=SHR
XXSYSLIN    DD      DSNAME=&&LOADSET,DISP=(OLD,DELETE)
```

Figure 8-8 A typical COBOL compile-and-go procedure

result, if I want to execute the program again, I'll have to compile the source program again. To avoid this, I can override the SYSLIN DD statement in both the compile and execute steps to refer to a permanent object library.

Compile-link-and-go

Figure 8-11 shows a typical PL/I compile-link-and-go procedure. This procedure consists of three steps and contains all of the elements of the other three types of procedures. Step 1 executes the PL/I compiler, step 2 executes the link-edit program, and step 3 executes the load module created in step 2. Here, the load module is executed directly (not indirectly as it was in the compile-and-go procedure).

If you execute the procedure in figure 8-11 without overriding any of the library DD names, the procedure will work, but the load

COBOL:

```
//COBGO    EXEC   PROC=COBUCG
//COB.SYSIN DD   *
     COBOL source program
/*
//GO.PRINTFLE DD  SYSOUT=A
//GO.CARDFLE  DD  *
     input data cards
/*
```

PL/I:

```
//PLIGO    EXEC   PROC=PLIXCG
//PLI.SYSIN DD   *
     PL/I source program
/*
//GO.PRINTFLE DD  SYSOUT=A
//GO.CARDFLE  DD  *
     input data cards
/*
```

FORTRAN:

```
//FORTGO   EXEC   PROC=FORTHCG
//FORT.SYSIN DD  *
     FORTRAN source program
/*
//GO.FT06F001 DD  SYSOUT=A
//GO.FT05F001 DD  *
     input data cards
/*
```

Assembler language:

```
//ASMGO    EXEC   PROC=ASMFCG
//ASM.SYSIN DD   *
     assembler language source program
/*
//GO.PRINTFLE DD  SYSOUT=A
//GO.CARDFLE  DD  *
     input data cards
/*
```

Figure 8-9 JCL to execute the compile-and-go procedure for COBOL, PL/I, FORTRAN, and assembler language

```
//COBGO      EXEC   PROC=COBUCG
XXCOB        EXEC   PGM=IKFCBL00,REGION=128K,
XX                  PARM='SUPMAP,NODMAP,NOPMAP,SIZE=131072,BUF=8192,NOXREF,
XX                  NOSTATE'
XXSYSUDUMP   DD     SYSOUT=A
XXSYSPRINT   DD     SYSOUT=A
XXSYSLIB     DD     DSNAME=CTI00.COPYLIB,DISP=SHR
XX           DD     DSNAME=IMS2.COPYLIBT,DISP=SHR
XXSYSLIN     DD     DSNAME=&&LOADSET,DISP=(MOD,PASS),UNIT=SYSDA,
XX                  DCB=(LRECL=80,BLKSIZE=800,RECFM=FB),
XX                  SPACE=(1600,(100,10),,CONTIG,ROUND)
XXSYSUT1     DD     UNIT=SYSDA,
XX                  SPACE=(1600,(600,600),,CONTIG,ROUND)
XXSYSUT2     DD     UNIT=SYSDA,
XX                  SPACE=(1600,(100,10),,CONTIG,ROUND)
XXSYSUT3     DD     UNIT=SYSDA,
XX                  SPACE=(1600,(100,10),,CONTIG,ROUND)
XXSYSUT4     DD     UNIT=SYSDA,
XX                  SPACE=(1600,(100,10),,CONTIG,ROUND)
//SYSIN DD   *
      COBOL source program
/*
XXGO         EXEC   PGM=LOADER,PARM='MAP,SIZE=120000',COND=(5,LT,COB),
XX                  REGION=128K
XXSYSUDUMP   DD     SYSOUT=A
XXSYSOUT     DD     SYSOUT=A
XXSYSLIB     DD     DSNAME=SYS1.COBLIB,DISP=SHR
XX           DD     DSNAME=SYS2.COBLIB,DISP=SHR
XXSYSLIN     DD     DSNAME=&&LOADSET,DISP=(OLD,DELETE)
//PRINTFLE   DD     SYSOUT=A
//CARDFLE    DD     *
      input data cards
/*
```

Figure 8-10 Effective JCL for the COBOL compile-and-go procedure

library will be deleted when the job completes. As a result, it's a good idea to override the SYSLMOD DD statement in the LKED step to name a permanent library just as you did in the compile-and-link procedure. For the GO step, you'll have to provide DD statements for the files used by your program just as you did in the compile-and-go procedure.

Executing the procedure Figure 8-12 shows the JCL to execute the compile-link-and-go procedure for COBOL, PL/I, FORTRAN, and assembler language. In each case, I've supplied a SYSLMOD DD statement for a permanent load library and DD statements for the program files.

Figure 8-13 shows the JCL as it's actually executed for the PL/I compile-link-and-go procedure. At the end of the execution, the source program will have been converted to a load module named PLIPROG and stored in a load library called MMA.USERLIB.

```
XXPLIXCLG  PROC      PLICOR=138K,LKEDCOR=138K,GOCOR=138K
XXPLI      EXEC      PGM=IELOAA,PARM='OBJECT,NODECK',REGION=&PLICOR
XXSYSPRINT DD        SYSOUT=A
XXSYSLIN   DD        DSN=&&LOADSET,DISP=(MOD,PASS),UNIT=SYSDA,
XX                   SPACE=(1600,(160,160),,CONTIG,ROUND)
XXSYSUT1   DD        DSN=&&SYSUT1,UNIT=SYSDA,DCB=BLKSIZE=1024,
XX                   SPACE=(1024,(200,50),,CONTIG,ROUND)
XXLKED     EXEC      PGM=HEWL,PARM='XREF,LIST',REGION=&LKEDCOR,
XX                   COND=(9,LT,PLI)
XXSYSLIB   DD        DSN=SYS1.PL1.BASELIB,DISP=SHR
XX         DD        DSN=SYS1.PL1.TASKLIB,DISP=SHR
XX         DD        DSN=SYS1.PL1.LINKLIB,DISP=SHR
XXSYSLMOD  DD        DSN=&&GOSET(GO),DISP=(MOD,PASS),UNIT=SYSDA,
XX                   SPACE=(1024,(600,,17),RLSE)
XXSYSUT1   DD        DSN=&&SYSUT1,UNIT=SYSDA,DCB=BLKSIZE=1024,
XX                   SPACE=(1024,(600,120),,CONTIG,ROUND)
XXSYSPRINT DD        SYSOUT=A
XXSYSLIN   DD        DSN=&&LOADSET,DISP=(OLD,DELETE)
XXGO       EXEC      PGM=*.LKED.SYSLMOD,COND=((9,LT,PLI),(5,LT,LKED)),
XX                   REGION=&GOCOR
```

Figure 8-11 A typical PL/I compile-link-and-go procedure

Terminology

language translator   compile-and-go procedure
compile-only procedure   compile-link-and-go procedure
object module   compiler option
compile-and-link procedure   procedure option
load module

Objective

Given a COBOL, PL/I, FORTRAN, or assembler language source program, write the JCL to execute a cataloged procedure to (1) compile the program for syntax errors only; (2) compile the program and link edit it into a load library; (3) compile the program and cause the object module to be executed without creating a load module; and (4) compile the program, link edit it into a load library, and execute the load module from that library.

Problems

1. Write the JCL to execute the assembler language compile-only procedure.

COBOL:

```
//COBGO     EXEC  PROC=COBUCLG
//COB.SYSIN DD  *
     COBOL source program
/*
//LKED.SYSLMOD DD  DSN=MNA.USERLIB(COBPROG),
//              DISP=(OLD,KEEP)
//GO.PRINTFLE DD  SYSOUT=A
//GO.CARDFLE  DD  *
     input data cards
/*
```

PL/I:

```
//PLIGO     EXEC  PROC=PLIXCLG
//PLI.SYSIN DD  *
     PL/I source program
/*
//LKED.SYSLMOD DD  DSN=MNA.USERLIB(PLIPROG),
//              DISP=(OLD,KEEP)
//GO.PRINTFLE DD  SYSOUT=A
//GO.CARDFLE  DD  *
     input data cards
/*
```

FORTRAN:

```
//FORTGO    EXEC  PROC=FORTHCLG
//FORT.SYSIN DD  *
     FORTRAN source program
/*
//LKED.SYSLMOD DD  DSN=MNA.USERLIB(FORTPROG),
//              DISP=(OLD,KEEP)
//GO.FT06F001 DD  SYSOUT=A
//GO.FT05F001 DD  *
     input data cards
/*
```

Assembler language:

```
//ASMGO     EXEC  PROC=ASMFCLG
//ASM.SYSIN DD  *
     assembler language source program
/*
//LKED.SYSLMOD DD  DSN=MNA.USERLIB(ASMPROG),
//              DISP=(OLD,KEEP)
//GO.PRINTFLE DD  SYSOUT=A
//GO.CARDFLE  DD  *
     input data cards
/*
```

Figure 8-12 JCL to execute the compile-link-and-go procedure for COBOL, PL/I, FORTRAN, and assembler language

```
//PLIGO       EXEC     PROC=PLIXCLG
XXPLI         EXEC     PGM=IEL0AA,PARM='OBJECT,NODECK',REGION=138K
XXSYSPRINT    DD       SYSOUT=A
XXSYSLIN      DD       DSN=&&LOADSET,DISP=(MOD,PASS),UNIT=SYSDA,
XX                     SPACE=(1600,(160,160),,CONTIG,ROUND)
XXSYSUT1      DD       DSN=&&SYSUT1,UNIT=SYSDA,DCB=BLKSIZE=1024,
XX                     SPACE=(1024,(200,50),,CONTIG,ROUND)
//SYSIN DD    *
       PL/I source program
/*
XXLKED        EXEC     PGM=HEWL,PARM='XREF,LIST',REGION=138K,
XX                     COND=(9,LT,PLI)
XXSYSLIB      DD       DSN=SYS1.PL1.BASELIB,DISP=SHR
XX            DD       DSN=SYS1.PL1.TASKLIB,DISP=SHR
XX            DD       DSN=SYS1.PL1.LINKLIB,DISP=SHR
X/SYSLMOD     DD       DSN=MMA.USERLIB(PLIPROG),
X/                     DISP=(OLD,KEEP)
XXSYSUT1      DD       DSN=&&SYSUT1,UNIT=SYSDA,DCB=BLKSIZE=1024,
XX                     SPACE=(1024,(600,120),,CONTIG,ROUND)
XXSYSPRINT    DD       SYSOUT=A
XXSYSLIN      DD       DSN=&&LOADSET,DISP=(OLD,DELETE)
XXGO          EXEC     PGM=*.LKED.SYSLMOD,COND=((9,LT,PLI),(5,LT,LKED)),
XX                     REGION=138K
//PRINTFLE    DD       SYSOUT=A
//CARDFLE     DD       *
       input data cards
/*
```

Figure 8-13 Effective JCL for the PL/I compile-link-and-go procedure

2. Write the JCL to execute the FORTRAN compile-and-link procedure. The load library name is MMA.USERLIB and the load module is FORT01.

3. Write the JCL to execute the PL/I compile-and-go procedure. The program requires two files: PLFILEIN as input and PLFILEOT as output. PLFILEIN is a cataloged sequential file with the data set name of EXPFILE. PLFILEOT is to be cataloged on a 3330 disk pack named TSTPAK, with 10 cylinders primary and 5 cylinders secondary space allocation. The data set name for PLFILEOT is ENTFILE. The DCB should request a record length of 95 bytes, block size of 1900 bytes, and record format of fixed blocked.

4. Write the JCL to execute the COBOL compile-link-and-go procedure. The load module library is MMA.USERLIB and the load module name is COB011. The program refers to two files: KXCYCLE as input and KXRPT as output. KXCYCLE is a cataloged sequential file with the data set name of KXMAST; KXRPT is a report to be printed on SYSOUT class A with a DCB indicating a block size of 133.

Solutions

1. Figure 8-14 is an acceptable solution.
2. Figure 8-15 is an acceptable solution.
3. Figure 8-16 is an acceptable solution.
4. Figure 8-17 is an acceptable solution.

```
//ASMCOMP  EXEC  PROC=ASMFC
//ASM.SYSIN DD  *
     assembler language source program
/*
```

Figure 8-14 Executing the assembler language compile-only procedure

```
//FORTLK   EXEC  PROC=FORTHCL
//FORT.SYSIN DD  *
     FORTRAN source program
/*
//LKED.SYSLMOD DD  DSN=MMA.USERLIB(FORT01),
//              DISP=(OLD,KEEP)
```

Figure 8-15 Executing the FORTRAN compile-and-link procedure

```
//PLICG    EXEC  PROC=PLIXCG
//PLI.SYSIN DD  *
     PL/I source program
/*
//GO.PLFILEIN DD  DSN=EXPFILE,
//              DISP=OLD
//GO.PLFILEOT DD  DSN=ENTFILE,
//              DISP=(NEW,CATLG),
//              UNIT=3330,
//              VOL=SER=TSTPAK,
//              SPACE=(CYL,(10,5),RLSE),
//              DCB=(LRECL=95,BLKSIZE=1900,RECFM=FB)
```

Figure 8-16 Executing the PL/I compile-and-go procedure

```
//COBL     EXEC  PROC=COBUCLG
//COB.SYSIN DD  *
    COBOL source program
/*
//LKED.SYSLMOD DD  DSN=MMA.USERLIB(COB011),
//             DISP=(OLD,KEEP)
//GO.KXCYCLE DD  DSN=KXMAST,
//             DISP=OLD
//GO.KXRPT DD  SYSOUT=A,
//             DCB=BLKSIZE=133
```

Figure 8-17 Executing the COBOL compile-link-and-go procedure

TOPIC 2   The Link-Edit Program

In topic 1, you learned how to execute the cataloged procedures to compile and link edit programs. All of the examples shown were standalone programs that neither called subprograms nor were themselves subprograms. In this topic, I'll show you the JCL and link-edit control statements to link separately compiled programs together as one load module.

THE FUNCTION OF THE LINK-EDIT PROGRAM

When a program is compiled, the output generated is an object module consisting of relocatable machine instructions, data, and unresolved references. *Relocatable machine instructions* are instructions that reference storage addresses relative to a starting point. In an object module, this starting point is not provided. Data consists of tables, headings, file definitions, and data definitions used by your program. They are also placed into areas relative to the starting point. *Unresolved references* are calls to subroutines that were not available to the compiler. As a result, the linkage is set up to pass control to the unresolved subroutine and to return control to the object module.

The starting point is provided by either the loader program (illustrated in the compile-and-go procedure in topic 1), or the link-edit program. The starting point assigned to a subprogram is an address location following the last address in the main program or another subprogram. Unresolved references are resolved by linking the main program and any called subprograms together into one load module by executing the link-edit program.

The link-edit program, then, uses the object module generated by a compile and assigns addresses, resolves external references (calls to subprograms), and connects the main program with any called subprograms it may refer to. When there are no subprograms involved, the cataloged procedures shown in topic 1 will be sufficient to link edit the program. However, when there are subprograms involved, you may have to supply additional information to the link-edit program.

There are three situations you'll encounter when working with subprograms. First, both the main program and all of the subprograms are in source code—that is, they haven't been compiled yet. The second situation is that either the main program or at least one of the subprograms has been compiled and is in object code. The third situation is that all of the programs have been compiled and are in object code.

Linking source code subprograms

When testing subprograms, it is common to keep both the main program and subprograms in source code. Then, the main program and subprograms are compiled and held in a temporary file for link editing. After the link-edit program combines the object modules into one load module, the entire program can be executed.

Figure 8-18 illustrates the JCL for this method of subprogram linkage. The first procedure executed is COBUC (the COBOL compile-only), which compiles the main program and stores the object module in a temporary data set named &&LOADSET. Then, the second procedure, COBUCL (the COBOL compile-and-link) compiles the subprogram and links it with the main program. If there were more subprograms, they would be compiled with the compile-only procedure before the compile-and-link procedure combines all the object modules into one load module. The SYSLMOD DD statement says to store the load module under the name COBMAIN in the library called MMA.USERLIB.

In order for the JCL to work correctly for a job like this, there are two key points you must note. First, the object module with which the program execution is to start must be compiled first. Since program execution is to begin with the first instruction of the main program, it is compiled first. Second, the SYSLIN DD statement in the COBUC procedure must have exactly the same parameters as the SYSLIN DD statement in the COB step of the COBUCL procedure. Then, since DISP=(MOD,PASS) is coded for this DD statement, the object modules created by the two compilations will be stored one behind the other on the temporary file named &&LOADSET.

```
//MGLINK   JOB  HE66YFNH,
//              'W. CLARY'
//MAINSTEP EXEC PROC=COBUC
//COB.SYSLIN DD DSN=&&LOADSET,
//              DISP=(MOD,PASS),
//              UNIT=SYSDA,
//              SPACE=(80,(500,100))
//COB.SYSIN DD  *
     COBOL source code for the main program
/*
//SUBSTEP  EXEC PROC=COBUCL
//COB.SYSIN DD  *
     COBOL source code for the subprogram
/*
//LKED.SYSLMOD DD  DSN=MMA.USERLIB(COBMAIN),
//              DISP=(OLD,KEEP)
```

Note: The SYSLIN DD statement in the main program compilation must be exactly like the SYSLIN DD statement in the cataloged COBUCL procedure.

Figure 8-18 JCL to link a main program with a subprogram when both are in source code

Although this example applies to the COBOL compiler, you should be able to adapt it to PL/I, FORTRAN, or assembler language. Refer to topic 1 or to a JCL listing of the compile-and-link procedure to determine the parameters to code in the SYSLIN DD statement.

Linking source code subprograms with object code subprograms

Figure 8-19 illustrates the JCL that can be used to link a main program with two subprograms that have been compiled and stored in a user object library. In this case, the COBOL compile-and-link (COBUCL) procedure is used alone.

The main point this JCL illustrates is the concatenation of the input data sets for the link-edit program. Here, the DD statement labeled LKED.SYSLIN is a duplicate of the link-edit input DD statement in the COBUCL procedure. It defines the temporary data set that was used by the compiler to pass the object module of the main program to the link-edit program. It is duplicated in this job so that the two DD statements that follow it (defining the two object modules in the object library) can be concatenated with the object module of the main program.

The result is that the two members of the MMAOBJ library (SUBPRG1 and SUBPRG2) are considered to be extensions of the

```
//DRLINK   JOB  HE66YFNH,
//              'W. CLARY'
//COMPILE  EXEC  PROC=COBUCL
//COB.SYSIN DD  *
     COBOL source code for the main program
/*
//LKED.SYSLIN DD   DSN=&&LOADSET,
//               DISP=OLD,
//               UNIT=SYSDA
//            DD  DSN=MMAOBJ(SUBPRG1),
//               DISP=SHR
//            DD  DSN=MMAOBJ(SUBPRG2),
//               DISP=SHR
```

Note: The SYSLIN DD statement in the LKED procedure step must be exactly like the SYSLIN DD statement in the corresponding step of the COBUCL procedure.

Figure 8-19 JCL to compile a main program that calls two subprograms from an object library

&&LOADSET data set. All three are read as input to the link-edit program in the sequence dictated by the order of the DD statements, and they are link edited together to form one load module.

If the main program has already been compiled and resides in an object library, and one of the subprograms is being compiled, you can use the same type of JCL. Figure 8-20 shows an example. In this case, the SYSLIN DD statement of the LKED step must first specify the main program member in the object library, then the temporary data set for the compiled object module of the subprogram. This can then be followed by other concatenated DD statements for other subprograms. Coding the concatenated DD statements in this order assures that execution will begin with the first instruction of the main program—not with the first instruction of a subprogram.

The INCLUDE statement Another method that can be used when some of the object modules are in libraries is to use *link-edit control statements*. Figure 8-21 illustrates the use of one such statement, the INCLUDE statement, to link a main program that calls two subprograms named SUBPRG1 and SUBPRG2. They are both stored in the object library MMAOBJ. Here, an instream data set (DD *) is concatenated with the LKED.SYSLIN DD statement. The instream file contains an INCLUDE statement telling the link-edit program to include the specified object modules in the load module. Once again, the order in which you code the INCLUDE statements and concatenated DD statements is significant to the proper link editing of the program.

```
//BANLINK  JOB   HE66YFNH,
//              'W. CLARY'
//COMPILE  EXEC  PROC=COBUCL
//COB.SYSIN DD  *
     COBOL source code for the subprogram (SUBPRG1)
/*
//LKED.SYSLIN DD  DSN=MMAOBJ(COBMAIN),
//               DISP=SHR
//           DD  DSN=&&LOADSET,
//               DISP=OLD,
//               UNIT=SYSDA
//           DD  DSN=MMAOBJ(SUBPRG2),
//               DISP=SHR
```

Figure 8-20 JCL to compile a COBOL subprogram and link it with the main program and another subprogram that both reside in an object library

```
//EMBLINK  JOB   HE66YFNH,
//              'W. CLARY'
//COMPILE  EXEC  PROC=COBUCL
//COB.SYSIN DD  *
     COBOL source code for the main program (COBMAIN)
/*
//LKED.SYSLIN DD  DSN=&&LOADSET,
//               DISP=OLD,
//               UNIT=SYSDA
//           DD  *
   INCLUDE MMAOBJ(SUBPRG1,SUBPRG2)
/*
```

Figure 8-21 Using the link-edit control statement INCLUDE to link a main program to its subprograms that reside in an object library

If you are including several members from the same object library, as in this example, you can specify each member name in parentheses after the library name. If you are including members from different object libraries, you must code a separate INCLUDE statement for each library.

Linking all object code subprograms

Figure 8-22 illustrates the JCL to link edit programs that are all in object code. Each of the object modules has been compiled and placed into a different object library. In this case, the link-edit program is

```
//SALINK    JOB   HE66YFNH,
//                'W. CLARY'
//LINK      EXEC  PGM=HEWL,
//                PARM='LIST,XREF',
//                REGION=128K
//SYSUDUMP  DD    SYSOUT=A
//SYSPRINT  DD    SYSOUT=A
//SYSUT1    DD    DSN=&&SYSUT1,
//                UNIT=SYSDA,
//                SPACE=(1024,(600,120),,CONTIG,ROUND)
//SYSLMOD   DD    DSN=MMA.USERLIB(SACOMP),
//                DISP=SHR
//SYSLIN    DD    DSN=MMAOBJ(SAMAIN),
//                DISP=SHR
//          DD    DSN=COMLIB(SASUB1),
//                DISP=SHR
//          DD    DSN=MMALIB(SASUB2),
//                DISP=SHR
```

Figure 8-22 Using concatenated LKED.SYSLIN DD statements to link three object modules that reside in different object libraries

executed by itself, instead of as part of a procedure, but the same method is used to concatenate the SYSLIN DD statement files together. As a result, the programs named SAMAIN, SASUB1, and SASUB2 are link edited into a single load module named SACOMP that is stored in MMA.USERLIB.

Figure 8-23 shows the JCL and link-edit INCLUDE statement to accomplish the same thing as figure 8-22. In this example, each object module requires an INCLUDE statement since each resides in a different library from all the others.

Terminology

relocatable machine instructions

unresolved references

link-edit control statement

Objectives

1. Given a main program and subprograms in source code, write the JCL to compile the source programs and link edit the object modules to produce one load module.
2. Given a main program and subprograms, one of which is in object code, write the JCL to compile the source program(s) and link edit the object modules to produce one load module.

```
//SALINK    JOB  HE66YFNH,
//               'W. CLARY'
//LINK      EXEC PGM=HEWL,
//               PARM='LIST,XREF',
//               REGION=128K
//SYSUDUMP  DD   SYSOUT=A
//SYSPRINT  DD   SYSOUT=A
//SYSUT1    DD   DSN=&&SYSUT1,
//               UNIT=SYSDA,
//               SPACE=(1024,(600,120),,CONTIG,ROUND)
//SYSLMOD   DD   DSN=MMA.USERLIB(SACOMP),
//               DISP=SHR
//SYSLIN    DD   *
   INCLUDE MMAOBJ(SAMAIN)
   INCLUDE COMLIB(SASUB1)
   INCLUDE MMALIB(SASUB2)
/*
```

Figure 8-23 Using the INCLUDE statement to link three object modules that reside in different object libraries

3. Given a main program and subprograms, all of which are in object code, write the JCL to link edit the object modules to produce one load module.

Problems

You may write the solutions based on the COBOL, PL/I, FORTRAN, or assembler procedures.

1. (Objective 1) Write the JCL to compile and link edit a main program named PARTPGM and its subprograms, PARTG1 and PARTG2. All of the programs are in source code. Place the load module (PARTCALC) in MMA.USERLIB.

2. (Objective 2) Write the JCL to compile a source language main program named PSYSRET, and link edit it with its subprograms PSYSL1 and PSYSL2. The subprograms have alredy been compiled and their object modules reside in a library named OUROBJ. Place the load module (PSYS) in a load library named OURLOAD.

    a. Solve the problem using only JCL (concatenated input to the link-edit program).
    b. Solve the problem using the link-edit INCLUDE statement.

3. (Objective 3) Write the JCL to link edit a main program named PUBLAD with its subprograms PUBSUB1 and PUBSUB2. All three

programs have been compiled and their object modules reside in a library named PUBLIB. Place the load module (PUBADDR) in a load library named PRODLIB.

a. Solve the problem using only JCL (concatenated input to the link-edit program).

b. Solve the problem using the link-edit INCLUDE statement.

Solutions

1. Figure 8-24 is an acceptable solution for a COBOL compiler. If you're using PL/I, FORTRAN, or assembler, the procedure names and the stepnames in the ddnames must be changed accordingly. Specifically, in the first two steps, you will execute a procedure named PLIXC, FORTHC, or ASMFC instead of COBUC; in the third step, the procedure will be PLIXCL, FORTHCL, or ASMFCL instead of COBUCL; and the stepname in the ddnames for the SYSLIN and SYSIN DD statements will be PLI, FORT, or ASM instead of COB.

```
//PROB1     JOB  HE66YFNH,
//               'W. CLARY'
//COMPILE1 EXEC  PROC=COBUC
//COB.SYSLIN DD  DSN=&&LOADSET,
//               DISP=(MOD,PASS),
//               UNIT=SYSDA,
//               SPACE=(80,(500,100))
//COB.SYSIN DD  *
     PARTPGM source program
/*
//COMPILE2 EXEC  PROC=COBUC
//COB.SYSLIN DD  DSN=&&LOADSET,
//               DISP=(MOD,PASS),
//               UNIT=SYSDA,
//               SPACE=(80,(500,100))
//COB.SYSIN DD  *
     PARTG1 source program
/*
//COMPILE3 EXEC  PROC=COBUCL
//COB.SYSIN DD  *
     PARTG2 source program
/*
//LKED.SYSLMOD DD  DSN=MMA.USERLIB(PARTCALC),
//                 DISP=(OLD,KEEP)
```

Figure 8-24 Linking programs in source code

2. a. Figure 8-25 is an acceptable solution. Here again, the COBUCL and COB values are for a COBOL compiler and will be different if you're using PL/I, FORTRAN, or assembler.
   b. Figure 8-26 is an acceptable solution for a COBOL compiler.

```
//PROB2A    JOB   HE66YFNH,
//                'W. CLARY'
//COMPILE  EXEC  PROC=COBUCL
//COB.SYSIN DD   *
      PSYSRET source program
/*
//LKED.SYSMOD DD  DSN=OURLOAD(PSYS),
//               DISP=SHR
//LKED.SYSLIN DD  DSN=&&LOADSET,
//               DISP=OLD,
//               UNIT=SYSDA
//            DD  DSN=OUROBJ(PSYSL1),
//               DISP=SHR
//            DD  DSN=OUROBJ(PSYSL2),
//               DISP=SHR
```

Figure 8-25 Linking a main program in source code with its subprograms in object code by concatenating LKED.SYSLIN

```
//PROB2B    JOB   HE66YFNH,
//                'W. CLARY'
//COMPILE  EXEC  PROC=COBUCL
//COB.SYSIN DD   *
      PSYSRET source program
/*
//LKED.SYSMOD DD  DSN=OURLOAD(PSYS),
//               DISP=SHR
//LKED.SYSLIN DD  DSN=&&LOADSET,
//               DISP=OLD,
//               UNIT=SYSDA
//            DD  *
   INCLUDE OUROBJ(PSYSL1,PSYSL2)
/*
```

Figure 8-26 Linking a main program in source code with its subprograms in object code by using the INCLUDE statement

3. a. Figure 8-27 is an acceptable solution. Since all three programs have already been compiled and are stored as object modules, there's nothing in the JCL that specifies any type of compiler. As a result, this JCL will work whether the programs were written in COBOL, PL/I, FORTRAN, or assembler.
   b. Figure 8-28 is an acceptable solution. Again, this JCL can be used no matter what language the programs were originally written in.

```
//PROB3A    JOB  HE66YFNH,
//               'W. CLARY'
//LINK      EXEC PGM=HEWL,
//               PARM='LIST,XREF',
//               REGION=128K
//SYSUDUMP  DD   SYSOUT=A
//SYSPRINT  DD   SYSOUT=A
//SYSUT1    DD   DSN=&&SYSUT1,
//               UNIT=SYSDA,
//               SPACE=(1024,(600,120),,CONTIG,ROUND)
//SYSLMOD   DD   DSN=PRODLIB(PUBADDR),
//               DISP=SHR
//SYSLIN    DD   DSN=PUBLIB(PUBLAD),
//               DISP=SHR
//          DD   DSN=PUBLIB(PUBSUB1),
//               DISP=SHR
//          DD   DSN=PUBLIB(PUBSUB2),
//               DISP=SHR
```

Figure 8-27 Linking programs that are in object code by concatenating LKED.SYSLIN

```
//PROB3B    JOB  HE66YFNH,
//               'W. CLARY'
//LINK      EXEC PGM=HEWL,
//               PARM='LIST,XREF',
//               REGION=128K
//SYSUDUMP  DD   SYSOUT=A
//SYSPRINT  DD   SYSOUT=A
//SYSUT1    DD   DSN=&&SYSUT1,
//               UNIT=SYSDA,
//               SPACE=(1024,(600,120),,CONTIG,ROUND)
//SYSLMOD   DD   DSN=PRODLIB(PUBADDR),
//               DISP=SHR
//SYSLIN    DD   *
   INCLUDE PUBLIB(PUBLAD,PUBSUB1,PUBSUB2)
/*
```

Figure 8-28 Linking programs that are in object code by using the INCLUDE statement

ZZZ,ZZZ.99	$ZZZ.ZZ $ZZZZ.ZZ $ZZZZ.99	$$$,$$$.99 $$$,$$$.99 $$$,$$$.99 $$$,$$$.99
Z,ZZZ.99		

			$**,**$.99

001234 -001234	001234 123456 000012 000000	142090 001242 000009 001234 -001012	142090

99V99	9(6) 99V99 99V99	99V99 99V99 99V99 99V99	99V99

9

Extended File Handling Capabilities of the DD Statement

As I've indicated throughout this book, OS JCL is a massive, complex subject. It consists of more operands than you would ever want to learn and allows you more control over the system than you would ever need to have. As a result, the JCL in this book is a subset of OS JCL; I've only covered the operands I think you'll need to know about and the applications in which you'll use them.

In this chapter, I'm going to present a few more parameters and subparameters for defining and handling files in the DD statement. But I want you to be aware that this material is extra information—I've already covered the important aspects of the subject in earlier chapters, in particular, chapters 2 through 4.

Frankly, most of the parameters covered here are rarely used. Then why present them at all? Although you'll probably never code most of these parameters, you may have occasion to work with packaged software systems that use them, or you may work on an application that requires one of them. As a result, I recommend that you read this chapter so you know what it covers and then use this material as a reference to those advanced DD parameters when you run across them.

The new DD parameters I'm going to cover in this chapter are the SEP, AFF, SUBALLOC, and SPLIT parameters. In addition, I'll present some additional subparameters for the UNIT, VOL, SPACE, and DCB parameters. This new JCL is shown in the abbreviated DD statement format in figure 9-1.

```
//ddname    DD   UNIT=(device,unit-count,DEFER,SEP=ddnames),
                     =AFF=ddname,
                 SEP=ddnames,
                 AFF=ddname,
                 SUBALLOC=(unit-of-measure,(primary,secondary,directory),
                          file-identifier),
                 SPLIT=formatting-specifications,
                 VOL=(PRIVATE,RETAIN,sequence,count,
                      SER/REF=serial-number/ddname/dsname),
                 SPACE=(unit-of-measure,(primary,secondary,directory/index),
                      RLSE,format,ROUND),
                 DCB=(BUFOFF=buffer-offset,
                      DEN=tape-density,
                      STACK=card-stacker,
                      PRTSP=print-spacing,
                      EROPT=error-options)
```

Figure 9-1 Abbreviated DD statement format showing only the parameters to be discussed in this chapter

THE SEP AND AFF PARAMETERS

As you learned in chapter 1, OS transmits data to and from I/O devices by means of *communication channels*. Each *channel* is the connector through which data must pass as it is being read and written. If a job step with two or more files uses the same type of UNIT, you can speed up the processing of the job by requesting OS to use separate channels for transmitting the data.

The *channel separation* (SEP) parameter tells OS to use a different channel from the ones used for other files. For example, in figure 9-2, the OUT1 DD statement is to be transmitted over a channel different from that used to transmit the files described by IN1 and IN2. In the EXRPT DD statement, the SEP parameter tells OS to use a channel separate from that used for OUT1 and IN1.

The OUT2 DD statement contains a *channel affinity* (AFF) parameter. This parameter tells OS to use the same channel separation for this file as is used for the file described by the DD statement referred to. In the example, AFF = OUT1 means that OS is to use the same channel separation for this file as it did for OUT1. AFF provides a shorthand way of repeating the SEP parameter. In other words, in the example, I could have coded SEP = (IN1,IN2) instead of AFF = OUT1.

The final result of the SEP and AFF parameters coded in figure 9-2 is this: IN1 and IN2 may or may not use the same channel; OUT1 and OUT2 may or may not use the same channel, but they will be

```
//PINSTEP   EXEC  PGM=RBBCON
//IN1       DD    DSN=RBBMAST,
//                DISP=OLD,
//                UNIT=3300,
//                VOL=SER=D00103
//IN2       DD    DSN=RBBINPT,
//                DISP=(NEW,PASS),
//                UNIT=3330,
//                VOL=SER=D00102,
//                SPACE=(CYL,(1,1),RLSE),
//                DCB=(LRECL=150,BLKSIZE=4500,RECFM=FB)
//OUT1      DD    DSN=NEWMAST,
//                DISP=(NEW,CATLG,DELETE),
//                UNIT=3330,
//                SEP=(IN1,IN2),
//                SPACE=(CYL,1,RLSE),
//                DCB=(LRECL=85,BLKSIZE=1700,RECFM=FB)
//OUT2      DD    DSN=HISTFILE,
//                DISP=(NEW,KEEP),
//                UNIT=3330,
//                AFF=OUT1,
//                DCB=*.OUT1
//EXRPT     DD    DSN=RPTFILE,
//                DISP=(NEW,PASS),
//                UNIT=3330,
//                SEP=(OUT1,IN1),
//                DCB=*.OUT1
```

Figure 9-2 Using the SEP and AFF parameters for channel separation and affinity

separate from IN1 and IN2; EXRPT may share a channel with IN2 or OUT2, but it will be separate from IN1 and OUT1. So at least three channels are required for this job.

If OS is unable to accommodate the channel separation you request, it will ask the operator to (1) modify the environment (by mounting devices or switching channels), (2) cancel the channel separation request, (3) cancel the job, or (4) cause OS to wait until devices or channels are available to accomplish the channel separation requested.

ALLOCATING SPACE

In chapter 2, you learned how to allocate space for direct-access files by coding the SPACE parameter. In this section, I'm going to introduce two other methods of obtaining direct-access space: suballocation (SUBALLOC) and cylinder splitting (SPLIT). The SPACE, SUBALLOC, and SPLIT parameters are mutually exclusive and can never be coded on the same DD statement.

The SUBALLOC parameter

Suballocation is a method of dividing an area on a direct-access volume among several files. In order to use this method, you must first define a file area and allocate space for it by coding the SPACE parameter. You can then suballocate that space to other files. As a result, it is possible to reduce access-mechanism movement, resulting in a faster I/O rate.

Figure 9-3 shows the format of the SUBALLOC parameter. Notice that it's similar to the SPACE parameter with the exception of the ddname at the end. This ddname is the name of the original file whose space is being suballocated. The primary allocation of the SUBALLOC parameter comes from this original file area; however, any secondary space requested comes from other available space on the volume.

An example of SUBALLOC is shown in figure 9-4. The pertinent statements are numbered, so let's walk through them.

1. SCALC is the name of the first job step. It executes a program that uses SCSRC as input and writes out SCOUT1 and SCOUT2.
2. SCAREA is the ddname that defines the area to be suballocated. Although it is not referred to by the program, it defines a file

```
             ⎧TRK         ⎫                            ⎧,ddname                          ⎫
SUBALLOC=( ⎨CYL          ⎬,(primary,secondary,directory)⎨,stepname.ddname                ⎬)
             ⎩block-length⎭                            ⎩,stepname.procstepname.ddname    ⎭
```

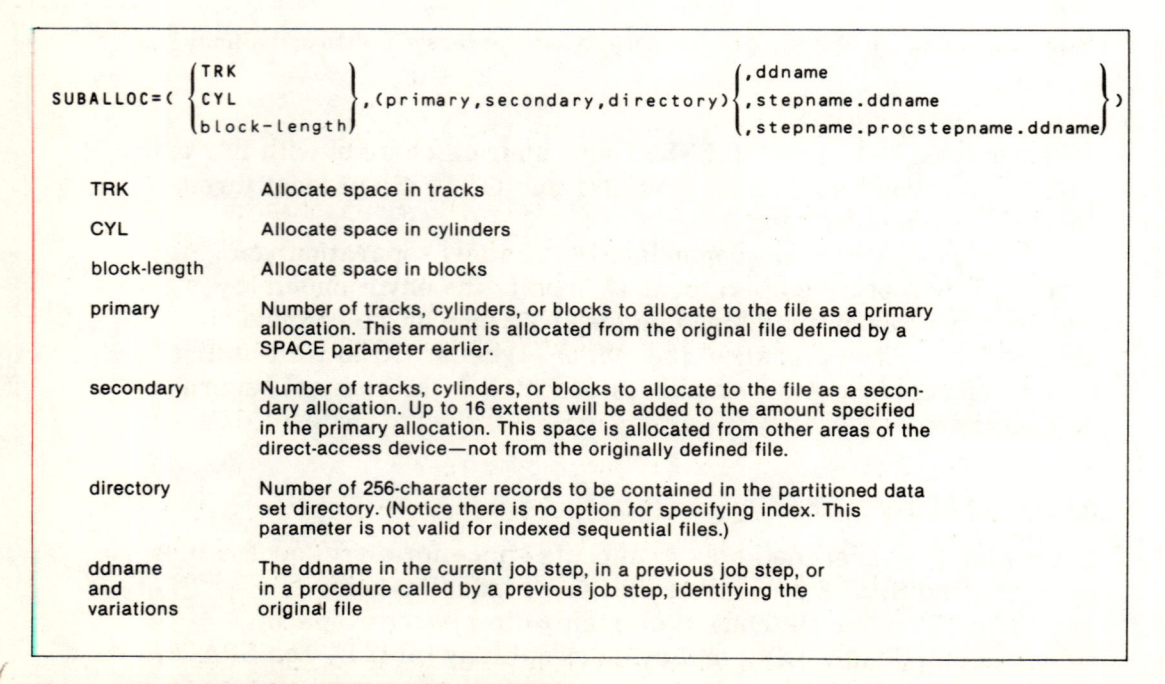

TRK	Allocate space in tracks
CYL	Allocate space in cylinders
block-length	Allocate space in blocks
primary	Number of tracks, cylinders, or blocks to allocate to the file as a primary allocation. This amount is allocated from the original file defined by a SPACE parameter earlier.
secondary	Number of tracks, cylinders, or blocks to allocate to the file as a secondary allocation. Up to 16 extents will be added to the amount specified in the primary allocation. This space is allocated from other areas of the direct-access device—not from the originally defined file.
directory	Number of 256-character records to be contained in the partitioned data set directory. (Notice there is no option for specifying index. This parameter is not valid for indexed sequential files.)
ddname and variations	The ddname in the current job step, in a previous job step, or in a procedure called by a previous job step, identifying the original file

Figure 9-3 Format of the SUBALLOC parameter

```
        //SCJOB    JOB   HE66YFNH,
        //              'W. CLARY'
        //JOBLIB   DD    DSN=NMA.USERLIB,
        //              DISP=SHR
1 //SCALC       EXEC   PGM=STDCALC
        //SCSRC    DD    DSN=STCMAST1,
        //              DISP=OLD
2 //SCAREA      DD    DSN=AREA1,
        //              DISP=(NEW,KEEP),
        //              UNIT=SYSDA,
        //              VOL=SER=DOG103,
        //              SPACE=(CYL,50,,CONTIG)
3 //SCOUT1      DD    DSN=SCDATA1,
        //              DISP=(NEW,KEEP),
        //              SUBALLOC=(CYL,(20,10),SCAREA),
        //              DCB=(LRECL=150,BLKSIZE=4500,RECFM=FB)
4 //SCOUT2      DD    DSN=SCDATA2,
        //              DISP=(NEW,KEEP),
        //              SUBALLOC=(TRK,5,SCAREA),
        //              DCB=*.SCOUT1
5 //SCUPDATE    EXEC   PGM=SCUPD
        //SCOUT    DD    DSN=*.SCALC.SCOUT1,
        //              DISP=OLD
6 //SCOUT3      DD    DSN=SCDATA3,
        //              DISP=(NEW,CATLG,DELETE),
        //              SUBALLOC=(4500,(50,10),SCALC.SCAREA),
        //              DCB=*.SCALC.SCOUT1
        //
```

Figure 9-4 Using the SUBALLOC parameter

area of 50 cylinders of contiguous space on a direct-access volume.

3. SCOUT1 is the ddname of the first file to be suballocated. It requests space in cylinders: 20 in the primary allocation and 10 in the secondary. The primary space is to be allocated from the area defined by SCAREA. Any secondary space will *not* be suballocated from SCAREA; it will be obtained from other space on the volume.

4. SCOUT2 requests five tracks of the area defined by SCAREA.

5. SCUPDATE is the name of the second job step.

6. SCOUT3 is the last file requesting some of the space allocated to SCAREA. It requests its space in blocks of data. According to the SUBALLOC parameter, it requires 50 blocks of 4500 bytes to be allocated from SCAREA.

If you look back at the format in figure 9-3, you'll see that the third value in the allocation subparameter tells how much space should be assigned to a directory only, not an index. That's because the SUBALLOC parameter can be coded for partitioned data sets but *not* for ISAM files.

The SPLIT parameter

The *cylinder splitting* technique is another way to reduce access-mechanism movement and increase the speed of I/O operations in your job. It provides for more than one file to share the tracks of one cylinder. For example, assume that a device has cylinders that contain 20 tracks each. You can split these tracks up between files by coding a SPLIT parameter.

Figure 9-5 illustrates the format of the SPLIT parameter. As you can see, the parameter has four different formats: formats 1 and 2 work together as do formats 3 and 4. You see, to split the tracks between files, you must code the DD statements for the files as a series. The SPLIT parameter (format 1 or 3) in the first DD statement in the series allocates the total amount of space for all of the files involved and sets aside the portion of each cylinder to be used by the first file. Each subsequent SPLIT parameter (format 2 or 4) in the series has only to specify the portion of each cylinder to be used by the file it defines.

Figure 9-6 shows two examples of the SPLIT parameter. In example 1, ENGOUT1 defines the first file and the allocation of the area for the three files in the series. It asks for space in cylinders: 25 in the primary allocation and two in the secondary allocation. Additionally, it tells OS to give the first five tracks of each cylinder to this file. ENGOUT2 asks for the next five tracks in each of the allocated cylinders. ENGOUT3 asks for the next seven tracks in each cylinder. As a result, there are three unused tracks left in each cylinder (20 tracks per cylinder).

Example 2 shows allocation in blocks using the SPLIT parameter. The number coded in each DD statement in the series is the *percentage* of tracks per cylinder to be allocated to that file. In other words, the allocation is made in percentage of tracks even though the allocation request is made in blocks. In example 2, APMAST requests enough space to hold 1000 blocks of data 4000 bytes in length. It also requests that 10 blocks be added each time more space is needed by a file in the series. Then, it asks for 20 percent of the tracks per cylinder to be allocated to the first file (ACCTPM). The second DD statement, APTAB1, requests 35 percent of the tracks per cylinder. The third DD statement, APTAB2, requests 40 percent of the tracks per cylinder. As a result, five percent of the tracks per cylinder are not used.

Format 1 (first DD statement):	`SPLIT=(number,CYL,(primary,secondary))`
Format 2 (other DD statements):	`SPLIT=number`
Format 3 (first DD statement):	`SPLIT=(percent,block-length,(primary,secondary))`
Format 4 (other DD statements):	`SPLIT=percent`

Format 1

number	Number of tracks per cylinder to be allocated to this file
CYL	Allocate space in cylinders
primary	Number of cylinders to be split among several files. Each file must be defined by a DD statement in this series.
secondary	Number of secondary cylinders to be allocated to a file if more space is required

Format 2

number	Number of tracks per cylinder to be allocated to this file. The allocation of cylinders was accomplished by the first DD statement in the series using Format 1.

Format 3

percent	Percentage of tracks per cylinder to be allocated to this file
block-length	Average block size indicating that space is to be allocated in blocks of data
primary	Number of blocks to be contained in the primary allocation to be split among several files. Each file must be defined by a DD statement in this series.
secondary	Number of blocks to be contained in each secondary extent for a file if more space is required. This area is not split among the files but is allocated in whole cylinders.

Format 4

percent	Percentage of tracks per cylinder to be allocated to this file. The allocation of blocks was accomplished by the first DD statement in the series using Format 3.

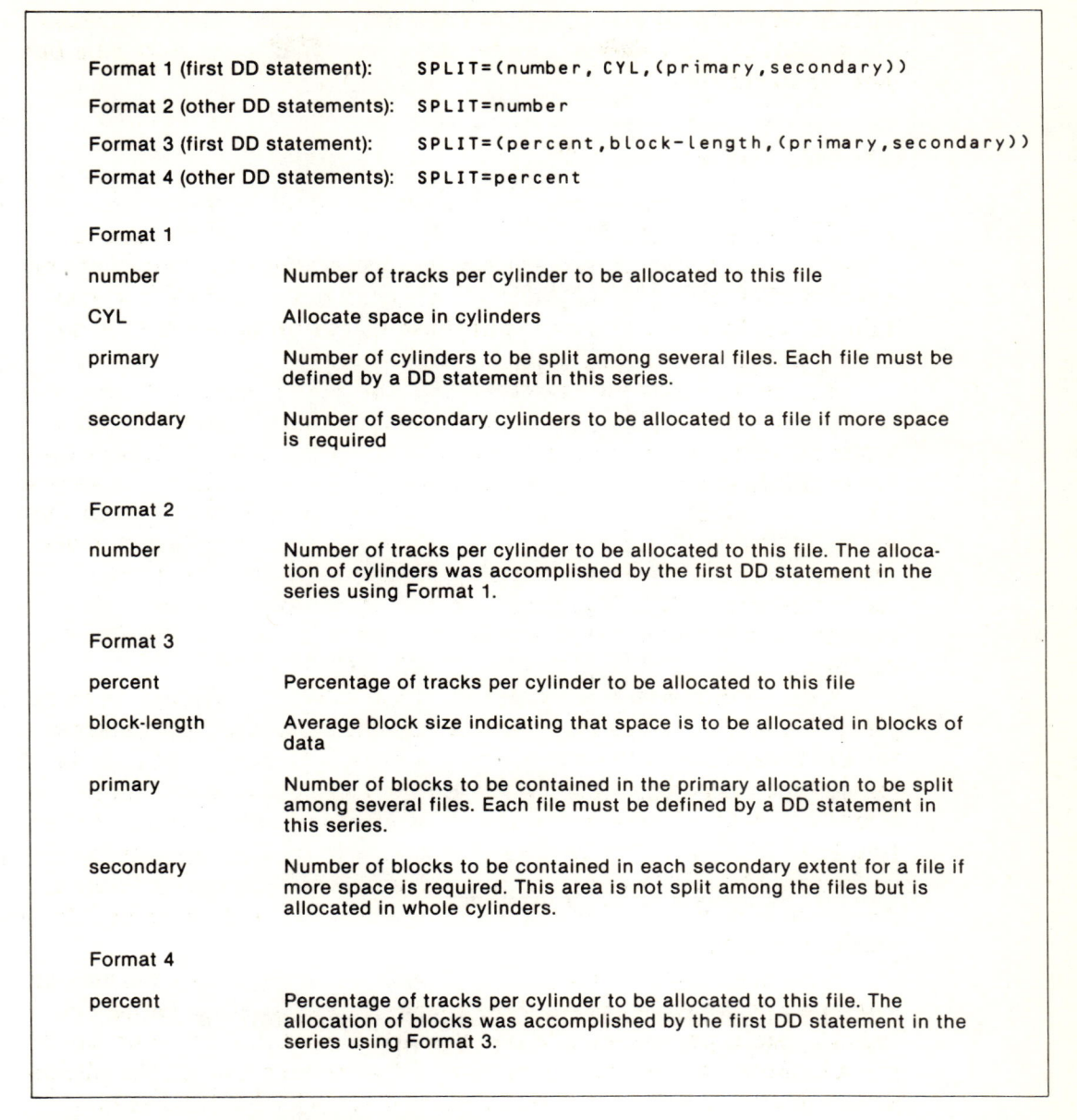

Figure 9-5 Format of the SPLIT parameter

In both of these examples, additional space required by a file described with the SPLIT parameter is obtained from the secondary allocation subparameter of the first DD statement in the series. However, the secondary space is not split. It is allocated in whole cylinders or blocks to the file that needs it. If a file needs more space and no secondary allocation is specified (or if it is used up), the job

```
Example 1
//ENGPRT    EXEC  PGM=ENGD504
//ENGIN     DD    DSN=ENGMAST,
//                DISP=OLD
//ENGOUT1   DD    DSN=FUNCCALC,
//                DISP=(NEW,KEEP),
//                UNIT=SYSDA,
//                VOL=SER=D00103,
//                SPLIT=(5,CYL,(25,2)),
//                DCB=(LRECL=30,BLKSIZE=900,RECFM=VB)
//ENGOUT2   DD    DSN=REALCOMP,
//                DISP=(NEW,PASS),
//                SPLIT=5,
//                DCB=*.ENGOUT1
//ENGOUT3   DD    DSN=OVERRIDE,
//                DISP=(NEW,KEEP),
//                SPLIT=7,
//                DCB=*.ENGOUT1


Example 2
//APSUM     EXEC  PGM=AP411
//APMAST    DD    DSN=ACCTPM,
//                DISP=(NEW,KEEP),
//                UNIT=SYSDA,
//                VOL=SER=D00102,
//                SPLIT=(20,4000,(1000,100)),
//                DCB=(LRECL=400,BLKSIZE=4000,RECFM=FB)
//APTAB1    DD    DSN=ACCTPT1,
//                DISP=(NEW,KEEP),
//                SPLIT=35,
//                DCB=*.APMAST
//APTAB2    DD    DSN=ACCTPT2,
//                DISP=(NEW,KEEP),
//                SPLIT=40,
//                DCB=*.APMAST
```

Figure 9-6 Examples of the SPLIT parameter

will be terminated. Like the SUBALLOC parameter, the SPLIT parameter *cannot* be used for ISAM files.

THE UNIT PARAMETER

As you know, the UNIT parameter tells OS what kind of device to make available for reading or writing a file. We covered the basic subparameters of the UNIT parameter in chapters 2 and 3. Now, I'll introduce you to subparameters that allow deferred mounting of volumes and unit separation and affinity. Figure 9-7 illustrates the expanded format of the UNIT parameter.

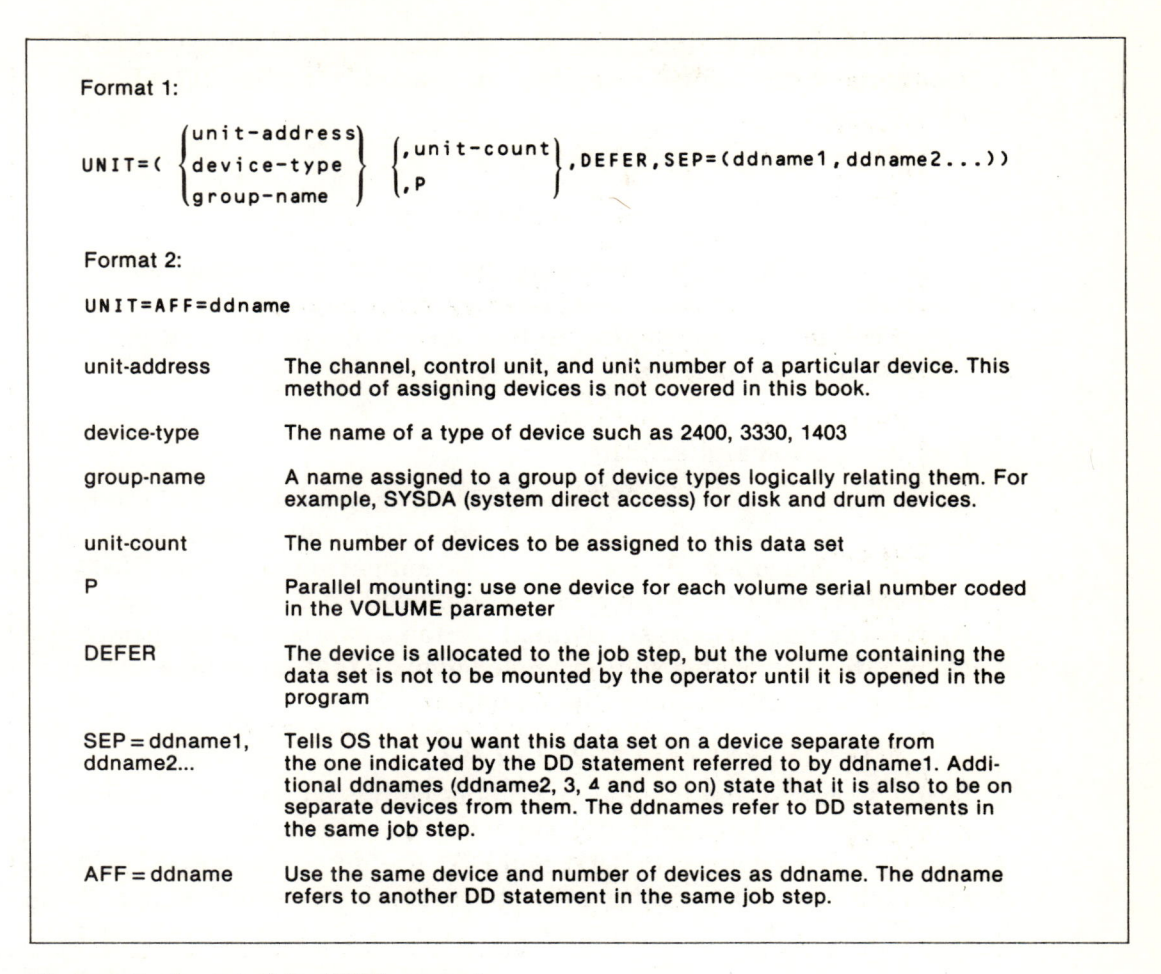

```
Format 1:
             ⎧unit-address⎫  ⎧,unit-count⎫
UNIT=( ⎨device-type ⎬  ⎨           ⎬,DEFER,SEP=(ddname1,ddname2...))
             ⎩group-name  ⎭  ⎩,P         ⎭

Format 2:
UNIT=AFF=ddname
```

unit-address	The channel, control unit, and unit number of a particular device. This method of assigning devices is not covered in this book.
device-type	The name of a type of device such as 2400, 3330, 1403
group-name	A name assigned to a group of device types logically relating them. For example, SYSDA (system direct access) for disk and drum devices.
unit-count	The number of devices to be assigned to this data set
P	Parallel mounting: use one device for each volume serial number coded in the VOLUME parameter
DEFER	The device is allocated to the job step, but the volume containing the data set is not to be mounted by the operator until it is opened in the program
SEP=ddname1, ddname2...	Tells OS that you want this data set on a device separate from the one indicated by the DD statement referred to by ddname1. Additional ddnames (ddname2, 3, 4 and so on) state that it is also to be on separate devices from them. The ddnames refer to DD statements in the same job step.
AFF=ddname	Use the same device and number of devices as ddname. The ddname refers to another DD statement in the same job step.

Figure 9-7 Format of the UNIT parameter

Deferred mounting

You can cause OS to allocate a device to your file and wait to mount the volume until the file is opened by the program. To do this, you code the DEFER subparameter in the UNIT parameter. You should only code this subparameter for volumes that can be mounted and de-mounted from the system. In other words, don't code it for a permanently resident disk pack or for a card reader. Additionally, DEFER cannot be coded for indexed sequential files or for files that are to be created on a direct-access device.

One good example of the use of DEFER is when you have an optional file that is occasionally used by your program. Perhaps it is a file associated with a transaction that is rarely used as input to an update program. In this case, you can eliminate the mounting and demounting of the volume when it's not needed by coding DEFER. Here's an example:

```
//UPFILEA  DD DSN=STUPFILE,
//            DISP=OLD,
//            UNIT=(2400,,DEFER)
```

In this example, we are assuming that the file is cataloged on magnetic tape. The two consecutive commas indicate the absence of the unit-count subparameter. In this case, if the program never opens the file, the operator doesn't have to mount the tape.

Unit separation and affinity

When we discussed the SEP and AFF parameters of the DD statement, we were describing *channel separation*. Here, we are discussing *unit separation*. By coding the SEP subparameter of the UNIT parameter, you can cause a file to be placed on a different volume from other files previously defined for the same type of device. Of course, the use of this subparameter implies that no volume serial number is specified. Here's an example:

```
UNIT=(SYSDA,SEP=(DD1,DD2))
```

In this example, the file described is to be placed on a system direct-access volume, but one that is separate from the volumes that DD1 and DD2 are assigned to. DD1 and DD2 are ddnames defined in the same job step. They may or may not reside on the same volume. (Note that if SEP is the only subparameter besides the group name, extra commas are not required.)

Unit affinity is just the opposite of unit separation. If you code AFF=ddname, the file defined will be placed on the same unit as the file defined by ddname. The ddname must refer to a DD statement in the same job step. Here's an example to illustrate:

```
//            UNIT=AFF=DD1
```

In this example, the file being described would be placed on the same unit as DD1.

If AFF refers to a tape unit, make sure your program has closed the first file before attempting to read or write the other. Since AFF tells OS to use the same device for two files that may be on separate volumes, you can't expect to alternately read data from both volumes.

The AFF subparameter is mutually exclusive of all other UNIT subparameters, and so, if coded, it must be the only subparameter. That's why it's shown in a separate format in figure 9-7.

UNIT examples

Figure 9-8 shows examples of the UNIT parameter and its subparameters. Example 1 is the UNIT parameter for a file assigned to three 2400 series magnetic tape units. The tapes are not to be mounted until the file is opened by the program. Example 2 shows a file contained on two tape volumes to be mounted on a separate device from files described by the ddnames DATA1 and DATA2. The volumes for this file are not to be mounted until the file is opened by the program. Example 3 illustrates the UNIT parameter for a file to be placed on a separate device from files described by UPSK1 and UPSK2 DD statements. Example 4 shows the UNIT parameter of a file assigned to magnetic tape that is not to be mounted until opened by the program. Finally, example 5 shows the UNIT parameter for a file assigned to a 3330 disk device, but not the same device assigned to a file defined by the GOODDATA DD statement.

THE VOLUME PARAMETER

In chapter 2, I discussed a limited application of the VOLUME parameter: assigning a file to one volume by coding its volume serial number. Then, in chapter 3, I showed you how to code multiple serial numbers and the VOL=REF format. In this chapter, I'll expand those concepts and introduce you to the full capabilities of the VOLUME parameter. Before we begin to look at the format and uses of this parameter, though, you should understand some basic information about the attributes of volumes.

```
Example 1
    //           UNIT=(2400,3,DEFER)
Example 2
    //           UNIT=(TAPE,2,DEFER,SEP=(DATA1,DATA2))
Example 3
    //           UNIT=SEP=(UPSK1,UPSK2)
Example 4
    //           UNIT=(2400,,DEFER)
Example 5
    //           UNIT=(3330,SEP=GOODDATA)
```

Figure 9-8 Examples of the UNIT parameter

Remember from chapter 1 that a volume is a tape reel, a drum, a disk pack, or some other unique storage entity. Each volume, when mounted on a device, is given certain attributes by OS. These attributes are derived from three sources: system generation commands, operator commands, and your JCL statements. When combined, the three main attributes of a volume are collectively called the *volume state*. The three main attributes of a volume are: mount attribute, use attribute, and non-sharable attribute.

Mount attribute The *mount attribute* indicates whether a volume is permanently resident (direct-access only), reserved, or removable. *Permanently resident volumes* are usually defined at system generation time through entries in the system parameter library. These volumes usually include those that are fixed (physically non-removable), those that contain the OS programs and support modules, and those that contain system files.

Reserved volumes are those volumes used by many different jobs. They include work disk packs or tape reels or other volumes that may contain files belonging to several organizations or functions. They remain mounted until the operator requests that they be demounted. As a result, the facility of reserved volumes eliminates the need for the operator to be continually mounting and demounting the commonly used volumes each time a job requests one.

A *removable volume* is mounted each time a job requests it and is demounted when that job step completes. In actual practice, most tape volumes are removable and most disk packs are reserved or permanently resident (although in a large installation, removable disk packs may be common).

Use attribute A volume can have one of four *use attributes*: public, private, storage, and scratch. The use attribute is one factor that controls the assignment of volumes to files. Only direct-access volumes can be public or storage. Only magnetic tape volumes can be scratch. Either magnetic tape or direct-access volumes may be private.

Public use indicates that any job requesting space on this direct-access volume (or being assigned space if a specific reference to the volume is not made) can place data on it. *Storage use* is the same as public use, except that a file can be stored on a storage volume by specific or non-specific volume requests regardless of whether the file is temporary or permanent. In contrast, to store a temporary file on a public volume, you must specifically request that volume. *Private use* indicates that only files that specifically request the volume can place data on it. In other words, if you code UNIT = SYSDA (or the unit name of the disk device) but don't provide the VOLUME information, the file will not be placed on a private disk pack. However, magnetic tape volumes are always private, even if you don't code the VOLUME parameter. *Scratch use* indicates that a magnetic tape volume is to be used to pass data to another step. Each volume is assigned a use attribute via systems commands at the time the volume is added to the installation.

Non-sharable attribute   The *non-sharable attribute* applies only to direct-access volumes and, more specifically, to volumes that can be mounted or demounted during the processing of the job step. A volume that is assigned the non-sharable attribute cannot be used for (1) another file that's defined in the same step with a non-specific volume request or (2) a file defined in another step that's being executed at the same time.

Permanently resident volumes, reserved volumes, and public volumes that are mounted to satisfy a non-specific volume request are *never* assigned the non-sharable attribute. Otherwise, a volume will be mounted with the non-sharable attribute if (1) you request multiple volumes in the VOLUME parameter, but the number of volumes is greater than the number of devices in the UNIT parameter; (2) you request unit affinity with another file, but the file resides on a volume that is not mounted; (3) you request deferred mounting of a direct-access volume; or (4) you make a non-specific volume request and code PRIVATE on the VOLUME parameter.

VOLUME parameter format

To control the volume's attributes, you can use the subparameters shown the format of the VOLUME parameter in figure 9-9. All of the subparameters are positional except SER and REF, so if you omit one, you must code a comma to indicate the position of subparameters that follow.

The PRIVATE subparameter indicates that the volume's use attribute is to be private. That is, only specific volume requests can cause files to be stored on the volume. It also causes the volume to be demounted at the completion of the job step (or at the end of the job if RETAIN is also coded).

The RETAIN subparameter indicates that the volume is not to be demounted after its use in the job step. It is to be left mounted until the entire job completes. This subparameter only applies to magnetic tape volumes and private removable direct-access volumes. It's useful when a number of job steps use the same private file; it relieves the operator from having to mount and demount the volume several times for one job.

```
                                                        ⎧,SER=(ser1,ser2...)      ⎫
⎧VOLUME⎫                                                ⎪         ⎧dsname   ⎫    ⎪
⎨      ⎬=(PRIVATE,RETAIN,volume-sequence-number,volume-count⎨,REF= ⎨         ⎬    ⎬)
⎩VOL   ⎭                                                ⎪         ⎩reference⎭    ⎪
```

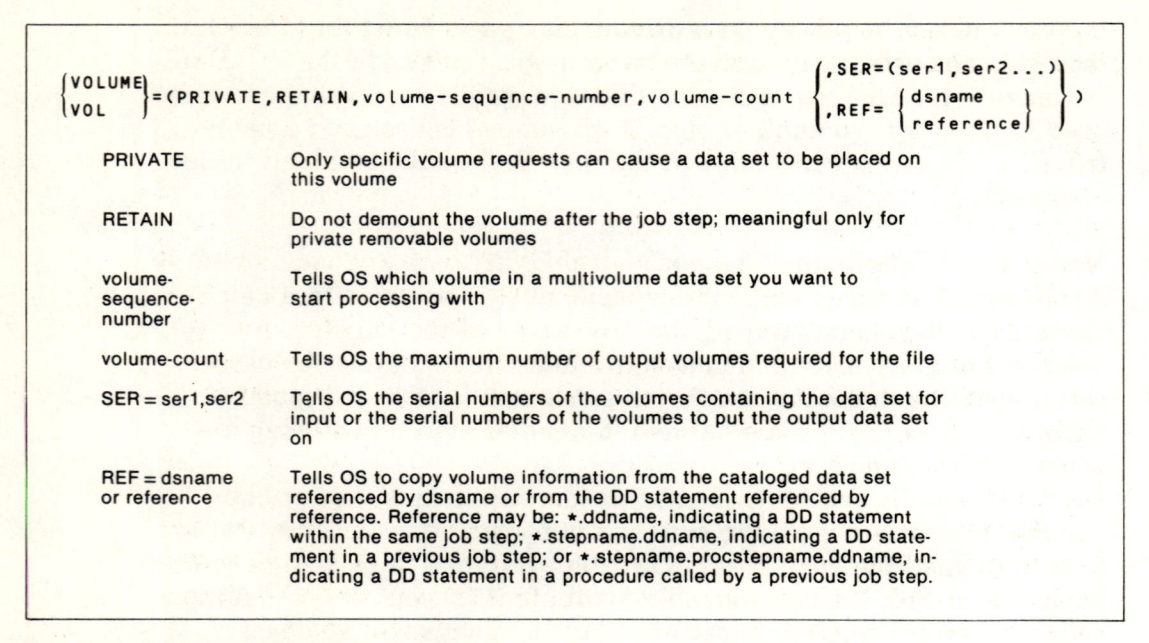

PRIVATE	Only specific volume requests can cause a data set to be placed on this volume
RETAIN	Do not demount the volume after the job step; meaningful only for private removable volumes
volume-sequence-number	Tells OS which volume in a multivolume data set you want to start processing with
volume-count	Tells OS the maximum number of output volumes required for the file
SER = ser1,ser2	Tells OS the serial numbers of the volumes containing the data set for input or the serial numbers of the volumes to put the output data set on
REF = dsname or reference	Tells OS to copy volume information from the cataloged data set referenced by dsname or from the DD statement referenced by reference. Reference may be: *.ddname, indicating a DD statement within the same job step; *.stepname.ddname, indicating a DD statement in a previous job step; or *.stepname.procstepname.ddname, indicating a DD statement in a procedure called by a previous job step.

Figure 9-9 Format of the VOLUME parameter

The volume-sequence-number subparameter is coded as a one- to three-digit number that specifies which volume of a multiple volume file you want to begin with. For example, suppose your job is to extract certain records from a cataloged file stored on several reels of magnetic tape. The file is in sequence by date, and you are to extract all records with dates later than 1975 for your report. Further, suppose that the first two reels of the history file contain records with dates prior to 1975. In such a case, you can code the VOLUME parameter like this:

```
//                VOL=(,,3)
```

In this example, OS will tell the operator to mount the tape corresponding to the third volume of the cataloged file. The two commas preceding the sequence number indicate that PRIVATE and RETAIN are omitted.

The volume-count subparameter is valid only for output files, and it specifies the maximum number of volumes required for an output file. For example, if you know that an output file will require no more than two volumes, you can code a VOLUME parameter like this:

```
//                VOL=(,,,2)
```

If you don't code the volume-count subparameter and the file requires more than one volume, the job may terminate abnormally. In the example above, the three consecutive commas indicate that PRIVATE, RETAIN, and volume sequence number are omitted.

Examples of the VOLUME parameter

Figure 9-10 illustrates some uses of the VOLUME parameter. And since the UNIT parameter and VOLUME parameter must be consistent, the UNIT parameter is shown in each of the examples. Let's look at each example and discuss the device allocation, volume state, and the consistency between the UNIT and VOLUME parameters coded.

Example 1 shows the parameters for a file on a direct-access device with the private use attribute. The volume serial number is D00102. This set of parameters will cause the operator to mount D00102 when the step begins and demount it when the step is completed.

Example 2 shows the subparameters for a magnetic tape volume. It is a private file, but it's not to be demounted after the job step completes. Code a VOLUME parameter like this when you want to pass data to a later job step using tape as the passing medium.

Example 3 shows an output tape file to be mounted when opened by the program. It is a private volume but should not be demounted until the end of the job. It will require that two tape volumes be mounted, one at a time, on one device. (If I had coded a unit count of 2 or P in the UNIT parameter, the volumes would be mounted on two different devices.) The serial numbers of the volumes are given.

THE SPACE PARAMETER

Figure 9-11 gives the complete format of the SPACE parameter. Most of the subparameters were covered in chapters 2 and 3. The only

```
    Example 1
        //              UNIT=SYSDA,
        //              VOL=(PRIVATE,,,,SER=D00102)
    Example 2
        //              UNIT=TAPE,
        //              VOL=(PRIVATE,RETAIN)
    Example 3
        //              UNIT=(TAPE,,DEFER),
        //              VOL=(PRIVATE,RETAIN,,2,SER=(0613,0614))
```

Figure 9-10 Examples of the UNIT and VOLUME parameters

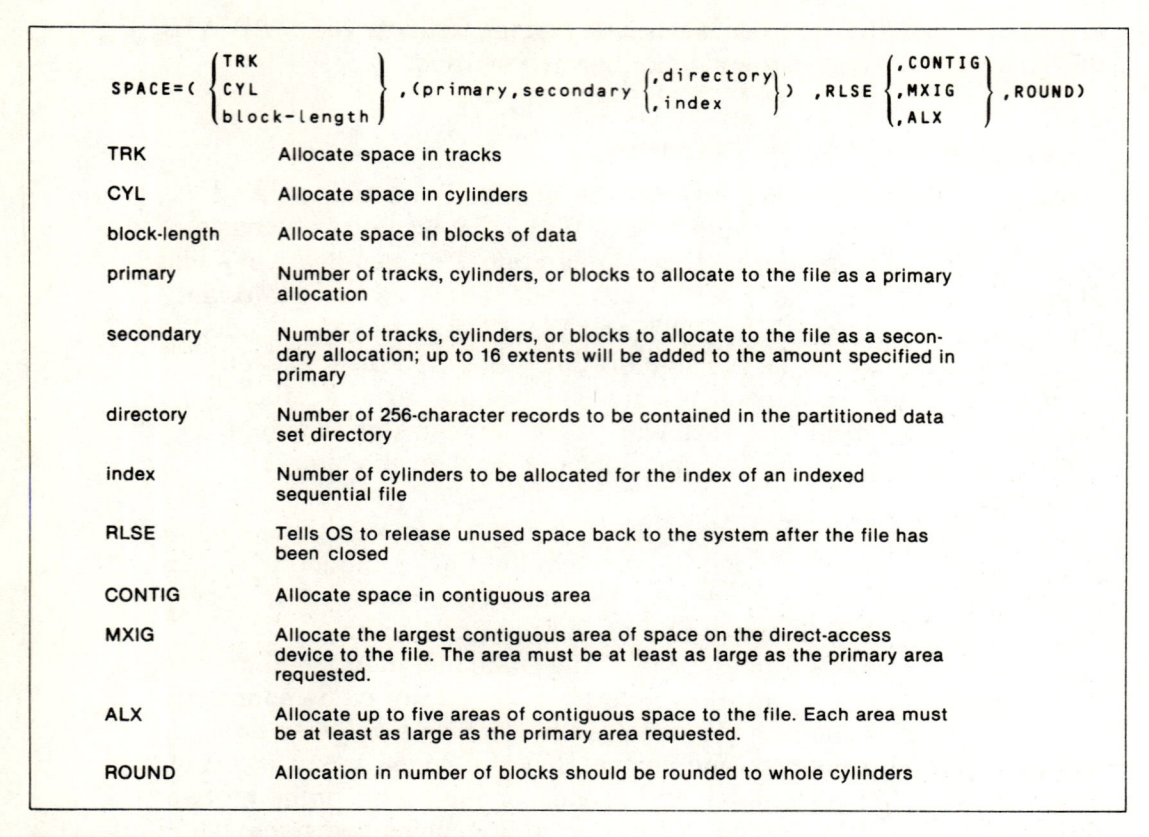

```
SPACE=( {TRK / CYL / block-length} ,(primary,secondary {,directory / ,index}) ,RLSE {,CONTIG / ,MXIG / ,ALX} ,ROUND)
```

TRK	Allocate space in tracks
CYL	Allocate space in cylinders
block-length	Allocate space in blocks of data
primary	Number of tracks, cylinders, or blocks to allocate to the file as a primary allocation
secondary	Number of tracks, cylinders, or blocks to allocate to the file as a secondary allocation; up to 16 extents will be added to the amount specified in primary
directory	Number of 256-character records to be contained in the partitioned data set directory
index	Number of cylinders to be allocated for the index of an indexed sequential file
RLSE	Tells OS to release unused space back to the system after the file has been closed
CONTIG	Allocate space in contiguous area
MXIG	Allocate the largest contiguous area of space on the direct-access device to the file. The area must be at least as large as the primary area requested.
ALX	Allocate up to five areas of contiguous space to the file. Each area must be at least as large as the primary area requested.
ROUND	Allocation in number of blocks should be rounded to whole cylinders

Figure 9-11 Format of the SPACE parameter

new ones are MXIG and ALX. Like CONTIG, these values control the format of the space that's allocated to a file. Unlike the CONTIG option, they *cannot* be coded for ISAM files.

The MXIG (maximum contiguous) subparameter goes one step beyond the CONTIG subparameter. Not only does it request contiguous space, but it requests the *largest* contiguous area available on the volume. This area must be as large as the primary allocation given for the file. If OS can't find such an area, the job is abnormally terminated.

The ALX (all extents) subparameter requests up to five different areas of contiguous space for the file. Again, each area must be at least as large as the primary allocation value. If OS can't find an area large enough to meet these requirements, the job will be abnormally terminated.

Figure 9-12 shows examples of SPACE parameters that use the MXIG and ALX values. In example 1, the space for the file is allocated in blocks of 1400 bytes: ten blocks in the primary allocation

```
Example 1
//              SPACE=(1400,(10,5),RLSE,ALX)
Example 2
//              SPACE=(CYL,(20,,2),,MXIG)
```

Figure 9-12 Examples of the SPACE parameter

and five in the secondary. The RLSE option causes unused space to be released to other files when the file is closed. The ALX option says the space must be contiguous and can consist of up to five areas on the volume. Each area must be large enough to hold the primary quantity of ten blocks of data (or 14,000 bytes).

Example 2 is the SPACE parameter for a file that can use 20 cylinders of primary space. This is a partitioned data set (MXIG can't be coded for ISAM files) whose directory contains two 256-byte directory records. The file space is to be allocated from the largest area of contiguous space that's available on the volume (MXIG). This area must consist of at least 20 cylinders.

THE DCB PARAMETER

Throughout this book, you've been learning how to code DCB values to define the characteristics of a file. And you've also learned that some DCB values can be coded for all files, while others are only used in certain situations. In this chapter, I'm going to cover five more subparameters. Four of them—BUFOFF, DEN, STACK, and PRTSP—are only used for files on certain devices. The fifth one—EROPT—lets you handle errors on sequential files. Figure 9-13 gives the formats and acceptable values for these subparameters.

BUFOFF At some time, you may have to work with tapes that are recorded in a code called ASCII, instead of the code used on standard IBM tapes. And some ASCII files contain a block prefix before each block of records—a prefix that is not present on standard IBM tape files. As a result, the I/O areas, or buffers, for the file must allow for the prefixes. So you will have to code the BUFOFF subparameter for such tapes. It tells OS how much the buffer needs to be adjusted, or offset, to allow for the block prefix. As you can see in figure 9-13, the value coded after BUFOFF= can be a one- or two-digit number from 0 to 99 specifying the length of the block prefix (for output files it must be 0). Or it can be the letter L, which indicates that the records are D-type (RECFM=D) containing a four-byte block prefix.

```
DCB=(BUFOFF= { nn
               L  },
     DEN=tape-density,
     STACK=card-stacker,
     PRTSP=print-spacing,
     EROPT=error-options)
```

nn	A number between 0 and 99 that specifies, in bytes, the length of the block prefix for an ASCII tape
L	Indicates the ASCII tape is D-type and has a four-byte block prefix
tape-density	0 = 200 bits per inch (7-track tape) 1 = 555 bits per inch (7-track tape) 2 = 800 bits per inch (7- or 9-track tape) 3 = 1600 bits per inch (9-track tape)
card-stacker	1 = stacker bin 1 2 = stacker bin 2
print-spacing	0 = no spacing 1 = single-spacing 2 = double-spacing 3 = triple-spacing
error-options	ABE Cause abnormal end of job ACC Accept the block causing the error SKP Skip the block causing the error

Figure 9-13 Format of the DCB parameter—the BUFOFF, DEN, STACK, PRTSP, and EROPT subparameters

DEN DEN is only used for magnetic tape files. It allows you to specify the recording density for the file. It can specify a value from 0 to 3, as shown in figure 9-13.

The default value for the DEN subparameter depends on the type of tape drive on your system. For seven-track tape drives and nine-track tape drives with single density, the default value is 800 bits per inch (DEN = 2); for nine-track tape drives with dual density or a phase-encoded feature, the default is 1600 bits per inch (DEN = 3).

STACK STACK tells OS which stacker bin is to receive a card after it has been read or punched. STACK = 1 indicates stacker bin 1; STACK = 2 indicates stacker bin 2. The default value is stacker bin 1. Naturally, this parameter is valid for card files only.

PRTSP PRTSP allows you to set the line spacing for a print (SYSOUT) file. You can set the printer so it will single-space, double-space, or triple-space between lines of print. The format and valid codes are as shown in figure 9-13; the default value is 1.

EROPT   EROPT is used only for sequential files. It allows you to request special error handling routines to be applied if an I/O error should occur when processing the file. As you can see in figure 9-13, you can use EROPT to (1) cause the job to terminate abnormally when an I/O error occurs, (2) accept the block that's causing the error, or (3) skip the block that's causing the error. The default value is ABE.

VS CONSIDERATIONS

Because of the way VS systems are managed, several of the JCL parameters presented in this chapter are not meaningful under VS. Specifically, the parameters requesting channel separation and affinity and unit separation are not supported. As a result, AFF, SEP, and UNIT = SEP are meaningless to the operating system. Similarly, SPLIT and SUBALLOC are not supported by OS/VS.

However, if any of these parameters are encountered in the job stream by the OS/VS interpreter, they are edited for syntax only, then ignored. In allocating space for files in an OS/VS system, the SPLIT and SUBALLOC parameters are changed to SPACE requests, so no cylinder splitting or space suballocation is performed.

Terminology

communication channel
channel
channel separation
channel affinity
suballocation
cylinder splitting
channel separation
unit separation
unit affinity
mount attribute

permanently resident volume
reserved volume
removable volume
use attribute
public use
storage use
private use
scratch use
non-sharable attribute

Objective

Given reference material and job specifications, code any of the parameters presented in this chapter.

Problems

1. Code a DD statement for an output file that is to be accessed through a channel separate from the one used for a file with the ddname IN1. The file is to be stored on system direct-access volume D00102. It should be allocated an initial area of one track, with one-track increments as needed. Any extra space is to be released to the system. The file contains fixed-length records, each 256 characters long, blocked five to a block.

2. Code the DD statements necessary to (1) allocate 50 contiguous tracks of 3330 space to a file area and (2) suballocate that area as shown in figure 9-14.

3. Code a DD statement for an output tape file to be cataloged under the data set name OUT24. It is to be mounted when opened by the program. It is a private volume, but it should not be demounted until the end of the job. It will require that two tape volumes be mounted, one at a time on the same device. The serial numbers are 00001 and 00002. The record length is 80, block size is 800, and record format is fixed blocked.

Files sharing space

AREA1　　⎧ PINFILE1　(16 primary, 4 secondary tracks)
(50 tracks)　⎨ PINFILE2　(10 primary, 5 secondary tracks)
　　　　　　⎩ PINFILE3　(20 primary, 10 secondary tracks)

Specifications

1. Allocate the area on a SYSDA volume named D00102.
2. Disposition for each file is (NEW,KEEP).
3. Use the names above as ddnames. The data set names are:
   a. AREA1—SPAREA
   b. PINFILE1—ABCFILE1
   c. PINFILE2—ABCFILE2
   d. PINFILE3—ABCFILE3
4. The DCB for all three files is: logical record length of 90 bytes, block size of 1800 bytes, and record format of fixed, blocked.

Figure 9-14 Specifications for suballocating space

```
//AREA1     DD  DSN=SPAREA,
//              DISP=(NEW,KEEP),
//              UNIT=SYSDA,
//              VOL=SER=D00102,
//              SPACE=(TRK,50,,CONTIG)
//PINFILE1 DD   DSN=ABCFILE1,
//              DISP=(NEW,KEEP),
//              SUBALLOC=(TRK,(16,4),AREA1),
//              DCB=(LRECL=90,BLKSIZE=1800,RECFM=FB)
//PINFILE2 DD   DSN=ABCFILE2,
//              DISP=(NEW,KEEP),
//              SUBALLOC=(TRK,(10,5),AREA1),
//              DCB=*.PINFILE1
//PINFILE3 DD   DSN=ABCFILE3,
//              DISP=(NEW,KEEP),
//              SUBALLOC=(TRK,(20,10),AREA1),
//              DCB=*.PINFILE1
```

Figure 9-15 Using the SUBALLOC parameter

Solutions

1.
```
//MYDD      DD  DSN=NAMEFILE,
                DISP=(NEW,KEEP),
                UNIT=SYSDA,
                SEP=IN1,
                VOL=SER=D00102,
                SPACE=(TRK,(1,1),RLSE),
                DCB=(LRECL=256,BLKSIZE=1280,RECFM=FB)
```

2. Figure 9-15 is an acceptable solution.

3.
```
//TAPEDD    DD  DSN=OUT24,
                DISP=(NEW,CATLG),
                UNIT=(TAPE,,DEFER),
                VOL=(PRIVATE,RETAIN,,2,SER=(00001,00002)),
                DCB=(LRECL=80,BLKSIZE=800,RECFM=FB)
```

```
JOB    HE66YFNH,
       'W. CLARY'
EXEC   PGM=IEBUPDTE,
       PARM=MOD
DD     SYSOUT=A
DD     DSN=MMA.EXAMPLIE
       DISP=OLD
DD     DSN=MMA.EXAMPLIE
       DISP=OLD
DD     *
NAME=EXAMP2,LEVEL=0C
NEW1=100,INCR=10
TIFICATION DIVISION.
RAM-ID.    PULLNMAN
```

Appendix

OS JCL Reference Summary

This appendix is simply a summary of the OS JCL statements and parameters that are covered in detail in the text. For each statement, the format is given in full. Then, to the left of the format, are two columns. The first column contains a notation whenever a parameter can only be used on a certain version of OS. The second column tells which chapter or chapters describe the parameter in detail. I hope you'll be able to use this as a quick reference when you need a refresher on how to code a statement or when you want to know where to look for a parameter in the text.

Appendix

The JOB statement:

Version of OS	Chapter reference	
	2	`//jobname  JOB  accounting-information,`
	2	`programmer-name,`
	2	`CLASS=job-class,`
	2	`PRTY=priority-number,`
	2	`MSGCLASS=message-class,`
	2	`MSGLEVEL=(statements,messages),`
MVT	2	`REGION=region-sizeK,`
	3	`COND=(number,relational-operator),`
	3	`TIME=(minutes,seconds),`
	3	`TYPRUN=HOLD,`
VS	6	`ADDRSP=VIRT,`
VS	6	`=REAL,`
VS	6	`PERFORM=performance-group`

Appendix

Version of OS	Chapter reference	The EXEC statement:
		`//stepname EXEC {PGM=program-name / PROC=procedure-name},`
	2	
	5	
MVT	2,7	`PARM=program-parameters,`
	2	`REGION=region-sizeK,`
	3	`COND=(number,relational-operator),`
	3	`=(number,relational-operator,stepname),`
	3	`=(number,relational-operator,stepname.procstepname),`
	3	`=EVEN,`
	3	`=ONLY,`
	3	`TIME=(minutes,seconds),`
VS	6	`ADDRSP=VIRT,`
VS	6	`=REAL,`
VS	6	`PERFORM=performance-group`

Appendix

The DD statement:

Format 1:

Version of OS	Chapter reference	
	2,3	`//ddname   DD   {DUMMY`
	2	`             DSN=filename}`
	3	`             =NULLFILE }`
	2	`   DISP=(status,normal-disposition,abnormal-disposition),`
	2,3,9	`   UNIT=(device,unit-count/P,DEFER,SEP=ddnames),`
	9	`        =AFF=ddname,`
MFT,MVT	9	`   SEP=ddnames,`
MFT,MVT	9	`   AFF=ddname,`
MFT,MVT	9	`   SUBALLOC=(unit-of-measure,(primary,secondary,directory),`
		`            filename),`
MFT,MVT	9	`   SPLIT=formatting-specifications,`
	2,3,9	`   VOL=(PRIVATE,RETAIN,sequence,count,`
		`        SER/REF=serial-numbers/ddname/dsname),`
	2,3,4,5,9	`   SPACE=(unit-of-measure,(primary,secondary,directory/index),`
		`          RLSE,format,ROUND),`
	3	`   LABEL=(data-set-sequence,format,password,IN/OUT,`
		`          expiration-date),`
	2	`   DCB=(LRECL=logical-record-length,`
	2	`        BLKSIZE=block-size`
	2	`        RECFM=record-format,`
	9	`        DEN=tape-density,`
	9	`        STACK=card-stacker,`
	9	`        PRTSP=print-spacing,`

4,5	DSORG=data-set-organization,
4	KEYLEN=key-length,
4	LIMCT=extended-search-limit,
4	RKP=relative-key-position,
4	CYLOFL=cylinder-overflow-size,
4	NTM=number-of-tracks-for-a-master-index,
9	ERROPT=error-options,
3,4	OPTCD=option-codes,
6 VS	FREE=CLOSE,
6 VS	=END,
6 VS	AMP=AMORG

Format 2 (for instream data):

```
             ⎧ *              ⎫
//ddname  DD ⎨ DATA           ⎬
             ⎩ DDNAME=ddname  ⎭
```

2	//ddname DD
2,5,7	*, DATA
5	DDNAME=ddname

Format 3 (for printed or punched output files):

2,3	//ddname DD SYSOUT=(sysout-class,program-name,form-id),
3	OUTLIM=output-limit

326 Appendix

Version of OS	Chapter reference		
		The delimiter (end-of-data) statement:	
	2	`/*`	
		The comment statement:	
	2	`//*`	
		The null statement:	
	2	`//`	
		Referback formats:	
		The EXEC statement:	
	3	`PGM=*.stepname`	
	3	`PGM=*.stepname.procstepname`	
		The DD statement:	
	3	$\begin{Bmatrix} \text{parameter} \\ \text{VOL=REF} \end{Bmatrix}$ `=*.ddname`	
	3	$\begin{Bmatrix} \text{parameter} \\ \text{VOL=REF} \end{Bmatrix}$ `=*.stepname.ddname`	
	3	$\begin{Bmatrix} \text{parameter} \\ \text{VOL=REF} \end{Bmatrix}$ `=*.stepname.procstepname.ddname`	

Index

Abnormal disposition, 63
Access cycle, 15, 24
Access mechanism, 10
Access method, 40
Access Method Services, 216
Accounting information, 55
Adding a DD statement to a procedure, 194
Adding procedure parameters, 193
ADDRSP parameter, 213, 214
AFF parameter, 300
AMP parameter, 216, 223
ASCII, 315
Assembler, 28, 47, 63, 263, 269, 275, 289

Backward reference, 92
BDAM, 40
BISAM, 40
Bit, 5
BLKSIZE, 71, 121, 138, 153
Block, 69, 315
Block prefix, 315
Block size, 71
Blocking, 6, 13
BPAM, 40
BSAM, 40
Buffer, 16, 315
BUFL, 153
BUFNO, 153
Byte, 5

Cataloged procedure, 183, 270
Cataloging, 38, 40
CATLG, 65
Central processing unit, 4
Channel affinity, 300
Channel command, 14
Channel separation, 300
Channel, 14, 300
CLASS parameter, 55
Cluster, 216
COBOL, 28, 38, 47, 62, 263, 269, 277, 288
Comment field, 48
Comment statement, 76
Communications channel, 300

Compile-and-go procedure, 270, 277
Compile-and-link procedure, 270, 275
Compile-link-and-go procedure, 270, 280
Compile-only procedure, 270, 272
Compiler options, 270
Computer operator, 23, 108, 301, 310
Concatenating files, 96
COND parameter, 105, 109, 249
CONTIG option, 116
Continuation character, 50
Continuing JCL parameters, 50
Control statement format, 48
Control word, 256
Core size, 262
CPU, 4, 23
CPU cycle, 31, 55
CPU time, 24
Cross-reference listing, 270
CYL, 69
Cylinder, 9, 12, 69, 132
Cylinder index, 132
Cylinder overflow, 134
Cylinder splitting, 301
CYLOFL, 140

Data control block (DCB), 39, 101
Data definition, 48
Data management services, 30, 37
Data set, 38
Data set label, 38, 119
Data set name, 62
Data set organization, 39
Data set storage control, 38
Data space, 216
Data transfer, 12
DCB (data control block), 39
DCB parameter, 71, 112, 121, 138, 153, 191, 315
DD *, 73, 233
DD DATA, 73, 233
DD statement, 48, 61, 111, 214, 299
    parameters:
        AFF, 300

AMP, 216, 223
DCB, 71, 112, 121, 138, 153, 191, 315
DDNAME, 195
DISP, 63, 137, 232, 260, 288
DSNAME, 62, 136, 232
DUMMY, 112, 189, 216, 223
FREE, 214
LABEL, 39, 118, 138
NULLFILE, 112
OUTLIM, 122
SEP, 300
SPACE, 41, 68, 116, 138, 260, 301, 313
SPLIT, 301
SUBALLOC, 301
SYSOUT, 121
UNIT, 67, 113, 137, 232, 306
VOLUME, 68, 114, 137, 232, 309
special ddnames:
    JOBCAT, 219
    JOBLIB, 75
    SORTIN, 258
    SORTLIB, 258
    SORTOUT, 260
    SORTWK, 260
    STEPCAT, 219
    STEPLIB, 75, 166
    SYSLIB, 277
    SYSLIN, 277
    SYSLMOD, 277, 288
    SYSOUT, 258
    SYSPRINT, 232
    SYSUDUMP, 75, 277
DD statement override, 191
Ddname, 62
DDNAME parameter, 195
DEFER, 307
Deferred mounting, 307
DEFINE command, 217
DELETE, 65
Delimiter statement, 77
Direct-access device, 7, 68
Direct-access organization, 39
Direct file, 39, 151
Directory, 166
Directory subparameter, 116

Index

Disk, 7, 9
DISP parameter, 63, 137, 232, 260, 288
Disposition of a file, 63
Drum, 8
DSCB, 101
DSNAME parameter, 62, 136, 232
DSORG, 140, 153
DUMMY parameter, 112, 189, 216, 223
Dynamic allocation, 34

Embedded overflow area, 136
Entry-sequenced VSAM cluster, 220
Error processing, 38, 42, 316
EVEN option, 110
EXEC statement, 48, 59, 109, 180, 214, 232
    parameters:
        ADDRSP, 214
        COND, 109, 249
        PARM, 59, 232, 237, 261, 270
        PERFORM, 214
        PGM, 59
        REGION, 60
        TIME, 111
EXEC statement override, 190
Expiration date, 119
Extended file handling, 299

File organization, 13
    direct, 39, 151
    ISAM, 132, 237
    partitioned, 39, 116, 166, 239
    physical sequential, 39
    VSAM, 216
FORTRAN, 28, 47, 63, 269, 272, 289
FREE parameter, 214

General overflow, 134
Generation data group index, 101
Generation data set, 41, 96
Generation number, 96
Generation processing, 38, 40
Group names of devices, 67

Hardware component, 4
Head, 10
Head switching, 12
HEWL, 276
High-level index, 93
High-level qualifier, 93

IDCAMS, 218

IDCAMS control statement rules, 217
IEBCOPY, 166, 234
IEBISAM, 134, 233, 236
IEBPTPCH, 166, 239
IEBUPDTE, 166
IEBUPDTE messages, 172
IEFBR14, 247
IEHMOVE, 166
IEHPROGM, 80, 101, 137, 166, 244
IEWL, 276
Independent overflow, 134
INDEX, 135
Index allocation subparameter, 116
Indexed sequential, 39, 116, 132
Initiator/terminator program, 22, 33
Input queue, 22, 36
Input/output device, 4
Instream procedure, 181
Interrecord gap, 5
I/O area, 16, 315
I/O device, 4, 26
I/O operation, 23
I/O routine, 38, 42
ISAM, 132, 237

JCL, 21, 47
JCL coding rules, 47
JCL coding techniques, 91
JCL for the sort/merge program, 258
JCL for utility programs, 231
JCL standards, 50
Job, 48
Job class, 26, 33
Job-control card, 20
Job-control language, 20, 47
Job-control statement, 20
Job deck, 21
Job name, 54
Job-scheduler program, 21
JOB statement, 48, 54, 104, 213
    parameters:
        accounting information, 55
        ADDRSP, 213
        CLASS, 55
        COND, 105
        MSGCLASS, 56
        MSGLEVEL, 57, 183
        PERFORM, 213
        programmer name, 55
        PRTY, 55
        REGION, 58
Job step, 48

JOBCAT, 219
JOBLIB, 75

K, 24
KEEP, 65
Key-sequenced VSAM cluster, 220
Key-word parameter, 49
KEYLEN, 140, 153

LABEL parameter, 39, 118, 138
Language translator, 28, 269
Library, 20, 30, 165, 280
Library maintenance, 30
LIMCT, 155
Line spacing, 316
Link-edit program, 28, 276, 280, 287
Link-pack area, 35, 211
Linkage-editor program, 28, 276, 280, 287
Load library, 165
Load module, 29, 280, 287
Loader program, 28, 277, 287
Logical record length, 71
LRECL, 71, 121, 138

Magnetic tape, 5, 38, 80, 312, 316
Maps, 270
Master catalog, 216
Master index, 132
Master-scheduler program, 23, 35
Maximum contiguous space, 314
Member, 166
MERGE, 255
MFT, 31
MOD, 65
Model data set control block, 101
MODLDSCB, 101
Mount attribute, 310
MSGCLASS parameter, 56
MSGLEVEL parameter, 57, 183
Multiplexor channel, 16
Multiprogramming, 23, 31
MVS, 36
MVT, 34

Name field, 48
Non-sharable attribute, 311
Normal disposition, 63
NTM, 140
Null statement, 77
NULLFILE parameter, 112
Nullifying procedure parameters, 193

Object library, 165
Object module, 29, 270

Index

ONLY option, 111
Operand field, 48
Operating system, 19
Operation field, 48
Operator console, 4, 23
OPTCD, 121, 140, 155
OS, 19
OS JCL, 47
OS JCL reference summary, 321
OS/MFT, 31
OS/MVS, 36
OS/MVT, 34
OS/VS systems, 207
OS/VS1, 34, 208
OS/VS2, 36, 211
OUTLIM parameter, 122
Output writer program, 22, 26, 211
Overflow area, 134
Overlap, 13
Override statement, 190
Overriding procedures, 190
OVFLOW, 135

Page, 208
Page frame, 208
Page frame management, 208
Page pool, 208
Pageable supervisor, 210
Paging, 208
PARM parameter, 59, 232, 237, 261, 270
Partition, 31, 211
Partitioned data set, 116, 166, 239
Partitioned organization, 39
PASS, 65
Password, 42, 119, 219
PDS, 166
PDS directory, 166
PDS member, 166
PEND statement, 181
PERFORM parameter, 213, 214
Performance group, 213
Permanently mounted volume, 310
PGM parameter, 59
Physical address, 151
Physical sequential file, 39
PL/I, 28, 47, 63, 263, 269, 280, 289
Positional parameter, 49
Primary allocation, 69, 314
PRIME, 135
Prime data area, 134
Priority, 26, 31
Private use attribute, 310

PROC statement, 181
Procedure, 178
    adding a DD statement, 194
    adding parameters, 193
    cataloged, 183
    general rules, 197
    instream, 181
    invoking, 180
    nullifying, 193
    overriding, 190
    statements, 183
    symbolic parameters, 185
Procedure library, 48, 165, 180
Procedure option, 270
Procedure statement, 183
Program library, 26
Programmer-name parameter, 55
PRTY parameter, 55
Public use attribute, 310

QISAM, 40
QSAM, 40
Qualified name, 93

Randomizing routine, 151
Read/write mechanism, 10
Reader/interpreter program, 22, 27, 33, 48, 54, 211
REAL, 213
Real storage, 27, 208
RECFM, 71, 121, 139, 155
Record format, 71
Record key, 132, 151
Referback, 92
Region, 35
REGION parameter, 58, 60
Relational operator, 106
Relative block address, 156
Relative file organization, 156
Relative generation number, 97
Relative-record VSAM cluster, 220
Relative track address, 151
Relocatable instructions, 287
Removable volume, 310
Reorganization, 134
Reserved volume, 310
Retention period, 118
Return code, 105, 249
RKP, 141
RLSE option, 68
Rotational delay, 12
ROUND option, 118
RPG, 28, 269

Scratch use attribute, 310
Secondary allocation, 69, 315

Secondary extent, 69
Security, 38, 42
Segment, 211
Selector channel, 16
SEP parameter, 300
Sequential processing, 7
Shared program, 24
SORT, 255
Sort/merge control statement, 255
Sort/merge program, 29, 254
SORTIN, 258
SORTLIB, 258
SORTOUT, 260
SORTWK, 260
Source library, 165
Space allocation, 38, 41
SPACE parameter, 41, 68, 116, 138, 260, 301, 313
Special ddname, 75
Special form, 121
SPLIT parameter, 301
Spooling, 26
Stacked-job processing, 20
Stacker, 316
Standalone sort, 263
Status of a file, 63
Step name, 59
STEPCAT, 219
STEPLIB, 75, 166
Storage access cycle, 15
Storage use attribute, 310
SUBALLOC parameter, 301
Suballocation, 301
Subprogram, 29, 288
Subroutine, 165, 287
Supervisor program, 20, 26, 32, 34, 208
Swapping, 208
Symbolic parameter, 185
    default value, 186
    nullifying, 187
SYNCSORT, 265
Syntax, language, 54
SYSABEND, 75
SYSLIB, 277
SYSLIN, 277
SYSLMOD, 277, 288
SYSOUT, 258
SYSOUT parameter, 121
SYSPRINT, 232
System library, 166
System message, 56
System-residence device, 20
System return code, 105
System/360-370, 4
SYSUDUMP, 75, 277

Tape drive, 6
Temporary file, 63
TIME parameter, 107, 111
Track, 9, 12, 69
Track index, 133
Transfer rate, 12
TRK, 69
TTR, 172
TYPRUN parameter, 108

UNCATLG, 65
Unit affinity, 308
Unit of measure, 69
UNIT parameter, 67, 113, 137, 232, 306
Unit separation, 308
Unresolved reference, 287
Use attribute, 310
User catalog, 218
User library, 166
User return code, 105
Utility control statement, 233
Utility program, 30, 134, 166, 231
    IEBCOPY, 166, 234
    IEBISAM, 134, 233, 236
    IEBPTPCH, 166, 239
    IEBUPDTE, 166
    IEFBR14, 247
    IEHMOVE, 166
    IEHPROGM, 80, 101, 137, 166, 244
Utility statements
    ADD, 168
    BLDG, 244
    CATLG, 244
    CHANGE, 170
    COPY, 234
    DELETE, 172
    ENDUP, 168
    EXCLUDE, 234
    MEMBER, 240
    NUMBER, 168
    PRINT, 240
    PUNCH, 240
    RECORD, 240
    RENAME, 244
    SCRATCH, 244
    SELECT, 234
    UNCATLG, 244

V = R area, 210
Variable length record, 72
Versions of OS
    OS/MFT, 31
    OS/MVS, 36
    OS/MVT, 34
    OS/VS1, 34, 208
    OS/VS2, 36, 211
VIRT, 213
Virtual equals real, 211
Virtual storage, 27, 34, 36, 39, 207
VOLUME parameter, 68, 114, 137, 232, 309
Volume sequence number, 312
Volume serial number, 68
Volume state, 310
Volume table of contents, 38
VS, 34, 207
VSAM, 216
VTOC, 38

Comment Form

Your opinions count

If you have comments, criticisms, or suggestions, I'm eager to get them. Your opinions today will affect our products of tomorrow. If you have questions, you can expect an answer within one week from the time we receive them. And if you discover any errors in this product, typographical or otherwise, please point them out so we can make corrections when the product is reprinted.

Thanks for your help.

Mike Murach
Fresno, California

Book title: OS JCL

Dear Mike: _____

_____
_____
_____
_____
_____
_____
_____
_____
_____
_____
_____
_____

Name and Title _____
Company (if any) _____
Address _____
City, State, & Zip _____

Fold where indicated and seal.
No postage necessary if mailed in the United States.

BUSINESS REPLY MAIL

First Class   Permit No. 3063   Fresno, CA

POSTAGE WILL BE PAID BY ADDRESSEE

Mike Murach & Associates, Inc.

4222 West Alamos, Suite 101

Fresno, California 93711

NO POSTAGE
NECESSARY
IF MAILED
IN THE
UNITED STATES

Order Form

> ### Our Guarantee
> You must be satisfied. If you ever feel that our books aren't effective, you can return them for a full refund . . . no matter how many you buy, no matter how long you've had them.

Name and Title _____

Company (if any) _____

Address _____

City, State, & Zip _____

Gentlemen: Please send the books I have indicated below. I understand I will be charged the appropriate book price plus freight (plus sales tax in California).

Quantity	Book Title	Unit Price	10 or More	25 or More
_____	Structured ANS COBOL (part 1)	$17.50	$16.00	$14.50
_____	Structured ANS COBOL (part 2)	17.50	16.00	14.50
_____	Report Writer	12.50	11.50	10.50
_____	Structured Programming for the COBOL Programmer	15.00	13.75	12.50
_____	The Structured Programming Cookbook (COBOL)	15.00	13.75	12.50
_____	System/360-370 Assembler Language (DOS)	18.50	17.00	15.50
_____	System/360-370 Assembler Language (OS)	18.50	17.00	15.50
_____	OS JCL	20.00	18.25	16.50

SEND CASH AND SAVE: Send cash with your order and we'll pay the freight. (California residents—Don't forget to add 6% sales tax to your order total.)

Fold where indicated and seal
No postage necessary if mailed in the United States.

BUSINESS REPLY MAIL

First Class   Permit No. 3063   Fresno, CA

POSTAGE WILL BE PAID BY ADDRESSEE

Mike Murach & Associates, Inc.

4222 West Alamos, Suite 101

Fresno, California 93711

NO POSTAGE
NECESSARY
IF MAILED
IN THE
UNITED STATES